EXPERIENCE
AND
NATURE
BY
JOHN
DEWEY

DOVER PUBLICATIONS, INC.
NEW YORK • NEW YORK

PUBLISHED ON THE FOUNDATION
ESTABLISHED IN MEMORY OF
PAUL CARUS
EDITOR OF THE OPEN COURT AND THE MONIST
1888-1919

This new Dover edition first published in 1958
is an unabridged and unaltered republication
of the second edition.

Library of Congress Catalog Card Number: 58-13673

Manufactured in the United States of America

Dover Publications, Inc.
180 Varick Street
New York 14, N. Y.

CONTENTS

THE PAUL CARUS FOUNDATION

Dr. Paul Carus was born in Ilsenburg, Germany, in 1852. He was educated at the Universities of Strassburg and Tübingen, from the latter of which he received the doctorate of philosophy in 1876. It was, however, in the United States, to which he shortly after removed, that his life-work was performed. He became editor of the *Open Court* in 1888, and later established *The Monist*, remaining throughout his career, editor of these two periodicals and Director of the editorial policies of the Open Court Company. He died in February, 1919, at La Salle, Illinois.

The primary interests which actuated Dr. Carus's life-work were in the field of philosophy, touching with almost equal weight the two great phases of modern speculative concern represented by the philosophy of science and comparative religion. To each of these he devoted numerous special studies, and to each he gave the influence of the press which he directed. This influence was in no sense narrow or specialistic. Dr. Carus was personally profoundly concerned for the broadening of that understanding in all intellectual fields which he felt must be the foundation of whatever is to be valuable in our future human culture; he saw his philosophy never as a closet pursuit, but always as a quest for the social illumination of mankind, in which his hope of betterment lay. In this interest he combatted prejudice, in religion and science alike, seeking to divest the spirit of truth of all cloaking of formula, and turning with eager and open eyes in every direction in which there was a suggestion of light and leading—to men and to thought of every complexion and to all levels of active human concern with matters of reflection. Dr. Carus was, in fact, strongly Socratic in disposition: he wished to bring philosophy down from the skies of a too studied abstraction and habituate it to the houses of men's souls and to the rich and changing tides of cultural interests. Certainly so far as America is concerned his service is a signal one. During much of his career he stood almost alone as a philosopher outside academic walls, a living exponent of the fact that philosophy is significant as a force as well as useful as an educational discipline. He looked to the cultivation of philosophy as a frame of mind open to all, lay and professional, who should come to see that social liberty is made secure only where there is growth of a sympathetic public intelligence.

It is with the spirit and intention of Dr. Carus's life-work in mind that his family have established in his memory the Paul Carus Lectures. In the United States, foundations devoted to the cultivation of philosophy are so confined to scholastic institutions that the whole field of philosophic concern tends to assume the slant of an immured and scholastic discipline; and the observer is tempted to say that the greatest gift that can befall philosophic liberalism is one that will cause its followers to forget their professional character. Such a gift, certainly, is more than suggested by a lectureship which comes with no institutional atmosphere to further the free play of the mind upon all phases of life. In the stipulations for the Carus lectures, the themes of the lectures are left without definition, for it is recognized that philosophy is a spirit of approach rather than a set of problems or theories; and the choice of the lecturers, while it is properly placed in the hands of those who make the study of philosophy their profession, is in no manner limited. The Foundation is free, and it asks of its beneficiaries no other response than the spirit of liberalism.

The conditions governing the lectures are few. They are established as a memorial and are to be called the "Paul Carus Lectures." The lecturers are to be chosen by committees appointed from the Divisions of the American Philosophical Association. The lecturer is recognized by an honorarium of one thousand dollars, and the lectures are to be published by the Open Court Company in a series of volumes, which, it is hoped, as the years pass, will become representative of the finest phases of our speculative thought. It is expected that series of lectures will be delivered biennially, the time and place being set by the committees to whom is delegated the selection of the lecturers. It is more than happy that the first series of the Paul Carus Lectures should have been delivered by John Dewey, for there is no living American philosopher of whom it can more truly be said that his influence is of the type which represents Dr. Carus's ideal.

HARTLEY BURR ALEXANDER.

PREFACE

The publication of this new edition has made it possible to rewrite completely the first chapter as well as to make a few minor corrections throughout the volume. The first chapter was intended as an introduction. It failed of its purpose; it was upon the whole more technical and harder reading than the chapters which it was supposed to introduce. It was also rather confused in mode of presentation, and at one important point in thought as well. It is hoped that its new form is both simpler and possessed of greater continuity. If the original intent is now better fulfilled, it is largely due to the help of kindly critics. I wish to record my especial indebtedness to Professor M. C. Otto of the University of Wisconsin and Mr. Joseph Ratner of Columbia University.

In addition to the complete revision of the first chapter, the new edition affords an occasion for inserting in these prefatory remarks what is not to be found in the earlier text; namely, a summary of the thought of the book in the order of its development. The course of the ideas is determined by a desire to apply in the more general realm of philosophy the thought which is effective in dealing with any and every genuine question, from the elaborate problems of science to the practical deliberations of daily life, trivial or momentous. The constant task of such thought is to establish working connections between old and new subject-matters. We cannot lay hold of the new, we cannot even keep it before our minds, much less understand it, save by the use

of ideas and knowledge we already possess. But just because the new *is* new it is not a mere repetition of something
already had and mastered. The old takes on new color and
meaning in being employed to grasp and interpret the new.
The greater the gap, the disparity, between what has become a familiar possession and the traits presented in new
subject-matter, the greater is the burden imposed upon
reflection; the distance between old and new is the measure
of the range and depth of the thought required.

Breaks and incompatibilities occur in collective culture
as well as in individual life. Modern science, modern industry and politics, have presented us with an immense
amount of material foreign to, often inconsistent with, the
most prized intellectual and moral heritage of the western
world. This is the cause of our modern intellectual perplexities and confusions. It sets the especial problem for
philosophy to-day and for many days to come. Every
significant philosophy is an attempt to deal with it; those
theories to which this statement seems to apply least are
attempts to bridge the gulf by seeking an escape or refuge.
I have not striven in this volume for a reconciliation between the new and the old. I think such endeavors are
likely to give rise to casualties to good faith and candor.
But in employing, as one must do, a body of old beliefs and
ideas to apprehend and understand the new, I have also
kept in mind the modifications and transformations that
are exacted of those old beliefs.

I believe that the method of empirical naturalism presented in this volume provides the way, and the only way—
although of course no two thinkers will travel it in just
the same fashion—by which one can freely accept the
standpoint and conclusions of modern science: the way by

which we can be genuinely naturalistic and yet maintain cherished values, provided they are critically clarified and reinforced. The naturalistic method, when it is consistently followed, destroys many things once cherished; but it destroys them by revealing their inconsistency with the nature of things—a flaw that always attended them and deprived them of efficacy for aught save emotional consolation. But its main purport is not destructive; empirical naturalism is rather a winnowing fan. Only chaff goes, though perhaps the chaff had once been treasured. An empirical method which remains true to nature does not "save"; it is not an insurance device nor a mechanical antiseptic. But it inspires the mind with courage and vitality to create new ideals and values in the face of the perplexities of a new world.

The new introductory chapter (Chapter I) accordingly takes up the question of method, especially with respect to the relation that exists between experience and nature. It points to faith in experience when intelligently used as a means of disclosing the realities of nature. It finds that nature and experience are not enemies or alien. Experience is not a veil that shuts man off from nature; it is a means of penetrating continually further into the heart of nature. There is in the character of human experience no index-hand pointing to agnostic conclusions, but rather a growing progressive self-disclosure of nature itself. The failures of philosophy have come from lack of confidence in the directive powers that inhere in experience, if men have but the wit and courage to follow them.

Chapter II explains our starting point: namely, that the things of ordinary experience contain within themselves a mixture of the perilous and uncertain with the settled and uniform. The need for security compels men to fasten upon the regular in order to minimize and to control the precarious and fluctuating. In actual experience this is a *practical* enterprise, made possible by knowledge of the recurrent and stable, of facts and laws. Philosophies have too often tried to forego the actual work that is involved in penetrating the true nature of experience, by setting up a purely *theoretical* security and certainty. The influence of this attempt upon the traditional philosophic preference for unity, permanence, universals, over plurality, change and particulars is pointed out, as well as its effect in creating the traditional notion of substance, now undermined by physical science. The tendency of modern science to substitute qualitative events, marked by certain similar properties and by recurrences, for the older notion of fixed substances is shown to agree with the attitude of naïve experience, while both point to the idea of matter and mind as significant characters of events, presented in different contexts, rather than underlying and ultimate substances.

Chapters III and IV discuss one of the outstanding problems in philosophy—namely, the question of laws, mechanical uniformities, on one hand and, on the other, ends, purposes, uses and enjoyments. It is pointed out that in actual experience the latter represent the consequences of series of changes in which the outcomes or ends have the value of consummation and fulfillment; and that because of this value there is a tendency to perpetuate them, render them stable, and repeat them. It is then shown that the foundation for value and the striving to realize it is found in nature, because when nature is viewed as consisting of events rather than substances, it is characterized by *histories,* that is, by continuity of change proceeding from beginnings to endings. Consequently, it is natural for genuine initiations and consummations to occur in experience. Owing to the presence of uncertain and precarious factors in these histories, attainment of ends, of goods, is unstable and evanescent. The only way to render them more secure is by ability to control the changes that intervene between the beginning and the end of a process. These intervening terms when brought under control are *means* in the literal and in the practical sense of the word. When mastered in actual experience they constitute tools, techniques, mechanisms, etc. Instead of being foes of purposes, they are means of execution; they are also tests for differentiating genuine aims from merely emotional and fantastic ideals.

The office of physical science is to discover those properties and relations of things in virtue of which they are capable of being used as instrumentalities; physical science makes claim to disclose not the inner nature of things but only those connections of things with one another that determine outcomes and hence can be used as means. The *intrinsic* nature of events is revealed in experience as the immediately felt qualities of things. The intimate coordination and even fusion of these qualities with the regularities that form the objects of knowledge, in the proper sense of the word "knowledge," characterizes intelligently directed experience, as distinct from mere casual and uncritical experience.

This conception of the instrumental nature of the objects of scientific knowing forms the pivot upon which further discussion turns (Chapter V). That character of everyday experience which has been most systematically ignored by philosophy is the extent to which it is saturated with the results of social intercourse and communication. Because this factor has been denied, meanings have either been denied all objective validity, or have been treated as miraculous extra-natural intrusions. If, however, language, for example, is recognized as the instrument of social cooperation and mutual participation, continuity is established between natural events (animal sound, cries, etc.) and the origin and development of meanings. Mind is seen to be a function of social interactions, and to be a genuine character of natural events when these attain the stage of widest and most complex interaction with one another. Ability to respond to meanings and to employ them, instead of reacting merely to physical contacts, makes the difference between man and other animals; it is the agency for elevating man into the realm of what is usually called the ideal and spiritual. In other words, the social participation affected by communication, through language and other tools, is the naturalistic link which does away with the often alleged necessity of dividing the objects of experience into two worlds, one physical and one ideal.

Chapter VI makes the transition from this realization that the social character of meanings forms the solid content of mind to considering mind as individual or "subjective." One of the most marked features of modern thought as distinct from ancient and medieval thought is its emphasis upon mind as personal or even private, its identification with selfhood. The connection of this underlying but misinterpreted fact with experience is made by showing that modern as distinct from ancient culture is characterized by the importance attached to initiation, invention and variation. Thus mind in its individual aspect is shown to be the method of change and progress in the significances and values attached to things. This trait is linked up to natural events by recurring to their particular and variable, their contingent, quality. In and of itself this factor is puzzling; it accounts for accidents and irrationalities. It was long treated as such in the history of mankind; the individual characteristics of mind were regarded as deviations from the normal, and as dangers against which society had to protect itself. Hence the long rule of custom, the rigid conservatism, and the still existing régime of conformity and intellectual standardization. The development of modern science began when there was recognized in certain technical fields a power to utilize variations as the starting points of new observations, hypotheses and experiments. The growth of the experimental as distinct from the dogmatic habit of mind is due to increased ability to utilize variations for constructive ends instead of suppressing them.

Life, as a trait of natural organisms, was incidentally treated in connection with the development of tools, of language and of individual variations. Its consideration as the link between physical nature and experience forms the topic of the mind-body problem (Chapter VII). The isolation of nature and experience from each other has rendered the undeniable connection of thought and effectiveness of knowledge and purposive action, with the body, an insoluble mystery. Restoration of continuity is shown to do away with the mind-body problem. It leaves us with an organism in which events have those qualities, usually called feelings, not realized in events that form inanimate things, and which, when living creatures communicate with

one another so as to share in common, and hence uni-
versalized, objects, take on distinctively mental properties.
The continuity of nature and experience is shown to resolve
many problems that become only the more taxing when
continuity is ignored.

The traits of living creatures are then considered (Chapter VIII) in connection with the conscious aspect of behavior and experience, the quality of immediacy attaching
to events when they are actualized in experience by means
of organic and social interactions. The difference and the
connection of mind and consciousness is set forth. The
meanings that form mind become consciousness, or ideas,
impressions, etc., when something within the meanings or
in their application becomes dubious, and the meaning in
question needs reconstruction. This principle explains
the focal and rapidly shifting traits of the objects of consciousness as such. A sensitive and vital mental career
thus depends upon being awake to questions and problems;
consciousness stagnates and becomes restricted and dull
when this interest wanes.

The highest because most complete incorporation of
natural forces and operations in experience is found in
art (Chapter IX). Art is a process of production in which
natural materials are re-shaped in a projection toward
consummatory fulfillment through regulation of trains
of events that occur in a less regulated way on lower levels
of nature. Art is "fine" in the degree in which ends, the
final termini, of natural processes are dominant and conspicuously enjoyed. All art is instrumental in its use of
techniques and tools. It is shown that normal artistic
experience involves bringing to a better balance than is
found elsewhere in either nature or experience the consum-

matory and instrumental phases of events. Art thus represents the culminating event of nature as well as the climax of experience. In this connection the usual sharp separation made between art and science is criticized; it is argued that science as method is more basic than science as subject-matter, and that scientific inquiry is an art, at once instrumental in control and final as a pure enjoyment of mind.

This recurrence to the topic of ends, or consummatory consequences, and of desire and striving for them, raises the question of the nature of values (Chapter X). Values are naturalistically interpreted as intrinsic qualities of events in their consummatory reference. The question of the control of the course of events so that it may yield, as ends or termini, objects that are stable and that tend toward creation of other values, introduces the topic of value-judgments or valuations. These constitute what is generically termed *criticism*. A return is made to the theme of the first chapter by emphasizing the crucial significance of criticism in all phases of experience for its intelligent control. Philosophy, then, is a generalized theory of criticism. Its ultimate value for life-experience is that it continuously provides instruments for the criticism of those values—whether of beliefs, institutions, actions or products—that are found in all aspects of experience. The chief obstacle to a more effective criticism of current values lies in the traditional separation of nature and experience, which it is the purpose of this volume to replace by the idea of continuity.

January, 1929, New York City.

JOHN DEWEY.

CHAPTER ONE

EXPERIENCE AND PHILOSOPHIC METHOD

The title of this volume, Experience and Nature, is intended to signify that the philosophy here presented may be termed either empirical naturalism or naturalistic empiricism, or, taking "experience" in its usual signification, naturalistic humanism.

To many the associating of the two words will seem like talking of a round square, so engrained is the notion of the separation of man and experience from nature. Experience, they say, is important for those beings who have it, but is too casual and sporadic in its occurrence to carry with it any important implications regarding the nature of Nature. Nature, on the other hand, is said to be complete apart from experience. Indeed, according to some thinkers the case is even in worse plight: Experience to them is not only something extraneous which is occasionally superimposed upon nature, but it forms a veil or screen which shuts us off from nature, unless in some way it can be "transcended." So something non-natural by way of reason or intuition is introduced, something supra-empirical. According to an opposite school experience fares as badly, nature being thought to signify something wholly material and mechanistic; to frame a theory of experience in naturalistic terms is, accordingly, to degrade and deny the noble and ideal values that characterize experience.

I know of no route by which dialectical argument can answer such objections. They arise from associations with words and cannot be dealt with argumentatively. One can only hope in the course of the whole discussion to disclose the meanings which are attached to "experience" and "nature," and thus insensibly produce, if one is fortunate, a change in the significations previously attached to them. This process of change may be hastened by calling attention to another context in which nature and experience get on harmoniously together—wherein experience presents itself as the method, and the only method, for getting at nature, penetrating its secrets, and wherein nature empirically disclosed (by the use of empirical method in natural science) deepens, enriches and directs the further development of experience.

In the natural sciences there is a union of experience and nature which is not greeted as a monstrosity; on the contrary, the inquirer must use empirical method if his findings are to be treated as genuinely scientific. The investigator assumes as a matter of course that experience, controlled in specifiable ways, is the avenue that leads to the facts and laws of nature. He uses reason and calculation freely; he could not get along without them. But he sees to it that ventures of this theoretical sort start from and terminate in directly experienced subject-matter. Theory may intervene in a long course of reasoning, many portions of which are remote from what is directly experienced. But the vine of pendant theory is attached at both ends to the pillars of observed subject-matter. And this experienced material is the same for the scientific man and the man in the street. The latter cannot follow the intervening reasoning without special preparation. But stars, rocks, trees, and creeping things are the same material of experience for both.

These commonplaces take on significance when the relation of experience to the formation of a philosophic theory of nature is in question. They indicate that experience, if scientific inquiry is justified, is no infinitesimally thin layer or foreground of nature, but that it penetrates into it, reaching down into its depths, and in such a way that its grasp is capable of expansion; it tunnels in all directions and in so doing brings to the surface things at first hidden—as miners pile high on the surface of the earth treasures brought from below. Unless we are prepared to deny all validity to scientific inquiry, these facts have a value that cannot be ignored for the general theory of the relation of nature and experience.

It is sometimes contended, for example, that since experience is a late comer in the history of our solar system and planet, and since these occupy a trivial place in the wide areas of celestial space, experience is at most a slight and insignificant incident in nature. No one with an honest respect for scientific conclusions can deny that experience as an existence is something that occurs only under highly specialized conditions, such as are found in a highly organized creature which in turn requires a specialized environment. There is no evidence that experience occurs everywhere and everywhen. But candid regard for scientific inquiry also compels the recognition that when experience does occur, no matter at what limited portion of time and space, it enters into possession of some portion of nature and in such a manner as to render other of its precincts accessible.

A geologist living in 1928 tells us about events that happened not only before he was born but millions of years before any human being came into existence on this earth. He does so by starting from things that are now the material of experience. Lyell revolutionized geology by perceiving that the sort of thing that can be experienced now in the operations of fire, water, pressure, is the sort of thing by which the earth took on its present structural forms. Visiting a natural history museum, one beholds a mass of rock and, reading a label, finds that it comes from a tree that grew, so it is affirmed, five million years ago. The geologist did not leap from the thing he can see and touch to some event in by-gone ages; he collated this observed thing with many others, of different kinds, found all over the globe; the results of his comparisons he then compared with data of other experiences, say, the astronomer's. He translates, that is, observed coexistences into non-observed, inferred sequences. Finally he dates his object, placing it in an order of events. By the same sort of method he predicts that at certain places some things not yet experienced will be observed, and then he takes pains to bring them within the scope of experience. The scientific conscience is, moreover, so sensitive with respect to the necessity of experience that when it reconstructs the past it is not fully satisfied with inferences drawn from even a large and cumulative mass of uncontradicted evidence; it sets to work to institute conditions of heat and pressure and moisture, etc., so as actually to reproduce in experiment that which he has inferred.

These commonplaces prove that experience is *of* as well as *in* nature. It is not experience which is experienced, but nature—stones, plants, animals, diseases, health, temperature, electricity, and so on. Things interacting in certain ways *are* experience; they are what is experienced. Linked in certain other ways with another natural object —the human organism—they are *how* things are experienced as well. Experience thus reaches down into nature; it has depth. It also has breadth and to an indefinitely elastic extent.   It stretches.   That stretch constitutes inference.

Dialectical difficulties, perplexities due to definitions given to the concepts that enter into the discussion, may be raised.   It is said to be absurd that what is only a tiny part of nature should be competent to incorporate vast reaches of nature within itself.   But even were it logically absurd one would be bound to cleave to it as a fact.   Logic, however, is not put under a strain.   The fact that something is an occurrence does not decide what kind of an occurrence it is; that can be found out only by examination.   To argue from an experience "being an experience" to what it is of and about is warranted by no logic, even though modern thought has attempted it a thousand times. A bare event is no event at all; *something* happens.   What that something is, is found out by actual study.   This applies to seeing a flash of lightning and holds of the longer event called experience.   The very existence of science is evidence that experience is such an occurrence that it penetrates into nature and expands without limit through it.

These remarks are not supposed to prove anything about experience and nature for philosophical doctrine; they are not supposed to settle anything about the worth of empirical naturalism.   But they do show that in the case of natural science we habitually treat experience as starting-point, and as method for dealing with nature, and as the goal in which nature is disclosed for what it is.   To realize this fact is at least to weaken those verbal associations which stand in the way of apprehending the force of empirical method in philosophy.

The same considerations apply to the other objection that was suggested: namely, that to view experience naturalistically is to reduce it to something materialistic, depriving it of all ideal significance. If experience actually presents esthetic and moral traits, then these traits may also be supposed to reach down into nature, and to testify to something that belongs to nature as truly as does the mechanical structure attributed to it in physical science. To rule out that possibility by some general reasoning is to forget that the very meaning and purport of empirical method is that things are to be studied on their own account, so as to find out what is revealed when they are experienced. The traits possessed by the subject-matters of experience are as genuine as the characteristics of sun and electron. They are *found*, experienced, and are not to be shoved out of being by some trick of logic. When found, their ideal qualities are as relevant to the philosophic theory of nature as are the traits found by physical inquiry.

To discover some of these general features of experienced things and to interpret their significance for a philosophic theory of the universe in which we live is the aim of this volume. From the point of view adopted, the theory of empirical method in philosophy does for experienced subject-matter on a liberal scale what it does for special sciences on a technical scale. It is this aspect of method with which we are especially concerned in the present chapter.

If the empirical method were universally or even generally adopted in philosophizing, there would be no need of referring to experience. The scientific inquirer talks and writes about particular observed events and qualities, about specific calculations and reasonings. He makes no allusion to experience; one would probably have to search a long time through reports of special researches in order to find the word. The reason is that everything designated by the word "experience" is so adequately incorporated into scientific procedures and subject-matter that to mention experience would be only to duplicate in a general term what is already covered in definite terms.

Yet this was not always so. Before the technique of empirical method was developed and generally adopted, it was necessary to dwell explicitly upon the importance of "experience" as a starting point and terminal point, as setting problems and as testing proposed solutions. We need not be content with the conventional allusion to Roger Bacon and Francis Bacon. The followers of Newton and the followers of the Cartesian school carried on a definite controversy as to the place occupied by experience and experiment in science as compared with intuitive concepts and with reasoning from them. The Cartesian school relegated experience to a secondary and almost accidental place, and only when the Galilean-Newtonian method had wholly triumphed did it cease to be necessary to mention the importance of experience. We may, if sufficiently hopeful, anticipate a similar outcome in philosophy. But the date does not appear to be close at hand; we are nearer in philosophic theory to the time of Roger Bacon than to that of Newton.

In short, it is the contrast of empirical method with other methods employed in philosophizing, together with the striking dissimilarity of results yielded by an empirical method and professed non-empirical methods that make the discussion of the methodological import of "experience" for philosophy pertinent and indeed indispensable.

This consideration of method may suitably begin with the contrast between gross, macroscopic, crude subject-matters in primary experience and the refined, derived objects of reflection. The distinction is one between what is experienced as the result of a minimum of incidental reflection and what is experienced in consequence of continued and regulated reflective inquiry. For derived and refined products are experienced only because of the intervention of systematic thinking. The objects of both science and philosophy obviously belong chiefly to the secondary and refined system. But at this point we come to a marked divergence between science and philosophy. For the natural sciences not only draw their material from primary experience, but they refer it back again for test. Darwin began with the pigeons, cattle and plants of breeders and gardeners. Some of the conclusions he reached were so contrary to accepted beliefs that they were condemned as absurd, contrary to common-sense, etc. But scientific men, whether they accepted his theories or not, employed his hypotheses as directive ideas for making new observations and experiments among the things of raw experience—just as the metallurgist who extracts refined metal from crude ore makes tools that are then set to work to control and use other crude materials. An Einstein working by highly elaborate methods of reflection, calculates theoretically certain results in the deflection of light by the presence of the sun. A technically equipped expedition is sent to South Africa so that by means of experiencing a thing—an eclipse—in crude, primary, experience, observations can be secured to compare with, and test the theory implied in, the calculated result.

The facts are familiar enough. They are cited in order to invite attention to the relationship between the objects of primary and of secondary or reflective experience. That the subject-matter of primary experience sets the problems and furnishes the first data of the reflection which constructs the secondary objects is evident; it is also obvious that test and verification of the latter is secured only by return to things of crude or macroscopic experience—the sun, earth, plants and animals of common, every-day life. But just what rôle do the objects attained in reflection play? Where do they come in? They *explain* the primary objects, they enable us to grasp them with *understanding,* instead of just having sense-contact with them. But how?

Well, they define or lay out a path by which return to experienced things is of such a sort that the meaning, the significant content, of what is experienced gains an enriched and expanded force because of the path or method by which it was reached. Directly, in immediate contact it may be just what it was before—hard, colored, odorous, etc. But when the secondary objects, the refined objects, are employed as a method or road for coming at them, these qualities cease to be isolated details; they get the meaning contained in a whole system of related objects; they are rendered continuous with the rest of nature and take on the import of the things they are now seen to be continuous with. The phenomena observed in the eclipse tested and, as far as they went, confirmed Einstein's theory of deflection of light by mass. But that is far from being the whole story. The phenomena themselves got a far-reaching significance they did not previously have. Perhaps they would not even have been noticed if the theory had not been employed as a guide or road to observation of them. But even if they had been noticed, they would have been dismissed as of no importance, just as we daily drop from attention hundreds of perceived details for which we have no intellectual use. But approached by means of theory these lines of slight deflection take on a significance as large as that of the revolutionary theory that lead to their being experienced.

This empirical method I shall call the *denotative* method. That philosophy is a mode of reflection, often of a subtle and penetrating sort, goes without saying. The charge that is brought against the non-empirical method of philosophizing is not that it depends upon theorizing, but that it fails to use refined, secondary products as a path pointing and leading back to something in primary experience. The resulting failure is three-fold.

First, there is no verification, no effort even to test and check. What is even worse, secondly, is that the things of ordinary experience do not get enlargement and enrichment of meaning as they do when approached through the medium of scientific principles and reasonings. This lack of function reacts, in the third place, back upon the philosophic subject-matter in itself. Not tested by being employed to see what it leads to in ordinary experience and what new meanings it contributes, this subject-matter becomes arbitrary, aloof—what is called "abstract" when that word is used in a bad sense to designate something which exclusively occupies a realm of its own without contact with the things of ordinary experience.

As the net outcome of these three evils, we find that extraordinary phenomenon which accounts for the revulsion of many cultivated persons from any form of philosophy. The objects of reflection in philosophy, being reached by methods that seem to those who employ them rationally mandatory are taken to be "real" in and of themselves—and supremely real. Then it becomes an insoluble problem why the things of gross, primary experience, should be what they are, or indeed why they should be at all. The refined objects of reflection in the natural sciences, however, never end by rendering the subject-matter from which they are derived a problem; rather, when used to describe a path by which some goal in primary experience is designated or denoted, they solve perplexities to which that crude material gives rise but which it cannot resolve of itself. They become means of control, of enlarged use and enjoyment of ordinary things. They may generate new problems, but these are problems of the same sort, to be dealt with by further use of the same methods of inquiry and experimentation. The problems to which empirical method gives rise afford, in a word, opportunities for more investigations yielding fruit in new and enriched experiences. But the problems to which non-empirical method gives rise in philosophy are blocks to inquiry, blind alleys; they are puzzles rather than problems, solved only by calling the original material of primary experience, "phenomenal," mere appearance, mere impressions, or by some other disparaging name.

Thus there is here supplied, I think, a first-rate test of the value of any philosophy which is offered us: Does it end in conclusions which, when they are referred back to ordinary life-experiences and their predicaments, render them more significant, more luminous to us, and make our dealings with them more fruitful? Or does it terminate in rendering the things of ordinary experience more opaque than they were before, and in depriving them of having in "reality" even the significance they had previously seemed to have? Does it yield the enrichment and increase of power of ordinary things which the results of physical science afford when applied in every-day affairs? Or does it become a mystery that these ordinary things should be what they are; and are philosophic concepts left to dwell in separation in some technical realm of their own? It is the fact, I repeat, that so many philosophies terminate in conclusions that make it necessary to disparage and condemn primary experience, leading those who hold them to measure the sublimity of their "realities" as philosophically defined by remoteness from the concerns of daily life, which leads cultivated common-sense to look askance at philosophy.

These general statements must be made more definite. We must illustrate the meaning of empirical method by seeing some of its results in contrast with those to which non-empirical philosophies conduct us. We begin by noting that "experience" is what James called a double-barrelled word.[1] Like its congeners, life and history, it includes *what* men do and suffer, *what* they strive for, love, believe and endure, and also *how* men act and are acted upon, the ways in which they do and suffer, desire and enjoy, see, believe, imagine—in short, processes of *experiencing*. "Experience" denotes the planted field, the sowed seeds, the reaped harvests, the changes of night and day, spring and autumn, wet and dry, heat and cold, that are observed, feared, longed for; it also denotes the one who plants and reaps, who works and rejoices, hopes, fears, plans, invokes magic or chemistry to aid him, who is downcast or triumphant. It is "double-barrelled" in that it recognizes in its primary integrity no division between act and material, subject and object, but contains them both in an unanalyzed totality. "Thing" and "thought," as James says in the same connection, are single-barrelled; they refer to products discriminated by reflection out of primary experience.[2]

It is significant that "life" and "history" have the same

---

[1] Essays in Radical Empiricism. p. 10.
[2] It is not intended, however, to attribute to James precisely the interpretation given in the text.

fullness of undivided meaning. Life denotes a function, a comprehensive activity, in which organism and environment are included. Only upon reflective analysis does it break up into external conditions—air breathed, food taken, ground walked upon—and internal structures— lungs respiring, stomach digesting, legs walking. The scope of "history" is notorious: it is the deeds enacted, the tragedies undergone; and it is the human comment, record, and interpretation that inevitably follow. Objectively, history takes in rivers, mountains, fields and forests, laws and institutions; subjectively it includes the purposes and plans, the desires and emotions, through which these things are administered and transformed.

Now empirical method is the only method which can do justice to this inclusive integrity of "experience." It alone takes this integrated unity as the starting point for philosophic thought. Other methods begin with results of a reflection that has already torn in two the subject-matter experienced and the operations and states of experiencing. The problem is then to get together again what has been sundered—which is as if the king's men started with the fragments of the egg and tried to construct the whole egg out of them. For empirical method the problem is nothing so impossible of solution. Its problem is to note how and why the whole is distinguished into subject and object, nature and mental operations. Having done this, it is in a position to see *to what effect* the distinction is made: how the distinguished factors function in the further control and enrichment of the subject-matters of crude but total experience. Non-empirical method starts with a reflective product as if it were primary, as if it were the originally "given." To non-empirical method, therefore, object and subject, mind and matter (or whatever words and ideas are used) are separate and independent. Therefore it has upon its hands the problem of how it is possible to know at all; how an outer world can affect an inner mind; how the acts of mind can reach out and lay hold of objects defined in antithesis to them. Naturally it is at a loss for an answer, since its premises make the fact of knowledge both unnatural and unempirical. One thinker turns metaphysical materialist and denies reality to the mental; another turns psychological idealist, and holds that matter and force are merely disguised psychical events. Solutions are given up as a hopeless task, or else different schools pile one intellectual complication on another only to arrive by a long and tortuous course at that which naïve experience already has in its own possession.

The first and perhaps the greatest difference made in philosophy by adoption respectively of empirical or non-empirical method is, thus, the difference made in what is selected as original material. To a truly naturalistic empiricism, the moot problem of the relation of subject and object is the problem of what consequences follow in and for primary experience from the distinction of the physical and the psychological or mental from each other. The answer is not far to seek. To distinguish in reflection the physical and to hold it in temporary detachment is to be set upon the road that conducts to tools and technologies, to construction of mechanisms, to the arts that ensue in the wake of the sciences. That these constructions make possible a better regulation of the affairs of primary experience is evident. Engineering and medicine, all the utilities that make for expansion of life, are the answer. There is better administration of old familiar things, and there is invention of new objects and satisfactions. Along with this added ability in regulation goes enriched meaning and value in things, clarification, increased depth and continuity—a result even more precious than is the added power of control.

The history of the development of the physical sciences is the story of the enlarging possession by mankind of more efficacious instrumentalities for dealing witth the conditions of life and action. But when one neglects the connection of these scientific objects with the affairs of primary experience, the result is a picture of a world of things indifferent to human interests because it is wholly apart from experience. It is more than merely isolated, for it is set in opposition. Hence when it is viewed as fixed and final in itself it is a source of oppression to the heart and paralysis to imagination. Since this picture of the physical universe and philosophy of the character of physical objects is contradicted by every engineering project and every intelligent measure of public hygiene, it would seem to be time to examine the foundations upon which it rests, and find out how and why such conclusions are come to.

When objects are isolated from the experience through which they are reached and in which they function, experience itself becomes reduced to the mere process of experiencing, and experiencing is therefore treated as if it were also complete in itself. We get the absurdity of an experiencing which experiences only itself, states and processes of consciousness, instead of the things of nature. Since the seventeenth century this conception of experience as the equivalent of subjective private consciousness set over against nature, which consists wholly of physical objects, has wrought havoc in philosophy. It is responsible for the feeling mentioned at the outset that "nature" and "experience" are names for things which have nothing to do with each other.

Let us inquire how the matter stands when these mental and psychical objects are looked at in their connection with experience in its primary and vital modes. As has been suggested, these objects are not original, isolated and self-sufficient. They represent the discriminated analysis of the process of experiencing from subject-matter experienced. Although breathing is in fact a function that includes both air and the operations of the lungs, we may detach the latter for study, even though we cannot separate it in fact. So while we always know, love, act for and against *things,* instead of experiencing ideas, emotions and mental intents, the attitudes themselves may be made a special object of attention, and thus come to form a distinctive subject-matter of reflective, although not of primary, experience.

We primarily observe things, not observations. But the *act* of observation may be inquired into and form a subject of study and become thereby a refined object; so may the acts of thinking, desire, purposing, the state of affection, reverie, etc. Now just as long as these attitudes are not distinguished and abstracted, they are incorporated into subject-matter. It is a notorious fact that the one who hates finds the one hated an obnoxious and despicable character; to the lover his adored one is full of intrinsically delightful and wonderful qualities. The connection between such facts and the fact of animism is direct.

The natural and original bias of man is all toward the objective; whatever is experienced is taken to be there independent of the attitude and act of the self. Its "thereness," its independence of emotion and volition, render the properties of things, whatever they are, cosmic. Only when vanity, prestige, rights of possession are involved does an individual tend to separate off from the environment and the group in which he, quite literally, lives, some things as being peculiarly himself. It is obvious that a total, un-analyzed world does not lend itself to control; that, on the contrary it is equivalent to the subjection of man to what-ever occurs, as if to fate. Until some acts and their con-sequences are discriminatingly referred to the human organism and other energies and effects are referred to other bodies, there is no leverage, no purchase, with which to regulate the course of experience. The abstraction of certain qualities of things as due to human acts and states is the *pou sto* of ability in control. There can be no doubt that the long period of human arrest at a low level of culture was largely the result of failure to select the human being and his acts as a special kind of object, having his own characteristic activities that condition specifiable consequences.

In this sense, the recognition of "subjects" as centres of experience together with the development of "subjectiv-ism" marks a great advance. It is equivalent to the emer-gence of agencies equipped with special powers of observa-tion and experiment, and with emotions and desires that are efficacious for production of chosen modifications of nature. For otherwise the agencies are submerged in nature and produce qualities of things which must be accepted and submitted to. It is no mere play on words to say that recognition of subjective minds having a special equipment of psychological abilities is a necessary factor in subjecting the energies of nature to use as instrumen-talities for ends.

Out of the indefinite number of possible illustrations of the consequences of reflective analysis yielding personal or "subjective" minds we cite one case. It concerns the influence of habitual beliefs and expectations in their social generation upon *what* is experienced. The things of primary experience are so arresting and engrossing that we tend to accept them just as they are—the flat earth, the march of the sun from east to west and its sinking under the earth. Current beliefs in morals, religion and politics similarly reflect the social conditions which present themselves. Only analysis shows that the *ways* in which we believe and expect have a tremendous affect upon *what* we believe and expect. We have discovered at last that these ways are set, almost abjectly so, by social factors, by tradition and the influence of education. Thus we discover that we believe many things not because the things are so, but because we have become habituated through the weight of authority, by imitation, prestige, instruction, the unconscious effect of language, etc. We learn, in short, that qualities which we attribute to objects ought to be imputed to our own ways of experiencing them, and that these in turn are due to the force of intercourse and custom. This discovery marks an emancipation; it purifies and remakes the objects of our direct or primary experience. The power of custom and tradition in scientific as well as in moral beliefs never suffered a serious check until analysis revealed the effect of personal ways of believing upon things believed, and the extent to which these ways are unwittingly fixed by social custom and tradition. In spite of the acute and penetrating powers of observation among the Greeks, their "science" is a monument of the extent to which the effects of acquired social habits as well as of organic constitution were attributed directly to natural events. The de-personalizing and de-socializing of some objects, to be henceforth the objects of physical science, was a necessary precondition of ability to regulate experience by directing the attitudes and objects that enter into it.

This great emancipation was coincident with the rise of "individualism," which was in effect identical with the reflective discovery of the part played in experience by concrete selves, with their ways of acting, thinking and desiring. The results would have been all to the good if they had been interpreted by empirical method. For this would have kept the eye of thinkers constantly upon the origin of the "subjective" out of primary experience, and then directed it to the function of discriminating what is usable in the management of experienced objects. But for lack of such a method, because of isolation from empirical origin and instrumental use, the results of psychological inquiry were conceived to form a separate and isolated mental world in and of itself, self-sufficient and self-enclosed. Since the psychological movement necessarily coincided with that which set up physical objects as correspondingly complete and self-enclosed, there resulted that dualism of mind and matter, of a physical and a psychical world, which from the day of Descartes to the present dominates the formulation of philosophical problems.

With the dualism we are not here concerned, beyond pointing out that it is the inevitable result, logically, of the abandoning of acknowledgment of the primacy and ultimacy of gross experience—primary as it is given in an uncontrolled form, ultimate as it is given in a more regulated and significant form—a form made possible by the methods and results of reflective experience. But what we are directly concerned with at this stage of discussion is the result of the discovery of subjective objects upon philosophy in creation of wholesale subjectivism. The outcome was, that while in actual life the discovery of personal attitudes and their consequences was a great liberating instrument, psychology became for philosophy, as Santayana has well put it, "malicious." That is, mental attitudes, *ways* of experiencing, were treated as self-sufficient and complete in themselves, as that which is primarily *given*, the sole original and therefore indubitable data. Thus the traits of genuine primary experience, in which natural things are the determining factors in production of all change, were regarded either as not-given dubious things that could be reached only by endowing the only certain thing, the mental, with some miraculous power, or else were denied all existence save as complexes of mental states, of impressions, sensations, feelings.[1]

One illustration out of the multitude available follows. It is taken almost at random, because it is both simple and typical. To illustrate the nature of experience, what experience really is, an author writes: "When I look at a chair, I say I experience it. But what I actually experience is only a very few of the elements that go to make up a chair, namely the color that belongs to the chair under these particular conditions of light, the shape which the chair displays when viewed from this angle, etc." Two points are involved in any such statement. One is that "experience" is reduced to the traits connected with the

[1] Because of this identification of the mental as the sole "given" in a primary, original way, appeal to experience by a philosopher is treated by many as necessarily committing one to subjectivism. It accounts for the alleged antithesis between nature and experience mentioned in the opening paragraph. It has become so deeply engrained that the empirical method employed in this volume has been taken by critics to be simply a re-statement of a purely subjective philosophy, although in fact it is wholly contrary to such a philosophy.

act of experiencing, in this case the act of seeing. Certain patches of color, for example, assume a certain shape or form in connection with qualities connected with the muscular strains and adjustments of seeing. These qualities, which define the act of seeing when it is made an object of reflective inquiry, *over against what is seen,* thus become the chair itself for immediate or direct experience. Logically, the chair disappears and is replaced by certain qualities of sense attending the act of vision. There is no longer any other object, much less the chair which was bought, that is placed in a room and that is used to sit in, etc. If we ever get back to this total chair, it will not be the chair of direct experience, of use and enjoyment, a thing with its own independent origin, history and career; it will be only a complex of directly "given" sense qualities as a core, plus a surrounding cluster of other qualities revived imaginatively as "ideas."

The other point is that, even in such a brief statement as that just quoted, there is compelled recognition of an *object* of experience which is infinitely other and more than what is asserted to be alone experienced. There is the *chair* which is looked at; the *chair displaying* certain colors, the *light* in which they are displayed; the angle of vision implying reference to an organism that possesses an optical apparatus. Reference to these *things* is compulsory, because otherwise there would be no meaning assignable to the sense qualities—which are, nevertheless, affirmed to be the sole data experienced. It would be hard to find a more complete recognition, although an unavowed one, of the fact that in reality the account given concerns only a selected portion of the actual experience, namely that part which defines the act of experiencing, to the deliberate omission, *for the purpose of the inquiry in hand,* of *what* is experienced.

The instance cited is typical of all "subjectivism" as a philosophic position. Reflective analysis of one element in actual experience is undertaken; its result is then taken to be primary; as a consequence the subject-matter of actual experience from which the analytic result was derived is rendered dubious and problematic, although it is assumed at every step of the analysis. Genuine empirical method sets out from the actual subject-matter of primary experience, recognizes that reflection discriminates a new factor in it, the *act* of seeing, makes an object of that, and then uses that new object, the organic response to light, to regulate, when needed, further experiences of the subject-matter already contained in primary experience.

The topics just dealt with, segregation of physical and mental objects, will receive extended attention in the body of this volume.[1] As respects *method*, however, it is pertinent at this point to summarize our results. Reference to the primacy and ultimacy of the material of ordinary experience protects us, in the first place, from creating artificial problems which deflect the energy and attention of philosophers from the real problems that arise out of actual subject-matter. In the second place, it provides a check or test for the conclusions of philosophic inquiry; it is a constant reminder that we must replace them, as secondary reflective products, in the experience out of which they arose, so that they may be confirmed or modified by the new order and clarity they introduce into it, and the new significantly experienced objects for which they furnish a method. In the third place, in seeing how they thus function in further experiences, the philosophical re-

[1] Chapters IV and VI.

sults themselves acquire empirical value; they are what they contribute to the common experience of man, instead of being curiosities to be deposited, with appropriate labels, in a metaphysical museum.

There is another important result for philosophy of the use of empirical method which, when it is developed, introduces our next topic. Philosophy, like all forms of reflective analysis, takes us away, for the time being, from the things had in primary experience as they directly act and are acted upon, used and enjoyed. Now the standing temptation of philosophy, as its course abundantly demonstrates, is to regard the results of reflection as having, in and of themselves, a reality superior to that of the material of any other mode of experience. The commonest assumption of philosophies, common even to philosophies very different from one another, is the assumption of the identity of objects of knowledge and ultimately real objects. The assumption is so deep that it is usually not expressed; it is taken for granted as something so fundamental that it does not need to be stated. A technical example of the view is found in the contention of the Cartesian school—including Spinoza—that emotion as well as sense is but confused thought which when it becomes clear and definite or reaches its goal is *cognition*. That esthetic and moral experience reveal traits of real things as truly as does intellectual experience, that poetry may have a metaphysical import as well as science, is rarely affirmed, and when it is asserted, the statement is likely to be meant in some mystical or esoteric sense rather than in a straightforward everyday sense.

Suppose however that we start with no presuppositions save that what is experienced, since it is a manifestation of nature, may, and indeed, must be used as testimony of the characteristics of natural events. Upon this basis, reverie and desire are pertinent for a philosophic theory of the true nature of things; the possibilities present in imagination that are not found in observation, are something to be taken into account. The features of objects reached by scientific or reflective experiencing are important, but so are all the phenomena of magic, myth, politics, painting, and penitentiaries. The phenomena of social life are as relevant to the problem of the relation of the individual and universal as are those of logic; the existence in political organization of boundaries and barriers, of centralization, of interaction across boundaries, of expansion and absorption, will be quite as important for metaphysical theories of the discrete and the continuous as is anything derived from chemical analysis. The existence of ignorance as well as of wisdom, of error and even insanity as well as of truth will be taken into account.

That is to say, nature is construed in such a way that all these things, since they are actual, are naturally possible; they are not explained away into mere "appearance" in contrast with reality. Illusions are illusions, but the occurrence of illusions is not an illusion, but a genuine reality. What is really "in" experience extends much further than that which at any time is *known*. From the standpoint of knowledge, objects must be distinct; their traits must be explicit; the vague and unrevealed is a limitation. Hence whenever the habit of identifying reality with the object of knowledge as such prevails, the obscure and vague are explained away. It is important for philosophic theory to be aware that the distinct and evident are prized and why they are. But it is equally important to note that the dark and twilight abound. For in any object of primary experience there are always potentialities which are not explicit; any object that is overt is charged with possible consequences that are hidden; the most overt act has factors which are not explicit. Strain thought as far as we may and not all consequences can be foreseen or made an express or known part of reflection and decision. In the face of such empirical facts, the assumption that nature in itself is all of the same kind, all distinct, explicit and evident, having no hidden possibilities, no novelties or obscurities, is possible only on the basis of a philosophy which at some point draws an arbitrary line between nature and experience.

In the assertion (implied here) that the great vice of philosophy is an arbitrary "intellectualism," there is no slight cast upon intelligence and reason. By "intellectualism" as an indictment is meant the theory that all experiencing is a mode of knowing, and that all subject-matter, all nature, is, in principle, to be reduced and transformed till it is defined in terms identical with the characteristics presented by refined objects of science as such. The assumption of "intellectualism" goes contrary to the facts of what is primarily experienced. For things are objects to be treated, used, acted upon and with, enjoyed and endured, even more than things to be known. They are things *had* before they are things cognized.

The isolation of traits characteristic of objects known, and then defined as the sole ultimate realities, accounts for the denial to nature of the characters which make things lovable and contemptible, beautiful and ugly, adorable and awful. It accounts for the belief that nature is an indifferent, dead mechanism; it explains why characteristics that are the valuable and valued traits of objects in actual experience are thought to create a fundamentally troublesome philosophical problem. Recognition of their genuine and primary reality does not signify that no thought and knowledge enter in when things are loved, desired and striven for; it signifies that the former are subordinate, so that the genuine problem is how and why, to what effect, things thus experienced are transformed into objects in which cognized traits are supreme and affectional and volitional traits incidental and subsidiary.

"Intellectualism" as a sovereign method of philosophy is so foreign to the facts of primary experience that it not only compels recourse to non-empirical method, but it ends in making knowledge, conceived as ubiquitous, itself inexplicable. If we start from primary experience, occurring as it does chiefly in modes of action and undergoing, it is easy to see what knowledge contributes—namely, the possibility of intelligent administration of the elements of doing and suffering. We are about something, and it is well to know what we are about, as the common phrase has it. To be intelligent in action and in suffering (enjoyment too) yields satisfaction even when conditions cannot be controlled. But when there is possibility of control, knowledge is the sole agency of its realization. Given this element of knowledge in primary experience, it is not difficult to understand how it may develop from a subdued and subsidiary factor into a dominant character. Doing and suffering, experimenting and putting ourselves in the way of having our sense and nervous system acted upon in ways that yield material for reflection, may reverse the original situation in which knowing and thinking were subservient to action-undergoing. And when we trace the genesis of knowing along this line, we also see that knowledge has a function and office in bettering and enriching the subject-matters of crude experience. We are prepared to under-

stand what we are about on a grander scale, and to understand what happens even when we seem to be the hapless
puppets of uncontrollable fate. But knowledge that is
ubiquitous, all-inclusive and all-monopolizing, ceases to
have meaning in losing all context; that it does not appear
to do so when made supreme and self-sufficient is because
it is literally impossible to exclude that context of non-
cognitive but experienced subject-matter which gives what
is *known* its import.

While this matter is dealt with at some length in further
chapters of this volume, there is one point worth mention-
ing here. When intellectual experience and its material
are taken to be primary, the cord that binds experience
and nature is cut. That the physiological organism with
its structures, whether in man or in the lower animals, is
concerned with making adaptations and uses of material
in the interest of maintenance of the life-process, cannot
be denied. The brain and nervous system are primarily
organs of action-undergoing; biologically, it can be asserted
without contravention that primary experience is of a corresponding type. Hence, unless there is breach of historic
and natural continuity, cognitive experience must originate
within that of a non-cognitive sort. And unless we start
from knowing as a factor in action and undergoing we are
inevitably committed to the intrusion of an extra-natural,
if not a supernatural, agency and principle. That professed non-supernaturalists so readily endow the organism
with powers that have no basis in natural events is a fact
so peculiar that it would be inexplicable were it not for the
inertia of the traditional schools. Otherwise it would be
evident that the only way to maintain the doctrine of
natural continuity is to recognize the secondary and derived character aspects of experience of the intellectual or

cognitive. But so deeply grounded is the opposite position in the entire philosophic tradition, that it is probably not surprising that philosophers are loath to admit a fact which when admitted compels an extensive reconstruction in form and content.

We have spoken of the difference which acceptance of empirical method in philosophy makes in the problem of subject-object and in that of the alleged all-inclusiveness of cognitive experience.[1] There is an intimate connection between these two problems. When real objects are identified, point for point, with knowledge-objects, all affectional and volitional objects are inevitably excluded from the "real" world, and are compelled to find refuge in the privacy of an experiencing subject or mind. Thus the notion of the ubiquity of all comprehensive cognitive experience results by a necessary logic in setting up a hard and fast wall between the experiencing subject and that nature which is experienced. The self becomes not merely a pilgrim but an unnaturalized and unnaturalizable alien in the world. The only way to avoid a sharp separation between the mind which is the centre of the processes of experiencing and the natural world which is experienced is to acknowledge that all modes of experiencing are ways in which some genuine traits of nature come to manifest realization.

The favoring of cognitive objects and their characteris-

[1] To avoid misapprehension, it may be well to add a statement on the latter point. It is not denied that any experienced subject-matter whatever may *become* an object of reflection and cognitive inspection. But the emphasis is upon "become"; the cognitive never *is* all-inclusive: that is, when the material of a prior non-cognitive experience is the object of knowledge, it and the act of knowing are themselves included within a new and and wider non-cognitive experience—and *this* situation can never be transcended. It is only when the temporal character of experienced things is forgotten that the idea of the total "transcendence" of knowledge is asserted.

tics at the expense of traits that excite desire, command action and produce passion, is a special instance of a principle of selective emphasis which introduces partiality and partisanship into philosophy. Selective emphasis, with accompanying omission and rejection, is the heart-beat of mental life. To object to the operation is to discard all thinking. But in ordinary matters and in scientific inquiries, we always retain the sense that the material chosen is selected for a purpose; there is no idea of denying what is left out, for what is omitted is merely that which is not relevant to the particular problem and purpose in hand.

But in philosophies, this limiting condition is often wholly ignored. It is not noted and remembered that the favored subject-matter is chosen for a purpose and that what is left out is just as real and important in its own characteristic context. It tends to be assumed that because qualities that figure in poetical discourse and those that are central in friendship do not figure in scientific inquiry, they have no reality, at least not the kind of unquestionable reality attributed to the mathematical, mechanical or magneto-electric properties that constitute matter. It is natural to men to take that which is of chief value to them at the time as *the* real. Reality and superior value are equated. In ordinary experience this fact does no particular harm; it is at once compensated for by turning to other things which since they also present value are equally real. But philosophy often exhibits a cataleptic rigidity in attachment to that phase of the total objects of experience which has become especially dear to a philosopher. *It* is real at all hazards and only it; other things are real only in some secondary and Pickwickian sense.

For example, certainty, assurance, is immensely valuable in a world as full of uncertainty and peril as that in which we live. As a result whatever is capable of certainty is assumed to constitute ultimate Being, and everything else is said to be merely phenomenal, or, in extreme cases, illusory. The arbitrary character of the "reality" that emerges is seen in the fact that very different objects are selected by different philosophers. These may be mathematical entities, states of consciousness, or sense data. That is, whatever strikes a philosopher from the angle of the particular problem that presses on him as being self-evident and hence completely assured, is selected by him to constitute reality. The honorable and dignified have ranked with the mundanely certain in determining philosophic definitions of the real. Scholasticism considered that the True and the Good, along with Unity, were the marks of Being as such. In the face of a problem, thought always seeks to unify things otherwise fragmentary and discrepant. Deliberately action strives to attain the good; knowledge is reached when truth is grasped. Then the goals of our efforts, the things that afford satisfaction and peace under conditions of tension and unrest, are converted into that which alone is ultimate real Being. Ulterior functions are treated as original properties.

Another aspect of the same erection of objects of selective preference into exclusive realities is seen in the addiction of philosophers to what is simple, their love for "elements." Gross experience is loaded with the tangled and complex; hence philosophy hurries away from it to search out something so simple that the mind can rest trustfully in it, knowing that it has no surprises in store, that it will not spring anything to make trouble, that it will stay put, having no potentialities in reserve. There is again the predilection for mathematical objects; there is Spinoza with his assurance that a true idea carries truth intrinsic in its bosom; Locke with his "simple idea"; Hume with his "impression"; the English neo-realist with his ultimate atomic data; the American neo-realist with his ready-made essences.

Another striking example of the fallacy of selective emphasis is found in the hypnotic influence exercised by the conception of the eternal. The permanent enables us to rest, it gives peace; the variable, the changing, is a constant challenge. Where things change something is hanging over us. It is a threat of trouble. Even when change is marked by hope of better things to come, that hope tends to project its object as something to stay once for all when it arrives. Moreover we can deal with the variable and precarious only by means of the stable and constant; "invariants"—for the time being—are as much a necessity in practice for bringing something to pass as they are in mathematical functions. The permanent answers genuine emotional, practical and intellectual requirements. But the demand and the response which meets it are empirically always found in a special context; they arise because of a particular need and in order to effect specifiable consequences. Philosophy, thinking at large, allows itself to be diverted into absurd search for an intellectual philosopher's stone of absolutely wholesale generalizations, thus isolating that which is permanent in a function and for a purpose, and converting it into the intrinsically eternal, conceived either (as Aristotle conceived it) as that which is the same at all times, or as that which is indifferent to time, out of time.

This bias toward treating objects selected because of their value in some special context as the "real," in a superior and invidious sense, testifies to an empirical fact of importance. Philosophical simplifications are due to choice, and choice marks an interest *moral* in the broad sense of concern for what is good. Our constant and unescapable concern is with prosperity and adversity, success and failure, achievement and frustration, good and bad. Since we are creatures with lives to live, and find ourselves within an uncertain environment, we are constructed to note and judge in terms of bearing upon weal and woe—upon value. Acknowledgment of this fact is a very different thing, however, from the transformation effected by philosophers of the traits they find good (simplicity, certainty, nobility, permanence, etc.) into fixed traits of real Being. The former presents something *to be accomplished,* to be brought about by the *actions* in which choice is manifested and made genuine. The latter ignores the need of action to effect the better and to prove the honesty of choice; it converts what is desired into antecedent and final features of a reality which is supposed to need only logical warrant in order to be contemplatively enjoyed as true Being.

For reflection the eventual is always better or worse than the given. But since it would also be better if the eventual good were now given, the philosopher, belonging by status to a leisure class relieved from the urgent necessity of dealing with conditions, converts the eventual into some kind of Being, something which *is,* even if it does not *exist.* Permanence, real essence, totality, order, unity, rationality, the *unum, verum et bonum* of the classic tradition, are eulogistic predicates. When we find such terms used to describe the foundations and proper conclusions of a philosophic system, there is ground for suspecting that an artificial simplification of existence has been performed. Reflection determining preference for an eventual

good has dialectically wrought a miracle of transubstantiation.

Selective emphasis, choice, is inevitable whenever reflection occurs. This is not an evil. Deception comes only
when the presence and operation of choice is concealed,
disguised, denied. Empirical method finds and points to
the operation of choice as it does to any other event. Thus
it protects us from conversion of eventual functions into
antecedent existence: a conversion that may be said to be
the philosophic fallacy, whether it be performed in behalf
of mathematical subsistences, esthetic essences, the purely
physical order of nature, or God. The present writer does
not profess any greater candor of intent than animates
fellow philosophers. But the pursuance of an empirical
method, is, he submits, the only way to secure execution of
candid intent. Whatever enters into choice, determining
its need and giving it guidance, an empirical method
frankly indicates what it is for; and the fact of choice,
with its workings and consequences, an empirical method
points out with equal openness.

The adoption of an empirical method is no guarantee
that all the things relevant to any particular conclusion
will actually be found, or that when found they will be
correctly shown and communicated. But empirical method
points out when and where and how things of a designated
description have been arrived at. It places before others
a map of the road that has been travelled; they may accordingly, if they will, re-travel the road to inspect the
landscape for themselves. Thus the findings of one may
be rectified and extended by the findings of others, with
as much assurance as is humanly possible of confirmation,
extension and rectification. The adoption of empirical
method thus procures for philosophic reflection something

of that cooperative tendency toward consensus which marks inquiry in the natural sciences. The scientific investigator convinces others not by the plausibility of his definitions and the cogency of his dialectic, but by placing before them the specified course of searchings, doings and arrivals, in consequence of which certain things have been found. His appeal is for others to traverse a similar course, so as to see how what they find corresponds with his report.

Honest empirical method will state when and where and why the act of selection took place, and thus enable others to repeat it and test its worth. Selective choice, denoted as an empirical event, reveals the basis and bearing of intellectual simplifications; they then cease to be of such a self-enclosed nature as to be affairs only of opinion and argument, admitting no alternatives save complete acceptance or rejection. Choice that is disguised or denied is the source of those astounding differences of philosophic belief that startle the beginner and that become the plaything of the expert. Choice that is avowed is an experiment to be tried on its merits and tested by its results. Under all the captions that are called immediate knowledge, or self-sufficient certitude of belief, whether logical, esthetic or epistemological, there is something selected for a purpose, and hence not simple, not self-evident and not intrinsically eulogizable. State the purpose so that it may be re-experienced, and its value and the pertinency of selection undertaken in its behalf may be tested. The purport of thinking, scientific and philosophic, is not to eliminate choice but to render it less arbitrary and more significant. It loses its arbitrary character when its quality and consequences are such as to commend themselves to the reflection of others after they have betaken themselves to the situations indicated; it becomes significant when reason for the choice is found to be weighty and its consequences momentous. When choice is avowed, others can repeat the course of the experience; it is an experiment to be tried, not an automatic safety device.

This particular affair is referred to here not so much as matter of doctrine as to afford an illustration of the nature of empirical method. Truth or falsity depends upon what men find when they warily perform the experiment of observing reflective events. An empirical finding is refuted not by denial that one finds things to be thus and so, but by giving directions for a course of experience that results in finding its opposite to be the case. To convince of error as well as to lead to truth is to assist another to see and find something which he hitherto has failed to find and recognize. All of the wit and subtlety of reflection and logic find scope in the elaboration and conveying of directions that intelligibly point out a course to be followed. Every system of philosophy presents the consequences of some such experiment. As experiments, each has contributed something of worth to our observation of the events and qualities of experienceable objects. Some harsh criticisms of traditional philosophy have already been suggested; others will doubtless follow. But the criticism is not directed at the experiments; it is aimed at the denial to them by the philosophic tradition of selective experimental quality, a denial which has isolated them from their actual context and function, and has thereby converted potential illuminations into arbitrary assertions.

This discussion of empirical method has had a double content. On one hand, it has tried to make clear, from the analogy of empirical method in scientific inquiry, what the method signifies (and does *not* signify) for philosophy.

Such a discussion would, however, have little definite import unless the *difference* that is made in philosophy by the adoption of empirical method is pointed out. For that reason, we have considered some typical ways and important places in which traditional philosophies have gone astray through failure to connect their reflective results with the affairs of every-day primary experience. Three sources of large fallacies have been mentioned, each containing within itself many more sub-varieties than have been hinted at. The three are the complete separation of subject and object, (of *what* is experienced from *how* it is experienced); the exaggeration of the features of known objects at the expense of the qualities of objects of enjoyment and trouble, friendship and human association, art and industry; and the exclusive isolation of the results of various types of selective simplification which are undertaken for diverse unavowed purposes.

It does not follow that the products of these philosophies which have taken the wrong, because non-empirical, method are of no value or little worth for a philosophy that pursues a strictly empirical method. The contrary is the case, for no philosopher can get away from experience even if he wants to. The most fantastic views ever entertained by superstitious people had some basis in experienced fact; they can be explained by one who knows enough about them and about the conditions under which they were formed. And philosophers have been not more but less superstitious than their fellows; they have been, as a class, unusually reflective and inquiring. If some of their products have been fantasies, it was not because they did not, even unwittingly, start from empirical method; it was not wholly because they substituted unchecked imagination for thought. No, the trouble has been that they have failed to note the empirical needs that generate their problems, and have failed to return the refined products back to the context of actual experience, there to receive their check, inherit their full content of meaning, and give illumination and guidance in the immediate perplexities which originally occasioned reflection.

The chapters which follow make no pretence, accordingly, of starting to philosophize afresh as if there were no philosophies already in existence, or as if their conclusions were empirically worthless. Rather the subsequent discussions rely, perhaps excessively so, upon the main results of great philosophic systems, endeavoring to point out their elements of strength and of weakness when their conclusions are employed (as the refined objects of all reflection must be employed) as guides back to the subject-matter of crude, everyday experience.

Our primary experience as it comes is of little value for purposes of analysis and control, crammed as it is with things that need analysis and control. The very existence of reflection is proof of its deficiencies. Just as ancient astronomy and physics were of little scientific worth, because, owing to the lack of apparatus and techniques of experimental analysis, they had to take the things of primary observation at their face value, so "common-sense" philosophy usually repeats current conventionalities. What is averred to be implicit reliance upon what is given in common experience is likely to be merely an appeal to prejudice to gain support for some fanaticism or defence for some relic of conservative tradition which is beginning to be questioned.

The trouble, then, with the conclusions of philosophy is not in the least that they are results of reflection and theorizing. It is rather that philosophers have borrowed from various sources the conclusions of special analyses, particularly of some ruling science of the day, and imported them direct into philosophy, with no check by either the empirical objects from which they arose or those to which the conclusions in question point. Thus Plato trafficked with the Pythagoreans and imported mathematical concepts; Descartes and Spinoza took over the presuppositions of geometrical reasoning; Locke imported into the theory of mind the Newtonian physical corpuscles, converting them into given "simple ideas"; Hegel borrowed and generalized without limit the rising historical method of his day; contemporary English philosophy has imported from mathematics the notion of primitive indefinable propositions, and given them a content from Locke's simple ideas, which had in the meantime become part of the stock in trade of psychological science.

Well, why not, as long as what is borrowed has a sound scientific status? Because in scientific inquiry, refined methods justify themselves by opening up new fields of subject-matter for exploration; they create new techniques of observation and experimentation. Thus when the Michelson-Moley experiment disclosed, as a matter of gross experience, facts which did not agree with the results of accepted physical laws, physicists did not think for a moment of denying the validity of what was found in that experience, even though it rendered questionable an elaborate intellectual apparatus and system. The coincidence of the bands of the interferometer was accepted at its face value in spite of its incompatibility with Newtonian physics. Because scientific inquirers accepted it at its face value they at once set to work to reconstruct their theories; they questioned their reflective premises, not the full "reality" of what they saw. This task of re-adjustment compelled not only new reasonings and calculations in the development of a more comprehensive theory, but opened up new ways of inquiry into experienced subject-matter. Not for a moment did they think of explaining away the features of an object in gross experience because it was not in logical harmony with theory—as philosophers have so often done. Had they done so, they would have stultified science and shut themselves off from new problems and new findings in subject-matter. In short, the material of refined scientific method is continuous with that of the actual world as it is concretely experienced.

But when philosophers transfer into their theories bodily and as finalities the refined conclusions they borrow from the sciences, whether logic, mathematics or physics, these results are not employed to reveal new subject-matters and illuminate old ones of gross experience; they are employed to cast discredit on the latter and to generate new and artificial problems regarding the reality and validity of the things of gross experience. Thus the discoveries of psychologies taken out of their own empirical context are in philosophy employed to cast doubt upon the reality of things external to mind and to selves, things and properties that are perhaps the most salient characteristics of ordinary experience. Similarly, the discoveries and methods of physical science, the concepts of mass, space, motion, have been adopted wholesale in isolation by philosophers in such a way as to make dubious and even incredible the reality of the affections, purposes and enjoyments of concrete experience. The objects of mathematics, symbols of relations having no explicit reference to actual existence, efficacious in the territory to which mathematical technique applies, have been employed in philosophy to determine the priority of essences to existence, and to create the insoluble problem of why pure essence ever descends into the tangles and tortuosities of existence.

What empirical method exacts of philosophy is two things: First, that refined methods and products be traced back to their origin in primary experience, in all its heterogeneity and fullness; so that the needs and problems out of which they arise and which they have to satisfy be acknowledged. Secondly, that the secondary methods and conclusions be brought back to the things of ordinary experience, in all their coarseness and crudity, for verification. In this way, the methods of analytic reflection yield material which form the ingredients of a method of designation, denotation, in philosophy. A scientific work in physics or astronomy gives a record of calculations and deductions that were derived from past observations and experiments. But it is more than a record; it is also an indication, an assignment, of further observations and experiments to be performed. No scientific report would get a hearing if it did not describe the apparatus by means of which experiments were carried on and results obtained; not that apparatus is worshipped, but because this procedure tells other inquirers how they are to go to work to get results which will agree or disagree in their experience with those previously arrived at, and thus confirm, modify and rectify the latter. The recorded scientific result is in effect a *designation* of a method to be followed and a *prediction* of what will be found when specified observations are set on foot. That is all a philosophy can be or do. In the chapters that follow I have undertaken a revision and reconstruction of the conclusions, the reports, of a number of historic philosophic systems, in order that they may be usable methods by which one may go to his own experience, and, discerning what is found by use of the method, come to understand better what is already within the common experience of mankind.

There is a special service which the study of philosophy may render. Empirically pursued it will not be a study of philosophy but a study, by means of philosophy, of life-experience. But this experience is already overlaid and saturated with the products of the reflection of past generations and by-gone ages. It is filled with interpretations, classifications, due to sophisticated thought, which have become incorporated into what seems to be fresh, naïve empirical material. It would take more wisdom than is possessed by the wisest historic scholar to track all of these absorbed borrowings to their original sources. If we may for the moment call these materials prejudices (even if they are true, as long as their source and authority is unknown), then philosophy is a critique of prejudices. These incorporated results of past reflection, welded into the genuine materials of first-hand experience, may become organs of enrichment if they are detected and reflected upon. If they are not detected, they often obfuscate and distort. Clarification and emancipation follow when they are detected and cast out; and one great object of philosophy is to accomplish this task.

An empirical philosophy is in any case a kind of intellectual disrobing. We cannot permanently divest ourselves of the intellectual habits we take on and wear when we assimilate the culture of our own time and place. But intelligent furthering of culture demands that we take some of them off, that we inspect them critically to see what they are made of and what wearing them does to us. We cannot achieve recovery of primitive naïveté. But there is attainable a cultivated naïveté of eye, ear and thought, one that can be acquired only through the discipline of severe thought. If the chapters which follow contribute to an artful innocence and simplicity they will have served their purpose.

I am loath to conclude without reference to the larger liberal humane value of philosophy when pursued with empirical method. The most serious indictment to be brought against non-empirical philosophies is that they have cast a cloud over the things of ordinary experience. They have not been content to rectify them. They have discredited them at large. In casting aspersion upon the things of everyday experience, the things of action and affection and social intercourse, they have done something worse than fail to give these affairs the intelligent direction they so much need. It would not matter much if philosophy had been reserved as a luxury of only a few thinkers. We endure many luxuries. The serious matter is that philosophies have denied that common experience is capable of developing from within itself methods which will secure direction for itself and will create inherent standards of judgment and value. No one knows how many of the evils and deficiencies that are pointed to as reasons for flight from experience are themselves due to the disregard of experience shown by those peculiarly reflective. To Waste of time and energy, to disillusionment with life that attends every deviation from concrete experience must be added the tragic failure to realize the value that intelligent search could reveal and mature among the things of ordinary experience. I cannot calculate how much of current cynicism, indifference and pessimism is due to these causes in the deflection of intelligence they have brought about. It has even become in many circles a sign of lack of sophistication to imagine that life is or can be a fountain of cheer and happiness. Philosophies no more than religions can be acquitted of responsibility for bringing this result to pass. The transcendental philosopher has probably done more than the professed sensualist and materialist to obscure the potentialities of daily experience for joy and for self-regulation. If what is written in these pages has no other result than creating and promoting a respect for concrete human experience and its potentialities, I shall be content.

CHAPTER TWO

EXISTENCE AS PRECARIOUS AND AS STABLE

It was suggested in the last chapter that experience has its equivalents in such affairs as history, life, culture. Reference to these other affairs enables us to put to one side the reminiscences which so readily give the word experience a sectarian and provincial content. According to Tylor, culture is "that complex whole which includes knowledge, belief, art, morals, custom, and any other capabilities acquired by a man as a member of society." It is, in some sense, a whole, but it is a complex, a diversified whole. It is differentiated into religion, magic, law, fine and useful art, science, philosophy, language, domestic and political relations, etc. Consider the following words of an anthropologist and ask if they do not fairly define the problem of philosophy, although intended for another purpose. "Cultural reality is never wholly deterministic nor yet wholly accidental, never wholly psychological nor yet wholly objective, never wholly of yesterday nor yet wholly of today, but combines all of these in its existential reality. . . . . A reconstructive synthesis re-establishes the synthetic unity necessarily lost in the process of analytic dismemberment."[1] I do not mean that philosophy is to be merged in an anthropological view of culture. But in a different context and by a different method, it has the task of analytic dismemberment and synthetic reconstruction of experience; the phenomena of culture as presented by

[1] Goldenweiser.

the anthropologist provide, moreover, precious material to aid the performance of this office, material more pertinent to the task of philosophizing than that of psychology isolated from a theory of culture.

A feature of existence which is emphasized by cultural phenomena is the precarious and perilous. Sumner refers to Grimm as authority for the statement that the Germanic tribes had over a thousand distinct sayings, proverbs and apothegms, concerning luck. Time is brief, and this statement must stand instead of the discourse which the subject deserves. Man finds himself living in an aleatory world; his existence involves, to put it baldly, a gamble. The world is a scene of risk; it is uncertain, unstable, uncannily unstable. Its dangers are irregular, inconstant, not to be counted upon as to their times and seasons. Although persistent, they are sporadic, episodic. It is darkest just before dawn; pride goes before a fall; the moment of greatest prosperity is the moment most charged with ill-omen, most opportune for the evil eye. Plague, famine, failure of crops, disease, death, defeat in battle, are always just around the corner, and so are abundance, strength, victory, festival and song. Luck is proverbially both good and bad in its distributions. The sacred and the accursed are potentialities of the same situation; and there is no category of things which has not embodied the sacred and accursed: persons, words, places, times, directions in space, stones, winds, animals, stars.

Anthropologists have shown incontrovertibly the part played by the precarious aspect of the world in generating religion with its ceremonies, rites, cults, myths, magic; and it has shown the pervasive penetration of these affairs into morals, law, art, and industry. Beliefs and dispositions connected with them are the background out of which philosophy and secular morals slowly developed, as well as more slowly those late inventions, art for art's sake, and business is business. Interesting and instructive as is this fact, it is not the ramifications which here concern us. We must not be diverted to consider the consequences for philosophy, even for doctrines reigning today, of facts concerning the origin of philosophies. We confine ourselves to one outstanding fact: the evidence that the world of empirical things includes the uncertain, unpredictable, uncontrollable, and hazardous.

It is an old saying that the gods were born of fear. The saying is only too likely to strengthen a misconception bred by confirmed subjective habits. We first endow man in isolation with an instinct of fear and then we imagine him irrationally ejecting that fear into the environment, scattering broadcast as it were, the fruits of his own purely personal limitations, and thereby creating superstition. But fear, whether an instinct or an acquisition, is a function of the environment. Man fears because he exists in a fearful, an awful world. The *world* is precarious and perilous. It is as easily accessible and striking evidence of this fact that primitive experience is cited. The voice is that of early man; but the hand is that of nature, the nature in which we still live. It was not fear of gods that created the gods.

For if the life of early man is filled with expiations and propitiations, if in his feasts and festivals what is enjoyed is gratefully shared with his gods, it is not because a belief in supernatural powers created a need for expiatory, propitiatory and communal offerings. Everything that man achieves and possesses is got by actions that may involve him in other and obnoxious consequences in addition to those wanted and enjoyed. His acts are trespasses upon the domain of the unknown; and hence atonement, if offered in season, may ward off direful consequences that haunt even the moment of prosperity—or that most haunt that moment. While unknown consequences flowing from the past dog the present, the future is even more unknown and perilous; the present by that fact is ominous. If unknown forces that decide future destiny can be placated, the man who will not study the methods of securing their favor is incredibly flippant. In enjoyment of present food and companionship, nature, tradition and social organization have coöperated, thereby supplementing our own endeavors so petty and so feeble without this extraneous reinforcement. Goods are by grace not of ourselves. He is a dangerous churl who will not gratefully acknowledge by means of free-will offerings the help that sustains him.

These things are as true today as they were in the days of early culture. It is not the facts which have changed, but the methods of insurance, regulation and acknowledgment. Herbert Spencer sometimes colored his devotion to symbolic experiences with a fact of dire experience. When he says that every fact has two opposite sides, "the one its near or visible side and the other its remote or invisible side," he expresses a persistent trait of every object in experience. The visible is set in the invisible; and in the end what is unseen decides what happens in the seen; the tangible rests precariously upon the untouched and ungrasped. The contrast and the potential maladjustment of the immediate, the conspicuous and focal phase of things, with those indirect and hidden factors which determine the origin and career of what is present, are indestructible features of any and every experience. We may term the way in which our ancestors dealt with the contrast superstitious, but the contrast is no superstition. It is a primary datum in any experience.

We have substituted sophistication for superstition, at least measurably so. But the sophistication is often as irrational and as much at the mercy of words as the superstition it replaces. Our magical safeguard against the uncertain character of the world is to deny the existence of chance, to mumble universal and necessary law, the ubiquity of cause and effect, the uniformity of nature, universal progress, and the inherent rationality of the universe. These magic formulae borrow their potency from conditions that are not magical. Through science we have secured a degree of power of prediction and of control; through tools, machinery and an accompanying technique we have made the world more conformable to our needs, a more secure abode. We have heaped up riches and means of comfort between ourselves and the risks of the world. We have professionalized amusement as an agency of escape and forgetfulness. But when all is said and done, the fundamentally hazardous character of the world is not seriously modified, much less eliminated. Such an incident as the last war and preparations for a future war remind us that it is easy to overlook the extent to which, after all, our attainments are only devices for blurring the disagreeable recognition of a fact, instead of means of altering the fact itself.

What has been said sounds pessimistic. But the concern is not with morals but with metaphysics, with, that is to say, the nature of the existential world in which we live. It would have been as easy and more comfortable to emphasize good luck, grace, unexpected and unwon joys, those unsought for happenings which we so significantly call happiness. We might have appealed to good fortune as evidence of this important trait of hazard in nature. Comedy is as genuine as tragedy. But it is traditional that comedy strikes a more superficial note than tragedy. And there is an even better reason for appealing to misfortunes and mistakes as evidence of the precarious nature of the world. The problem of evil is a well recognized problem, while we rarely or never hear of a problem of good. Goods we take for granted; they are as they should be; they are natural and proper. The good is a recognition of our deserts. When we pull out a plum we treat it as evidence of the *real* order of cause and effect in the world. For this reason it is difficult for the goods of existence to furnish as convincing evidence of the uncertain character of nature as do evils. It is the latter we term accidents, not the former, even when their adventitious character is as certain.

What of it all, it may be asked? In the sense in which an assertion is true that uncontrolled distribution of good and evil is evidence of the precarious, uncertain nature of existence, it is a truism, and no problem is forwarded by its reiteration. But it is submitted that just this predicament of the inextricable mixture of stability and uncertainty gives rise to philosophy, and that it is reflected in all its recurrent problems and issues. If classic philosophy says so much about unity and so little about unreconciled diversity, so much about the eternal and permanent, and so little about change (save as something to be resolved into combinations of the permanent), so much about necessity and so little about contingency, so much about the comprehending universal and so little about the recalcitrant particular, it may well be because the ambiguousness and ambivalence of reality are actually so pervasive. Since these things form the problem, solution is more apparent (although not more actual), in the degree in which whatever of stability and assurance the world presents is fastened upon and asserted.

Upon their surface, the reports of the world which form our different philosophies are various to the point of stark contrariness. They range from spiritualism to materialism, from absolutism to relativistic phenomenalism, from transcendentalism to positivism, from rationalism to sensationalism, from idealism to realism, from subjectivism to bald objectivism, from Platonic realism to nominalism. The array of contradictions is so imposing as to suggest to sceptics that the mind of man has tackled an impossible job, or that philosophers have abandoned themselves to vagary. These radical oppositions in philosophers suggest however another consideration. They suggest that all their different philosophies have a common premise, and that their diversity is due to acceptance of a common premise. Variant philosophies may be looked at as different ways of supplying recipes for denying to the universe the character of contingency which it possesses so integrally that its denial leaves the reflecting mind without a clew, and puts subsequent philosophising at the mercy of temperament, interest and local surroundings.

Quarrels among conflicting types of philosophy are thus family quarrels. They go on within the limits of a too domestic circle, and can be settled only by venturing further afield, and out of doors. Concerned with imputing complete, finished and sure character to the world of real existence, even if things have to be broken into two disconnected pieces in order to accomplish the result, the character desiderated can plausibly be found in reason or in mechanism; in rational conceptions like those of mathematics, or brute things like sensory data; in atoms or in essences; in consciousness or in a physical externality which forces and overrides consciousness.

As against this common identification of reality with what is sure, regular and finished, experience in unsophisticated forms gives evidence of a different world and points to a different metaphysics. We live in a world which is an impressive and irresistible mixture of sufficiencies, tight completenesses, order, recurrences which make possible prediction and control, and singularities, ambiguities, uncertain possibilities, processes going on to consequences as yet indeterminate. They are mixed not mechanically but vitally like the wheat and tares of the parable. We may recognize them separately but we cannot divide them, for unlike wheat and tares they grow from the same root. Qualities have defects as necessary conditions of their excellencies; the instrumentalities of truth are the causes of error; change gives meaning to permanence and recurrence makes novelty possible. A world that was wholly risky would be a world in which

adventure is impossible, and only a living world can include death.   Such facts have been celebrated by thinkers like Heracleitus and Laotze; they have been greeted
by theologians as furnishing occasions for exercise of
divine grace; they have been elaborately formulated by
various schools under a principle of relativity, so defined as to become itself final and absolute.   They have
rarely been frankly recognized as fundamentally significant for the formation of a naturalistic metaphysics.

Aristotle perhaps came the nearest to a start in that
direction.   But his thought did not go far on the road,
though it may be used to suggest the road which he
failed to take. Aristotle acknowledges contingency,
but he never surrenders his bias in favor of the fixed,
certain and finished.   His whole theory of forms and
ends is a theory of the superiority in Being of rounded-
out fixities.   His physics is a fixation of ranks or grades
of necessity and contingency so sorted that necessity
measures dignity and equals degree of reality, while contingency and change measure degrees of deficiency of
Being.   The empirical impact and sting of the mixture
of universality and singularity and chance is evaded by
parcelling out the regions of space so that they have
their natural abode in different portions of nature.   His
logic is one of definition and classification, so that its
task is completed when changing and contingent things
are distinguished from the necessary, universal and fixed,
by attribution to inferior species of things.   Chance appears in thought not as a calculus of probabilities in pre-
dicting the observable occurrence of any and every
event, but as marking an inferior type of syllogism.
Things that move are intrinsically different from things

that exhibit eternal regularity. Change is honestly
recognized as a genuine feature of *some* things, but the
point of the recognition is avoided by imputing alteration to inherent deficiency of Being over against complete Being which never changes. Changing things belong to a purgatorial realm, where they wander aimlessly
until redeemed by love of finality of form, the acquisition of which lifts them to a paradise of self-sufficient
Being. With slight exaggeration, it may be said that
the thoroughgoing way in which Aristotle defined, distinguished and classified rest and movement, the finished
and the incomplete, the actual and potential, did more
to fix tradition, *the* genteel tradition one is tempted to
add, which identifies the fixed and regular with reality
of Being and the changing and hazardous with deficiency
of Being than ever was accomplished by those who took
the shorter path of asserting that change is illusory.

His philosophy was closer to empirical facts than most
modern philosophies, in that it was neither monistic nor
dualistic but openly pluralistic. His plurals fall however,
within a grammatical system, to each portion of which
a corresponding cosmic status is allotted. Thus his
pluralism solved the problem of how to have your cake
and eat it too, for a classified and hierarchically ordered
set of pluralities, of variants, has none of the sting of the
miscellaneous and uncoördinated plurals of our actual
world. In this classificatory scheme of separation he has
been followed, though perhaps unwittingly, by many
philosophers of different import. Thus Kant assigns all
that is manifold and chaotic to one realm, that of sense,
and all that is uniform and regular to that of reason. A
single and all embracing dialectic problem of the com-

bination of sense and thought is thereby substituted for the concrete problems that arise through the mixed and varied union in existence of the variable and the constant, the necessary and that which proceeds uncertainly.

The device is characteristic of a conversion such as has already been commented upon of a moral insight to be made good in action into an antecedent metaphysics of existence or a general theory of knowledge. The striving to make stability of meaning prevail over the instability of events is the main task of intelligent human effort. But when the function is dropped from the province of art and treated as a property of given things, whether cosmological or logical, effort is rendered useless, and a premium is put upon the accidental good-fortune of a class that happens to be furnished by the toil of another class with products that give to life its dignity and leisurely stability.

The argument is not forgetful that there are, from Heracleitus to Bergson, philosophies, metaphysics, of change. One is grateful to them for keeping alive a sense of what classic, orthodox philosophies have whisked out of sight. But the philosophies of flux also indicate the intensity of the craving for the sure and fixed. They have deified change by making it universal, regular, sure. To say this is not, I hope, verbal by-play. Consider the wholly eulogistic fashion in which Hegel and Bergson, and the professedly evolutionary philosophers of becoming, have taken change. With Hegel becoming is a rational process which defines logic although a new and strange logic, and an absolute, although new and strange, God. With Spencer, evolution is but the transitional process of attaining a fixed and universal equilibrium of harmonious adjustment. With Bergson, change is the creative operation of God, or *is* God—one is not quite sure which. The change of change is not only cosmic pyrotechnics, but is a process of divine, spiritual, energy. We are here in the presence of prescription, not description. Romanticism is an evangel in the garb of metaphysics. It sidesteps the painful, toilsome labor of understanding and of control which change sets us, by glorifying it for its own sake. Flux is made something to revere, something profoundly akin to what is best within ourselves, will and creative energy. It is not, as it is in experience, a call to effort, a challenge to investigation, a potential doom of disaster and death.

If we follow classical terminology, philosophy is love of wisdom, while metaphysics is cognizance of the generic traits of existence. In this sense of metaphysics, incompleteness and precariousness is a trait that must be given footing of the same rank as the finished and fixed. Love of wisdom is concerned with finding its implications for the conduct of life, in devotion to what is good. On the cognitive side, the issue is largely that of measure, of the ratio one bears to others in the situations of life. On the practical side, it is a question of the use to be made of each, of turning each to best account. Man is naturally philosophic, rather than metaphysical or coldly scientific, noting and describing. Concerned with prudence if not with what is honorifically called wisdom, man naturally prizes knowledge only for the sake of its bearing upon success and failure in attaining goods and avoiding evils. This is a fact of our structure and nothing is gained by recommending it as an ideal truth, and equally nothing is gained by attributing to intellect an intrinsic relationship to pure truth for its own sake or bare fact on its own account. The first method encourages dogma, and the second expresses a myth. The love of knowledge for its own sake is an ideal of morals; it is an integral condition of the wisdom that rightly conceives and effectually pursues the good. For wisdom as to ends depends upon acquaintance with conditions and means, and unless the acquaintance is adequate and fair, wisdom becomes a sublimated folly of self-deception.

Denial of an inherent relation of mind to truth or fact for its own sake, apart from insight into what the fact or truth exacts of us in behavior and imposes upon us in joy and suffering; and simultaneous affirmation that devotion to fact, to truth, is a necessary moral demand, involve no inconsistency. Denial relates to natural events as independent of choice and endeavor; affirmation relates to choice and action. But choice and the reflective effort involved in it are themselves such contingent events and so bound up with the precarious uncertainty of other events, that philosophers have too readily assumed that metaphysics, and science of fact and truth, are themselves wisdom, thinking thus to avoid the necessity of either exercising or recognizing choice. The consequence is that conversion of unavowed morals or wisdom into cosmology, and into a metaphysics of nature, which was termed in the last chapter *the* philosophic fallacy. It supplies the formula of the technique by which thinkers have relegated the uncertain and unfinished to an invidious state of unreal being, while they have systematically exalted the assured and complete to the rank of true Being.

Upon the side of wisdom, as human beings interested in good and bad things in their connection with human conduct, thinkers are concerned to mitigate the instability of life, to introduce moderation, temper and economy, and when worst comes to worst to suggest consolations and compensations. They are concerned with rendering more stable good things, and more unstable bad things; they are interested in how changes may be turned to account in the consequences to which they contribute. The facts of the ungoing, unfinished and ambiguously potential world give point and poignancy to the search for absolutes and finalities. Then when philosophers have hit in reflection upon a thing which is stably good in quality and hence worthy of persistent and continued choice, they hesitate, and withdraw from the effort and struggle that choice demands:—namely, from the effort to give it some such stability in observed existence as it possesses in quality when thought of. Thus it becomes a refuge, an asylum for contemplation, or a theme for dialectical elaboration, instead of an ideal to inspire and guide conduct.

Since thinkers claim to be concerned with knowledge of existence, rather than with imagination, they have to make good the pretention to knowledge. Hence they transmute the imaginative perception of the stably good object into a definition and description of true reality in contrast with lower and specious existence, which, being precarious and incomplete, alone involves us in the necessity of choice and active struggle. Thus they remove from actual existence the very traits which generate philosophic reflection and which give point and bearing to its conclusions. In briefest formula, "reality" becomes what we wish existence to be, after we have analyzed its defects and decided upon what would remove them; "reality" is what existence would be if our reasonably justified preferences were so completely established in nature as to exhaust and define its entire being and thereby render search and struggle unnecessary. What is left over, (and since trouble, struggle, conflict, and error still empirically exist, something *is* left over) being excluded by definition from full reality is assigned to a grade or order of being which is asserted to be metaphysically inferior; an order variously called appearance, illusion, mortal mind, or the merely empirical, against what really and truly is. Then the problem of metaphysics alters: instead of being a detection and description of the generic traits of existence, it becomes an endeavor to adjust or reconcile to each other two separate realms of being. Empirically we have just what we started with: the mixture of the precarious and problematic with the assured and complete. But a classificatory device, based on desire and elaborated in reflective imagination, has been introduced by which the two traits are torn apart, one of them being labelled reality and the other appearance. The genuinely moral problem of mitigating and regulating the troublesome factor by active employment of the stable factor then drops out of sight. The dialectic problem of logical reconciliation of two notions has taken its place.

The most widespread of these classificatory devices, the one of greatest popular appeal, is that which divides existence into the supernatural and the natural. Men may fear the gods but it is axiomatic that the gods have nothing to fear. They lead a life of untroubled serenity, the life that pleases them. There is a long story between the primitive forms of this division of objects of experience and the dialectical imputation to the divine of omnipotence, omniscience, eternity and infinity, in contrast with the attribution to man and experienced nature of finitude, weakness, limitation, struggle and change. But in the make-up of human psychology the later history is implicit in the early crude division. One realm is the home of assured appropriation and possession; the other of striving, transiency and frustration. How many persons are there today who conceive that they have disposed of ignorance, struggle and disappointment by pointing to man's "finite" nature—as if finitude signifies anything else but an abstract classificatory naming of certain concrete and discriminable traits of nature itself—traits of nature which generate ignorance, arbitrary appearance and disappearance, failure and striving. It pleases man to substitute the dialectic exercise of showing how the "finite" can exist with or within the "infinite" for the problem of dealing with the contingent, thinking to solve the problem by distinguishing and naming its factors. Failure of the exercise is certain, but the failure can be flourished as one more proof of the finitude of man's intellect, and the needlessness because impotency of endeavor of "finite" creatures to attack ignorance and oppressive fatalities. Wisdom then consists in administration of the temporal, finite and human in its relation to the eternal and infinite, by means of dogma and cult, rather than in regulation of the events of life by understanding of actual conditions.

It does not demand great ingenuity to detect the inversion here. The starting point is precisely the existing mixture of the regular and dependable and the unsettled and uncertain. There are a multitude of recipes for obtaining a vicarious possession of the stable and final without getting involved in the labor and pain of intellectual effort attending regulation of the conditions upon which these fruits depend.

This situation is worthy of remark as an exemplification of how easy it is to arrive at a description of existence via a theory of wisdom, of reflective insight into goods. It has a direct bearing upon a metaphysical doctrine which is not popular, like the division into the supernatural, and natural, but which is learned and technical. The philosopher may have little esteem for the crude forms assumed by the popular metaphysics of earth and heaven, of God, nature, and man. But the philosopher has often proceeded in a manner analogous to that which resulted in this popular metaphysics; some of the most cherished metaphysical distinctions seem to be but learned counterparts, dependent upon an elaborate intellectual technique, for these rough, crude notions of supernatural and natural, divine and human, in popular belief. I refer to such things as the Platonic division into ideal archetypes and physical events; the Aristotelian division into form which is actuality and matter which is potential, when that is understood as a distinction of ranks of reality; the noumenal things, things-in-themselves of Kant in contrast with natural objects as phenomenal; the distinction, current among contemporary absolute idealists, of reality and appearance.

The division however is not confined to philosophers
with leanings toward spiritualistic philosophies. There
is some evidence that Plato got the term Idea, as a name
for essential form, from Democritus. Whether this be
the case or no, the Idea of Democritus, though having a
radically diverse structure from the Platonic Idea, had
the same function of designating a finished, complete,
stable, wholly unprecarious reality. Both philosophers
craved solidity and both found it; corresponding to the
Platonic phenomenal flux are the Democritean things
as they are in custom or ordinary experience: corresponding to the ideal archetypes are substantial indi-
visible atoms. Corresponding, again to the Platonic
theory of Ideas is the modern theory of mathematical
structures which are alone independently real, while
the empirical impressions and suggestions to which they
give rise is the counterpart of his realm of phenomena.

Apart from the materialistic and spirtualistic schools,
there is the Spinozistic division into attributes and modes;
the old division of essence and existence, and its modern
counterpart subsistence and existence. It is impossible
to force Mr. Bertrand Russell into any one of the pigeon-
holes of the cabinet of conventional philosophic schools.
But moral, or philosophical, motivation is obvious in his
metaphysics when he says that mathematics takes us
"into the region of absolute necessity, to which not only
the actual world but every possible world must conform."
Indeed with his usual lucidity, he says, mathematics
"finds a habitatio,1 eternally standing, where our ideals
are fully satisfied and our best hopes are not thwarted."
When he adds that contemplation of such objects is the
"chief means of overcoming the terrible sense of impo-

tence, of weakness, of exile amid hostile power, which is too apt to result from acknowledging the all but omnipotence of alien forces," the presence of moral origin is explicit.

No modern thinker has pointed out so persuasively as Santayana that "every phase of the ideal world emanates from the natural," that "sense, art, religion, society express nature exuberantly." And yet unless one reads him wrong, he then confounds his would-be disciples and confuses his critics by holding that nature is *truly* presented only in an esthetic contemplation of essences reached by physical science, an envisagement reached through a dialectic which "is a transubstantiation of matter, a passage from existence to eternity." This passage moreover is so utter that there is no road back. The stable ideal meanings which are the fruit of nature are forbidden, in the degree in which they are its highest and truest fruits, from dropping seeds in nature to its further fructification.

The perception of genetic continuity between the dynamic flux of nature and an eternity of static ideal forms thus terminate in a sharp division, in reiteration of the old tradition. Perhaps it is a caricature to say that the ultimate of reason is held to be ability to behold nature as a complete mechanism which generates and sustains the beholding of the mechanism, but the caricature is not wilful. If the separation of contingency and necessity is abandoned, what is there to exclude a belief that science, while it is grasp of the regular and stable mechanism of nature, is also an organ of regulating and enriching, through its own expansion, the more exuberant and irregular expressions of nature in human intercourse, the arts, religion, industry, and politics?

To follow out the latter suggestion would take us to a theme reserved for later consideration. We are here concerned with the fact that it is the intricate mixture of the stable and the precarious, the fixed and the unpredictably novel, the assured and the uncertain, in existence which sets mankind upon that love of wisdom which forms philosophy. Yet too commonly, although in a great variety of technical modes, the result of the search is converted into a metaphysics which denies or conceals from acknowledgment the very characters of existence which initiated it, and which give significance to its conclusions. The form assumed by the denial is, most frequently, that striking division into a superior true realm of being and lower illusory, insignificant or phenomenal realm which characterizes metaphysical systems as unlike as those of Plato and Democritus, St. Thomas and Spinoza, Aristotle and Kant, Descartes and Comte, Haeckel and Mrs. Eddy.

The same jumble of acknowledgment and denial attends the conception of Absolute Experience: as if any experience could be more absolutely experience than that which marks the life of humanity. This conception constitutes the most recent device for first admitting and then denying the combinedly stable and unstable nature of the world. Its plaintive recognition of our experience as finite and temporal, as full of error, conflict and contradiction, is an acknowledgment of the precarious uncertainty of the objects and connections that constitute nature as it emerges in history. Human experience however has also the pathetic longing for truth, beauty and order. There is more than the longing: there are moments of achievement. Experience exhibits ability to possess harmonious objects. It evinces an ability, within limits, to safeguard the excellent objects and to deflect and reduce the obnoxious ones. The concept of an absolute experience which is only and always perfect and good, first explicates these desirable implications of things of actual experience, and then asserts that they alone are real. The experienced occurrences which give poignancy and pertinency to the longing for a better world, the experimental endeavors and plans which make possible actual betterments within the objects of actual experience, are thus swept out of real Being into a limbo of appearances.

The notion of Absolute Experience thus serves as a symbol of two facts. One is the ineradicable union in nature of the relatively stable and the relatively contingent. The division of the movement and leadings of things which are experienced into two parts, such that one set constitutes and defines absolute and eternal experience, while the other set constitutes and defines finite experience, tells us nothing about absolute experience. It tells us a good deal about experience as it exists: namely, that it is such as to involve permanent and general objects of reference as well as temporally changing events; the possibility of truth as well as error; conclusive objects and goods as well as things whose purport and nature is determinable only in an indeterminate future. Nothing is gained—except the delights of a dialectic problem—in labelling one assortment absolute experience and the other finite experience. Since the appeal of the adherents of the philosophy of absolute and phenomenal experience is to a logical criterion, namely, to the implication in every judgment, however erroneous, of a standard of consistency which excludes any possibility of contradictoriness, the inherent logical contradictions in the doctrine itself are worth noting.

In the first place, the contents as well as the form of ultimate Absolute Experience are derived from and based upon the features of actual experience, the very experience which is then relegated to unreality by the supreme reality derived from its unreality. It is "real" just long enough to afford a spring-board into ultimate reality and to afford a hint of the essential contents of the latter and then it obligingly dissolves into mere appearance. If we start from the standpoint of the Absolute Experience thus reached, the contradiction is repeated from its side. Although absolute, eternal, all-comprehensive, and pervasively integrated into a whole so logically perfect that no separate patterns, to say nothing of seams and holes, can exist in it, it proceeds to play a tragic joke upon itself—for there is nothing else to be fooled—by appearing in a queer combination of rags and glittering gew-gaws, in the garb of the temporal, partial and conflicting things, mental as well as physical, of ordinary experience. I do not cite these dialectic contradictions as having an inherent importance. But the fact that a doctrine which avowedly takes logical consistence for its method and criterion, whose adherents are noteworthy for dialectic acumen in specific issues, should terminate in such thoroughgoing contradictions may be cited as evidence that after all the doctrine is merely engaged in an arbitrary sorting out of characters of things which in nature are always present in conjunction and interpenetration.

The union of the hazardous and the stable, of the incomplete and the recurrent, is the condition of all experienced satisfaction as truly as of our predicaments and problems. While it is the source of ignorance, error and failure of expectation, it is the source of the delight which fulfillments bring. For if there were nothing in the way, if there were no deviations and resistances, fulfillment would be at once, and in so being would fulfill nothing, but merely be. It would not be in connection with desire or satisfaction. Moreover when a fulfillment comes and is pronounced good, it is *judged* good, distinguished and asserted, simply because it is in jeopardy, because it occurs amid indifferent and divergent things. Because of this mixture of the regular and that which cuts across stability, a good object once experienced acquires ideal quality and attracts demand and effort to itself. A particular ideal may be an illusion, but having ideals is no illusion. It embodies features of existence. Although imagination is often fantastic it is also an organ of nature; for it is the appropriate phase of indeterminate events moving toward eventualities that are now but possibilities. A purely stable world permits of no illusions, but neither is it clothed with ideals. It just exists. To be good is to be better than; and there can be no better except where there is shock and discord combined with enough assured order to make attainment of harmony possible. Better objects when brought into existence are existent not ideal; they retain ideal quality only retrospectively as commemorative of issue from prior conflict and prospectively, in contrast with forces which make for their destruction. Water that slakes thirst, or a conclusion that solves a problem have ideal character as long as thirst or problem persists in a way which qualifies the result. But water that is not a satisfaction of need has no more ideal quality than water running through pipes into a reservoir; a solution ceases to be a solution and becomes a bare incident of existence when its antecedent generating conditions of doubt, ambiguity and search are lost from its context. While the precarious nature of existence is indeed the source of all trouble, it is also an indispensable condition of ideality, becoming a sufficient condition when conjoined with the regular and assured.

We long, amid a troubled world, for perfect being. We forget that what gives meaning to the notion of perfection is the events that create longing, and that, apart from them, a "perfect" world would mean just an unchanging brute existential thing. The ideal significance of esthetic objects is no exception to this principle. Their satisfying quality, their power to compose while they arouse, is not dependent upon definite prior desire and effort as is the case with the ideally satisfying quality of practical and scientific objects. It is part of their peculiar satisfying quality to be gratuitous, not purchased by endeavor. The contrast to other things of this detachment from toil and labor in a world where most realizations have to be bought, as well as the contrast to trouble and uncertainty, give esthetic objects their peculiar traits. If all things came to us in the way our esthetic objects do, none of them would be a source of esthetic delight.

Some phases of recent philosophy have made much of need, desire and satisfaction. Critics have frequently held that the outcome is only recurrence to an older subjective empiricism, though with substitution of affections and volitional states for cognitive sensory states. But need and desire are exponents of natural being. They are, if we use Aristotelian phraseology, actualizations of its contingencies and incompletenesses; as such nature itself is wistful and pathetic, turbulent and passionate. Were it not, the existence of wants would be a miracle. In a world where everything is complete, nothing requires anything else for its completion. A world in which events can be carried to a finish only through the coinciding assistance of other transitory events, is already necessitous, a world of begging as well as of beggarly elements. If human experience is to express and reflect this world, it must be marked by needs; in becoming aware of the needful and needed quality of things it must project satisfactions or completions. For irrespective of whether a satisfaction is conscious, a satisfaction or non-satisfaction is an objective thing with objective conditions. It means fulfillment of the demands of objective factors. Happiness may *mark* an awareness of such satisfaction, and it may *be* its culminating form. But satisfaction is not subjective, private or personal: it is conditioned by objective partialities and defections and made real by objective situations and completions.

By the same logic, necessity implies the precarious and contingent. A world that was all necessity would not be a world of necessity; it would just be. For in its being, nothing would be necessary for anything else. But where some things are indigent, other things are necessary if demands are to be met. The common failure to note the fact that a world of complete being would be a world in which necessity is meaningless is due to a rapid shift from one universe of discourse to another. First we postulate a whole of Being; then we shift to a part; now since a "part" is logically dependent as such in its existence and its properties, it is necessitated by other parts. But we have unwittingly introduced contingency in the very fact of marking off something as just a part. If the logical implications of the original notion are held to firmly, a part is already a part-of-a-whole. Its being what it is, is not necessitated by the whole or by other parts: its being what it is, is just a name for the whole being what it is. Whole and parts alike are but names for existence there as just what it is. But wherever we can say *if* so-and-so, then something else, there is necessity, because partialities are implied which are not just parts-of-a-whole. A world of "ifs" is alone a world of "musts" —the "ifs" express real differences; the "musts" real connections. The stable and recurrent is needed for the fulfillment of the possible; the doubtful can be settled only through its adaptation to stable objects. The necessary is always necessary for, not necessary in and of itself; it is conditioned by the contingent, although itself a condition of the full determination of the latter.

One of the most striking phases of the history of philosophic thought is the recurrent grouping together of unity, permanence (or "the eternal"), completeness and rational thought, while upon another side full multiplicity, change and the temporal, the partial, defective, sense and desire. This division is obviously but another case of violent separation of the precarious and unsettled from the regular and determinate. One aspect of it however, is worthy of particular attention: the connection of thought and unity. Empirically, all reflection sets out from the problematic and confused. Its aim is to clarify and ascertain. When thinking is successful, its career closes in transforming the disordered into the orderly, the mixed-up into the distinguished or placed, the unclear and ambiguous into the defined and unequivocal, the disconnected into the systematized. It is empirically assured that the goal of thinking does not remain a mere ideal, but is attained often enough so as to render reasonable additional efforts to achieve it.

In these facts we have, I think, the empirical basis of the philosophic doctrines which assert that reality is really and truly a rational system, a coherent whole of relations that cannot be conceived otherwise than in terms of intellect. Reflective inquiry moves in each particular case from differences toward unity; from indeterminate and ambiguous position to clear determination, from confusion and disorder to system. When thought in a given case has reached its goal of organized totality, of definite relations of distinctly placed elements, its object is the accepted starting point, the defined subject matter, of further experiences; antecedent and outgrown conditions of darkness and of unreconciled differences are dismissed as a transitory state of ignorance and inadequate apprehensions. Retain connection of the goal with the thinking by which it is reached, and then identify it with true reality in contrast with the merely phenomenal, and the outline of the logic of rational and "objective" idealisms is before us. Thought like Being, has two forms, one real; the other phenomenal. It is compelled to take on *reflective* form, it involves doubt, inquiry and hypothesis, because it sets out from a subject-matter conditioned by sense, a fact which proves that thought, intellect, is not pure in man, but restricted by an animal organism that is but one part linked with other parts, of nature. But the conclusion of reflection affords us a pattern and guarantee of thought which is *constitutive;* one with the system of objective reality. Such in outline is the procedure of all ontological logics.

A philosophy which accepts the denotative or empirical method accepts at full value the fact that reflective thinking transforms confusion, ambiguity and discrepancy into illumination, definiteness and consistency. But it also points to the contextual situation in which thinking occurs. It notes that the starting point is the actually *problematic,* and that the problematic phase resides in some actual and specifiable situation.

It notes that the means of converting the dubious into the assured, and the incomplete into the determinate, is use of assured and established things, which are just as empirical and as indicative of the nature of experienced things as is the uncertain. It thus notes that thinking is no different in kind from the use of natural materials and energies, say fire and tools, to refine, re-order, and shape other natural materials, say ore. In both cases, there are matters which as they stand are unsatisfactory and there are also adequate agencies for dealing with them and connecting them. At no point or place is there any jump outside empirical, natural objects and their relations. Thought and reason are not specific powers. They consist of the procedures intentionally employed in the application to each other of the unsatisfactorily confused and indeterminate on one side and the regular and stable on the other. Generalizing from such observations, empirical philosophy perceives that thinking is a continuous process of temporal re-organization within one and the same world of experienced things, not a jump from the latter world into one of objects constituted once for all by thought. It discovers thereby the empirical basis of rational idealism, and the point at which it empirically goes astray. Idealism fails to take into account the specified or concrete character of the uncertain situation in which thought occurs; it fails to note the empirically concrete nature of the subject-matter, acts, and tools by which determination and consistency are reached; it fails to note that the conclusive eventual objects having the latter properties are themselves as many as the situations dealt with. The conversion of the logic of reflection into an ontology of rational being is thus due to arbitrary conversion of an eventual natural function of unification into a causal antecedent reality; this in turn is due to the tendency of the imagination working under the influence of emotion to carry unification from an actual, objective and experimental enterprise, limited to particular situations where it is needed, into an unrestricted, wholesale movement which ends in an all-absorbing dream.

The occurrence of reflection is crucial for dualistic metaphysics as well as for idealistic ontologies. Reflection occurs only in situations qualified by uncertainty, alternatives, questioning, search, hypotheses, tentative trials or experiments which test the worth of thinking. A naturalistic metaphysics is bound to consider reflection as itself a natural event occurring *within* nature because of traits of the latter. It is bound to inference from the empirical traits of thinking in precisely the same way as the sciences make inferences from the happening of suns, radio-activity, thunder-storms or any other natural event.

Traits of reflection are as truly indicative or evidential of the traits of *other* things as are the traits of these events. A theory of the nature of the occurrence and career of a sun reached by denial of the obvious traits of the sun, or by denial that these traits are so connected with the traits of other natural events that they can be used as evidence concerning the nature of these other things, would hardly possess scientific standing. Yet philosophers, and strangely enough philosophers who call themselves realists, have constantly held that the traits which are characteristic of thinking, namely, uncertainty, ambiguity, alternatives, inquiring, search, selection, experimental reshaping of external conditions, do not possess the same existential character as do the objects of valid knowledge. They have denied that these traits are evidential of the character of the world within which thinking occurs. They have not, as realists, asserted that these traits are mere appearances; but they have often asserted and implied that such things are only personal or psychological in contrast with a world of objective nature. But the interests of empirical and denotative method and of naturalistic metaphysics wholly coincide. The world must actually be such as to generate ignorance and inquiry; doubt and hypothesis, trial and temporal conclusions; the latter being such that they develop out of existences which while wholly "real" are not as satisfactory, as good, or as significant, as those into which they are eventually re-organized. The ultimate evidence of genuine hazard, contingency, irregularity and indeterminateness in nature is thus found in the occurrence of thinking. The traits of natural existence which generate the fears and adorations of superstitious barbarians generate the scientific procedures of disciplined civilization. The superiority of the latter does not consist in the fact that they are based on "real" existence, while the former depend wholly upon a human nature different from nature in general. It consists in the fact that scientific inquiries reach *objects* which are better, because reached by method which controls them and which adds greater control to life itself, method which mitigates accident, turns contingency to account, and releases thought and other forms of endeavor.

The conjunction of problematic and determinate characters in nature renders every existence, as well as every idea and human act, an experiment in fact, even though not in design. To be intelligently experimental is but to be conscious of this intersection of natural conditions so as to profit by it instead of being at its mercy. The Christian idea of this world and this life as a probation is a kind of distorted recognition of the situation; distorted because it applied wholesale to one stretch of existence in contrast with another, regarded as original and final. But in truth anything which can exist at any place and at any time occurs subject to tests imposed upon it by surroundings, which are only in part compatible and reinforcing. These surroundings test its strength and measure its endurance. As we can discourse of change only in terms of velocity and acceleration which involve relations to other things, so assertion of the permanent and enduring is comparative. The stablest thing we can speak of is not free from conditions set to it by other things. That even the solid earth mountains, the emblems of constancy, appear and disappear like the clouds is an old theme of moralists and poets. The fixed and unchanged being of the Democritean atom is now reported by inquirers to possess some of the traits of his non-being, and to embody a temporary equilibrium in the economy of nature's compromises and adjustments. A thing may endure *secula seculorum* and yet not be everlasting; it will crumble before the gnawing tooth of time, as it exceeds a certain measure. Every existence is an event.

This fact is nothing at which to repine and nothing to gloat over. It is something to be noted and used. If it is discomfiting when applied to good things, to our friends, possessions and precious selves, it is consoling also to know that no evil endures forever; that the longest lane turns sometime, and that the memory of loss of nearest and dearest grows dim in time. The eventful character of all existences is no reason for consigning them to the realm of mere appearance any more than it is a reason for idealizing flux into a deity. The important thing is measure, relation, ratio, knowledge of the comparative tempos of change. In mathematics some variables are constants in some problems; so it is in nature and life. The rate of change of some things is so slow, or is so rhythmic, that these changes have all the advantages of stability in dealing with more transitory and irregular happenings—if we know enough. Indeed, if any one thing that concerns us is subject to change, it is fortunate that all other things change. A thing "absolutely" stable and unchangeable would be out of the range of the principle of action and reaction, of resistance and leverage as well as of friction. Here it would have no applicability, no potentiality of use as measure and control of other events. To designate the slower and the regular rhythmic events structure, and more rapid and irregular ones process, is sound practical sense. It expresses the function of one in respect to the other.

But spiritualistic idealism and materialism alike treat this relational and functional distinction as something fixed and absolute. One doctrine finds structure in a framework of ideal forms, the other finds it in matter. They agree in supposing that structure has some superlative reality. This supposition is another form taken by preference for the stable over the precarious and uncompleted. The fact is that all structure is structure *of* something; anything defined as structure is a character of *events*, not something intrinsic and *per se*. A set of traits is called structure, because of its limiting function in relation to other traits of events. A house has a structure; in comparison with the disintegration and collapse that would occur without its presence, this structure is fixed. Yet it is not something external to which the changes involved in building and using the house have to submit. It is rather an arrangement of changing events such that properties which change slowly, limit and direct a series of quick changes and give them an order which they do not otherwise possess. Structure is constancy of means, of things used for consequences, not of things taken by themselves or absolutely. Structure is what makes construction possible and cannot be discovered or defined except in some realized construction, construction being, of course, an evident order of changes. The isolation of structure from the changes whose stable ordering it is, renders it mysterious—something that is metaphysical in the popular sense of the word, a kind of ghostly queerness.

The "matter" of materialists and the "spirit" of idealists is a creature similar to the constitution of the United States in the minds of unimaginative persons. Obviously the real constitution is certain basic relationships among the activities of the citizens of the country; it is a property or phase of these processes, so connected with them as to influence their rate and direction of change. But by literalists it is often conceived of as something external to them; in itself fixed, a rigid framework to which *all* changes must accommodate themselves. Similarly what we call matter is that character of natural events which is so tied up with changes that are sufficiently rapid to be perceptible as to give the latter a characteristic rhythmic order, the causal sequence. It is no cause or source of events or processes; no absolute monarch; no principle of explanation; no substance behind or underlying changes—save in that sense of substance in which a man well fortified with this world's goods, and hence able to maintain himself through vicissitudes of surroundings, is a man of substance. The name designates a character in operation, not an entity.

That structure, whether of the kind called material or of the kind summed up in the word mental, is stable or permanent relationally and in its office, may be shown in another way. There is no action without reaction; there is no exclusively one-way exercise of conditioning power, no mode of regulation that operates wholly from above to below or from within outwards or from without inwards. Whatever influences the changes of other things is itself changed. The idea of an activity proceeding only in one direction, of an unmoved mover, is a survival of Greek physics. It has been banished from science, but remains to haunt philosophy.   The vague and mysterious properties assigned to mind and matter, the very conceptions of mind and matter in traditional thought, are ghosts walking underground.   The notion of matter actually found in the practice of science has nothing in common with the matter of materialists—and almost everybody is still a materialist as to matter, to which he merely adds a second rigid structure which he calls mind.   The matter of science is a character of natural events and changes as they change; their character of regular and stable order.

Natural events are so complex and varied that there is nothing surprising in their possession of different characterizations, characters so different that they can be easily treated as opposites.

Nothing but unfamiliarity stands in the way of thinking of both mind and matter as different characters of natural events, in which matter expresses their sequential order, and mind the order of their meanings in their logical connections and dependencies.   Processes may be eventful for functions which taken in abstract separation are at opposite poles, just as physiological processes eventuate in both anabolic and katabolic functions.   The idea that matter and mind are two sides or "aspects" of the same things, like the convex and the concave in a curve, is literally unthinkable.

A curve is an intelligible object and concave and convex are defined in terms of this object; they are indeed but names for properties involved in its meaning.   We do not start with convexity and concavity as two independent things and then set up an unknown *tertium quid* to unite two disparate things.   In spite of the literal absurdity of the comparison, it may be understood however in a way which conveys an inkling of the truth. That to which both mind and matter belong is the complex of events that constitute nature. This becomes a mysterious *tertium quid*, incapable of designation, only when mind and matter are taken to be static structures instead of functional characters. It is a plausible prediction that if there were an interdict placed for a generation upon the use of mind, matter, consciousness as nouns, and we were obliged to employ adjectives and adverbs, conscious and consciously, mental and mentally, material and physically, we should find many of our problems much simplified.

We have selected only a few of the variety of the illustrations that might be used in support of the idea that the significant problems and issues of life and philosophy concern the rate and mode of the conjunction of the precarious and the assured, the incomplete and the finished, the repetitious and the varying, the safe and sane and the hazardous. If we trust to the evidence of experienced things, these traits, and the modes and tempos of their interaction with each other, are fundamental features of natural existence. The experience of their various consequences, according as they are relatively isolated, unhappily or happily combined, is evidence that wisdom, and hence that love of wisdom which is philosophy, is concerned with choice and administration of their proportioned union. Structure and process, substance and accident, matter and energy, permanence and flux, one and many, continuity and discreteness, order and progress, law and liberty, uniformity and growth, tradition and innovation, rational will and impelling desires, proof and discovery, the actual and the possible, are names given to various phases of their conjunction, and the issue of living depends upon the art with which these things are adjusted to each other.

While metaphysics may stop short with noting and registering these traits, man is not contemplatively detached from them. They involve him in his perplexities and troubles, and are the source of his joys and achievements. The situation is not indifferent to man, because it forms man as a desiring, striving, thinking, feeling creature. It is not egotism that leads man from contemplative registration of these traits to interest in managing them, to intelligence and purposive art. Interest, thinking, planning, striving, consummation and frustration are a drama enacted by these forces and conditions. A particular choice may be arbitrary; this is only to say that it does not approve itself to reflection. But choice is not arbitrary, not in a universe like this one, a world which is not finished and which has not consistently made up its mind where it is going and what it is going to do. Or, if we call it arbitrary, the arbitrariness is not ours but that of existence itself. And to call existence arbitrary or by any moral name, whether disparaging or honorific, is to patronize nature. To assume an attitude of condescension toward existence is perhaps a natural human compensation for the straits of life. But it is an ultimate source of the covert, uncandid and cheap in philosophy. This compensatory disposition it is which forgets that reflection exists to guide choice and effort. Hence its love of wisdom is but an unlaborious transformation of existence by dialectic, instead of an opening and enlarging of the ways of nature in man. A true wisdom, devoted to the latter task, discovers in thoughtful observation and experiment the method of administering the unfinished processes of existence so that frail goods shall be substantiated, secure goods be extended, and the precarious promises of good that haunt experienced things be more liberally fulfilled.

CHAPTER THREE

Nature, Ends and Histories

Human experience in the large, in its coarse and conspicuous features, has for one of its most striking features preoccupation with direct enjoyment, feasting and festivities; ornamentation, dance, song, dramatic pantomime, telling yarns and enacting stories. In comparison with intellectual and moral endeavor, this trait of experience has hardly received the attention from philosophers that it demands. Even philosophers who have conceived that pleasure is the sole motive of man and the attainment of happiness his whole aim, have given a curiously sober, drab, account of the working of pleasure and the search for happiness. Consider the utilitarians how they toiled, spun and wove, but who never saw man arrayed in joy as the lilies of the field. Happiness was to them a matter of calculation and effort, of industry guided by mathematical book-keeping. The history of man shows however that man takes his enjoyment neat, and at as short range as possible.

Direct appropriations and satisfactions were prior to anything but the most elementary and exigent prudence, just as the useful arts preceded the sciences. The body is decked before it is clothed. While homes are still hovels, temples and palaces are embellished. Luxuries prevail over necessities except when necessities can be festally celebrated. Men make a game of their fishing and hunting, and turn to the periodic and disciplinary labor of agriculture only when inferiors, women and slaves, cannot be had to do the work. Useful labor is, whenever possible, transformed by ceremonial and ritual accompaniments, subordinated to art that yields immediate enjoyment; otherwise it is attended to under the compulsion of circumstance during abbreviated surrenders of leisure. For leisure permits of festivity, in revery, ceremonies and conversation. The pressure of necessity is, however, never wholly lost, and the sense of it led men, as if with uneasy conscience at their respite from work, to impute practical efficacy to play and rites, endowing them with power to coerce events and to purchase the favor of rulers of events.

But it is possible to magnify the place of magical exercise and superstitious legend. The primary interest lies in staging the show and enjoying the spectacle, in giving play to the ineradicable interest in stories which illustrate the contingencies of existence combined with happier endings for emergencies than surrounding conditions often permit. It was not conscience that kept men loyal to cults and rites, and faithful to tribal myths. So far as it was not routine, it was enjoyment of the drama of life without the latter's liabilities that kept piety from decay. Interest in rites as means of influencing the course of things, and the cognitive or explanation office of myths were hardly more than an embroidery, repeating in pleasant form the pattern which inexpugnable necessities imposed upon practice. When rite and myth are spontaneous rehearsal of the impact and career of practical needs and doings, they must also seem to have practical force. The political significance of July Fourth, 1776, is perhaps renewed by the juvenile celebrations of Independence Day, but this effect hardly accounts for the fervor of the celebration.   Any excuse serves for a holiday and the more the holiday is decked out with things that contrast with the pressure of workaday life while re-enacting its form, the more a holiday it is.   The more unrestrained the play of fancy the greater the contrast.   The supernatural has more thrills than the natural, the customary; holidays and holy-days are indistinguishable.   Death is an occasion for a wake, and mourning is acclaimed with a board of funeral meats.

Reflected upon, this phase of experience manifests objects which are final.   The attitude involved in their appreciation is esthetic.   The operations entering into their production is fine art, distinguished from useful art. It is dangerous however to give names, especially in discourse that is far aloof from the things named—direct enjoyment of the interplay of the contingent and the effective, purged of practical risks and penalties.   Esthetic, fine art, appreciation, drama have an eulogistic flavor. We hesitate to call the penny-dreadful of fiction artistic, so we call it debased fiction or a travesty on art.   Most sources of direct enjoyment for the masses are not art to the cultivated, but perverted art, an unworthy indulgence. Thus we miss the point.   A passion of anger, a dream, relaxation of the limbs after effort, swapping of jokes, horse-play, beating of drums, blowing of tin whistles, explosion of firecrackers and walking on stilts, have the same quality of immediate and absorbing finality that is possessed by things and acts dignified by the title of esthetic.   For man is more preoccupied with enhancing life than with bare living; so that a sense of living when it attends labor and utility is borrowed not intrinsic, having been generated in those periods of relief when activity was dramatic.

To say these things is only to say that man is naturally more interested in consummations than he is in preparations; and that consummations have first to be hit upon spontaneously and accidentally—as the baby gets food and all of us are warmed by the sun—before they can be objects of foresight, invention and industry. Consciousness so far as it is not dull ache and torpid comfort is a thing of the imagination. The extensions and transformations of existence generated in imagination may come at last to attend work so as to make it significant and agreeable. But when men are first at the height of business, they are too busy to engage either in fancy or reflective inquiry. At the outset the hunt was enjoyed in the feast, or in the calm moments of shaping spears, bows and arrows. Only later was the content of these experiences carried over into hunting itself, so that even its dangers might be savored. Labor, through its structure and order, lends play its pattern and plot; play then returns the loan with interest to work, in giving it a sense of beginning, sequence and climax. As long as imagined objects are satisfying, the logic of drama, of suspense, thrill and success, dominates the logic of objective events. Cosmogonies are mythological not because savages indulge in defective scientific explanations, but because objects of imagination are consummatory in the degree in which they exuberantly escape from the pressure of natural surroundings, even when they re-enact its crises. The congenial is first form of the consistent.

As Goldenweiser says, if supernaturalism prevails in early culture it is largely because, "the phantasmagoria of supernaturalism is esthetically attractive, it has beauty of thought and form and of movement, it abounds in delightful samples of logical coherence, and is full of fascination for the creator, the systematizer and the beholder." And it is safe to add, that the esthetic character of logical coherence rather than its tested coherence with fact is that which yields the delight. Again speaking of the place of ceremonialism in early culture, Goldenweiser well characterizes it as a kind of "psychic incandescence;" because of its presence, there is "no cooling of the ever glowing mass (the conglomerate of customs) no flagging of the emotions, no sinking of the cultural associations to the more precarious level of purely ideational connections."

Modern psychiatry as well as anthropology have demonstrated the enormous rôle of symbolism in human experience. The word symbolism, however, is a product of reflection upon direct phenomena, not a description of what happens when so-called symbols are potent. For the feature which characterizes symbolism is precisely that the thing which later reflection calls a symbol is not a symbol, but a direct vehicle, a concrete embodiment, a vital incarnation. To find its counterpart we should betake ourselves not to signal flags which convey information, ideas and direction, but to a national flag in moments of intense emotional stir of a devout patriot. Symbolism in this sense dominates not only all early art and cult but social organization as well. Rites, designs, patterns are all charged with a significance which we may call mystic, but which is immediate and direct to those who have and celebrate them. Be the origin of the totem what it may, it is not a cold, intellectual sign of a social organization; it is that organization made present and visible, a centre of emotionally charged behavior. It is not otherwise with the symbolism uncovered in dreams and neurotic states by psychological analysis.   Such symbols are not indicative or intellectual signs; they are condensed substitutes of actual things and events, which embody actual things with more direct and enchanced import than do the things themselves with their distractions, imposition, and irrelevances.   Meanings are intellectually distorted and depressed, but immediately they are heightened and concentrated.

Jesperson speaks of the origin of language in similar terms.   He says that many linguistic philosophers appear to "imagine our primitive ancestors after their own image as serious and well meaning men, endowed with a large share of common sense. . . . . They leave you with the impression that these first framers of speech were sedate citizens with a strong interest in the purely business and matter of fact aspects of life."   But Jesperson finds that the prosaic side of early culture was capable only " of calling forth short monosyllabic interjections; they are the most immutable portions of language, and remain now at essentially the same standpoint as thousands of years ago."   He concludes that the "genesis of language is found . . . . in the poetic side of life; the source of speech is not gloomy seriousness, but merry play and youthful hilarity."   And no one would deny, I suppose that literature rather than business and science has developed and fixed our present linguistic resources.

It would be difficult to find a fact more significant of the traits of nature, more instructive for a naturalistic metaphysics of existence, than this cleavage of the things of human experience into actual but hard objects, and enjoyed but imagined objects.   One might think that philosophers in their search for some datum that possesses properties that put it beyond doubt, might have directed their attention to this direct phase of experience, in which objects are not a matter of sensations, ideas, beliefs or knowledge, but are something had and enjoyed. All that "self-evidence" can intelligibly mean is obviousness of presence; commonplaces like human interest in the things of sport and celebration are the most conspicuously obvious of all. In comparison, the "self-evident" things of philosophers are recondite and technical.

The other most self-evident thing in experience is useful labor and its coercive necessity. As direct appreciative enjoyment exhibits things in their consummatory phase, labor manifests things in their connections of things with one another, in efficiency, productivity, furthering, hindering, generating, destroying. From the standpoint of enjoyment a thing is what it directly does for us. From that of labor a thing is what it will do to other things—the only way in which a tool or an obstacle can be defined. Extraordinary and subtle reasons have been assigned for belief in the principle of causation. Labor and the use of tools seem, however, to be a sufficient empirical reason: indeed, to be the only empirical events that can be specifically pointed to in this connection. They are more adequate grounds for acceptance of belief in causality than are the regular sequences of nature or than a category of reason, or the alleged fact of will. The first thinker who proclaimed that every event is effect of something and cause of something else, that every particular existence is both conditioned and condition, merely put into words the procedure of the workman, converting a mode of practice into a formula. External regularity is familiar, customary, taken for granted, not thought of, embodied in thoughtless routine. Regularity, orderly sequence, in productive labor presents itself to thought as a controlling principle. Industrial arts are the type-forms of experience that bring to light the sequential connections of things with one another.

In contrast, the enjoyment (with which suffering is to be classed) of things is a declaration that natural exist-ences are not mere passage ways to another passage way, and so on *ad infinitum.* Thinkers interested in esthetic experience are wont to point out the absurdity of the idea that things are good or valuable only for something else; they dwell on the fact vouchsafed by esthetic appreciation that there are things that have their goodness or value in themselves, which are not cherished for the sake of any-thing else. These philosophers usually confine this obser-vation however to human affairs isolated from nature, which they interpret exclusively in terms of labor, or causal connections. But in every event there is some-thing obdurate, self-sufficient, wholly immediate, neither a relation nor an element in a relational whole, but termi-nal and exclusive. Here, as in so many other matters, materialists and idealists agree in an underlying meta-physics which ignores in behalf of relations and relational systems, those irreducible, infinitely plural, undefinable and indescribable qualities which a thing must *have* in order to be, and in order to be capable of becoming the subject of relations and a theme of discourse. Immediacy of existence is ineffable. But there is nothing mystical about such ineffability; it expresses the fact that of direct existence it is futile to say anything to one's self and impossible to say anything to another. Discourse can but intimate connections which if followed out may lead one to *have* an existence.   Things in their immediacy are unknown and unknowable, not because they are remote or behind some impenetrable veil of sensation of ideas, but because knowledge has no concern with them.   For knowledge is a memorandum of conditions of their appearance, concerned, that is, with sequences, coexistences, relations.   Immediate things may be *pointed to* by words, but not described or defined.   Description when it occurs is but a part of a circuitous method of pointing or denoting; index to a starting point and road which if taken may lead to a direct and ineffable presence.   To the empirical thinker, immediate enjoyment and suffering are the conclusive exhibition and evidence that nature has its finalities as well as its relationships.

Many modern thinkers, influenced by the notion that knowledge is the only mode of experience that grasps things, assuming the ubiquity of cognition, and noting that immediacy or qualitative existence has no place in authentic science, have asserted that qualities are always and only states of consciousness.   It is a reasonable belief that there would be no such thing as "consciousness" if events did not have a phase of brute and unconditioned "isness," of being just what they irreducibly are.   Consciousness as sensation, image and emotion is thus a particular case of immediacy occurring under complicated conditions.   And also without immediate qualities those relations with which science deals, would have no footing in existence and thought would have nothing beyond itself to chew upon or dig into.   Without a basis in qualitative events, the characteristic subject-matter of knowledge would be algebraic ghosts, relations that do not relate. To dispose of things in which relations terminate by calling them elements, is to discourse within a relational and logical scheme.   Only if elements are more than just elements in a whole, only if they have something qualitatively their own, can a relational system be prevented from complete collapse.

The Greeks were more naïve than we are. Their thinkers were as much dominated by the esthetic characters of experienced objects as modern thinkers are by their scientific and economic (or relational) traits.   Consequently they had no difficulty in recognizing the importance of qualities and of things inherently closed or final.   They thought of mind as a realization of natural existence or a participation in it.   Thus they were saved from the epistemological problem of how things and mind, defined antithetically, can have anything to do with each other.   If existence in its immediacies could speak it would proclaim, "I may *have* relatives but *I* am not related."   In esthetic objects, that is in all immediately enjoyed and suffered things, in things directly possessed, they thus speak for themselves; Greek thinkers heard their voice.

Unfortunately however, these thinkers were not content to speak as artists, of whom they had a low opinion. Since they were thinkers, aiming at truth or knowledge, they put art on a lower plane than science; and the only enjoyment they found worth serious attention was that of objects of thought.   In consequence they formulated a doctrine in which the esthetic and the rational are confused on principle, and they bequeathed the confusion as an intellectual tradition to their successors.   Aristotle spoke more truly than he was aware when he said that philosophy began in leisure "when almost all the necessaries and things that make for comfort and recreation were present." For it was philosophic, rather than scientific "knowledge" which thus began. Philosophy was a telling of the story of nature after the style of all congenial stories, a story with a plot and climax, given such coherent properties as would render it congenial to minds demanding that objects satisfy logical canons.

Objects are certainly none the worse for having wonder and admiration for their inspiration and art for their medium. But these objects are distorted when their affiliation with the epic, temple and drama is denied, and there is claimed for them a rational and cosmic status independent of piety, drama and story. In the classic philosophy of Greece the picture of the world that was constructed on an artistic model preferred itself as being the result of intellectual study. A story composed in the interests of a refined type of enjoyment, ordered by the needs of consistency in discourse, or dialectic, became cosmology and metaphysics. Its authors took toward art and rite much the same sort of superior attitude that the modern esthete takes to vulgar forms of esthetic satisfaction. A claim for superiority in subject matter and mode of artistic treatment was indeed legitimate; but a claim was made for difference in kind. Art was an embellished imitation of the everyday or empirical affairs of life in their natural setting; philosophy was science, an envisagement of realities behind all copies, all phenomena; or a grasp of essences within them forming their valid substance. The delight attending the insight was attributed to the final intrinsic dignity of the cosmic objects perceived by reason, instead of being frankly recognized to be due to a selection and arrangement of things with a view to enhancement of tranquil enjoyment.

Devotion to rites, stories and revery springs on its magical side from practical desire to control the contingent; but in larger measure it embodies the happiness that attends the sense of successful issue from the uncertainly hazardous. Imagination is primarily dramatic, rather than lyric, whether it takes the form of the play enacted on the stage, of the told story or silent soliloquy. The constant presence of instability and trouble gives depth and poignancy to the situations in which are pictured their subordination to final issues possessed of calm and certainty. To re-enact the vicissitudes, crises and tragedies of life under conditions that deprive them of their overt dangers, is the natural rôle of "consciousness," which is tamed to respect actualities only when circumstance enforces the adoption of the method of labor, a discipline that is fortunate if it retain some of the liberation from immediate exigencies which characterizes dramatic imagination.

Modern critics of esthetics have criticized the conception of Plato and Aristotle that art is imitation. But in its original statement, this conception was a description of the observed facts of drama, music and epic rather than theoretical interpretation. For these thinkers were not so stupid as to hold that art is an imitation of inert things; they held that it was a mimesis of the critical and climatic behavior of natural forces within human career and destiny. Such a reproduction is naturally in a new and liberal medium; it permits idealization, but the idealization is of natural events. It is self-sufficing, an end in itself, while the events seem to exist only to render the perfection of an idealized reproduction possible and pertinent. Resort to esthetic objects is the spontaneous human escape and consolation in a trying and difficult world. A world that consisted entirely of stable objects directly presented and possessed would have no esthetic qualities; it would just be, and would lack power to satisfy and to inspire. Objects are actually esthetic when they turn hazard and defeat to an issue which is above and beyond trouble and vicissitude. Festal celebration and consummatory delights belong only in a world that knows risk and hardship.

Greek philosophy as well as Greek art is a memorial of the joy in what is finished, when it is found amid a world of unrest, struggle, and uncertainty in what, since it is ended, does not commit us to the uncertain hazards of what is still going on. Without such experiences as those of Greek art it is hardly conceivable that the craving for the passage of change into rest, of the contingent, mixed and wandering into the composed and total, would have found a model after which to design a universe like the cosmos of Platonic and Aristotelian tradition. Form was the first and last word of philosophy because it had been that of art; form is change arrested in a prerogative object. It conveys a sense of the imperishable and time-less, although the material in which it is exemplified is subject to decay and contingency. It thus conveys an intimation of potentialities completely actualized in a happier realm, where events are not events, but are arrested and brought to a close in an eternal self-sustaining activity. Such a realm is intrinsically one of secure and self-possessed meaning. It consists of objects of immediate enjoyment hypostasized into transcendent reality. Such was the conversion of Greek esthetic contemplation effected by Greek reflection.

The technical structure of the resulting metaphysics is familiar. The cosmically real is one with the finished, the perfect, or wholly done. Even with Aristotle, a coldly defining theory, called metaphysics, of the traits of Being, becomes a theology, or science of ultimate and eternal reality to which only ecstatic predicates are attributable. It consists of pure forms, self-sufficient, self-enclosed and self-sustaining; self-movement or life at eternal full-tide. Forms are ideal, and the ideal is the rational apprehended by reason. The material for this point of view was found empirically in what is consummatory and final; and the dominion exercised by art in Greek culture fostered and enhanced attention to objects of this immediately enjoyed kind. To the spectator, artistic objects are given; they need only to be envisaged; Greek reflection, carried on by a leisure class in the interest of liberalizing leisure, was preëminently that of the spectator, not that of the participator in processes of production. Labor, production, did not seem to create form, it dealt with matter or changing things so as to furnish an occasion for incarnation of antecedent forms in matter. To artisans form is alien, unperceived and unenjoyed; absorbed in laboring with material, they live in a world of change and matter, even when their labors have an end in manifestation of form. Plato was so troubled by the consequences of this ignorance of form on the part of all who live in the world of practice, industrial and political, that he elaborated a plan by which their activities might be regulated by those who, above labor and entanglement in change and practice, provide in laws forms to shape the habits of those who work. Aristotle escaped the dilemma by putting nature above art, and endowing nature with skilled purpose that for the most part achieves ends or completions. Thus the rôle of the human artisan whether in industry or politics became relatively negligible, and the miscarriages of human art a matter of relative insignificance.

The Aristotelian conception of four-fold "causation" is openly borrowed from the arts, which for the artisan are utilitarian and menial, and are "fine" or liberal only for the cultivated spectator who is possessed of leisure—that is, is relieved from the necessity of partaking laboriously in change and matter. Nature is an artist that works from within instead of from without. Hence all change, or matter, is potentiality for finished objects. Like other artists, nature first possesses the forms which it afterwards embodies. When arts follow fixed models, whether in making shoes, houses, or dramas, and when the element of individual invention in design is condemned as caprice, forms and ends are necessarily external to the individual worker. They preceded any particular realization. Design and plan are anonymous and universal, and carry with them no suggestion of a designing, purposive mind. Models are objectively given and have only to be observed and followed. Thus there was no difficulty, such as one may feel to-day, in ascribing definite and regulative forms to the changes of nature, which are actualized in objects that are finalities, closures of change. The actualization in an organic body of the forms that are found in things constitutes mind as the end of nature. Their immediate possession and celebration constitutes consciousness, as far as the idea of consciousness is found in Greek thought.

This doctrine was not an arbitrary speculation; it flowed naturally from the fact that Greek thinkers were fortunate to find ready-made to hand and eye a realm of esthetic objects with traits of order and proportion, form and finality. The arts were pursued upon the basis of a fund of realized, objective and impersonal designs and plans, which were prior to individual devising and execution rather than products of individual purpose and invention. The philosophers did not create out of their own speculations, the idea of materials subdued to the acceptance and manifestation of objective forms. They found the fact in the art of their period, translating it into an intellectual formula. Philosophers were not the authors of an identification of objects informed with ideal order and proportion with a final and arresting outcome of processes of antecedent change. That identification was at least implicit in the operation of artisans. Nor were the philosophers the originators of the idea that mental appropriation of some objects is intrinsically a state of elevated satisfaction. That fact was given to them in the esthetic culture of their civilization. What the philosophers are responsible for is a peculiar one-sided interpretation of these empirical facts, an interpretation, however, which has its roots in features, although less admirable ones, of Greek culture.

For the Greek community was marked by a sharp separation of servile workers and free men of leisure, which meant a division between acquaintance with matters of fact and contemplative appreciation, between unintelligent practice and unpractical intelligence, between affairs of change and efficiency— or instrumentality—and of rest and enclosure—finality. Experience afforded therefore no model for a conception of experimental inquiry and of reflection efficacious in action. In consequence, the sole notability, intelligibility, of nature was conceived to reside in objects that were ends, since they set limits to change. Changing things were not capable of being known on the basis of relationship to one another, but only on the basis of their relationship to objects beyond change, because marking its limit, and immediately precious. The terminal objects lent changing objects the properties which made them knowable; such stability of character as they possessed was derived from the form of the end-objects toward which they moved. Hence an inherent appetition or nisus toward these terminal and static objects was attributed to them. The whole scheme of cosmic change was a vehicle for attaining ends possessed of properties which caused them to be objects of attraction of all lesser things, rendering the latter uneasy and restless until they attained the end-object which constitutes their real nature. Thus an immediate contemplative possession and enjoyment of objects, dialectically ordered, was interpreted as defining both true knowledge and the highest end and good of nature. A doctrine of morals, of what is better in reflective choice, was thus converted into a metaphysics and science of Being, the moral aspect being disguised to the modern mind by the fact that the highest good was conceived esthetically, instead of in the social terms which upon the whole dominate modern theories of morality.

The doctrine that objects as ends are the proper objects of science, because they are the ultimate forms of real being, met its doom in the scientific revolution of the seventeenth century. Essences and forms were attacked as occult; "final causes" were either wholly denied or relegated to a divine realm too high for human knowledge. The doctrine of natural ends was displaced by a doctrine of designs, ends-in-view, conscious aims constructed and entertained in individual minds independent of nature. Descartes, Spinoza and Kant are upon this matter at least in agreement with Bacon, Hume and Helvetius. The imputation to natural events of cosmic appetition towards ends, the notion that their changes were to be understood as efforts to reach a natural state of rest and perfection, were indicated as the chief source of sterility and fantasy in science; the syllogistic logic connected with the doctrine was discarded as verbal, polemical, and at its best irrelevant to the subtle operations of nature; purpose and contingency were alike relegated to the purely human and personal; nature was evacuated of qualities and became a homogeneous mass differentiated by differences of homogeneous motion in a homogeneous space. Mechanical relations, which Greek thought had rejected as equivalent to the chaotic reign of pure accident, became the head corner-stone of the conception of law, of uniformity and order. If ends were recognized at all, it was only under the caption of design, and design was defined as conscious aim rather than as objective order and architechtonic form. Wherever the influence of modern physics penetrated, the classic theory became remote, faded, factitious, with its assertion that natural changes are inherent movements toward objects which are their fulfillments or perfections, so that the latter are true objects of knowledge, supplying the forms or characters under which alone changes may be known. With the decay of this doctrine, departed also belief in cosmic qualitative differences and kinds, so that of necessity quality and immediacy had no recourse, expelled from objective nature, save to take refuge in personal consciousness.

Is this reversal of classic theories of existence inevitable? Must belief in ends involved in nature itself be surrendered, or be asserted only by means of a roundabout examination of the nature of knowledge which starting from conscious intent to know, finally infers that the universe is a vast, non-natural fulfillment of a conscious intent? Or is there an ingredient of truth in ancient metaphysics which may be extracted and re-affirmed? Empirically, the existence of objects of direct grasp, possession, use and enjoyment cannot be denied. Empirically, things are poignant, tragic, beautiful, humorous, settled, disturbed, comfortable, annoying, barren, harsh, consoling, splendid, fearful; are such immediately and in their own right and behalf. If we take advantage of the word esthetic in a wider sense than that of application to the beautiful and ugly, esthetic quality, immediate, final or self-enclosed, indubitably characterizes natural situations as they empirically occur. These traits stand in themselves on precisely the same level as colors, sounds, qualities of contact, taste and smell. Any criterion that finds the latter to be ultimate and "hard" data will, impartially applied, come to the same conclusion about the former. *Any* quality as such is final; it is at once initial and terminal; just what it is as it exists. It may be referred to other things, it may be treated as an effect or as a sign. But this involves an extraneous extension and use. It takes us beyond quality in its immediate qualitativeness. If experienced things are valid evidence, then nature in having qualities within itself has what in the literal sense must be called ends, terminals, arrests, enclosures.

It is dangerous to venture at all upon the use of the word "ends" in connection with existential processes. Apologetic and theological controversies cluster about it and affect its signification. Barring this connotation, the word has an almost inexpugnable honorific flavor, so that to assert that nature is characterized by ends, the most conspicuous of which is the life of mind, seems like engaging in an eulogistic, rather than an empirical account of nature. Something much more neutral than any such implication is, however, meant. We constantly talk about things coming or drawing to a close; getting ended, finished, done with, over with. It is a commonplace that no *thing* lasts forever. We may be glad or we may be sorry but that is wholly a matter of the kind of history which is being ended. We may conceive the end, the close, as due to fulfillment, perfect attainment, to satiety, or to exhaustion, to dissolution, to something having run down or given out. Being an end may be indifferently an ecstatic culmination, a matter-of-fact consummation, or a deplorable tragedy. Which of these things a closing or terminal object is, has nothing to do with the property of being an end.

The genuine implications of natural ends may be brought out by considering beginnings instead of endings. To insist that nature is an affair of beginnings is to assert that there is no one single and all-at-once beginning of everything. It is but another way of saying that nature is an affair *of* affairs, wherein each one, no matter how linked up it may be with others, has its *own* quality. It does not imply that every beginning marks an advance or improvement; as we sadly know accidents, diseases, wars, lies and errors, begin.   Clearly the fact and idea of beginning is neutral, not eulogistic; temporal, not absolute. And since wherever one thing begins something else ends, what is true of beginnings is true of endings.   Popular fiction and drama shows the bias of human nature in favor of happy endings, but by being fiction and drama they show with even greater assurance that unhappy endings are natural events.

To minds inured to the eulogistic connotation of ends, such a neutral interpretation of the meaning of ends as has just been set forth may seem to make the doctrine of ends a matter of indifference.   If ends are only endings or closings of temporal episodes, why bother to call attention to ends at all, to say nothing of framing a theory of ends and dignifying it with the name of natural teleology? In the degree, however, in which the mind is weaned from partisan and ego-centric interest, acknowledgement of nature as a scene of incessant beginnings and endings, presents itself as the source of philosophic enlightenment. It enables thought to apprehend causal mechanisms and temporal finalities as phases of the same natural processes, instead of as competitors where the gain of one is the loss of the other.   Mechanism is the order involved in an historic occurrence, capable of definition in terms of the order which various histories sustain to each other. Thus it is the instrumentality of control of any particular termination since a sequential order involves the last term.

The traditional conception of natural ends was to the effect that nature does nothing in vain; the accepted meaning of this phrase was that every change is for the sake of something which does not change, occurring in its behalf. Thus the mind started with a ready-made list of good things or perfections which it was the business of nature to accomplish. Such a view may verbally distinguish between something called efficient causation and something else called final causation. But in effect the distinction is only between the causality of the master who contents himself with uttering an order and the efficacy of the servant who actually engages in the physical work of execution. It is only a way of attributing ultimate causality to what is ideal and mental—the directive order of the master—, while emancipating it from the supposed degradation of physical labor in carrying it out, as well as avoiding the difficulties of inserting an immaterial cause within the material realm. But in a legitimate account of ends as endings, all directional order resides in the sequential order. This no more occurs for the sake of the end than a mountain exists for the sake of the peak which is its end. A musical phrase has a certain close, but the earlier portion does not therefore exist for the sake of the close as if it were something which is done away with when the close is reached. And so a man is not an adult until after he has been a boy, but childhood does not exist for the sake of maturity.

By the nature of the case, causality, however it be defined, consists in the sequential order itself, and not in a last term which as such is irrelevant to causality, although it may, of course be, in addition, an initial term in another sequential order. The view held—or implied—by some "mechanists", which treats an initial term as if it had an inherent generative force which it somehow emits and bestows upon its successors, is all of a piece with the view held by teleologists which implies that an end brings about its own antecedents. Both isolate an event from the history in which it belongs and in which it has its character. Both make a factitiously isolated position in a temporal order a mark of true reality, one theory selecting initial place and the other final place. But in fact causality is another name for the sequential order itself; and since this is an order of a history having a beginning and end, there is nothing more absurd than setting causality over against either initiation or finality.

The same considerations permit a naturalistic interpretation of the ideas of dynamic and static. Every end is as such static; this statement is but a truism; changing into something else, a thing is obviously transitive, not final. Yet the thing which is a close of one history is always the beginning of another, and in this capacity the thing in question is transitive or dynamic. This statement also is tautology, for dynamic does not mean possessed of "force" or capable of emitting it so as to stir up other things and set them in motion; it means simply change in a connected series of events. The traditional view of force points necessarily to something transcendental, because outside of events, whether called God or Will or The Unknowable. So the traditional view of the static points to something fixed and rigid, incapable of change, and therefore also outside the course of things and consequently non-empirical. Empirically, however, there is a history which is a succession of histories, and in which any event is at once both beginning of one course and close of another; is both transitive and static. The phrase constantly in our mouths, "state of affairs" is accurately descriptive, although it makes sheer nonsense in both the traditional spiritual and mechanistic theories. There are no changes that do not enter into an affair, *Res*, and there is no affair that is not bounded and thereby marked off as a state or condition. When a state of affairs is perceived, the perceiving-of-a-state-of-affairs is a further state of affairs. Its subject-matter is a thing in the idiomatic sense of thing, *res*, whether a solar-system, a stellar constellation, or an atom, a diversified and more or less loosely interconnection of events, falling within boundaries sufficiently definite to be capable of being approximately traced. Such is the unbiased evidence of experience in gross, and such in effect is the conclusion of recent physics as far as a layman can see. For this reason, and not because of any unique properties of a separate kind of existence, called psychic or mental, every situation or field of consciousness is marked by initiation, direction or intent, and consequence or import. What is unique is not these traits, but the property of awareness or perception. Because of this property, the initial stage is capable of being judged in the light of its probable course and consequence. There is anticipation. Each successive event being a stage in a serial process is both expectant and commemorative. What is more precisely pertinent to our present theme, the terminal outcome when anticipated (as it is when a moving cause of affairs is perceived) becomes an end-in-view, an aim, purpose, a prediction usable as a plan in shaping the course of events. In classic Greek thought, the perception of ends was simply an esthetic contemplation of the forms of objects in which natural processes were completed. In most modern thought, it is an arbitrary creation of private mental operations guided by personal desire, the theoretical alternative being that they are finite copies of the fulfilled intentions of an infinite mind. In empirical fact, they are projections of possible consequences; they are ends-in-view. The in-viewness of ends is as much conditioned by antecedent natural conditions as is perception of *contemporary* objects external to the organism, trees and stones, or whatever. That is, natural processes must have actually terminated in specifiable consequences, which give those processes definition and character, before ends can be mentally entertained and be the objects of striving desire. In so far, we must side with Greek thought. But empirical ends-in-view are distinguished in two important respects from ends as they are conceived in classic thought. They are not objects of contemplative possession and use, but are intellectual and regulative means, degenerating into reminiscences or dreams unless they are employed as plans within the state of affairs. And when they are attained, the objects which they inform are conclusions and fulfillments, *only* as these objects are the consequence of prior reflection, deliberate choice and directed effort are they fulfillments, conclusions, completions, perfections. A natural end which occurs without the intervention of human art is a terminus, a de facto boundary, but it is not entitled to any such honorific status of completions and realizations as classic metaphysics assigned them.

When we regard conscious experience, that is to say, the *object* and *qualities* characteristic of conscious life, as a natural end, we are bound to regard *all* objects impartially as distinctive ends in the Aristotelian sense. We cannot pick or choose; when we do pick and choose we are obviously dealing with practical ends—with objects and qualities that are deemed worthy of selection by reflective, deliberate choice.   These "ends" are not the less natural, if we have an eye to the continuity of experienced objects with other natural occurrences, but they are not ends without the intervention of a special affair, reflective survey and choice.   But popular thought, in accord with the Greek tradition, picks and chooses among all ends those which it likes and honors, at the same time ignoring and implicitly denying the act of choice.   Like those who regard a happy escape from a catastrophe as a providential intervention, neglecting all who have not escaped, popular teleology regards *good* objects as natural ends, *bad* objects and qualities being regarded as mere accidents or incidents, regrettable mechanical excess or defect. Popular teleology like Greek metaphysics, has accordingly been apologetic, justificatory of the beneficence of nature; it has been optimistic in a complacent way.

Primitive man like naïve common sense imputes terminating qualities to nature—in which it follows a sound realistic metaphysics.   But it also imputes to them the property of causal determination, an imputation rejected by science.   Rejection by science does not prove these qualities to be mere "subjective" or "private" appearances; it only shows that they are termini, closings of serial events.   Events that achieve and possess them are linked, mediatory, transitive, indicative, and the proper material of knowledge.   From the standpoint of causal sequence, or the order with which science is concerned, qualities are superfluous, irrelevant and immaterial.   We could never predict their occurrence from the fullest acquaintance with the properties that form the objects of knowledge as such.

From the standpoint of the latter, the relational orders, ends are abrupt and interruptive.   Hence to a philosophy that takes the subject-matter of knowledge to be exclusive and exhaustive—as so much of modern philosophy has done—they form a most perplexing problem, a mystery. For with extrusive and superfluous status they combine the property of being permeating and absorbing.   They alone, as we say, are of interest, and they are the cause of taking interest in other things.   For living creatures they form the natural platform for regarding other things. They are the basis, directly and indirectly, of active response to things.   As compared with them, other things are obstacles and means of procuring and avoiding the occurrence of situations having them.   When the word "consciousness" is—as it often is—used for a short name for the sum total of such immediate qualities as actually present themselves, it is the end or terminus of natural events.   As such it is also gratuitous, superfluous and inexplicable when reality is defined in terms of the relational objects of science.

By "ends" we also mean ends-in-view, aims, things viewed after deliberation as worthy of attainment and as evocative of effort.   They are formed from objects taken in their immediate and terminal qualities; objects once having occurred as endings, but which are not now in existence and which are not likely to come into existence save by an action which modifies surroundings.   Classic metaphysics is a confused union of these two sense of ends, the primarily natural and the secondarily natural, or practical, moral.   Each meaning is intelligible, grounded, legitimate in itself.   But their mixture is one of the Great Bads of philosophy.   For it treats as natural ends apart from reflection just those objects that are worthy and excellent to reflective choice. Popular teleology has unknowingly followed the leadings that controlled Greek thought; spiritualistic quasi-theological metaphysics has consciously adopted the latter's point of view.

The features of this confused metaphysics are: First, elimination from the status of natural ends of all objects that are evil and troublesome; Secondly, the grading of objects selected to constitute natural ends into a fixed, unchangeable hierarchical order. Objects that possess and import qualities of struggle, suffering and defeat are regarded not as ends, but as frustrations of ends, as accidental and inexplicable deviations. Theology has resorted to an act of original sin to make their occurrence explicable, Greek metaphysics resorted to the presence in nature of a recalcitrant, obdurate, factor. To this provincially exclusive view of natural termini, popular teleology adds a ranking of objects according to which some are more completely ends than others, until there is reached an object which is only end, never eventful and temporal—*the* end. The hierarchy is explicit in Greek thought: first, and lowest are vegetative ends, normal growth and reproduction; second in rank, come animal ends, locomotion and sensibility; third in rank, are ideal and rational ends, of which the highest is blissful contemplative possession in thought of all the forms of nature. In this gradation, each lower rank while an *end* is also means or preformed condition of higher ends. Empirical things, things of useful arts, belonging to the second class but, affected by an adventitious mixture of thought, are ultimately instrumentalities potential for the life of pure rational possession of ideal objects. Modern teleologies are much less succinct and definite, they agree however in the notion of rows of inferior ends which prepare for and culminate in something which is *the* end.

Such a classificatory enterprise is naturally consoling to those who enjoy a privileged status, whether as philosophers, as saints or scholars, and who wish to justify their special status. But its consoling apologetics should not blind us to the fact that to think of objects as more or less ends is nonsense. They either have immediate and terminal quality; or they do not: quality as such is absolute not comparative. A thing may be of some shade of blue when compared with some quality that is wanted and striven for; but its blue is not itself more or less blue nor than blueness, and so with the quality of being terminal and absorbing. Objects may be more or less absorptive and arresting and thus possess degrees of intensity with respect to finality. But this difference of intensity is not, save as subject to reflective choice, a distinction in rank or class of finality. It applies to different toothaches as well as to different objects of thought; but it does not apply, inherently, to the difference between a tooth-ache and an ideal object—save that a thing like a toothache is often possessed of greater intensity of finality. If we follow the clew of the latter fact, we shall probably conclude that search for pure and unalloyed finality carries us to inarticulate sensation and overwhelming passion. For such affairs are the best instances of things that are complete in themselves with no outleadings.

If then rational essences or meanings are better objects of contemplation than are seizures by sensory and passionate objects, it is not because the former are fulfillments of higher or more "real" antecedent processes.

They are not graded on the basis of being lesser or greater actualizations. It is because they present themselves to reflective appraisal as more worthy to be striven for. And this rational character implies that the *things* which have the better qualities possess also transitiveness, instrumentality, as well as immediacy and finality. They are potential and productive. They lead somewhere, perhaps to other affairs having qualities to be envisaged and deeply meditated. If dialectic were not so esthetically enjoyable to some, it would never have played the role it has played in liberating man from the dominion of sensation and impulse. This shows that the esthetic object may be useful and an useful one esthetic, or that immediacy and efficacy[1] though distinguishable qualities are not disjoined existentially. But it is no reason for making contemplative knowledge or any other particular affair the highest of all natural ends. Whether the given or the deliberately constructed is a better or higher end is not a question of intrinsic quality, but a matter of reflectively determined judgment. It is conceivable that just because certain objects are immediately good, that which secures and extends their occurrence may itself become for reflective choice a supreme immediate good.

---

[1] To avoid misapprehension it should perhaps be explicitly stated the term "efficacy" employed here and elsewhere, does not imply an interpretation in terms of the old theory of something engaged in emitting force. It is used purely denotatively; it designates empirical position in a course of affairs having a specifiable ending; its meaning is defined not by any theory, but by such affairs as that to get a fire, a match is applied and that it is applied not to a stone but to paper or shavings. The words agency, instrumentality, causal condition, which appear frequently in these pages are to be similarly translated.

History is full of ingratitude. All existences are something more than products; they have qualities of their own and assert independent life. There is something of King Lear's daughters in all offspring. This ingratitude is reproachable only when it turns to deny its ancestry. That Plato and Aristotle should have borrowed from the communal objects of the fine arts, from ceremonies, worship and the consummatory objects of Greek culture, and should have idealized their borrowings into new objects of art is something to be thankful for. That, after having enforced the loan, they spurned the things from which they derived their models and criteria is not so admirable. This lack of piety concealed from them the poetic and religious character of their own constructions, and established in the classic Western philosophic tradition the notions that immediate grasp and incorporation of objects is knowledge; that things are placed in graded reality in accordance with their capacity to afford a cultivated mind such a grasp or beholding; and that the order of reality in Being is coincident with a predetermined rank of Ends.

If we recognize that all qualities directly had in conscious experience apart from use made of them, testify to nature's characterization by immediacy and finality, there is ground for unsophisticated recognition of use and enjoyment of things as natural, as belonging to the things as well as to us. *Things* are beautiful and ugly, lovely and hateful, dull and illuminated, attractive and repulsive. Stir and thrill in us is as much theirs as is length, breadth, and thickness. Even the utility of things, their capacity to be employed as means and agencies, is first of all not a relation, but a quality possessed, immediately possessed, it is as esthetic as any other quality.   If labor transforms an orderly sequence into a means of attaining ends, this not only converts a casual ending into a fulfillment, but it also gives labor an immediate quality of finality and consummation.   Art, even fine art, is long, as well as a joy.

From the standpoint of control and utilization, the tendency to assign superior reality to causes is explicable. A "cause" is not merely an antecedent; it is that antecedent which if manipulated regulates the occurrence of the consequent.   This is why the sun rather than night is the causal condition of day.   Knowing that consequences will take care of themselves if conditions can be had and managed, an ineradicable natural pragmatism indulges in a cheap and short conversion, and conceives the cause as intrinsically more primary and necessary.   This practical tendency is increased by the fact that time is a softener and dignifier; present troubles lose their acuteness when they are no longer present.   Old times are proverbially the good old times, and history begins with a Garden of Paradise or a Golden Age.   Good, being congenial, is held to be normal; and what is suffered is a deviation, creating the problem of evil.   Thus the earlier gets moral dignity as well as practical superiority.   But in existence, or metaphysically, cause and effect are on the same level; they are portions of one and the same historic process, each having immediate or esthetic quality and each having efficacy, or serial connection.   Since existence is historic it can be known or understood only as each portion is distinguished and related.   For knowledge "cause" and "effect" alike have a partial and truncated being.   It is as much a part of the real being of atoms that they give rise in time, under increasing complication of relationships, to qualities of blue and sweet, pain and beauty, as that they have at a cross-section of time extension, mass, or weight.

The problem is neither psychological nor epistemological. It is metaphysical or existential. It is whether existence consists of events, or is possessed of temporal quality, characterized by beginning, process and ending. If so, the affair of later and earlier, however important it is for particular practical matters, is indifferent to a theory of valuation of existence. It is as arbitrary to assign complete reality to atoms at the expense of mind and conscious experience as it is to make a rigid separation between here and there in space. Distinction is genuine and for some purpose necessary. But it is not a distinction of kinds or degrees of reality. Space here is joined to space there, and events then are joined to events now; the reality is as much in the joining as in the distinction. In order to control the course of events it is indispensable to know their conditions. But to characterize the conditions, it is necessary to have followed them to some term, which is not fully followed till we arrive at something enjoyed or suffered, had and used, in conscious experience. Vital and conscious events exhibit actualization of properties that are not fully displayed in the simpler relationships that are by definition termed physical.

Temporal quality is however not to be confused with temporal order. Quality is quality, direct, immediate and undefinable. Order is a matter of relation, of definition, dating, placing and describing. It is discovered in reflection, not directly had and denoted as is temporal quality. Temporal order is a matter of science; temporal quality is an immediate trait of every occurrence whether in or out of consciousness. Every event as such is passing into other things, in such a way that a later occurrence is an integral part of the *character* or *nature* of present existence. An "affair", *Res*, is always at issue whether it concerns chemical change, the emergence of life, language, mind or the episodes that compose human history. Each comes from something else and each when it comes has its own initial, unpredictable, immediate qualities, and its own similar terminal qualities. The later is never just resolved into the earlier. What we call such resolution is merely a statement of the order by means of which we regulate the passage of an earlier into the later. We may explain the traits of maturity by better knowledge of childhood, but maturity is never just infancy plus.

It is not easy to distinguish between ends as *de facto* endings, and ends as fulfillments, and at the same time to bear in mind the connection of the latter with the former. We respond so directly to some objects in experience with intent to preserve and perpetuate them that it is difficult to keep the conception of a thing as terminus free from the element of deliberate choice and endeavor; when we think of it or discourse about it, we introduce connection. Since we turn away from trouble and suffering, since these things are not the objects of choice and effort save in avoidance, it seems forced to call them ends. To name them such appears an impropriety of language. I am quite willing to concede the linguistic point, provided its implications are acknowledged and adhered to. For in this case we are left, apart from a deliberately directed course of events, only with objects immediately used, enjoyed and suffered but having in themselves no claim to the title of ends. Health in this case is not in itself an end of any natural process; much less an end-in-itself. It is an enjoyed good when it happens just as disease is a suffered ill. Similarly, truth of belief and statement is an affair that has the quality of good; but it is not an end just because it is good; it becomes an end only when, because of its goodness, it is actively sought for and reached as a conclusion. On this basis, all ends are ends-in-view; they are no longer ideal as characters of Being, as they were when they were in Greek theory, but are the objects of conscious intent. When achieved in existence they are ends because they are then conclusions attained through antecedent endeavor, just as a post is not a goal in itself, but becomes a goal in relation to a runner and his race. Either we must consistently stick to the equivalence of ends with objectives of conscious endeavor, or admit that all things directly possessed of irreducible and self-sufficing quality, red and blue, pain, solidity, toughness, smoothness and so on through the list, are natural ends.

There is however nothing self-evident, or even clear, in the exclusive identification of ends with ends-in-view and of the latter with psychic states. The identification isolates conscious life from objective nature. It was a particular historic situation that effected the division. Modern science made it clear that nature has no preference for good things over bad things; its mills turn out any kind of grist indifferently. If Greek thought had contented itself with asserting that all immediacy of existence has a certain ultimacy and finality, a certain incommensurability and incommutability, if it had cited conscious experience as a striking instance of the indifference of natural processes to termini of good and evil.

modern science would have had no destructive impact upon the doctrine of natural ends. It would rather have added resourcefulness to this doctrine. In explicit discovery of just the conditions antecedent to this good and that bad, it puts in our hands means of regulating the occurrence of things possessed of these qualities. But discovery of the indifference of natural energies to the production of good and bad endings, and the discovery of the over lapping and intermixture of processes leading to different outcomes, so completely overthrew the classic doctrine of ends, that it seemed to abolish any and every conception of natural ends. The logical result was to cut off "consciousness," as the collectivity of immediate qualities, from nature, and to create the dualism of physical nature and mind which is the source of modern epistemological problems.

A reconsideration of the theory of natural termini, is in historic sequel necessary to a correct envisagement of the connection of conscious life with nature. "Consciousness" in one of its many significations, is identical with direct apparition, obvious and vivid presence of qualities and of meanings. Take these apparitions as something else than emphatic characters of natural events and physical events, and objects become themselves remote and uncertain in existence arrived at only through the mediation of consciousness. Moreover, while quality is immediate and absolute, any particular quality is notoriously unstable and transitory. Immediate objects are the last word of evanescence. Consciousness, in the sense just indicated, is flux in which nothing abides. Persistence, "substance" is found only in some unapproachable things, which have to be invoked to supply this flux with a substratum and locus. Thus we are confronted with the perplexing riddles familiar in epistemological theory. It suffices at this time to note but one. The realm of immediate qualities contains everything of worth and significance. But it is uncertain, unstable and precarious. The first consideration induces us to prize consciousness supremely; the second leads us to deny reality to it as compared with alleged underlying things with their fixity and permanence. Since immediate qualities come and go without inherent rhyme and reason, since life is more unstable than inanimate things and conscious life is even more evanescent than life physiologically considered, since the coming and going of immediate qualities is susceptible of regulation only through the medium of things out of consciousness, "consciousness" becomes an anomaly. "Matter" as a complex of indirect, not immediately given, and in some sense unknowable, things becomes alone real and solid.

If we discount practical bias toward the regular and repeated, and hence toward "causes" as opposed to consequences, all that is indicated by the transiency of immediate qualitative affairs is that immediacy is immediacy. By the nature of the case the occurrence of the immediate is at the mercy of the sequential order. In the case of the things which appeal to common-sense as substances, properties like mass and inertia, unchanged solidity and extension, count most. Rate of change is slow; and presents itself as a matter of attrition and accumulation; spatial qualities which are static chiefly figure. Time is of comparative indifference to the change of solid substances; a million years is a day. But whatever depends for its existence upon the interaction of a large number of independent variables is in unstable equilibrium; its rate of change is rapid; successive qualities have no obvious connection with one another; any shift of any part may alter the whole pattern. Thus, while light and water are "substances," a rainbow, depending upon a highly specialized conjunction of light and vapor, and being transient, is only a "phenomenon."   Such immediate qualities as red and blue, sweet and sour, tone, the pleasant and unpleasant, depend upon an extraordinary variety and complexity of conditioning events; hence they are evanescent. They are never exactly reduplicated, because the exact combination of events of which they are termini does not precisely recur. Hence they are even more "phenomenal" than a rainbow; they must be hitched to substance as its "modes" to get standing in "reality."

Thus the things that are most precious, that are final, being just the things that are unstable and most easily changing, seem to be different in kind from good, solid, old-fashioned substance. Matter has turned out to be nothing like as lumpy and chunky as unimaginative prejudice conceived it to be. But as compared with the changes of immediate qualities it seems in any case solid and substantial; a fact which accounts, I suppose, for the insertion of an immaterial sort of substance, after the analogy of matter-substance, underneath mental affairs. But when it is recognized that the latter are eventual and consummatory to highly complicated interactions of natural events, their transiency becomes itself intelligible; it is no ground of argument for a radical difference from the physical, the latter being also resolvable into a character of the course of events. While "consciousness" as the conspicuous and vivid presence of immediate qualities and of meanings, is alone of direct worth, things not immediately present, whose intrinsic qualities are not directly had, are primary from the standpoint of control. For just because the things that are directly had are both precious and evanescent, the only thing that can be thought of is the conditions under which they are had. The common, pervasive and repeated *is* of superior rank from the standpoint of safeguarding and buttressing the having of terminal qualities. Directly we can do nothing with the latter save have, enjoy and suffer them. So reflection is concerned with the order which conditions, prevents and secures their occurrence. The irony of many historic systems of philosophy is that they have so inverted the actualities of the case. The general, recurrent and extensive has been treated as the worthy and superior kind of Being; the immediate, intensive, transitory, and qualitatively individualized taken to be of importance only when it is imputed to something ordinary, which is all the universal can denotatively mean. In truth, the universal and stable are important because they are the instrumentalities, the efficacious conditions, of the occurrence of the unique, unstable and passing.

The system which Aristotle bequeathed to the modern world through Latin Christianity expresses the consequences of taking the universal which is instrumental, as if it were final. Actually, consummatory objects instead of being a graded series of numerable and unalterable species or kinds of existence ranked under still fewer genera, are infinitely numerous, variable and individualized affairs. Poets who have sung of despair in the midst of prosperity, and of hope amid darkest gloom, have been the true

metaphysicians of nature.   The glory of the moment and
its tragedy will surely pass.   The contingent, uncertain
and incomplete give depth and scope to consummatory
objects while things not directly had, things approach-
able only through reflective imagination and rational
constructions are the conditions of such regulation of their
occurrence as is feasible.

The richer and fuller are the terminal qualities of an
object the more precarious is the latter, because of its
dependence upon a greater diversity of events.   At the
best, therefore, control is partial and experimental.   All
prediction is abstract and hypothetical.   Given the stability of other events, and it follows that certain conditions, selected in thought, determine the predictability
of the occurrence of say, red.   But since the other conditions do not remain unalterably put, what actually
occurs is never just what happens in thought; the thing of
mere redness does not happen, but some thing with just
this shade and tinge of red, in just this unduplicable content.   Thus something unpredictable, spontaneous, unformulable and ineffable is found in any terminal object.
Standardizations, formulae, generalizations, principles,
universals, have their place, but the place is that of being
instrumental to better approximation to what is unique
and unrepeatable.

We owe to Romanticism the celebration of this fact;
no fact apparently being fully discovered and communicated save as it is too much celebrated.   Aversion to
Romanticism as a system is quite justifiable; but even an
obnoxious system may hit upon a truth unknown to
soberer schemes.   Call the facts romantic or by some
sweeter sounding name, and it still remains true that

immediate and terminal qualities (whether or not called consciousness) form an unpredictable and unformulable flow of immediate, shifting, impulsive, adventured finalities, with respect to which the universal and regular objects and principles celebrated in classic thought are instrumental.

Perhaps we may prudently close this chapter with a reminder. To point out something as a fact is not the same thing as to commend or eulogize the fact. I am not saying that it is a fine and noble thing that whatever is immediately consummatory and precious should be also evanescent and unique, never completely subject to principle and rule. A reporter is not necessarily to blame for the state of thing that he reports. The fact hereby reported is so unescapable and so obvious to a candid empiricist that there is no occasion for either eulogy or condemnation. The only question is what is going to be done about the various instances of it which compose our lives, and give them humor and tragedy. The question is urgent for reflection; it is urgent for the most practical of acts in "getting a living," where the need to do something is constantly imperative. Materials used in reflection change even more rapidly than materials employed in meeting hunger and thirst. Their metabolism is at a quicker pace. Genuinely to think of a thing is to think of implications that are no sooner thought of than we are hurried on to *their* implications. There is no rest for the thinker, save in the *process* of thinking. Possibly it is for this reason that reflection upon the whole has been identified in human culture with onerous labor, with the sombre and melancholic. Reverie travels fast, but in reverie the labor of making connections taut and consistent is not involved. Only in circumstances as for-

tunate as those of ancient Greece does effort to understand become a rich and full delight, so that it may be
conceived of not only as an end of nature, but as its end of
ends, for the sake of which all else happens.

Participation in this consummatory activity has, however, been confined to a few. Since it was conceived of
as an end given spontaneously or "naturally" to a few,
not as a practical and reflective conclusion to be achieved,
it was concluded that some men are servile by nature,
having as sole function to supply the materials which made
it possible for other men to indulge in pure theoretical
activity, without distraction by the need of making a
living. Thus the conception that thought is the final and
complete end of nature became a "rationalization" of an
existing division of classes in society. The division of
men into the thoughtless and the inquiring was taken to
be the intrinsic work of nature; in effect it was identical
with the division between workers and those enjoying
leisure. Philosophers and scientific inquiries became the
utmost acme of nature's perfection, being the least dependent upon outward acts and connections.

In a sense, this occurrence of thought and leisurely
insight was natural; it happened in the course of natural
processes. It was "given." Like any finality it had to
be hit upon, achieved without premeditation before it
might become an object of reflective choice and endeavor.
But when it came to be reflected upon, its terms were mis-
conceived. The conception that contemplative thought
is *the* end in itself was at once a compensation for inability
to make reason effective in practice, and a means for perpetuating a division of social classes. A local and temporal polity of historical nature became a metaphysics
of everlasting being. Thought when it achieves truth

may, indeed, be said to fulfill the regularities and universalities of nature; to be their natural end. But its incarnation as an end in some, not others, does not partake of any universality. It is contingent, accidental; its achievement is a rational fulfillment only when it is the product of deliberate arts of politics and education.

Since nothing in nature is exclusively final, rationality is always means as well as end. The doctrine of the universality and necessity of rational ends can be validated only when those in whom the good is actualized employ it as a means to modify conditions so that others may also participate in it, and its universality exist in the course of affairs. The more it is asserted that thought and understanding are "ends in themselves," the more imperative is it that thought should discover why they are realized only in a small and exclusive class. The ulterior problem of thought is to make thought prevail in experience, not just the results of thought by imposing them upon others, but the active process of thinking. The ultimate contradiction in the classic and genteel tradition is that while it made thought universal and necessary and the culminating good of nature, it was content to leave its distribution among men a thing of accident, dependent upon birth, economic, and civil status. Consistent as well as humane thought will be aware of the hateful irony of a philosophy which is indifferent to the conditions that determine the occurrence of reason while it asserts the ultimacy and universality of reason. In as far as qualities of objects are found worthy of finality, the finding must eventuate in arts. Only thereby will thinking and knowing take their full place as events falling within natural processes, not only in their origin but also in their outcome.

CHAPTER FOUR

NATURE, MEANS AND KNOWLEDGE

No mythology is more familiar than that which tells how labor is due to trespass of man upon divine prerogatives, an act that brought curse upon the earth and woe to man. Because of this primeval rebellion against God, men toil amid thorns to gain an uncertain livelihood, and women bring forth children in pain. The tale is touching evidence that man finds it natural that nature should support his activities, and unnatural that the burden of continued and hard endeavor should be placed upon him. Festivity is spontaneous; labor needs to be accounted for. There is a long distance between the birth of the old legend and the formulation of classic political economy; but the doctrine of the latter that labor which is the source of value signifies cost, onerous sacrifice of present consummation to attainment of later good, expresses the same human attitude.

Yet, in fact, it was not enjoyment of the apple but the enforced penalty of labor that made man as the gods, *knowing* good and evil instead of just having and enjoying them. The exacting conditions imposed by nature, that have to be observed in order that work be carried through to success, are the source of all noting and recording of nature's doings. They supply the discipline that chastens exuberant fancy into respect for the operation of events, and that effect subjection of thought to a pertinent order of space and time. While leisure is the mother of drama, sport and literary spell-binding, necessity is the mother of invention, discovery and consecutive reflection. While at happy junctures the course of extraordinary events may be bound or wheedled by enjoyed rite and ceremony, only work places a conclusive spell upon homely, everyday affairs. Spears, snares, gins, traps, utensils, baskets and webs may have their potency enhanced by adherence to ceremonial design, but the design is never a complete substitute for conformity to the efficacious resistances and adaptations of natural materials. Acumen, shrewdness, inventiveness, accumulation and transmission of information are products of the necessity under which man labors to turn away from absorption in direct having and enjoying, so as to consider things in their active connections as means and as signs. The same need converts immediate emotion irrelevant to everything save its own thrill into ordered interest in the movements and possibilities of natural events. Everything is done to bedeck utilities, instrumentalities, with reminders of consummatory events so as to lessen their burden, but useful arts in return supply ceremonial arts with their materials, appliances and patterns.

Tools, means, agencies are the characteristic thing in industry; such a statement is tautology. By its nature technology is concerned with things and acts in their instrumentalities, not in their immediacies. Objects and events figure in work not as fulfillments, realizations, but in behalf of other things of which they are means and predictive signs. A tool is a particular thing, but it is more than a particular thing, since it is a thing in which a connection, a sequential bond of nature is embodied. It possesses an objective relation as its own defining property. Its perception as well as its actual use takes the mind to other things. The spear suggests the feast not directly but through the medium of other external things, such as the game and the hunt, to which the sight of the weapon transports imagination. Man's bias towards himself easily leads him to think of a tool solely in relation to himself, to his hand and eyes, but its primary relationship is toward other external things, as the hammer to the nail, and the plow to the soil. Only through this objective bond does it sustain relation to man himself and his activities. A tool denotes a perception and acknowledgment of sequential bonds in nature.

Classic philosophy was conceived in wonder, born in leisure and bred in consummatory contemplation. Hence it noted the distinction between objects consummatory or final in the fine arts and instrumental and operative in the industrial. It then employed the distinction to interpret nature in terms of a dialectical physics. Useful arts are *possible* because things have observable efficiencies; but they are *necessary* because of lack, privation, imperfection, Non-being. This deficiency is manifest in sensation and appetite; the very transitiveness of materials which renders them capable of transformation into serviceable forms is evidence that they too lack fullness of Being. Things have potentialities or are instrumental because they are not Being, but rather Being in process of becoming. They lend themselves to operative connections that fulfill them because they are not themselves Real in an adequate sense. This point of view protected Greek thought from that modern onesidedness which conceives tools as mere subjective conveniences. But the safeguard was at the expense of the introduction into nature of a split in Being itself, its division into some things which are inherently defective, changing, relational, and other things which are inherently perfect, permanent, self-possessed. Other dualisms such as that between sensuous appetite and rational thought, between the particular and universal, between the mechanical and the telic, between experience and science, between matter and mind, are but the reflections of this primary metaphysical dualism.

The counterpart of the conversion of esthetic objects into objects of science, into the one, true and good, was the conversion of operative and transitive objects into things which betray absence of full Being. This absence causes their changing instability which is, none the less, after the model of materials of the useful arts, potentially useful for ends beyond themselves. The social division into a laboring class and a leisure class, between industry and esthetic contemplation, became a metaphysical division into things which are mere means and things which are ends. Means are menial, subservient, slavish; and ends liberal and final; things as means testify to inherent defect, to dependence, while ends testify to independent and intrinsically self-sufficing being. Hence the former can never be *known* in themselves but only in their subordination to objects that are final, while the latter can be known in and through themselves by self-enclosed reason. Thus the identification of knowledge with esthetic contemplation and the exclusion from science of trial, work, manipulation and administration of things, comes full circle.

The ingratitude displayed by thinkers to artists who by creation of harmoniously composed objects supplied idealistic philosophy with empirical models of their ultimately real objects, was shown in even greater measure to artisans. The accumulated results of the observations and procedures of farmers, navigators, builders furnished matter-of-fact information about natural events, and also supplied the pattern of logical and metaphysical subordination of change to directly possessed and enjoyed fulfillments. While thinkers condemned the industrial class and despised labor, they borrowed from them the facts and the conceptions that gave form and substance to their own theories. For apart from processes of art there was no basis for introducing the idea of fulfillment, realization, into the notion of end nor for interpreting antecedent operations as potentialities.

Yet we should not in turn exhibit ingratitude. For if Greek thinkers did not achieve science, they achieved the idea of science. This accomplishment was beyond the reach of artist and artisan. For no matter how solid the content of their own observations and beliefs about natural events, that content was bound down to occasions of origin and use. The relations they recognized were of local areas in time and place. Subject-matter underwent a certain distortion when it was lifted out of this context, and placed in a realm of eternal forms. But the idea of knowledge was thereby liberated, and the scheme of logical relationships among existences held up as an ideal of inquiry. Thinking was uncovered as an enterprize having its own objects and procedures; and the discovery of thought as method of methods in all arts added a new dimension to all subsequent experience. It would be an academic matter to try to balance the credit items due to the discovery of thought and of logic as a free enterprise, against the debit consequences resulting from the hard and fast separation of the instrumental and final.

A great change took place in Greek experience between the time of Homer and Hesiod and the fifth century before Christ. The earlier period evinces a gloomy temper of life. The sense of the sovereignty of fortune, largely ill-fortune, is prevalent. The temper is shown by such quotations as the following: "Thus the gods have decided for unhappy mortals that men should live in misery while they themselves live free from suffering." "A thousand woes traverse the abode of man; the earth is gorged with them and the sea filled; day and night bring grief. They come in silence for prudent Zeus has taken away their voice." "Men favored by Hecate have no need for knowledge, memory or effort to achieve success; she acts alone without the assistance of her favorites." Divination of the intent of unseen powers and pious sacrifice are man's only resource, but this is of no avail. Reckon no man happy till after his death. The gods have indeed bestowed arts on man to ameliorate his hard lot, but their issue is uncertain. The ends rests with the gods and with fate who rules even the gods, a fate to be neither bribed with offerings nor yet compelled by knowledge and art.

By the days of the Sophists and their great Athenian successors there is marked change in mood. The conditions then existed that have occasioned the myth of Greek serenity. The Sophists taught that man could largely control the fortunes of life by mastery of the arts. No one has exceeded Plato in awareness of present ills. But since they are due to ignorance and opinion, they are remediable, he holds, by adequate knowledge. Philosophy should terminate in an art of social control. The great rival of Plato taught that fortune "is a fantom which men have invented to excuse their own imprudence. Fortune does not easily resist thought and for the most part an instructed and far-seeing soul will attain its goal." In short arts based on knowledge coöperate with nature and render it amenable to human happiness. The gods recede into twilight. Divination has a powerful competitor. Worship becomes moral. Medicine, war, and the crafts desert the temple and the altar of the patron-god of the guild, as inventions, tools, techniques of action and works multiply.

This period of confident expansion did not endure. It soon gave way; it was succeeded by what Gilbert Murray has so well named the failure of nerve, and a return to the supernatural, philosophy changing from a supreme art into a way of access to the supernatural. Yet the episode even if brief is more than historically significant. It manifests another way open to man in the midst of an uncertain, incomplete and precarious universe; another way, that is, in addition to that of celebrating such moments of respite and festal joy as occur in the troubled life of man. Through instrumental arts, arts of control based on study of nature, objects which are fulfilling and good, may be multiplied and rendered secure. This road after almost two millenia of obscuration and desertion was refound and retaken; its rediscovery marks what we call the modern era. Consideration of the significance of science as a resource in a world of mixed uncertainty, peril, and of uniformity, stability, furnishes us with the theme of this chapter of experience.

That the sciences were born of the arts, the physical sciences of the crafts and technologies of healing, navigation, war and the working of wood, metals, leather, flax and wool; the mental sciences of the arts of political management, is I suppose, an admitted fact. The distinctively intellectual attitude which marks scientific inquiry was generated in efforts at controlling persons and things so that consequences, issues, outcomes would be more stable and assured. The first step away from oppression by immediate things and events was taken when man employed tools and appliances, for manipulating things so as to render them contributory to desired objects. In responding to things not in their immediate qualities but for the sake of ulterior results, immediate qualities are dimmed, while those features which are signs, indices of something else, are distinguished. A thing is more significantly what it makes possible than what it immediately is. The very conception of cognitive meaning, intellectual significance, is that things in their immediacy are subordinated to what they portend and give evidence of. An intellectual sign denotes that a thing is not taken immediately but is referred to something that may come in consequence of it. Intellectual meanings may themselves be appropriated, enjoyed and appreciated; but the character of intellectual meaning is instrumental. Fortunate for us is it that tools and their using can be directly enjoyed; otherwise all work would be drudgery. But this additive fact does not alter the definition of a tool; it remains a thing used as an agency for some concluding event.

The first groping steps in defining spatial and temporal qualities, in transforming purely immediate qualities of local things into generic relationships, were taken through the arts.   The finger, the foot, the unit of walking were used to measure space; measurements of weight originated in the arts of commercial exchange and manufacture.   Geometry, beginning as agricultural art, further emancipated space from being a localized quality of immediate extensity.   But the radically different ways of conceiving geometry found in ancient and in modern science is evidence of the slowness of the process of emancipation of even geometrical forms from direct or esthetic traits.   In Greek astronomy the intrinsic qualities of figures always dominated their instrumental significance in inquiry; they were forms to which phenomena had to conform instead of means of indirect measurements.   Hardly till our own day did spatial relations get emancipated from esthetic and moral qualities, and become wholly intellectual and relational, abstracted from immediate qualifications, and thereby generalized to their limit.

Anything approaching a history of the growth of recognition of things in their intellectual or instrumental phase is far beyond our present scope.   We can only point out some of its net results.   In principle the step is taken whenever objects are so reduced from their status of complete objects as to be treated as signs or indications of other objects.   Enter upon this road and the time is sure to come when the appropriate object-of-knowledge is stripped of all that is immediate and qualitative, of all that is final, self-sufficient.   Then it becomes an anatomized epitome of just and only those traits which are of indicative or instrumental import.   Abstraction is not a psychological incident; it is a following to its logical conclusion of interest in those phases of natural existence which are dependable and fruitful signs of other things; which are means of prediction by formulation in terms implying other terms. Self-evidence ceases to be a characteristic trait of the fundamental objects of either sensory or noetic objects. Primary propositions are statements of objects in terms which procure the simplest and completest forming and checking of other propositions. Many systems of axioms and postulates are possible, the more the merrier, since new propositions as consequences are thus brought to light. Genuine science is impossible as long as the object esteemed for its own intrinsic qualities is taken as the object of knowledge. Its completeness, its immanent meaning, defeats its use as indicating and implying.

Said William James, "Many were the ideal prototypes of rational order: teleological and esthetic ties between things . . . . as well as logical and mathematical relations. The most promising of these things at first were of course the richer ones, the more sentimental ones. The baldest and least promising were mathematical ones; but the history of the latter's application is a history of steadily advancing successes, while that of the sentimentally richer ones is one of relative sterility and failure. Take those aspects of phenomena which interest you as a human being most . . . . and barren are all your results. Call the things of nature as much as you like by sentimental moral and esthetic names, no natural consequences follow from the naming. . . . . But when you give the things mathematical and mechanical names and call them so many solids in just such positions, describing just such paths with just such velocities, all is changed. . . . . Your "things" realize the consequences of the names by which you classed them."[1]

A fair interpretation of these pregnant sentences is that as long as objects are viewed telically, as long as the objects of the truest knowledge, the most real forms of being, are thought of as ends, science does not advance. Objects are possessed and appreciated, but they are not *known*. To know, means that men have become willing to turn away from precious possessions; willing to let drop what they own, however precious, in behalf of a grasp of objects which they do not as yet own. Multiplied and secure ends depend upon letting go existent ends, reducing them to indicative and implying means. The great historic obstacle to science was unwillingness to make the surrender, lest moral, esthetic and religious objects suffer. To large groups of persons, the bald and dry objects of natural science are still objects of fear. The mechanical or mathematical-logical object presents itself as a rival of the ideal and final object. Then philosophy becomes a device for conserving "the spiritual values of the universe" by devices of interpretation which converts the material and mechanical into mind. By means of a dialectic of the implications of the possibility of knowledge, the physical is transformed into something mental, psychic—as if psychic existence were sure to be inherently more ideal than the physical.

The net result of the new scientific method was conception of nature as a mathematical-mechanical object. If modern philosophy, reflecting the tendencies of the

---

[1] James, Principles of Psychology, Vol. II, pp. 605–06.

new science, abolished final causes from nature, it was because concern with qualitative ends, already existing objects of possession and enjoyment, blocked inquiry, discovery and control, and ended in barren dialectical disputes about definitions and classifications. A candid mind can hardly deny that sensory qualities, colors, moist and dry, hard and soft, light and heavy are genuine natural ends. In them the potentialities of the body are brought into functioning, while the activity of the body thus achieved brings in turn to completion potentialities in nature outside of the body. Nevertheless the theory that final objects are the appropriate objects of knowledge, in assimilating knowledge to esthetic contemplation had fatal consequences for science. All natural phenomena had to be known in terms of qualities. Hot and cold, wet and dry, up and down, light and heavy were things to know with and by. They were essential forms, active principles of nature. But Galileo and his scientific and philosophical followers (like Descartes and Hobbes) reversed the method by asserting that these sensory forms are things to be known, challenges to inquiry, problems, not solutions nor terms of solution. The assertion was a general one; it necessitated *search* for objects of knowledge. Dependable material with which to know was found in a different realm of being; in spatial relations, positions, masses, mathematically defined, and in motion as change of space having direction and velocity. Qualities were no longer things to do with; they were things already done, effects, requiring to be known by statement and description in mathematical and mechanical relations. The only world which defines and describes and explains was a world of masses in motion, arranged in a system of Cartesian coördinates.

When we view experientially this change, what occurs is the kind of thing that happens in the useful arts when natural objects, like crude ores, are treated as materials for getting something else. Their character ceases to lie in their immediate qualities, in just what they are and as directly enjoyed. Their character is now representative; some pure metal, iron, copper, etc. is their essence, which may be extracted as their "true" nature, their "reality." To get at this reality many existent constituents have to be got rid of. From the standpoint of the *object*, pure metal, these things to be eliminated are "false," irrelevant and obstructive. They stand in the way, and in the existent thing those qualities are alone significant which indicate the ulterior objective and which offer means for attaining it.

Modern science represents a generalized recognition and adoption of the point of view of the useful arts, for it proceeds by employment of a similar operative technique of manipulation and reduction. Physical science would be impossible without the appliances and procedures of separation and combinations of the industrial arts. In useful arts, the consequence is increase of power, multiplication of ends appropriated and enjoyed, and an enlarged and varied flexibility and economy in means used to achieve ends. Metal can be put to thousands of uses, while the crude ore can only be beheld for whatever esthetic qualities it happens to present, or be hurled bodily at game or an enemy. Reduction of natural existences to the status of means thus presents nothing inherently adverse to possessed and appreciated ends, but rather renders the latter a more secure and extensive affair.

Why then has it been so often assumed in modern philosophy that the advance of physical science has created a serious metaphysical problem; namely, that of the relation of a mechanical world as the object of knowledge to ends; the reconciliation of antithetical worlds of description and appreciation? In empirical fact, the advance of mechanistic science has multiplied and diversified ends; has increased wants and satisfactions, and has multiplied and diversified the means of attaining them. Why the problem? There are two historical empirical reasons to be given in answer. In the first place, the Aristotelian metaphysics of potentiality and actuality, of objects consummatory of natural processes, was intricately entangled with an astronomy and physics which had become incredible. It was also entangled with doctrines and institutions in politics and economics which were fast getting out of relationship to current social needs. The simplest recourse was to treat the classic tradition as the Jonah of science and throw it bodily overboard. The method was imperious and impatient, but it served a need. By a single act it relieved scientific inquiries of notions that were hampering, even paralyzing investigation into nature and that were limiting new practices by outworn sanctions.

By itself alone, however, this cause would hardly have created more than a passing historic episode. The reason that rendered the abandonment of any theory of natural ends something more than a gesture of impatient haste lies in the persistence of the classic theory of knowledge. Greek thought regarded possession, contemplation, as the essence of science, and thought of the latter as such a complete possession of reality as incorporates it with

mind. The notion of knowledge as immediate possession of Being was retained when knowing as an actual
affair radically altered. Even when science had come
to include a method of experimental search and finding, it
was still defined as insight into, grasp of, real being as
such, in comparison with which other modes of experience
are imperfect, confused and perverted. Hence a serious
problem. If the proper object of science is a mathematico-mechanical world (as the achievements of science
have proved to be the case) and if the object of science
defines the true and perfect reality (as the perpetuation
of the classic tradition asserted), then how can the objects
of love, appreciation—whether sensory or ideal—and devotion be included within true reality?

Efforts to answer this question constitute a large part
of the technical content of modern metaphysical thought.
Given the premises, its import covers almost every
thing from the problem of freedom, ideals and ideas to
the relation of the physical and the mental. With respect to the latter, there is the causal problem of their
existential relation; and there is the cognitive problem
of how one order of existence can refer to the other in
such a way as to know it. We are not concerned here
with the voluminous literature and various (controversial
and controverted) points of view that have emerged. It is
pertinent, however, to recall the source of the problems;
and to register the statement that without the underlying
dubious assumption, we are not called upon to find solutions; they cease to be perplexities as soon as certain premises are surrendered. The premise which concerns us
here is that science is grasp of reality in its final self-
sufficing form. If the proper object of knowledge has the

character appropriate to the subject matter of the useful arts, the problem in question evaporates. The objects of science, like the direct objects of the arts, are an order of relations which serve as tools to effect immediate havings and beings. Goods, objects with qualities of fulfillment are the natural fruition of the discovery and employment of means, when the connection of ends with a sequential order is determined. Immediate empirical things are just what they always were: endings of natural histories. Physical science does not set up another and rival realm of antithetical existence; it reveals the state or order upon which the occurrence of immediate and final qualities depends. It adds to casual having of ends an ability to regulate the date, place and manner of their emergence. Fundamentally, the assertion that this condition of ordered relationships is mathematic, mechanical, is tautology; that is, the meaning of anything which is such that perception and use of it enables us to regulate consequences or attain terminal qualities is a mathematical, mechanical—or if you please —logical order. If we did not discover those which we have found, we should have to find another, if deliberate planning and execution are to occur.

If science be perfect grasp, or envisagement of being, and if science terminate with a mathematico-mechanical world, then, in the second place, we have upon our hands the problems of reality and appearance. In ancient thought, the problem occurred in a simple form. There were higher and lower forms of knowledge; but all stages of knowledge were alike realizations of some level of Being, so that appearance in contrast with reality meant only a lower degree of Being, being imperfect or not fully actualized. In modern science, with its homogenous natural world, this contrast of perfect and defective Being is meaningless. It is a question of knowledge or error, not of differences of cognitive grasp in one to one correspondence with different levels of Being. In the ancient view, sensation and opinion are good forms of knowledge in their place; *what* they know, their place, is just an inferior grade of Being. To the modern mind, they are not knowledge of anything unless they are brought to agree with the deliverances of science. Is matter an appearance of mind as true reality? Or is the mental only an appearance of the physical as the final reality? Or are both of them appearances of some still more ultimate reality?

Such questions are as necessary as they are unanswerable, given the premise which defines knowledge as direct grasp and envisagement. They vanish if the proper objects of science are nature in its instrumental characters. Any immediate object then *becomes* for inquiry, as something *to be* known, an appearance. To call it "appearance" denotes a functional status, not a kind of existence. Any quality in its immediacy is doubly an appearance. In the first place it appears; it is evident, conspicuous, outstanding, it is, to recur to language already used, *had*. A thing appears in the sense in which a bright object appears in a dark room, while other things remain obscure, hidden. The affair is one of physical and physiological limits of vision and audition, etc. We see islands floating as it were upon the sea; we call them islands because of their apparent lack of continuity with the medium that immediately surrounds them. But they are projections of the very earth upon which we walk; the connecting links do not ordinarily appear; they are there, but are not had. The difference between the appearing and the unappearing is of immense practical and theoretical import, imposing upon us need for inference, which would not exist if things appeared to us in their full connections, instead of with sharply demarcated outlines due to limits of perceptibility. But the ground of the difference is as physical as that between solid, liquid and gas. The endings of organic events, seeing, hearing, etc. are for the time being, or immediately, endings of the history of all natural events. To re-establish a connection of histories within a longer course of events and a more inclusive state of affairs, requires delving, probing, and extension by artifice beyond the apparent. To link the things which are immediately and apparitionally had with one another by means of what is not immediately apparent and thus to create new historic successions with new initiations and new endings depends in turn upon the system of mathematical-mechanical systems which form the proper objects of science as such.

The empirical basis of the distinction between the apparent and the non-apparent thus lies in the need for inference. When we take the outstandingly evident as evidence, its status is subordinate to that of unperceived things. For the nonce, it is a way of establishing something more fundamental than it is itself with respect to the object of inquiry. If we conceive of the world of immediately apparent things as an emergence of peaks of mountains which are submerged except as to their peaks or endings, and as a world of initial climbings whose subsequent career emerges above the surface only here and there and by fits and starts; and if we give attention to the fact that any ability of control whatever depends upon ability to unite these disparate appearances into a serial history, and then give due attention to the fact that connection into a consecutive history can be effected only by means of a scheme of constant relationships (a condition met by the mathematical-logical-mechanical objects of physics), we shall have no difficulty in seeing why it is that the immediate things from which we start lend themselves to interpretation as signs or appearances of the objects of physics; while we also recognize that it is only with respect to the function of instituting connection that the objects of physics can be said to be more "real." In the total situation in which they function, they are means to weaving together otherwise disconnected beginnings and endings into a consecutive history. Underlying "reality" and surface "appearance" in this connection have a meaning fixed by the function of inquiry, not an intrinsic metaphysical meaning.

To treat therefore the object of science—which in effect is the object of physics—as a complete and self-sufficient object, the end of knowing, is to burden ourselves with an unnecessary and insoluble problem. It commits us on one side to a realm of immediately apparent things, the socalled perceptual order which is an order only by courtesy, and on the other to a realm of inferred and logically constructed real objects. These two realms are rivals of each other. If knowledge is possession or grasp, then there are two incompatible kinds of knowledge, one sensible, the other rational. Which is the genuine article and which the counterfeit? If we say sensible knowledge is the genuine, then we are committed to phenomenalism of a somewhat chaotic kind, unless we follow Berkeley and invoke deity to hold the immediate things together.

If we say rational knowledge is the genuine article, then true reality becomes the reality of materialism or of logical realism or of objective idealism, according to training and temperament. To follow the clues of experience is to see that the socalled sensible world is a world of immediate beginnings and endings; not at all an affair of cases of knowledge but a succession of qualitative events; while the socalled conceptual order is recognized to be the proper object of science, since it constitutes the scheme of constant relationships by means of which spare, scattered and casual events are bound together into a connected history. These emergent immediate events remain the beginning and the end of knowledge; but since their *occurrence* is one with their being sensibly, affectionally and appreciatively *had*, they are not themselves things known. That the qualities and characters of these immediate apparitions are tremendously modified when they are linked together by 'physical objects'— that is, by means of the mathematical-mechanical objects of physics—is a fact of the same nature as that a steel watch-spring is a modification of crude iron ore. The objects of physics subsist precisely in order to bring about this transformation—to change, that is, casual endings into fulfillments and conclusions of an ordered series, with the development of meaning therein involved.

Practically all epistemological discussion depends upon a sudden and unavowed shift to and fro from the universe of having to the universe of discourse. At the outset, ordinary empirical affairs, chairs, tables, stones, sticks, etc., are called physical objects—which is obviously a term of theoretical interpretation when it so applied, carrying within itself a complete metaphysical commitment. Then physical objects are defined as the objects of physics, which is, I suppose, the only correct mode of designation. But such objects are clearly very different things from the plants, lamps, chairs, thunder and light-ning, rocks etc. that were first called physical objects. So another transformation phantasmagoria in the tab-leau is staged. The original "physical things," ordinary empirical objects, not being the objects of physics, are not physical at all but mental. Then comes the grand dissolving climax in which objects of physics are shown as themselves hanging from empirical objects now dressed up as mental, and hence as themselves mental.

Everything now being mental, and the term having lost its original contrasting or differential meaning, a new and different series of transformation scenes is exhibited. Immediate empirical things are resolved into hard sensory data, which are called the genuine physical things, while the objects of physical science are treated as are logical constructions; all that remains to constitute mental existence is images and feelings. It is not neces-sary to mention other permutations and combinations, familiar to the student of theories of the possibility of knowledge. The samples mentioned are illustrations of the sort of thing which happens when the having of immediate objects, whether sensible, affectional or ap-preciatoral, is treated as a mode of knowledge.

If objects which are colored, sonorous, tactile, gusta-tory, loved, hated, enjoyed, admired, which are attrac-tive and repulsive, exciting, indifferent and depressive, in all their infinitely numerous modes, are beginnings and endings of complex natural affairs, and if physical ob-jects (defined as objects of physical science) are constituted by a mathematical-mechanical order; then physical objects instead of involving us in the predicament of having to choose between opposing claimants to reality, have precisely the characters which they should have in order to serve effectively as means for securing and avoiding immediate objects. Four of these characters may be noted. First, immediate things come and go; events in the way of direct seeing, hearing, touching, liking, enjoying, and the rest of them are in rapid change; the subject-matter of each has a certain uniqueness, unrepeatedness. Spatial-temporal orders, capable of mathematical formulation are, by contrast, constant. They present stability, recurrence at its maximum, raised to the highest degree. Qualitative affairs like red and blue, although in themselves unlike, are subject to comparison in terms of objects of physics; on the basis of connection with orders of sequence, a qualitative spectrum or scale becomes a scheme of numerable variations of a common unit.

The second character of objects of science follows from this feature. The possibility of regulating the occurrence of any event depends upon the possibility of instituting substitutions. By means of the latter, a thing which is within grasp is used to stand for another thing which is not immediately had, or which is beyond control. The technique of equations and other functions characteristic of modern science is, taken generically, a method of thoroughgoing substitutions. It is a system of exchange and mutual conversion carried to its limit.[2] The

[2] The modern mathematical conception of infinity as correspondence of part and whole appears to represent this function in its generalized form.

cognitive result is the homogeneous natural world of modern science, in its contrast with the qualitatively heterogeneous world of ancient science; the latter being made up of things different in inherent kinds and in qualities of movement, such up and down, lateral and circular, and heterogeneous according to periods of time, such as earlier and later. These become amenable to transformations in virtue of reciprocal substitutions.

In the third place, objects of knowledge as means explain the importance attached to elements, or numerically discrete units. Control of beginnings and ends by means is possible only when the individual, the unique, is treated as a composite of parts, made by sequential differentiations and integrations.[3] In its own integrity an immediate thing just exists as it exists; it stays or it passes; it is enjoyed or suffered. That is all that can be said. But when it is treated as the outcome of a complex convergence or coincidence of a large number of elementary independent variables, points, moments, numerical units, particles of mass and energy or more elementary space-times, (which in spite of their independence are capable of one to one correspondence with one another) the situation changes. The simples or elements are in effect the last pivots upon which regulation of conditions, turns; last, that is to say, as far as present appliances permit.

[3] Leibniz, whose monadism is the first philosophical manifestation of this notion, and the prototype of analytic realism, or theory of external relations, asserted the existence of monads on the ground that every composite implies elements. Surely. But he omitted to note that metaphysically the case was begged as soon as an affair, no matter how elaborate in structure, is regarded as *being* composite. To *be* a composite is one thing; to be capable of reduction to a composite by certain measures, is another thing.

Preoccupation with elementary units is as marked in logic, biology, and psychology, as in physics and chemistry. Sometimes it seems to have resulted in taking merely dialectical entities for actual unitary elements; but that is not logically necessary. Such an outcome signifies only that the right units were not found. Serious objection holds when the instrumental character of the elements is forgotten; and they are treated as independent, ultimate; when they are treated as metaphysical finalities, insoluble epistemological problems result. Whatever are designated as elements, whether logical, mathematical, physical or mental, depend especially upon the existence of immediate, qualitatively integral objects. Search for elements starts with such empirical objects already possessed. Sensory data, whether they are designated psychic or physical, are thus not starting points; they are the products of analysis. Denial of the primary reality of immediate empirical objects logically terminates in an abrogation of the reality of elements; for sensory data, or sensa and *sensibilia*, are the residua of analysis of these primary things. Moreover every step of analysis depends upon continual reference to these empirical objects. Drop them from mental view for a moment and any clew in search for elements is lost. Unless macroscopic things are recognized, cells, electrons, logical elements become meaningless. The latter have meaning only as elements *of*. Since, for example, only propositions have implications, a proposition cannot be a mere conjunction of terms; terms having no implications, a proposition so formed would have no significance. Terms must have a significance and since that they have only in a proposition, they depend upon some prior unity. In similar fashion, a purely unitary physical element would have no efficacy; it could not act or be acted upon.

We quote from a psychiatric writer speaking of his own field, in dealing with a particular matter on its own merits. With reference to one stage in the development of the theory of mental disorders, Dr. Adolph Meyer said that "there was a quest for elements of mind and their immediate correlation with the latest discoveries in the structure of the brain. The centre theory and the cell and neuronic theory seemed obligatory standpoints. Today we have become shy of such a one-sided not sufficiently functional materialism. . . . . . There is always a place for elements, but there is certainly also a place for the large momentous facts of human life just as we find it. . . . . . The psychopathologist had to learn to do more than the so-called "elementalist," who always goes back to the elements and smallest units and then is apt to shirk the responsibility of making an attempt to solve the concrete problems of greater complexity. The psychiatrist has to study individuals and groups as wholes, as complex units, as the "you" or "he" or "she" or "they" we have to work with. We recognize that throughout nature we have to face the general principle of unit-formation, and the fact that new units need not be a mere sum of the component parts, but can be an actually new entity not wholly predictable from the component parts and known only through actual experience with the specific product."[4]

Lastly, the instrumental nature of objects of knowledge accounts for the central position of laws, relations.

[4] Adolph Meyer, A Psychiatric Milestone, p. 32. P. 38.

These are the formulations of the regularities upon which intellectual and other regulation of things as immediate apparitions depends. Variability of elements in mathematical science is specious; elements vary independently of one another, but not independently of a *relation* to others, the relation or law being the constancy among variations. It is a truism that mathematics is the method by which elements can be stated as terms in constant relations, and be subjected to equations and other functions of transformation and substitution. An element is appropriately represented by a mathematical variable; for since any variable falls within some equation, it is treated as a constant function of other variables. The shift from variability to constancy is repeated as often as is needed. It is thus only *pro forma* that the variable is variable. It is not variable in the sense in which unique individualized existences are variable. The inevitable consequence is the subjection of individuals or unique modes of variation to external relations, to laws of uniformity; that is to say, the elimination of individuality. Bear in mind the instrumental nature of the relation of elements, and this abrogation of individuality merely means a temporary neglect—an abstracted gaze—in behalf of attending to conditions under which individualities present themselves. Convert the objects of knowledge into real things by themselves, and individuals become anomalous or unreal; they are not individualized for science but are instances, cases, specimens, of some generical relation or law.

The difficulty under which morals labor in this case is evident. They can be "saved" only by the supposition of another kind of Being from that with which natural sciences are concerned. History and anthropology are implicated in a similar predicament. The former has for subject-matter not only individual persons but unduplicated situations and events. The attempt to escape the dilemma by recourse to uniform and unilinear laws of sequence or "evolution" is inept; it contradicts the premises assumed, and is not borne out by facts. Contemporary anthropologists have made clear the historical nature of the phenomena with which they deal. Cultures are in many respects individual or unique, and their manifestations are "explained" by correlations with one another and by borrowings due to chance contacts. The chief, even if not sole, law of their changes is that of transmission from other individualized cultures.

It is no wonder that *Historismus* has become the preoccupying problem of a whole school of thinkers, many of whom now hold that the only attitude which can be taken toward historic situations and characters is non-intellectual, being esthetic appreciation, or sympathetic artistic rehabilitation. The theory which identifies knowledge with the beholding or grasp of self-sufficient objects reaches an impasse where it comes to deal with historical science in contrast with physics. Windelband justly draws the conclusion that Being and knowledge compel "antinomianism," certain problems inevitably force themselves upon us, but all efforts at solution are hopeless.[5]

[5] "It remains an unsolved problem why timeless reality needs realization in the temporal course of the event or why it tolerates in itself an event in the temporal course of which there is something that differs from its own nature. We do not understand why that which is also has nevertheless to happen; and still less why something different happens from that which is in itself without time."

Introduction to Philosophy, English translation, p. 299.

Empirically, individualized objects, unique affairs, exist. But they are evanescent, unstable. They tremble on the verge of disappearance as soon as they appear. Useful arts prove that, within limits, neglect of their uniqueness and attention to what is common, recurrent, irrelevant to time, procures and perpetuates the happening of some of these unique things. Timeless laws, *taken by themselves*, like all universals, express dialectic intent, not any matter of fact existence. But their ultimate implication is application; they are methods, and when applied as methods they regulate the precarious flow of unique situations. Objects of natural science are not metaphysical rivals of historical events; they are means of directing the latter. Events change; one individual gives place to another. But individually qualified things have some qualities which are pervasive, common, stable. They are out of time in the sense that a particular temporal quality is irrelevant to them. If anybody feels relieved by calling them eternal, let them be called eternal. But let not "eternal" be then conceived as a kind of absolute perduring existence or Being. It denotes just what it denotes: irrelevance to existence in its temporal quality. These non-temporal, mathematical or logical qualities are capable of abstraction, and of conversion into relations, into temporal, numerical and spatial *order*.[6] As such they are dialectical, non-existential.

[6] For a convincing discussion see Brown's essay, Intelligence and Mathematics, in the volume, Creative Intelligence, especially the section entitled Things, Relations, and Quantities. "Instead of reducing qualities to relations, it seems to me a much more intelligible view to conceive relations as abstract ways of taking qualities in general, as qualities thought of in their function of bridging a gap or making a transition between two bits of reality that have previously been taken as separate

But also as such they are tools, instrumentalities applicable historic events to help regulate their course.

This entire discussion has but a single point. It aims to show that the problems which constitute modern epistemology with its rival, materialistic, spiritualistic, dualistic doctrines, and rival realistic, idealistic, representational theories; and rival doctrines of relation of mind and matter occasionalism, pre-established harmony, paralellism, panpsychism, etc., have a single origin in the dogma which denies temporal quality to reality as such. Such a theory is bound to regard things which are causally explanatory as superior to results and outcomes; for the temporal dependence of the latter cannot be disguised, while "causes" can be plausibly converted into independent beings, or laws, or other non-temporal forms. As has been pointed out, this denial of change to true Being had its source in bias in favor of objects of contemplative enjoyment, together with a theory that such objects are the adequate subject-matter of science.

The bias is spontaneous and legitimate. The accompanying theory of knowledge and reality is a distortion. The legitimate implication of the preference for worthy objects of appreciation is the necessity of art, or control of the sequential order upon which they depend; a necessity which carries with it the further implication that this order, which is to be discovered by inquiry and confirmed by experimental action, is the proper object of knowledge.

things." P. 159. Thus "terms, (elements) and relations are both (p. 160) abstract replacements of qualitatively heterogeneous realities of such a sort as "to symbolize their *effective* nature in particular respect." The word "effective" brings out the agreement of the text with this point of view, for which I am much indebted to Dr. Brown.

Such a recognition would, however, have conceded the dependence of the contemplative functions of the leisure class upon the appliances and technique of artisans— among whom all artists were included. And since in olden time the practice of the arts was largely routine, fixed by custom and ready-made patterns, such a recognition would have carried with it the need of transforming the arts themselves, if the occurrence of ends was to be a real fulfillment, a realization, and not a contingent accident. The introduction of inventive thought into the arts and the civil emancipation of the industrial class at last made the transformation possible.

When the appliances of a technology that had grown more deliberate were adopted in inquiry, and the lens, pendulum, magnetic needle, lever were used as tools of knowing, and their functions were treated as models to follow in interpreting physical phenomena, science ceased to be identified with appreciative contemplation of noble and ideal objects, was freed from subjection to esthetic perfections, and became an affair of time and history intelligently managed. Ends were in consequence no longer determined by physical accident and social traditions. Anything whatsoever for which means could be found was an end to be averted or to be secured. Liberation from a fixed scheme of ends made modern science possible. In large affairs, practice precedes the possibility of observation and formulation; the results of practice must accumulate before mind has anything to observe. There is little cause for wonder therefore that long after the objects of science had become instrumentalities rather than things in their own rights, the old theory persisted, and philosophy spent much of its effort in the effort to reconcile the traditional theory of knowledge as immediate possession with the terms and conclusions of the new method of practice.

It is characteristic of the inevitable moral pre-possession of philosophy, together with the subjective turn of modern thought, that many critics take an "instrumental" theory of knowledge to signify that the value of knowing is instrumental to the knower. This is a matter which is as it may be in particular cases; but certainly in many cases the pursuit of science is sport, carried on, like other sports, for its own satisfaction. But "instrumentalism" is a theory not about personal disposition and satisfaction in knowing, but about the proper objects of science, what is "proper" being defined in terms of physics.

The distinction between tools (or things in their objectivities) and fulfilled products of the use of tools accounts for the distinction between known objects on one side and objects of appreciation and affection on the other. But the distinction primarily concerns objects themselves; only secondarily does it apply to attitudes, dispositions, motivations. Making and using tools may be intrinsically delightful. Prior to the introduction of machinery for quantitative production and sale of commodities for profit, utensils were themselves usually works of art, esthetically satisfying. This fact does not however define them *as* utensils; it does not confer upon them their characteristic property. In like manner, the pursuit of knowledge is often an immediately delightful event; its attained products possess esthetic qualities of proportion, order, and symmetry. But these qualities do not mark off or define the characteristic and appropriate *objects* of science. The character of the object is like that of a tool, say a lever; it is an order of determination of sequential changes terminating in a foreseen consequence.

We are brought to the question of method. In ancient science the essence of science was demonstration; the life blood of modern science is discovery. In the former, reflective inquiry existed for the sake of attaining a stable subject-matter; in the latter systematized knowledge exists in practice for the sake of stimulating, guiding and checking further inquiries. In ancient science, "learning" belonged in the realm of inferior being, of becoming, change; it was transitive, and ceased in the actualization of final and fixed objects. It was thought of after the analogy of master and disciple; the former was already in possession of the truth, and the learner merely appropriated what already is there in the store house of the master. In modern science, learning is finding out what nobody has previously known. It is a transaction in which nature is teacher, and in which the teacher comes to knowledge and truth only through the learning of the inquiring student.

Characteristic differences in logic thus accompany the change from "knowledge" whose subject-matter is final affairs to knowledge dealing with instrumental objects. Where the objects of knowledge are taken to be final, perfect, complete, metaphysical fulfillments of nature, proper method consists in definition and classification; learning closes with demonstration of the rational necessity of definitions and classifications. Demonstration is an exhibition of the everlasting, universal, final and fixed nature of objects. Investigation denoted merely the accumulation of material with which to fill in gaps in an antecedent ready-made hierarchy of species. Discovery was merely the perception that some particular material hitherto unclassified by the learner came under a universal form already known. The universal is already known because given to thought; and the particular is already known, because given to perception; learning merely brings these two given forms into connection, so that what is "discovered" is the subsumption of particular under its universal.

Apart from their theories, or in spite of them, the Greeks were possessed by a lively curiosity, and their practice was better than their logic. In the medieval Christian period, the logic was taken literally. Revelation, scriptures, church fathers and other authentic sources, increased the number of given universal truths, and also of given particular facts and events. The master-teacher was God, who taught not through the dim instrumentality of rational thought alone, but directly through official representatives. The form of apprehension of truth remained the demonstrative syllogism; the store of universal truths was supplemented by the gracious gift of revelation, and the resources of the minor premise extended by divinely established historic facts. Truth was given to reason and faith; and the part of the human mind was to humble itself to hearken, accept and obey.

The scheme was logically complete; it carried out under new circumstances the old idea that the highest end and good of man is knowledge of true Being, and that such knowledge in the degree of its possession effects an assimilation of the mind to the reality known. It added to old theoretical premises such institutions and practices as were practically required to give them effect, so that the humblest of human creatures might at least start on the road to that knowledge the possession of which is salvation and bliss. In comparison, most modern theories are an inconsistent mixture; dialectically the modernist is easy prey to the traditionalist; he carries so many of the conceptions of the latter in his intellectual outfit that he is readily confuted. It is his practice not his theory that gets him ahead. His professed logic is still largely that of antecedent truths, demonstration and certitude; his practice is doubting, forming hypotheses, conducting experiments. When he surrenders antecedent truths of reason it is usually only to accept antecedent truths of sensation. Thus John Stuart Mill conceives of an inductive logic in which certain canons shall bear exactly the same relation to inquiry into fact that the rules of the syllogism bore to classic "deductive" proof or dialectic. He recognizes that science is a matter of inference, but he is as certain as was Aristotle that inference rests upon certain truths which are immediately possessed, differing only about the organ through which they come into our possession.

But in the practice of science, knowledge is an affair of *making* sure, not of grasping antecedently given sureties. What is already known, what is accepted as truth, is of immense importance; inquiry could not proceed a step without it. But it is held subject to use, and is at the mercy of the discoveries which it makes possible. It has to be adjusted to the latter and not the latter to it. When things are defined as instruments, their value and validity reside in what proceeds from them; consequences not antecedents supply meaning and verity. Truths already possessed may have practical or moral certainty, but logically they never lose a hypothetic quality. They are true *if:* if certain other things eventually present themselves; and when these latter things occur they in turn suggest further possibilities; the operation of doubt-inquiry-finding recurs. Although science is concerned in practice with the contingent and its method is that of making hypotheses which are then tried out in actual experimental change of physical conditions, its traditional formulation persists in terms of necessary and fixed objects. Hence all kinds of incoherences occur. The more stubbornly the traditional formulation is clung to, the more serious become these inconsistencies.

Leonardo virtually announced the birth of the method of modern science when he said that true knowledge begins with opinion. The saying involves a revolution; no other statement could be so shocking to the traditional logic. Not that opinion as such is anything more than opinion or an unconfirmed and unwarranted surmise; but that such surmises may be used; when employed as hypotheses they induce experimentation. They then become fore-runners of truth, and mind is released from captivity to antecedent beliefs. Opinion, in the classic conception, was concerned with what was inherently contingent and variable as to possibility and probability, in contrast with knowledge concerned with the inherently necessary and everlasting. It therefore was as ultimate and unquestionable *in its proper sphere* as science was in its place. But opinion as a venture, as an "it seems to me probable," is an occasion of new observations, an instigator of research, an indispensable organ in deliberate discovery. Taken in this fashion, opinion was the source of new histories, the beginning of operations that terminated in new conclusions. Its worth lay neither in itself nor in a peculiar realm of objects to which it was applied, but in the direction of inquiries which it set agoing. It was a starting point, and like any beginning of any history was altered and displaced in the history of which it was the initiation.

Sometimes discovery is treated as a proof of the opposite of which it actually shows. It is viewed as evidence that the object of knowledge is already there in full-fledged being and that we just run across it; we uncover it as treasure-hunters find a chest of buried gold. That there is existence antecedent to search and discovery is of course admitted; but it is denied that as such, as other than the conclusion of the historical event of inquiry in its connection with other histories, it is already the object of knowledge. The Norsemen are said to have discovered America. But in what sense? They landed on its shores after a stormy voyage; there was discovery in the sense of hitting upon a land hitherto untrod by Europeans. But unless the newly found and seen object was used to modify old beliefs, to change the sense of the old map of the earth, there was no discovery in any pregnant intellectual sense, any more than mere stumbling over a chair in the dark is discovery till used as basis of inference which connects the stumbling with a body of meanings. Discovery of America involved insertion of the newly touched land in a map of the globe. This insertion, moreover, was not merely additive, but transformative of a prior picture of the world as to its surfaces and their arrangements. It may be replied that it was not the world which was changed but only the map. To which there is the obvious retort that after all the map is part of the world, not something outside it, and that its meaning and bearings are so important that a change in the map involves other and still more important objective changes.

It was not simply states of consciousness or ideas inside the heads of men that were altered when America was actually discovered; the modification was one in the public meaning of the world in which men publicly act. To cut off this meaning from the world is to leave us in a situation where it makes no difference what change takes place in the world; one wave more or less in a puddle is of no account. Changing the meaning of the world effected an existential change. The map of the world is something more than a piece of linen hung on a wall. A new world does not appear without profound transformations in the old one; a discovered America was a factor interacting with Europe and Asia to produce consequences previously impossible. A potential object of further exploration and discoveries now existed in Europe itself; a source of gold; an opportunity for adventure; an outlet for crowded and depressed populations, an abode for exiles and the discounted, an appeal to energy and invention: in short, an agency of new events and fruitions, at home as well as abroad. In some degree, every genuine discovery creates some such transformation of both the meanings and the existences of nature.

Modern idealistic theories of knowledge have displayed some sense of the method and objective of science. They have apprehended the fact that the object of knowledge implies that the found rather than the given is the proper subject matter of science. Recognizing the part played by intelligence in this finding, they have framed a theory of the constitutive operation of mind in the determination of real objects. But idealism, while it has had an intimation of the constructively instrumental office of intelligence, has mistranslated the discovery. Following the old tradition, in its exclusive identification of the object of knowledge with reality, equating truth and Being, it was forced to take the work of thought absolutely and wholesale, instead of relatively and in detail. That is, it took re-constitution to be constitution; re-construction to be construction. Accepting the premise of the equivalence of Reality with the attained object of knowledge, idealism had no way of noting that thought is intermediary between some empirical objects and others. Hence an office of transformation was converted into an act of original and final creation. A conversion of actual immediate objects into *better*, into more secure and significant, objects was treated as a movement from merely apparent and phenomenal Being to the truly Real. In short, idealism is guilty of neglect that thought and knowledge are histories.

To call action of thought in constituting objects direct is the same as to say that it is miraculous. For it is not thought as idealism defines thought which exercises the reconstructive function. Only action, interaction, can change or remake objects. The analogy of the skilled artist still holds. His intelligence is a factor in forming new objects which mark a fulfillment. But this is because intelligence is incarnate in overt action, using things as means to affect other things. "Thought," reason, intelligence, whatever word we choose to use, is existentially an adjective (or better an adverb), not a noun. It is disposition of activity, a quality of that conduct which foresees consequences of existing events, and which uses what is foreseen as a plan and method of administering affairs.

This theory, explicitly about thought as a condition of science, is actually a theory about nature. It involves attribution to nature of three defining characteristics. In the first place, it is implied that some natural events are endings whether enjoyed or obnoxious, which occur, apart from reflective choice and art, only casually, without control. In the second place, it implies that events, being events and not rigid and lumpy substances, are ongoing and hence as such unfinished, incomplete, indeterminate. Consequently they possess a possibility of being so managed and steered that ends may become fulfilments not just termini, conclusions not just closings. Suspense, doubt, hypotheses, experiment with alternatives are exponents of this phase of nature. In the third place, regulation of ongoing and incomplete processes in behalf of selected consequences, implies that there are orders of sequence and coexistence involved; these orders or relations when ascertained are intellectual means which enable us to use events as concrete means of directing the course of affairs to forecast conclusions. The belief that these orders of relation, which are the appropriate object of science, are therefore the sole ultimately "real" objects is the source of that assertion of a symmetrical dovetailed and completed universe made by both traditional materialism and idealism. The belief is due to neglect of the fact that such relations are always relations of ongoing affairs characterized by beginnings and endings which mark them off into unstable individuals. Yet this neglected factor is empirically so pervasive and conspicuous that it has to be acknowledged in some form; it is usually acknowledged in a back-handed way—and one which confuses subsequent reflection—by attributing all qualities inconsistent with nature thus defined to "finite" mind, in order to account for ignorance, doubt, error and the need of inference and inquiry.

If nature is as finished as these schools have defined it to be, there is no room or occasion in it for such a mind; it and the traits it is said to possess are literally supernatural or at least extra-natural.

A realist may deny this particular hypothesis that, existentially, mind designates an instrumental method of directing natural changes.   But he cannot do so in virtue of his realism; the question at issue is what the real is.   If natural existence is qualitatively individualized or genuinely plural, as well as repetitious, and if things have both temporal quality and recurrence or uniformity, then the more realistic knowledge is, the more fully it will reflect and exemplify these traits.   Science seizes upon whatever is so uniform as to make the changes of nature rhythmic, and hence predictable.   But the contingencies of nature make discovery of these uniformities with a view to prediction needed and possible.   Without the uniformities, science would be impossible.   But if they alone existed, thought and knowledge would be impossible and meaningless.   The incomplete and uncertain gives point and application to ascertainment of regular relations and orders.   These relations in themselves are hypothetical, and when isolated from application are subject-matter of mathematics (in a non-existential sense).   Hence the *ultimate* objects of science are *guided* processes of change.

Sometimes the use of the word "truth" is confined to designating a logical property of propositions; but if we extend its significance to designate character of existential reference, this is the meaning of truth: processes of change so directed that they achieve an intended consummation. Instrumentalities are actually such only in operation; when they operate, an end in-view is in process of actualization. The means is fully a means only *in* its end. The instrumental objects of science are completely themselves only as they direct the changes of nature toward a fulfilling object. Thus it may be said intelligibly and not as mere tautology that the end of science is knowledge, implying that knowledge is more than science, being its fruit.

Knowledge is a word of various meanings. Etymologically, "science" may signify tested and authentic instance of knowledge. But knowledge has also a meaning more liberal and more humane. It signifies events understood, events so discriminately penetrated by thought that mind is literally at home in them. It means comprehension, or inclusive reasonable agreement. What is sometimes termed "applied" science, may then be more truly science than is what is conventionally called pure science. For it is directly concerned with not just instrumentalities, but instrumentalities at work in effecting modifications of existence in behalf of conclusions that are reflectively preferred. Thus conceived the characteristic subject-matter of knowledge consists of fulfilling objects, which as fulfillments are connected with a history to which they give character. Thus conceived, knowledge exists in engineering, medicine and the social arts more adequately than it does in mathematics, and physics.

Thus conceived, history and anthropology are scientific in a sense in which bodies of information that stop short with general formulae are not.

"Application" is a hard word for many to accept. It suggests some extraneous tool ready-made and complete, which is then put to uses that are external to its nature. To call the arts applications of science is then to introduce something foreign to the sciences which the latter irrelevantly and accidentally serve. Since the application is in human use, convenience, enjoyment and improvement, this view of application as something external and arbitrary reflects and strengthens the theories which detach man from nature, which, in the language of philosophy, oppose subject and object. But if we free ourselves from preconceptions, application of "science" means application *in*, not application *to*. Application *in* something signifies a more extensive interaction of natural events with one another, an elimination of distance and obstacles; provision of opportunities for interactions that reveal potentialities previously hidden and that bring into existence new histories with new initiations and endings. Engineering, medicine, social arts realize relationships that were unrealized in actual existences. Surely in their new context the latter are understood or known as they are not in isolation. Prejudice against the abstract, as something remote and technical, is often irrational; but there is sense in the conviction that in the abstract there is something lacking which should be recovered. The serious objection to "applied" science lies in limitation of the application, as to private profit and class advantage.

"Pure" science is of necessity relational and abstract: it fulfills its meaning and gains full truth when included within a course of concrete events. The proposition that "pure" science is non-existential is a tacit admission that only "applied" science is existential. Something else than history and anthropology lose all scientific standing when standards of "purity" are set up as ultimate; namely, all science of existential events. There is superstitious awe reflected in the current estimate of science. If we could free ourselves from a somewhat abject emotion, it would be clear enough that what makes any proposition scientific is its power to yield understanding, insight, intellectual at-homeness, in connection with any existential state of affairs, by filling events with coherent and tested meanings. The case of history is typical and basic. Upon the current view, it is a waste of time to discuss whether there can be such a thing as a science of history. History and science are by definition at opposite poles. And yet if all natural existences *are* histories, divorce between history and the logical mathematical schemes which are the appropriate objects of pure science, terminates in the conclusion that of existences there is no science, no adequate knowledge. Aside from mathematics, all knowledge is historic; chemistry, geology, physiology, as well as anthropology and those human events to which, arrogantly, we usually restrict the title of history. Only as science is seen to be fulfilled and brought to itself in intelligent management of historical processes in their continuity can man be envisaged as within nature, and not as a supernatural extrapolation. Just because nature is what it is, history is capable of being more truly known

—understood, intellectually realized—than are mathematical and physical objects. Do what we can, there always remains something recondite and remote in the latter, until they are restored in the course of affairs from which they have been sequestrated. While the humanizing of science contributes to the life of humanity, it is even more required in behalf of science, in order that it may be intelligible, simple and clear; in order that it may have that correspondence with reality which true knowledge claims for itself.

One can understand the sentiment that animates the bias of scientific inquirers against the idea that all science is ultimately applied. It is justified in the sense in which it is intended; for it is directed against two conceptions which are harmful, but which, also, are irrelevant to the position here taken. One of these conceptions is that the concern or personal motive of the inquirer should be in each particular inquiry some specific practical application. This is just as it happens to be. Doubtless many important scientific discoveries have been thus instigated, but that is an incident of human history rather than of scientific inquiry as such. And upon the whole, or if this animating interest were to become general, the undoubted effect is limitation of inquiry and thereby in the end of the field of application. It marks a recurrence to the dogma of fixed predetermined ends, while emancipation from the influence of this dogma has been the chief service rendered modern scientific methods.

The evil thus effected is increased by the second notion, namely, that application is identical with "commercialized" use. It is an incident of human history, and a rather appalling incident, that applied science has been so largely made an equivalent of use for private and economic class purposes and privileges. When inquiry is narrowed by such motivation or interest, the consequence is in so far disastrous both to science and to human life. But this limitation does not spring from nor attach to the conception of "application" which has been just presented. It springs from defects and perversions of morality as that is embodied in institutions and their effects upon personal disposition. It may be questioned whether the notion that science is pure in the sense of being concerned exclusively with a realm of objects detached from human concerns has not conspired to reinforce this moral deficiency. For in effect it has established another class-interest, that of intellectualists and aloof specialists. And it is of the nature of any class-interest to generate and confirm other class-interests, since division and isolation in a world of continuities are always reciprocal. The institution of an interest labelled ideal and idealistic in isolation tends of necessity to evoke and strengthen other interests lacking ideal quality. The genuine interests of "pure" science are served only by broadening the idea of application to include all phases of liberation and enrichment of human experience.

CHAPTER FIVE

Nature, Communication and Meaning

Of all affairs, communication is the most wonderful. That things should be able to pass from the plane of external pushing and pulling to that of revealing themselves to man, and thereby to themselves; and that the fruit of communication should be participation, sharing, is a wonder by the side of which transubstantiation pales. When communication occurs, all natural events are subject to reconsideration and revision; they are re-adapted to meet the requirements of conversation, whether it be public discourse or that preliminary discourse termed thinking. Events turn into objects, things with a meaning. They may be referred to when they do not exist, and thus be operative among things distant in space and time, through vicarious presence in a new medium. Brute efficiencies and inarticulate consummations as soon as they can be spoken of are liberated from local and accidental contexts, and are eager for naturalization in any non-insulated, communicating, part of the world. Events when once they are named lead an independent and double life. In addition to their original existence, they are subject to ideal experimentation: their meanings may be infinitely combined and re-arranged in imagination, and the outcome of this inner experimentation—which is thought—may issue forth in interaction with crude or raw events. Meanings having been deflected from the rapid and roaring stream of events into a calm and traversible canal, rejoin the main stream, and color, temper and compose its course. Where communication exists, things in acquiring meaning, thereby acquire representatives, surrogates, signs and implicates, which are infinitely more amenable to management, more permanent and more accommodating, than events in their first estate.

By this fashion, qualitative immediacies cease to be dumbly rapturous, a possession that is obsessive and an incorporation that involves submergence: conditions found in sensations and passions. They become capable of survey, contemplation, and ideal or logical elaboration; when something can be said of qualities they are purveyors of instruction. Learning and teaching come into being, and there is no event which may not yield information. A directly enjoyed thing adds to itself meaning, and enjoyment is thereby idealized.   Even the dumb pang of an ache achieves a significant existence when it can be designated and descanted upon; it ceases to be merely oppressive and becomes important; it gains importance, because it becomes representative; it has the dignity of an office.

In view of these increments and transformations, it is not surprising that meanings, under the name of forms and essences, have often been hailed as modes of Being beyond and above spatial and temporal existence, invulnerable to vicissitude; nor that thought as their possession has been treated as a non-natural spiritual energy, disjoined from all that is empirical. Yet there is a natural bridge that joins the gap between existence and essence; namely communication, language, discourse. Failure to acknowledge the presence and operation of natural interaction in the form of communication creates the gulf between existence and essence, and that gulf is factitious and gratuitous.

The slight respect paid to larger and more pervasive kinds of empirical objects by philosophers, even by professed empiricists, is apparent in the fact that while they have discoursed so fluently about many topics they have discoursed little about discourse itself. Anthropologists, philologists and psychologists have said most that has been said about saying. Nevertheless it is a fact of such distinction that its occurrence changed dumb creatures—as we so significantly call them—into thinking and knowing animals and created the realm of meanings. Speaking from the standpoint of anthropology Franz Boas says: "The two outer traits in which the distinction between the minds of animals and man finds expression are the existence of organized articulate speech in man and the use of utensils of varied application."[1] It is antecedently probable that sole external marks of difference are more than external; that they have intimate connection with such intrinsic differences as religion, art and science, industry and politics. "Utensils" were discussed in the last chapter, in connection with the useful arts and knowledge, and their indispensable relation with science pointed out. But at every point appliances and application, utensils and uses, are bound up with directions, suggestions and records made possible by speech; what has been said about the role of tools is subject to a condition supplied by language, the tool of tools.

Upon the whole, professed transcendentalists have been more aware than have professed empiricists of the fact that language makes the difference between brute and man. The trouble is that they have lacked naturalistic conception of its origin and status. Logos has been cor-

[1] The Mind of Primitive Man, p. 98.

rectly identified with mind; but logos and hence mind was conceived supernaturally. Logic was thereby supposed to have its basis in what is beyond human conduct and relationships, and in consequence the separation of the physical and the rational, the actual and the ideal, received its traditional formulation.

In protest against this view empirical thinkers have rarely ventured in discussion of language beyond reference to some peculiarity of brain structure, or to some psychic peculiarity, such as tendency to "outer expression" of "inner" states. Social interaction and institutions have been treated as products of a ready-made *specific* physical or mental endowment of a self-sufficing individual, wherein language acts as a mechanical go-between to convey observations and ideas that have prior and independent existence. Speech is thus regarded as a practical convenience but not of fundamental intellectual significance. It consists of "mere words," sounds, that happen to be associated with perceptions, sentiments and thoughts which are complete prior to language. Language thus, "expresses" thought as a pipe conducts water, and with even less transforming function than is exhibited when a wine-press "expresses" the juice of grapes. The office of signs in creating reflection, foresight and recollection is passed by. In consequence, the occurrence of ideas becomes a mysterious parallel addition to physical occurrences, with no community and no bridge from one to the other.

It is safe to say that psychic events, such as are anything more than reactions of a creature susceptible to pain and diffuse comfort, have language for one of their conditions. It is altogether likely that the "ideas" which Hume found in constant flux whenever he looked within himself were a succession of words silently uttered. Primary to these events there was, of course, a substratum of organic psycho-physical actions. But what made the latter identifiable objects, events with a perceptible character, was their concretion in discourse. When the introspectionist thinks he has withdrawn into a wholly private realm of events disparate in kind from other events, made out of mental stuff, he is only turning his attention to his own soliloquy. And soliloquy is the product and reflex of converse with others; social communication not an effect of soliloquy. If we had not talked with others and they with us, we should never talk to and with ourselves. Because of converse, social give and take, various organic attitudes become an assemblage of persons engaged in converse, conferring with one another, exchanging distinctive experiences, listening to one another, over-hearing unwelcome remarks, accusing and excusing. Through speech a person dramatically identifies himself with potential acts and deeds; he plays many rôles, not in successive stages of life but in a contemporaneously enacted drama. Thus mind emerges.

It is significant of the differences between Greek and modern experience, that when their respective philosophers discovered discourse, they gave such different accounts of it. The moderns made of it a world separate from spatial and material existences, a separate and private world made of sensations, images, sentiments. The Greeks were more nearly aware that it was *discourse* they had discovered. But they took the structure of discourse for the structure of things, instead of for the forms which things assume under the pressure and opportunity of social cooperation and exchange. They overlooked the fact that meanings as objects of thought are entitled to be called complete and ultimate only because they are not original but are a happy outcome of a complex history. They made them primitive and independent forms of things, intrinsically regulative of processes of becoming. They took a work of social art to be nature independent of man. They overlooked the fact that the import of logical and rational essences is the consequence of social interactions, of companionship, mutual assistance, direction and concerted action in fighting, festivity, and work. Hence they conceived of ideal meanings as the ultimate framework of events, in which a system of substances and properties corresponded to subjects and predicates of the uttered proposition. Things conformed naturally and exactly to parts of speech, some being inherently subject-matter of nouns, proper and common; others of verbs, of which some expressed self-activity, while others designated adjectival and adverbial changes to which things are exposed on account of their own defects; some being external relations in which substances stand to one another, and subject-matter of prepositions.

The resulting theory of substances, essential properties, accidental qualities and relations, and the identification of Being, (by means of the copula "is") with the tenses of the verb, (so that the highest Being was, is now, and ever shall be, in contrast to existence now and then, occasional, wholly past, merely just now, or possibly at some passing time in the future) controlled the whole scheme of physics and metaphysics, which formed the philosophic tradition of Europe. It was a natural consequence of the insight that things, meanings, and words correspond.

The insight was perverted by the notion that the correspondence of things and meanings is prior to discourse and social intercourse. Hence, every true affirmation was an assertion of the fixed belonging to one another of two objects in nature; while every true denial was an assertion of intrinsic exclusion of one object by another. The consequence was belief in ideal essences, individually complete, and yet connected in a system of necessary subordinations and dependencies. Dialectic of their relationships, definition, classification, division in arranging essences, constituted scientific truth about the inmost constituents of nature. Thus a discovery which is the greatest single discovery of man, putting man in potential possession of liberation and of order, became the source of an artificial physics of nature, the basis of a science, philosophy and theology in which the universe was an incarnate grammatical order constructed after the model of discourse.

The modern discovery of inner experience, of a realm of purely personal events that are always at the individual's command, and that are his exclusively as well as inexpensively for refuge, consolation and thrill is also a great and liberating discovery. It implies a new worth and sense of dignity in human individuality, a sense that an individual is not a mere property of nature, set in place according to a scheme independent of him, as an article is put in its place in a cabinet, but that he adds something, that he marks a contribution. It is the counterpart of what distinguishes modern science, experimental, hypothetical; a logic of discovery having therefore opportunity for individual temperament, ingenuity, invention. It is the counterpart of modern politics, art, religion and industry where individuality is given room and movement, in contrast to the ancient scheme of experience, which held individuals tightly within a given order subordinated to its structure and patterns. But here also distortion entered in. Failure to recognize that this world of inner experience is dependent upon an extension of language which is a social product and operation led to the subjectivistic, solipsistic and egotistic strain in modern thought. If the classic thinkers created a cosmos after the model of dialectic, giving rational distinctions power to constitute and regulate, modern thinkers composed nature after the model of personal soliloquizing.

Language considered as an experienced event enables us to interpret what really happened when rational discourse and logic were discovered by the ancients, and when 'inner' experience and its interest were discovered by moderns. Language is a natural function of human association; and its consequences react upon other events, physical and human, giving them meaning or significance. Events that are objects or significant exist in a context where they acquire new ways of operation and new properties. Words are spoken of as coins and money. Now gold, silver, and instrumentalities of credit are first of all, prior to being money, physical things with their own immediate and final qualities. But as money they are substitutes, representations, and surrogates, which embody relationships. As a substitute, money not merely facilitates exchange of such commodities as existed prior to its use, but it revolutionizes as well production and consumption of all commodities, because it brings into being new transactions, forming new histories and affairs. Exchange is not an event that can be isolated. It marks the emergence of production and consumption into a new medium and context wherein they acquire new properties.

Language is similarly not a mere agency for economizing energy in the interaction of human beings. It is a release and amplification of energies that enter into it, conferring upon them the added quality of meaning. The quality of meaning thus introduced is extended and transferred, actually and potentially, from sounds, gestures and marks, to all other things in nature. Natural events become messages to be enjoyed and administered, precisely as are song, fiction, oratory, the giving of advice and instruction. Thus events come to possess characters; they are demarcated, and noted. For character is general and distinguished.

When events have communicable meaning, they have marks, notations, and are capable of con-notation and de-notation. They are more than mere occurrences; they have implications. Hence inference and reasoning are possible; these operations are reading the message of things, which things utter because they are involved in human associations. When Aristotle drew a distinction between sensible things that are more noted—known— to us and rational things that are more noted—known— in themselves, he was actually drawing a distinction between things that operate in a local, restricted universe of discourse, and things whose marks are such that they readily enter into indefinitely extensive and varied discourse.

The interaction of human beings, namely, association, is not different in origin from other modes of interaction. There is a peculiar absurdity in the question of how individuals become social, if the question is taken literally. Human beings illustrate the same traits of both immediate uniqueness and connection, relationship, as do other things. No more in their case than in that of atoms and physical masses is immediacy the whole of existence and therefore an obstacle to being acted upon by and effecting other things. Everything that exists in as far as it is known and knowable is in interaction with other things. It is associated, as well as solitary, single. The catching up of human individuals into association is thus no new and unprecedented fact; it is a manifestation of a commonplace of existence. Significance resides not in the bare fact of association, therefore, but in the consequences that flow from the distinctive patterns of human association. There is, again, nothing new or unprecedented in the fact that assemblage of things confers upon the assembly and its constituents, new properties by means of unlocking energies hitherto pent in. The significant consideration is that assemblage of organic human beings transforms sequence and coexistence into participation.

Gestures and cries are not primarily expressive and communicative. They are modes of organic behavior as much as are locomotion, seizing and crunching. Language, signs and significance, come into existence not by intent and mind but by over-flow, by-products, in gestures and sound. The story of language is the story of the *use* made of these occurrences; a use that is eventual, as well as eventful. Those rival accounts of the origin of language that go by the nicknames of bow-wow, pooh-pooh, and ding-dong theories are not in fact theories of the origin of *language*. They are accounts, of some plausibility, of how and why certain sounds rather than others were selected to signify objects, acts and situations. If the mere existence of sounds of these kinds constituted language, lower animals might well converse more subtly and fluently than man. But they became language only when used within a context of mutual assistance and direction. The latter are alone of prime importance in considering the transformation of organic gestures and cries into names, things with significance, or the origin of language.

Observable facts of animal experience furnish us with our starting point. "Animals respond to certain stimuli . . . . by the contraction of certain muscles whose functioning is of no direct consequence to the animal itself, but affects other animals by stimulating them to act. . . . . Let us call this class the signaling reflexes. A few, but very diversified examples of the signaling reflexes, are the lighting of a fire-fly, the squeezing out of a black liquid from the ink bladder of a cuttle-fish, the crowing of a rooster . . . . the spreading of its tail by a peacock. These reflex activities affect other animals by stimulating them. . . . . If no other animals are present, or these other animals fail to respond by their own reflexes, the former reflex actions are completely wasted."[2]

Sub-human animals thus behave in ways which have no *direct* consequences of utility to the behaving animal, but which call out certain characteristic responses, sexual, protective, food-finding (as with the cluck of a hen to her chicks), in other animals. In some cases, the act evoked

[2] Max Meyer, The Psychology Of The Other One, 1922, p. 195; a statement of behavioristic psychology that has hardly received the attention it intrinsically deserves.

in other animals has in turn an important consequence for the first agent. A sexual act or a combined protective act against danger is furthered. In other cases, the consequences turn out useful to the species, to a numerically indeterminate group including individuals not yet born. Signaling acts evidently form the basic *material* of language. Similar activities occur without intent in man; thus a babe's scream attracts the attention of an adult and evokes a response useful to the infant, although the cry itself is an organic overflow having no intent. So too a man's posture and facial changes may indicate to another things which the man himself would like to conceal, so that he "gives himself away." "Expression," or signs, communication of meaning, exists in such cases for the observer, not for the agent.

While signaling acts are a material condition of language they are not language nor yet are they its *sufficient* condition. Only from an external standpoint, is the original action even a signal; the response of other animals to it is not to a sign, but, by some preformed mechanism, to a direct stimulus. By habit, by conditioned reflex, hens run to the farmer when he makes a clucking noise, or when they hear the rattle of grain in a pan. When the farmer raises his arms to throw the grain they scatter and fly, to return only when the movement ceases. They act as if alarmed; his movement is thus not a sign of food; it is a stimulus that evokes flight. But a human infant learns to discount such movements; to become interested in them as events preparatory to a desired consummation; he learns to treat them as signs of an ulterior event so that his response is to their meaning. He treats them as means to consequences. The hen's activity is ego-cen-

tric; that of the human being is participative.   The latter
puts himself at the standpoint of a situation in which two
parties share.   This is the essential peculiarity of language, or signs.

A requests *B* to bring him something, to which *A* points,
say a flower.   There is an original mechanism by which
B may react to *A*'s movement in pointing.   But natively
such a reaction is to the movement, not to the *pointing*,
not to the object pointed out.   But *B* learns that the
movement *is* a pointing; he responds to it not in itself,
but as an index of something else.   His response is transferred from *A*'s direct movement to the *object* to which *A*
points.   Thus he does not merely execute the natural
acts of looking or grasping which the movement might
instigate on its own account.   The motion of *A* attracts
his gaze to the thing pointed to; then, instead of just
transferring his response from *A*'s movement to the
native reaction he might make to the thing as stimulus, he
responds in a way which is a function of *A*'s *relationship*,
actual and potential, to the thing.   The characteristic
thing about *B*'s understanding of *A*'s movement and
sounds is that he responds to the thing from the standpoint of *A*.   He perceives the thing as it may function in
A's experience, instead of just ego-centrically.   Similarly,
A in making the request conceives the thing not only in
its direct relationship to himself, but as a thing capable
of being grasped and handled by *B*.   He sees the thing
as it may function in *B*'s experience.   Such is the essence
and import of communication, signs and meaning.   Something is literally made common in at least two different
centres of behavior.   To understand is to anticipate
together, it is to make a cross-reference which, when acted

upon, brings about a partaking in a common, inclusive, undertaking.

Stated in greater detail; B upon hearing A, makes a preparatory reaction of his eyes, hands and legs in view of the consummatory act of A's possession; he engages in the act of grasping, carrying and tendering the flower to A. At the same time, A makes a preparatory response to B's consummatory act, that of carrying and proffering the flower. Thus neither the sounds uttered by A, his gesture of pointing, nor the sight of the thing pointed to, is the occasion and stimulus of B's act; the stimulus is B's anticipatory share in the consummation of a transaction in which both participate. The heart of language is not "expression" of something antecedent, much less expression of antecedent thought. It is communication; the establishment of cooperation in an activity in which there are partners, and in which the activity of each is modified and regulated by partnership. To fail to understand is to fail to come into agreement in action; to misunderstand is to set up action at cross purposes. Take speech as behavioristically as you will, including the elimination of all private mental states, and it remains true that it is markedly distinguished from the signaling acts of animals. Meaning is not indeed a psychic existence; it is primarily a property of behavior, and secondarily a property of objects. But the behavior of which it is a quality is a distinctive behavior; cooperative, in that response to another's act involves contemporaneous response to a thing as entering into the other's behavior, and this upon both sides. It is difficult to state the exact physiological mechanism which is involved. But about the fact there is no doubt. It constitutes the intelligibility of acts and things. Possession of the capacity to engage in such activity is intelligence. Intelligence and meaning are natural consequences of the peculiar form which interaction sometimes assumes in the case of human beings.

Primarily meaning is intent and intent is not personal in a private and exclusive sense. *A* proposes the consummatory possession of the flower through the medium or means of *B*'s action; *B* proposes to cooperate—or act adversely—in the fulfillment of *A*'s proposal. Secondarily, meaning is the acquisition of significance by things in their status in making possible and fulfilling shared cooperation. In the first place, it is the *motion and sounds* of *A* which have meaning, or are signs. Similarly the movements of *B*, while they immediate to him, are signs to *A* of *B*'s cooperation or refusal. But secondarily the *thing* pointed out by *A* to *B* gains meaning. It ceases to be just what it brutely is at the moment, and is responded to in its potentiality, as a means to remoter consequences. The flower pointed to for example, *is* portable; but apart from language portability is a brute contingency waiting for its actualization upon circumstance. But when *A* counts upon the understanding and cooperation of *B*, and *B* responds to the intent of *A*, the flower *is* contemporaneously portable though not now actually in movement. Its potentiality, or conditioning of consequences, is an immediately recognized and possessed trait; the flower *means* portability instead of simply *being* portable. Animism, the attribution of desire and intent to inanimate things, is no mysterious projection of psychical traits; it is a misinterpretation of a natural fact, namely, that significant things are things actually implicated in situations of shared or social purpose and execution.

The logic of animism is simple. Since words act upon things indirectly, or as signs, and since words express the significant consequences of things, (the traits for the sake of which they are used), why should not words act also directly upon things to release their latent powers? Since we "call" things by their names, why should they not answer? And if they assist us as our friends do when appealed to, is not this proof they are animated by friendly intent; or if they frustrate us, proof that they are filled with the same traits which inspirit our enemies? "Animism" is thus the consequence of a direct transfer of properties of a social situation to an immediate relationship of natural things to a person. Its legitimate and constant form is poetry, in which things and events are given voice and directly communicate with us.

If we consider the *form* or scheme of the situation in which meaning and understanding occur, we find an involved simultaneous presence and cross-reference of immediacy and efficiency, overt actuality and potentiality, the consummatory and the instrumental. *A* in making the request of *B*, at the same time makes the incipient and preparatory response of receiving the thing at the hands of *B;* he performs in readiness the consummatory act. *B*'s understanding of the meaning of what *A* says, instead of being a mere reaction to sound, is an anticipation of a consequence, while it is also an immediate activity of eyes, legs, and hands in getting and giving the flower to *A*. The flower is the thing which it immediately is, and it also is means of a conclusion. All of this is directly involved in the existence of intelligible speech. No such simultaneous presence of finality and agency, is possible in things as *purely* physical—in abstraction, that is, of potential presence in a situation of communication. Since we have discovered that all things have a phase of potential communicability, that is, that any conceivable thing may enter into discourse, the retrospective imputation of meanings and logical relationships to bare things is natural; it does no harm, save when the imputation is dogmatic and literal. What a physical event immediately is, and what it *can* do or its relationship are distinct and incommensurable. But when an event has meaning, its potential consequences become its integral and funded feature. When the potential consequences are important and repeated, they form the very nature and essence of a thing, its defining, identifying, and distinguishing form. To recognize the thing is to grasp its definition. Thus we become capable of perceiving things instead of merely feeling and having them. To *perceive* is to acknowledge unattained possibilities; it is to refer the present to consequences, apparition to issue, and thereby to behave in deference to the *connections* of events. As an attitude, perception or awareness is predictive expectancy, wariness. Since potential consequences also *mark* the thing itself, and form its nature, the event thus marked becomes an object of contemplation; as meaning, future consequences already belong to the thing. The act of striving to bring them existentially into the world may be commuted into esthetic enjoyed possession of form.

Essence, as has been intimated, is but a pronounced instance of meaning; to be partial, and to assign *a* meaning to a thing as *the* meaning is but to evince human subjection to bias. Since consequences differ also in their consequence and hence importance, practical good sense may attach to this one-sided partiality, for the meaning seized upon as essence may designate extensive and recurrent consequences. Thus is explained the seeming paradox of the distinction and connection of essence and existence. Essence is never existence, and yet it is the essence, the distilled import, of existence; the significant thing about it, its intellectual voucher, the means of inference and extensive transfer, and object of esthetic intuition. In it, feeling and understanding are one; the meaning of a thing is the sense it makes.

Since the consequences which are liked have an emphatic quality, it is not surprising that many consequences, even though recognized to be inevitable, are regarded as if they were accidental and alien. Thus the very essence of a thing is identified with those consummatory consequences which the thing has when conditions are felicitous. Thus *the* essence, one, immutable and constitutive, which *makes* the thing *what* it is, emerges from the various meanings which vary with varying conditions and transitory intents. When essence is then thought to contain existence as the perfect includes the imperfect, it is because a legitimate, practical measure of reality in terms of importance is illegitimately altered into a theoretical measure.

Discourse itself is both instrumental and consummatory. Communication is an exchange which procures something wanted; it involves a claim, appeal, order, direction or request, which realizes want at less cost than personal labor exacts, since it procures the cooperative assistance of others. Communication is also an immediate enhancement of life, enjoyed for its own sake. The dance is accompanied by song and becomes the drama; scenes of danger and victory are most fully savored when they are told.   Greeting becomes a ceremonial with its prescribed rites.   Language is always a form of action and in its instrumental use is always a means of concerted action for an end, while at the same time it finds in itself all the goods of its possible consequences.   For there is no mode of action as fulfilling and as rewarding as is concerted consensus of action.   It brings with it the sense of sharing and merging in a whole.   Forms of language are unrivalled in ability to create this sense, at first with direct participation on the part of an audience; and then, as literary forms develop, through imaginative identification.   Greek thinkers had distinguished patterns in Greek literary art of consummatory uses of speech, and the meanings that were discovered to be indispensable to communication were treated as final and ultimate in nature itself.   Essences were hypostatized into original and constitutive forms of all existence.

The idea put forth about the connection of meaning with language is not to be confused with traditional nominalism.   It does not imply that meaning and essence are adventitious and arbitrary.   The defect of nominalism lies in its virtual denial of interaction and association.   It regarded the word not as a mode of social action with which to realize the ends of association, but as an expression of a ready-made, exclusively individual, mental state; sensation, image or feeling, which, being an existence, is necessarily particular.   For the sound, gesture, or written mark which is involved in language is a particular existence.   But as such it is not a *word*, and it does not become a word by declaring a mental existence; it becomes a word by gaining meaning; and it gains meaning when its use stablishes a genuine community of action. Interaction, operative relationship, is as much a fact about events as are particularity and immediacy. Language and its consequences are characters taken on by natural interaction and natural conjunction in specified conditions of organization. Nominalism ignores organization, and thus makes nonsense of meanings.

Language is specifically a mode of interaction of at least two beings, a speaker and a hearer; it presupposes an organized group to which these creatures belong, and from whom they have acquired their habits of speech. It is therefore a relationship, not a particularity. This consideration alone condemns traditional nominalism. The meaning of signs moreover always includes something common as between persons and an object. When we attribute meaning to the speaker as *his* intent, we take for granted another person who is to share in the execution of the intent, and also something, independent of the persons concerned, through which the intent is to be realized. Persons and thing must alike serve as means in a common, shared consequence. This community of partaking is meaning.

The invention and use of tools have played a large part in consolidating meanings, because a tool is a thing used as means to consequences, instead of being taken directly and physically. It is intrinsically relational, anticipatory, predictive. Without reference to the absent, or "transcendence," nothing is a tool. The most convincing evidence that animals do not "think" is found in the fact is that they have no tools, but depend upon their own relatively-fixed bodily structures to effect results.

Because of such dependence they have no way of distinguishing the immediate existence of anything from its potential efficiencies; no way of projecting its consequences to define a nature or essence. Anything whatever used as a tool exhibits distinction and identification. Fire existentially burns; while fire which is employed in order to cook and keep warm, especially after other things, like rubbing sticks together, are used as means to generate it, is an existence having meaning and potential essence. The presence of inflammation and terror or discomfort is no longer the whole story; an occurrence is now an object; and while it is absurd to hold (as idealism virtually does) that the meaning of an existence is the real substance of the existence, it is equally absurd not to recognize the full transformative import of what has happened.

As to be a tool, or to be used as means for consequences, is to have and to endow with meaning, language, being the tool of tools, is the cherishing mother of all significance. For other instrumentalities and agencies, the things usually thought of as appliances, agencies and furnishings, can originate and develop only in social groups made possible by language. Things become tools ceremonially and institutionally. The notoriously conventionalized and traditional character of primitive utensils and their attendant symbolizations demonstrate this fact. Moreover, tools and artifices of agency are always found in connection with some division of labor which depends upon some device of communication. The statement can be proved in a more theoretical way. Immediacy as such is transient to the point of evanescence, and its flux has to be fixed by some easily recoverable and recurrent act within control of the organism, like gesture and spoken sounds, before things can be intentionally utilized. A creature might accidentally warm itself by a fire or use a stick to stir the ground in a way which furthered the growth of food-plants. But the effect of comfort ceases with the fire, existentially; a stick even though once used as a lever would revert to the status of being just a stick, unless the *relationship* between it and its consequence were distinguished and retained. Only language, or some form of artificial signs, serves to register the relationship and make it fruitful in other contexts of particular existence. Spears, urns, baskets, snares may have originated accidentally in some consummatory consequence of natural events. But only repetition through concerted action accounts for their becoming institutionalized as tools, and this concert of action depends upon the use of memoranda and communication. To make another aware of the possibility of a use or objective relationship is to perpetuate what is otherwise an incident as an agency; communication is a condition of consciousness.

Thus every meaning is generic or universal. It is something common between speaker, hearer and the thing to which speech refers. It is universal also as a means of generalization. For a meaning is a method of action, a way of using things as means to a shared consummation, and method is general, though the things to which it is applied are particular. The meaning, for example, of portability is something in which two persons and an object share. But portability after it is once apprehended becomes a way of treating other things; it is extended widely. Whenever this is a chance, it is applied; application ceases only when a thing refuses to be treated in this way. And even then refusal may be only a challenge to develop the meaning of portability until the thing can be transported. Meanings are rules for using and interpreting things; interpretation being always an imputation of potentiality for some consequence.

It would be difficult to imagine any doctrine more absurd than the theory that general ideas or meanings arise by the comparison of a number of particulars, eventuating in the recognition of something common to them all. Such a comparison may be employed to check a suggested widened application of a rule. But generalization is carried spontaneously as far as it will plausibly go; usually much further than it will actually go. A newly acquired meaning is forced upon everything that does not obviously resist its application, as a child uses a new word whenever he gets a chance or as he plays with a new toy. Meanings are self-moving to new cases. In the end, conditions force a chastening of this spontaneous tendency. The scope and limits of application are ascertained experimentally in the process of application. The history of science, to say nothing of popular beliefs, is sufficient indication of the difficulty found in submitting this irrational generalizing tendency to the discipline of experience. To call it *a priori* is to express a fact; but to impute the *a priori* character of the generalizing force of meanings to *reason* is to invert the facts. Rationality is acquired when the tendency becomes circumspect, based upon observation and tested by deliberate experiment.

Meaning is objective as well as universal. Originating as a concerted or combined method of using or enjoying things, it indicates a possible interaction, not a thing in separate singleness. A meaning may not of course have the particular objectivity which is imputed to it, as whistling does not actually portend wind, nor the ceremonial sprinkling of water indicate rain. But such magical imputations of external reference testify to the objectivity of meaning as such. Meanings are naturally the meaning of something or other; difficulty lies in discriminating the right thing. It requires the discipline of ordered and deliberate experimentation to teach us that some meanings delightful or horrendous as they are, are meanings communally developed in the process of communal festivity and control, and do not represent the polities, and ways and means of nature apart from social arts. Scientific meanings were superadded to esthetic and affectional meanings when objects instead of being defined in terms of their consequences in social interactions and discussion were defined in terms of their consequences with respect to one another. This discrimination permitted esthetic and affective objects to be freed from magical imputations, which were due to attributing to them *in rerum natura* the consequences they had in the transmitted culture of the group.

Yet the truth of classic philosophy in assigning objectivity to meanings, essences, ideas remains unassailable. It is heresy to conceive meanings to be private, a property of ghostly psychic existences. Berkeley with all his nominalism, saw that "ideas," though particular in existence, are general in function and office. His attribution of the ideas which are efficacious in conduct to an order established by God, while evincing lack of perception of their naturalistic origin in communication or communal interaction, manifests a sounder sense of the objectivity of meanings than has been shown by those who eliminated his theology while retaining his psychology. The inconsistency of the sensationalists who, stopping short of extreme scepticism, postulate that some associations of ideas correspond to conjunctions among things is also reluctantly extorted evidence of how intimation of the objectivity of ideas haunts the mind in spite of theory to the contrary.

Meanings are objective because they are modes of natural interaction; such an interaction, although primarily between organic beings, as includes things and energies external to living creatures. The regulative force of legal meanings affords a convenient illustration. A traffic policeman holds up his hand or blows a whistle. His act operates as a signal to direct movements. But it is more than an episodic stimulus. It embodies a rule of social action. Its proximate meaning is its near-by consequences in coordination of movements of persons and vehicles; its ulterior and permanent meaning—essence—is its consequence in the way of security of social movements. Failure to observe the signal subjects a person to arrest, fine or imprisonment. The essence embodied in the policeman's whistle is not an occult reality superimposed upon a sensuous or physical flux and imparting form to it; a mysterious subsistence somehow housed within a psychical event. Its essence is the rule, comprehensive and persisting, the standardized habit, of social interaction, and for the sake of which the whistle is used. The pattern, archetype, that forms the essence of the whistle as a particular noise is an orderly arrangement of the movements of persons, and vehicles established by social agreement as its consequence. This meaning is independent of the psychical landscape, the sensations and imagery, of the policeman and others concerned. But it is not on that account a timeless spiritual ghost nor pale logical subsistence divorced from events.

The case is the same with the essence of any non-human event, like gravity, or virtue, or vertebrate. Some consequences of the interaction of things concern us; the consequences are not *merely* physical; they enter finally into human action and destiny. Fire burns and the burning is of moment. It enters experience; it is fascinating to watch swirling flames; it is important to avoid its dangers and to utilize its beneficial potencies. When we name an event, calling it fire, we speak proleptically; we do not name an immediate event; that is impossible. We employ a term of discourse; we invoke a meaning, namely, the potential consequences of the existence. The ultimate meaning of the noise made by the traffic officer is the total consequent system of social behavior, in which individuals are subjected, by means of noise, to social coördination; its proximate meaning is a coördination of the movements of persons and vehicles in the neighborhood and directly affected. Similarly the ultimate meaning, or essence, denominated fire, is the consequences of certain natural events within the scheme of human activities, in the experience of social intercourse, the hearth and domestic altar, shared comfort, working of metals, rapid transit, and other such affairs. "Scientifically," we ignore these ulterior meanings. And quite properly; for when a sequential order of changes is determined, the final meaning in immediate enjoyments and appreciations is capable of control.

While classic thought, and its survival in later idealisms, assumed that the ulterior human meanings, meanings of direct association in discourse, are forms of nature apart from their place in discourse, modern thought is given to marking a sharp separation between meanings determined in terms of the causal relationship of things and meanings in terms of human association. Consequently, it treats the latter as negligible or as purely private, not the meanings of natural events at all. It identifies the proximate meanings with the only valid meanings, and abstract relations become an idol. To pass over in science the human meanings of the consequences of natural interactions is legitimate; indeed it is indispensable. To ascertain and state meanings in abstraction from social or shared situations is the only way in which the latter can be intelligently modified, extended and varied. Mathematical symbols have least connection with distinctively human situations and consequences; and the finding of such terms, free from esthetic and moral significance, is a necessary part of the technique. Indeed, such elimination of ulterior meanings supplies perhaps the best possible empirical definition of mathematical relations. They are meanings without direct reference to human behavior. Thus an essence becomes wholly "intellectual" or scientific, devoid of consummatory implication; it expresses the purely instrumental without reference to the objects to which the events in question are instrumental. It then becomes the starting point of reflection that may terminate in ends or consequences in human suffering and enjoyment not previously experienced. Abstraction from any particular consequence (which is the same thing as taking instrumentality generally), opens the way to new uses and consequences.

This is what happens when the meaning of the traffic officer's signal is detached from its own context, and taken up into, say, written and published language, a topic of independent consideration by experts or by civic administrators.   In being placed in a context of other meanings, (theoretically and scientifically discussed), it is liberated from the contingencies of its prior use.   The outcome may be the invention of a new and improved system of semaphores which exercise regulation of human interaction more effectively.   Deliberate abstraction, however, from all ulterior human use and consequence is hardly likely to occur in the case of discourse about a signal system.   In physical science, the abstraction or liberation is complete. Things are defined by means of symbols that convey only their consequences with respect to one another.   'Water' in ordinary experience designates an essence of something which has familiar bearings and uses in human life, drink and cleansing and the extinguishing of fire.   But H_2O gets away from these connections, and embodies in its essence only instrumental efficiency in respect to things independent of human affairs.

The counterpart of classic thought which took ends, enjoyments, uses, not simply as genuine termini of natural events (which they are), but as the essence and form of things independent of human experience, is a modern philosophy which makes reality purely mechanical and which regards the consequences of things in human experience as accidental or phenomenal by-products.   In truth, abstraction from human experience is but a liberation from familiar and specific enjoyments, it provides means for detecting hitherto untried consequences, for invention, for the creation of new wants, and new modes of good and evil. In any sense in which the conception of essence is legitimate, these human consequences are the essence of natural events. Water still has the meanings of water of everyday experience when it becomes the essence H_2O, or else H_2O would be totally meaningless, a mere sound, not an intelligible name.

Meaning, fixed as essence in a term of discourse, may be imaginatively administered and manipulated, experimented with. Just as we overtly manipulate things, making new separations and combinations, thereby introducing things into new contexts and environments, so we bring together logical universals in discourse, where they copulate and breed new meanings. There is nothing surprising in the fact that dialectic (or deduction, as it is termed by moderns) generates new objects; that, in Kantian language, it is "synthetic," instead of merely explicating what is already had. All discourse, oral or written, which is more than a routine unrolling of vocal habits, says things that surprise the one that says them, often indeed more than they surprise any one else. Systematic logical discourse, or ratiocination, is the same sort of thing conducted according to stricter rules. Even under the condition of rigid rules the emergence of new meanings is much more similar to what happens in genial conversation than is conventionally supposed. Rules of logical order and consistency appertain to economy and efficiency of combination and separation in generating new meanings; not to meanings as such. They are rules of a certain kind of experimentation. In trying new combinations of meanings, satisfactory consequences of new meanings are hit upon; then they may be arranged in a system. The expert in thought is one who has skill in making experiments to introduce an old meaning into different situations and who has a sensitive ear for detecting resultant harmonies and discords. The most "deductive" thought in actual occurrence is a series of trials, observations and selections. In one sense of the ambiguous word intuition, it is a "series of intuitions," and logic is *ex post facto*, expressing a wit that formulates economically the congruities and incongruities that have manifested themselves. Any "syllogism" which is such *ab initio* is performed better by a machine that manipulates symbols automatically than by any "thinker."

This capacity of essences to enter readily into any number of new combinations, and thereby generate further meanings more profound and far reaching than those from which they sprang, gives them a semblance of independent life and career, a semblance which is responsible for their elevation by some thinkers into a realm separate from that of existence and superior to it. Consider the interpretations that have been based upon such essences as four, plus, the square root of minus one. These are at once so manipulable and so fertile in consequences when conjoined with others that thinkers who are primarily interested in their performances treat them not as significant terms of discourse, but as an order of entities independent of human invention and use. The fact that we can watch them and register what happens when they come together, and that the things that happen are as independent of our volition and expectation as are the discoveries of a geographic exploration, is taken as evidence that they constitute entities having subsistent Being independently not only of us but of all natural events whatever.

Alternatives are too narrowly conceived. Because meanings and essences are not states of mind, because they are as independent of immediate sensation and imagery as are physical things, and because nevertheless they are not physical things, it is assumed that they are a peculiar kind of thing, termed metaphysical, or "logical" in a style which separates logic from nature. But there are many other things which are neither physical nor psychical existences, and which are demonstrably dependent upon human association and interaction. Such things function moreover in liberating and regulating subsequent human intercourse; their essence is their contribution to making that intercourse more significant and more immediately rewarding. Take the sort of thing exemplified in the regulation of traffic. The sound of a whistle is a particular existential event numerically separate, with its own peculiar spatial temporal position. This may not be said of the rule or method of social co-operative interaction which it manifests and makes effective. A continuous way of organized action is not a particular, and hence is not a physical or psychical existence. Yet the consequences of using the method of adjusting movements, so that they do not interfere with one another, have both a physical and a mental phase. Physically, there is modification of the changes in space which would otherwise occur. Mentally, there are enjoyments and annoyances which would not otherwise happen. But no one of these incidents nor all of them put together form the essence or ulterior meaning of the sound of the whistle; they are qualifications of a more secure concert of human activity which, as a consequence of a legal order incarnate in the whistling, forms its significance.

Discussion of meaning and essence has reached such an impasse and is barbed with such entanglements, that it is further worth while to suggest consideration of legal entities as indicative of escape from the disjunction of essence from existence. What is a Corporation, a Franchise? A corporation is neither a mental state nor a particular physical event in space and time. Yet it is an objective reality, not an ideal Realm of Being. It is an objective reality which has multitudinous physical and mental consequences. It is something to be studied as we study electrons; it exhibits as does the latter unexpected properties, and when introduced into new situations behaves with new reactions. It is something which may be conducted, facilitated and obstructed, precisely as may be a river. Nevertheless it would not exist nor have any meaning and potency apart from an interaction of human beings with one another, an interaction in which external things are implicated. As legal essence, or concerted method of regulated interaction, corporation has its own and its developing career.

Again juridical rule implies jurisdiction; a particular body of persons within a certain territory to whom it applies. The legal significance of an act depends upon *where* it takes place. Yet an act is an interaction, a transaction, not isolated, self-sufficient. The initial stage of an act and the terminating consequences which, between them, determine its meaning, may be far apart in place as well as in time. Where then is the act? What is its locus? The readiest reply is in terms of the beginning of the act. The act was performed where the agent bodily was at the time of its occurrence. Suppose, however, that before discovery, the agent in a criminal transaction changes his abode and resides within another jurisdiction. The need of security leads to the generation, in its union with the conception of jurisdiction, of a new conception or essence, that of extradition, of comity of jurisdictions. New procedures with corresponding new technical concepts or meanings then develop by means of which a person charged with crime may be requisitioned and removed. The concept of jurisdiction in combination with that of security, justice, etc., deductively generates other concepts.

The process does not stop here. An agent implies a patient. Suppose a person in New York State shoots a bullet across the New Jersey line, and kills some one in that State; or sends poisoned candy by mail to some one in California who dies from eating it. *Where* is the crime committed? The guilty person is not within the jurisdiction of the State where the death resulted; hence, his crime by definition, was not committed in that State. But since the death did not occur where he was bodily present at the time, no crime occurred in that jurisdiction, locus being defined in terms of the abode of the agent. The essence, extradition, does not apply because there is no crime for which to extradite him. In short, because of the accepted meaning of jurisdiction, no crime has been committed anywhere. Such an outcome is evidently prejudicial to the integrity and security of human association and intercourse. Thus the element of *transaction* in an act is noted; an act initiated within a given jurisdiction becomes a crime when its obnoxious consequences occur outside. The locus of the act now extends all the way from New York to California. Thus two independ-

ent particular events capable of direct observation, together with a connection between them which is inferred,
not directly observable, are now included in so simple
a meaning as that of the locus of an act.   In the traditional language of philosophy, the essence is now ideal or
rational, non-sensible.   Furthermore a system of legal
meanings is developed by modifying different ones with
a view to consistency or logical order.   Thus the meanings
get more independent of the events that led up to them;
they may be taught and expounded as a logical system,
whose portions are deductively connected with one
another.

In civil cases, however, the concept of locus even as
thus extended fails to take care of all the consequences
which are found to require regulation, by attachment of
rights and liabilities to certain classes of acts.   A transaction may concern goods or funds which operate in a
jurisdiction different to that of either of the parties
directly concerned in it.   Its consequences include persons
living in a third jurisdiction.   The ultimate result is a
tendency in some case to reverse the earlier and more
immediately physical (or spatially limited) concept of
jurisdiction with respect to place.   Jurisdiction comes to
mean "power to deal legally" with a certain specific
affair, rather than an "area within which action has
occurred": that is, area is defined by power to act, which
in turn is determined with respect to consequences found
desirable, while originally a concept of fixed area had been
employed to fix power of legal action.   If it be asked,
"where" a transaction is located, the only possible answer,
on the basis of legal procedure, appears in many cases to

be that it is located wherever it has consequences which it is deemed socially important to regulate.[3]

Juridical institutions everywhere embody essences which are as objective and coercive with respect to opinions, emotions and sensations of individuals as are physical objects; essences which are general, capable of independent examination; of fruitful connection with one another; and of extension to concrete phenomena not previously related to them.   At the same time the origin and nature of such meanings can be empirically described by reference to social interactions and their consequences. They are means of regulating consequences, through establishing a present cross-reference to one another of the diverse acts of interacting agents.   If we bear in mind the capacity to transfer such a regulative method to new and previously unconnected universes of discourse, there is nothing astonishing in the fact that a stain may mean an anatomical structure, a change in the size of a mercury column changes in atmospheric pressure and thus probable rain.   There is nothing astonishing therefore in the fact that meanings expressed in symbols are capable of yielding a vast and growing system of mathematics.   An essence which is a method of procedure can be linked to other methods of procedure so as to yield

[3] In this respect the actual tendency of law (though not always its doctrinal formulations) is further advanced than are views current among philosophers.   Compare the discussions as to "where" an illusion is; or what is the locus of past experience, and "where" unrealized possibilities exist.   Some writers find satisfaction in locating them "in" the mind, although they also deny that mind is spatial.   Then, realizing that the psychical existence "in" which these affairs are located is itself a present particular existence, they find it necessary to place an "essence" or meaning within the skin of the psychical state.

new methods; to bring about a revision of old methods, and form a systematic and ordered whole—all without reference to any application of any method to any particular set of concrete existences, and in complete abstraction from any particular consequences which the methods or logical universals are to regulate.   For mathematics, they are as much independent objects as is the material with which a zoologist deals.   Comparison with machines like a self-binding reaper or a telephone system is useful. Machines are evolved in human experience, not prior to it or independently of it.   But they are objective and compelling with respect to present particular physical and psychical processes; they are general methods of reaching consequences; they are interactions of previously existing physical existences.   Moreover, they depend for their efficacy upon other and independent natural existences; they produce consequences only when used in connection with other existences which limit and test their operation.   When machines have attained a certain stage of development, engineers may devote themselves to the construction of new machines and to improvements in old machines without specific reference to concrete uses and applications.   That is, inventors are guided by the inherent logic of existing machines, by observation of the consistency of relationships which parts of the machine bear to one another and to the pattern of the entire machine.   An invention may thus result from purely mathematical calculations.   Nevertheless the machine is still a machine, an instrumental device for regulating interactions with reference to consequences.

When the "concept" of a machine, its meaning or essence embodied in a symbol, deductively generates plans of new machines, essence is fruitful because it was first devised for a purpose. Its subsequent success or failure in fulfilling its purpose, in delivering the desired consequences, together with reflection upon the reason therefore, supply a basis for revising, extending, and modifying the essence in question; thus it has a career and consequence of its own. If we follow the lead of empirically verifiable cases, it would then appear that mathematical and moral essences may be dialectically fruitful, because like other machines they have been constructed for the purpose of securing certain consequences with the minimum of waste and the maximum of economy and efficiency.

Communication is consummatory as well as instrumental. It is a means of establishing coöperation, domination and order. Shared experience is the greatest of human goods. In communication, such conjunction and contact as is characteristic of animals become endearments capable of infinite idealization; they become symbols of the very culmination of nature. That God is love is a more worthy idealization than that the divine is power. Since love at its best brings illumination and wisdom, this meaning is as worthy as that the divine is truth. Various phases of participation by one in another's joy, sorrows, sentiments and purposes, are distinguished by the scope and depth of the objects that are held in common, from a momentary caress to continued insight and loyalty. When a psychologist like Bain reduced the "tender emotions" to sensations of contact he indicated a natural organic basis. But he failed to connect even organic contact with its vital function, assimilation and fruitful union; while (what is of greater import) he failed to note the transformation that this biological function undergoes when its consequences, being noted, become an objective meaning incorporated as its essence in a natural physiological occurrence.

If scientific discourse is instrumental in function, it also is capable of becoming an enjoyed object to those concerned in it. Upon the whole, human history shows that thinking in being abstract, remote and technical has been laborious; or at least that the process of attaining such thinking has been rendered painful to most by social circumstances. In view of the importance of such activity and its objects, it is a priceless gain when it becomes an intrinsic delight. Few would philosophize if philosophic discourse did not have its own inhering fascination. Yet it is not the satisfactoriness of the activity which defines science or philosophy; the definition comes from the structure and function of subject-matter. To say that knowledge as the fruit of intellectual discourse is an end in itself is to say what is esthetically and morally true for some persons, but it conveys nothing about the structure of knowledge; and it does not even hint that its objects are not instrumental. These are questions that can be decided only by an examination of the things in question. Impartial and disinterested thinking, discourse in terms of scrutinized, tested, and related meanings, is a fine art. But it is an art as yet open to comparatively few. Letters, poetry, song, the drama, fiction, history, biography, engaging in rites and ceremonies hallowed by time and rich with the sense of the countless multitudes that share in them, are also modes of discourse that, detached from immediate instrumental consequences of assistance and coöperative action, are ends for most persons. In them discourse is both instrumental and final. No person remains unchanged and has the same future efficiencies, who shares in situations made possible by communication. Subsequent consequences may be good or bad, but they are there. The part of wisdom is not to deny the causal fact because of the intrinsic value of the immediate experience. It is to make the immediately satisfactory object the object which will also be most fertile.

The saying of Matthew Arnold that poetry is a criticism of life sounds harsh to the ears of some persons of strong esthetic bent; it seems to give poetry a moral and instrumental function. But while poetry is not a criticism of life in intent, it is in effect, and so is all art. For art fixes those standards of enjoyment and appreciation with which other things are compared; it selects the objects of future desires; it stimulates effort. This is true of the objects in which a particular person finds his immediate or esthetic values, and it is true of collective man. The level and style of the arts of literature, poetry, ceremony, amusement, and recreation which obtain in a community, furnishing the staple objects of enjoyment in that community, do more than all else to determine the current direction of ideas and endeavors in the community. They supply the meanings in terms of which life is judged, esteemed, and criticized. For an outside spectator, they supply material for a critical evaluation of the life led by that community.

Communication is uniquely instrumental and uniquely final. It is instrumental as liberating us from the otherwise overwhelming pressure of events and enabling us to live in a world of things that have meaning. It is final as a sharing in the objects and arts precious to a community, a sharing whereby meanings are enhanced, deepened and solidified in the sense of communion.   Because of its characteristic agency and finality, communication and its congenial objects are objects ultimately worthy of awe, admiration, and loyal appreciation.   They are worthy as means, because they are the only means that make life rich and varied in meanings.   They are worthy as ends, because in such ends man is lifted from his immediate isolation and shares in a communion of meanings. Here, as in so many other things, the great evil lies in separating instrumental and final functions.   Intelligence is partial and specialized, because communication and participation are limited, sectarian, provincial, confined to class, party, professional group.   By the same token, our enjoyment of ends is luxurious and corrupting for some; brutal, trivial, harsh for others; exclusion from the life of free and full communication excluding both alike from full possession of meanings of the things that enter experience.   When the instrumental and final functions of communication live together in experience, there exists an intelligence which is the method and reward of the common life, and a society worthy to command affection, admiration, and loyalty.[4]

[4] Since the above was originally written I have found the following by Dr. Malinowski in Ogden and Richards, The Meaning of Meaning: "A word, signifying an important utensil, is used in action, not to comment on its nature or reflect on its properties, but to make it appear, be handed over to the speaker, or to direct another man to its proper use.   The meaning of the thing is made up of experiences of its active uses and not of intellectual contemplation. . . . . A word *means* to a native the proper use of the thing for which it stands, exactly as an implement *means* something when it can be handled and means nothing when no active experience is at hand.   Similarly a verb, a word for an action, re-

ceives its meaning through active participation in this action. A word is used when it can produce an action, and not to describe one, still less to translate thoughts." (Pp. 488–9.) I know of no statement about language that brings out with the same clearness and appreciation of the force of the fact that language is primarily a mode of action used for the sake of influencing the conduct of others in connection with the speaker. As he says "The manner in which I am using language now, in writing these words, the manner in which the author of a book or a papyrus or hewn inscription has to use it, is a very far-fetched and derivative function of language. In its primitive uses, language functions as a link in concerted human activity, as a piece of human behavior." (P. 474.) He shows that to understand the meaning of savage language, we have to be able to re-instate the whole social context which alone supplies the meaning. While he lists narrative and ceremonial speech as well as active, he shows that the same principle permeates them. "When incidents are told or discussed among a group of listeners, there is, first, the situation of that moment made up of the respective social, intellectual and emotional attitudes of those present. Within this situation, the narrative creates new bonds and sentiments by the emotional appeal of the words. In every case, narrative speech is primarily a mode of social action rather than a mere reflection of thought." (P. 475.) Then there is the use of language "in free, aimless, social intercourse." "In discussing the function of speech in mere sociabilities, we come to one of the bed rock aspects of human nature in society. There is in all human beings the well-known tendency to congregate, to be together, to enjoy each other's company. . . . . Taciturnity means not only unfriendliness but directly a bad character. The breaking of silence, the communion of words, is the first act to establish links of fellowship." (Pp. 476–7.) Here speech has both the instrumental use of re-assurance and the consummatory good of enhanced sense of membership in a congenial whole. Thus communication is not only a means to common ends but is the sense of community, communion actualized. Nothing more important for philosophers to hearken to has been written than Dr. Malinowski's conclusion: "Language is little influenced by thought, but Thought on the contrary having to borrow from action its tool—that is language—is largely influenced thereby. To sum up we can say that the fundamental grammatical categories, universal to all human languages, can be understood only with reference to the pragmatic *Weltanschauung* of primitive man and that, through the use of language, the barbarous primitive categories must have deeply influenced the later philosophies of man." (P. 498.) He goes on to show its influence in framing categories of (nouns) substance, of action centering around (verbs) objects, and spatial relations—prepositions. And he closes with an express warning against "the old realist fallacy that a word vouches for, or contains, the reality of its meaning. The migration of roots into improper places has given to the imaginary reality of hypostatized meaning a special solidity of its own. For since early experience warrants the substantival existence of anything found within the category of crude substance, of *Protousia*, and subsequent linguistic shifts introduce there such roots as "going", "rest", "motion", etc., the obvious inference is that such abstract entities or ideas live in a world of their own." (P. 509.) Here we have the source of the classic hypostatizing of essence which is described in the text as due to isolating important meanings of things from their context in human interaction.

CHAPTER SIX

NATURE, MIND AND THE SUBJECT

Personality, selfhood, subjectivity are eventual functions that emerge with complexly organized interactions, organic and social. Personal individuality has its basis and conditions in simpler events. Plants and non-human animals act *as if* they were concerned that their activity, their characteristic receptivity and response, should maintain itself. Even atoms and molecules show a selective bias in their indifferencies, affinities and repulsions when exposed to other events. With respect to some things they are hungry to the point of greediness; in the presence of others they are sluggish and cold. It is not surprising that naïve science imputed appetition to their own consummatory outcome to all natural processes, and that Spinoza identified inertia and momentum with inherent tendency on the part of things to conserve themselves in being, and achieve such perfection as belongs to them. In a genuine although not psychic sense, natural beings exhibit preference and centeredness.

In regard to the nature of the individual, as in so many other respects, classic and modern philosophies have pursued opposite paths. In Greek reflection, love of perfection, or self-completion, was attributed to Being. The state of self-sufficiency excluding deficiency constituted the individual, significant change being thought of as the coming into being of such a whole. In consequence, in view of the obvious instability of particular existences such as moderns usually term individuals, a species im-

mutable in time and having form was the true individual.
What moderns call individuals were particulars, transient, partial, and imperfect specimens of the true individual. Mankind as species is more truly an individual than was this or that man. Although Aristotle
criticized his master for giving Being to the genus or
universal separate from particulars, he never doubted
that the species was a real entity, a metaphysical or existential whole including and characterizing all particulars.
A type-form had no separate being; but, being embodied
in particulars, it made them an intrinsically unified and
marked out class, which as a class was ungenerated and
indestructible, perfect and complete.

Modern science has made the conception strange.
Yet it was a natural interpretation of things found in
ordinary experience. The immediate qualitative differences of things cannot be recognized without noting
that things possessed of these qualitative traits fall into
kinds, or families. That the family is more lasting, important, and real than any of its members; that the
family confers upon its constituents their standing and
character, so that those who have no family are outcasts
and wanderers, represents a notable situation in most
forms of human culture. In such a cultural scheme, those
peculiar differences that constitute for us personal individuality are only accidental variations from the family
type, the form which marks a kind enables a particular
person to be placed, known, identified. The modern
habit of using self, "I," mind, and spirit interchangeably
is inconceivable when family and commune are solid
realities. To the Greeks, a kind was an organized
system in which an ideal form unites varying particulars

into a genuine whole, and gives to them distinctive and recognizable character. The presence in things of the generic form renders them knowable. Mind is but the ordered system of all the characters which constitute kinds, differing among men, differing according to differences of organic constitutions. Upon such a view, subjectivity, individuality of mind marks an anomaly; a failure of realization of objective forms on the part of the indwelling family to impress itself adequately, owing to stubborn resisting material constitution. What is prized and exalted by moderns as individual was just the defect which is the source of ignorance, opinion, and error.

Such a marked difference in the estimate of the status of individuality is proof of difference in the empirical content of ancient and modern culture. In primitive cultures, experience is dominated by what a contemporary French school has called categories of participation and incorporation. Life and being belong in a significant sense to the tribe and family; particular creatures are only members of a consolidated whole. This state of social affairs formed the pattern in accord with which all natural events were construed. One need not endorse all the details of the theories of this French school or even accept its general principles, in order to recognize a predominantly collectivistic character in early culture, and to perceive its influence upon early beliefs and modes of thought. An individual was a member of a group-whole; in this membership were almost exhausted his accomplishments and possibilities. From birth, he was a subject for assimilation and incorporation of group traditions and customs; his personal measure was the extent in which he became their vehicle. Private belief and invention, were a deviation, a dangerous eccentricity, signs of disloyal disposition. The private was an equivalent of the illicit; and all innovations and departures from custom are illicit:—witness the fact that children have to be educated and inducted into tradition and custom. This need of education, moreover, and of maintenance of tradition against deviation serve to bring otherwise unconscious customs to mind, and to render consciousness of them acute and emotional.[1] Thereby, customs are more than mere overt ways of action; tradition is more than external imitation and reproduction of what obtains in outward behavior. Custom is Nomos, lord and king of all, of emotions, beliefs, opinions, thoughts as well as deeds.

Yet mind in an individualized mode has occasionally some constructive operation. Every invention, every improvement in art, technological, military and political, has its genesis in the observation and ingenuity of a particular innovator. All utensils, traps, tools, weapons, stories, prove that some one exercised at sometime initiative in deviating from customary models and standards. Accident played its part; but *some one* had to observe and utilize the accidental change before a new tool and custom emerged. Men were not wholly and merely subdued to the demands of custom, even when innovations were looked upon as threats to the welfare of the group, defiances of its gods.

As Goldenweiser has said: "Whether it is a pot, basket or blanket that is being manufactured, or the soil

---

[1] See Boas, The Mind of Primitive Man. Chapter VIII of this book seems to me to supply what is sound in the view of the French school alluded to, free from its exaggerations.

that is being tilled, or an animal that is being hunted or fought—in all of these situations man faces an individual, technical task.   In all of these directions there is room for the development and exhibition of skill.   In industry and the chase, in a sea-faring expedition and a war raid, things can be done well and less well. . . . . There is opportunity for comparison of individual efforts, there is rivalry."[2]   As a fruit of this rivalry of individuals, pace-making occurs; those who excel set a standard for others to come up to; they furnish models of technique to be adopted by others, till gradually or suddenly they initiate a new custom.   Even in cultures most committed to reproduction, there is always occurring some creative production, through specific variations, that is, through individuals.   Thus, while negatively individuality means something to be subdued, positively it denotes the source of change in institutions and customs.   While the negative side is most conscious and most asserted, the positive phase is there and is taken advantage of, even though by stealth and under cover.   Upon the whole the imagination and effort of individual technicians and artists were submerged; in idea, the doctrine of fixed wholes with their fixed patterns prevailed.   We may well follow the further statements of Dr. Goldenweiser. "When tradition is a matter of the spoken word, the advantage is all on the side of age.   The elder is in the saddle;" because he is the most experienced man and the one who best embodies the net experience of the group. The group is small enough to be homogeneous; innovations are conspicuous and focus resentment; customary activities are moreover enmeshed in ceremonialism and have supernatural sanctions; variations when once they

[2] Early Civilization, pp. 407-8.

are adopted become automatic group habits; they endure not as ideas or because of insight into principles, but as "motor habits which represent nothing but knowledge and technical experience rendered mechanical through habituation;" individual "consciousness and ratiocination quickly are incorporated in objective results which are handed down while the thinking perishes; inventions become part of the technical equipment of behavior, not of thought and understanding." Under such circumstances, individual variations of thought remain private reveries or are soon translated into objective established institutions through gradual accumulation of imperceptible variations. The exceptional character of creative individuality is reflected in attribution of the origin of the arts, industrial and political, to gods and semi-divine heroes.

Thus the artist and artisan merely observe, as has been noted in another connection, ready-made models and patterns, and unquestioningly follow procedures antecedently established. Patterns and methods are accepted as belonging to the objective nature of things; there is next to no sense of any connection between them and personal desire and thought; to introduce such a connection would evince a dangerously subversive spirit. The point of view therein displayed is so far from that which animates modern psychology and philosophy that it is not easily recoverable; yet we do not have even today to go far to find a like notion regulative of action and belief. The mechanic who follows blueprints and a procedure dictated by his machine in the production of standardized commodities would, if he were both articulate and uncognizant of inventions by others, say the same thing.   Legal formalities consciously adopt similar realistic conceptions in politics and morals, and find the exhibition of the spirit which they take for granted in science and industry to be anarchistic and destructive in less technical fields.   Standards and patterns seem to them to be given in the nature of things; the intervention of initiative and invention, of individuality, are counted contrary to reason as well as to sincerity and loyalty.

When experience is of this sort, an individual worker or demiurge has only to observe and conform.   He is but a case to be subsumed in a fixed whole as far as may be; what is left over is merely quantitative and accidental. Plato found in the arts exemplifications of fixed archetypes governing particular processes of change through imparting to them measure and proportion; hence changes as far as knowable were subject in advance to the dialectic of geometry.   As in the Philebus, measure comes first; then comes the measured, the symmetrical and beautiful; conscious mind and wisdom are in the third rank as observation of measure and the measured antecedently established.   In similar fashion, Aristotle could draw his account of the four fundamental affairs of nature from analysis of the procedure of artisan, with no suspicion that he was thereby subjecting his metaphysics to an anthropomorphic rendering of nature; setting up the cumulative deposit of individual variations of insight and skill as the measure of nature.   It is inept to charge these thinkers with hypostatizing psychical states and processes.   Since their own experience exhibited subordination of individualized mind to objects, operations, patterns and ends that were preëstablished and presented ready-made and complete, their metaphysic and logic were in so far a faithful report of what they found. Greek philosophy converted not psychological conditions but positive institutional affairs into cosmic realities. The idea that generalization, purposes, etc., are individual mental processes did not originate until experience had registered such a change that the functions of individualized mind were productive of objective achievements and hence capable of external observation.

When this happened, an extraordinary revolution occurred. The conception of the individual changed completely. No longer was the individual something complete, perfect, finished, an organized whole of parts united by the impress of a comprehensive form. What was prized as individuality was now something moving, changing, discrete, and above all initiating instead of final. As long as deviation of particulars from established order meant disorder, the metaphysics and logic of subordination of parts to the form of a pre-formed whole was reasonable. Mind as individualized could be recognized in other than a pejorative sense only when its variations were social, utilized in generating greater social security and fullness of life. This was possible only when social relationships were heterogeneous and expansive, when demand for initiative, invention and variation exceeded that for adherence and conformity. It is noteworthy that even Plato with all his zeal for a fixed organized whole could not imagine its coming into being save through the effort of some happily constituted and fortunately placed individual. Social heterogeneity alone does not promote a functioning of variations for socially desirable consequences, and thereby constitute individuality as something objective and socially acknowledged. It may signify only a break up of pious adherence to a cumulative and conserved outcome of prior history. But let there be a situation in which the tradition of order and unity is still vital while the actual state of affairs is one of variation and conflict, and there is a situation in which dependence must perforce be placed on individuality. Even though its office be conceived at first as merely restorative, a return to an earlier and better state of affairs, as Italians thinkers would return to Greco-Roman culture and the early protestant to primitive Christianity, yet the operation of individuals rather than that of collective tradition is the hope and reliance. Under such circumstances, particularized centres of initiation and energy are prized because being emancipated from the net work of current forces, they are free to direct change to new objective consequences.

Individualism in modern life has been understood in diverse ways. To those retaining the classic tradition, it is a revolt of undisciplined barbarians, reverting to the spontaneous petulant egotism of childhood; in another version of this underlying idea, it is rebellion of unregenerate human nature against divine authority, established among men for their salvation. To still others, it is emancipation, the achieving of voluntary maturity; courageous independence in throwing off all external yokes and bondages, in asserting that every human being is an end in himself; in effect a transfer to each conscious unit of honorific predicates previously reserved for the class, species, universal. In any case, an individual is no longer just a particular, a part without meaning save in an inclusive whole, but is a subject, self, a distinctive centre of desire, thinking and aspiration.

An adherent of empirical denotative method can hardly accept either the view which regards subjective mind as an aberration or that which makes it an independent creative source. Empirically, it is an agency of novel reconstruction of a preëxisting order. Criticism of the history of political theory during the formation of modern European states may bring out the difference between such a view and that of both classic universalism and extreme modern subjectivism. The older theory had asserted that the state exists by nature. The modern declared that it existed by means of agreements between individuals who willed the institution of civil order. We may imagine reformers of the seventeenth century saying that the states they found about them did indeed exist by nature—that was precisely what was the matter with them. Because they were natural products, they were products of force, chance, fraud, tyranny. Hence they were naturally the scene of war, foreign and domestic, of servitudes and inequities, of intrigue and harsh coercion —one huge historical accident. A just and good state would be one brought into existence by voluntary convention; by promises exchanged and obligations mutually undertaken. A good state exists not by nature but by the contriving activities of individual selves in behalf of the satisfaction of their needs. It implies art, not nature; a clear perception by individuals of what they want and of the conditions through which their wants can be satisfied. In detail, thinkers divided into opposite schools. Some held that by nature individuals are non-social, becoming social when subjected to discipline by artificial and instituted law to which they are naturally adverse. Others attributed to the natural individual some degree of friendly and genial inclination. Both schools agreed that just political order, legitimate authority and subordination, is a product of voluntary conjunction of individuals naturally exempt from the universal of civil law.

The truth of which the social compact was a symbol is that social institutions as they exist can be bettered only through the deliberate interventions of those who free their minds from the standards of the order which obtains. The underlying fact was the perception of the possibility of a change, a change for the better, in social organization. The fact that the intent of the perception was veiled and distorted by the myth of an aboriginal single and one-for-all decisive meeting of wills is instructive as an aberration, but the myth should not disguise the intent and consequence. Social conditions were altered so that there were both need and opportunity for inventive and planning activities, initiated by innovating thought, and carried to conclusion only as the initiating mind secured the sympathetic assent of other individuals.

I say individual minds, not just individuals with minds. The difference between the two ideas is radical. There is an easy way by which thinkers avoid the necessity of facing a genuine problem. It starts with a self, whether bodily or spiritual being immaterial for present purposes, and then endows or identifies that self with mind, a formal capacity of apprehension, devising and belief. On the basis of this assumption, any mind is open to entertain any thought or belief whatever. There is here no problem involved of breaking loose from the weight of tradition and custom, of initiating observations and reflections, forming designs and plans, undertaking experiments on the basis of hypotheses, diverging from accepted doctrines and traditions. Or when it is observed that this departure occurs infrequently and is not easy, some vague reference to genius and originality disposes of the question. But the whole history of science, art and morals proves that the mind that appears *in* individuals is not as such individual mind. The former is in itself a system of belief, recognitions, and ignorances, of acceptances and rejections, of expectancies and appraisals of meanings which have been instituted under the influence of custom and tradition.

It is not easy to break away from current and established classifications and interpretations of the world. The difficulty in this respect, however, is eased by the notion that after all it is only error that the mind needs to cut loose from, and that it can do this by direct appeal to nature, by applying pure observation and reflection to pure objects. This notion of course is fiction; objects of knowledge are not given to us defined, classified, and labeled, ready for labels and pigeon-holes. We bring to the simplest observation a complex apparatus of habits, of accepted meanings and techniques. Otherwise observation is the blankest of stares, and the natural object is a tale told by an idiot, full only of sound and fury. In the case of social objects and patterns, institutions and arrangements, we have not the benefit of the mitigating fiction of direct correction by appeal of transparent mind to the court of nature. There *is* a contrast between physical objects and objects as they are believed to be, even though what they are believed to be is an unescapable medium in observing what they are. Where is such a contrast to be found in the case of existing social institutions and standards? The contrast is not, as it seems to be in the case of knowledge of physical existence, between a belief which is defective or false and an existence which is real; it is between an existence which is actual, and a belief, desire and aspiration for something which is better but non-existent.

Such facts exemplify the difference between a bodily or a psychic self *with* a mind and mind *as* individual. Either the better social object is sheer illusion, or else individual thought and desire denote a distinctive and unique mode of existence, an object held in solution, undergoing transformation, to emerge finally as an established and public object. Reference to imagination is pertinent. But the reference is too frequently used to disguise and avoid recognition of the essential fact and the problems involved in it. Imagination as mere reverie is one thing, a natural and additive event, complete in itself, a terminal object rich and consoling, or trivial and silly, as may be. Imagination which terminates in a modification of the objective order, in the institution of a new object is other than a merely added occurrence. It involves a dissolution of old objects and a forming of new ones in a medium which, since it is beyond the old object and not yet in a new one, can properly be termed subjective.

The point in placing emphasis upon the rôle of individual desire and thought in social life has in part been indicated. It shows the genuinely intermediate position of subjective mind: it proves it to be a mode of natural existence in which objects undergo directed reconstitution. Reference to the place of individual thought in political theory and practice has another value. Unless subjective intents and thoughts are to terminate in picturesque utopias or dogmas irrelevant to constructive action, they are subject to objective requirements and tests. Even in the crudest form of the contract theory, men had to *do* something. They had at least to meet together, come to agreement, give guarantees, and govern their subsequent conduct by agreements reached, or else suffer a tangible penalty. Thinking and desiring, no matter how subjective, are a preliminary, tentative and inchoate mode of action. They are "overt" behavior of a communicated and public form in process of construction, and behavior involves change of objects which tests the meanings animating behavior.

There is a peculiar intrinsic privacy and incommunicability attending the preparatory intermediate stage. When an old essence or meaning is in process of dissolution and a new one has not taken shape even as a hypothetical scheme, the intervening existence is too fluid and formless for publication, even to one's self. Its very existence is ceaseless transformation. Limits from which and to which are objective, generic, stateable; not so that which occurs between these limits. This process of flux and ineffability is intrinsic to any thought which is subjective and private. It marks "consciousness" as bare event. It is absurd to call a recognition or a conception subjective or mental because it takes place through a physically or socially numerically distinct existence; by this logic a house disappears from the spatial and material world when it becomes *my* house; even a physical movement would then be subjective when referred to particles.

Recognition of an object, conception of a meaning may be mine rather than yours; yours rather than his, at a particular moment; but this fact is about me or you, not about the object and essence perceived and conceived. Acknowledgment of this fact is compatible however with the conviction that after all there would be no *objects* to be perceived, no meanings to be conceived, if at some period of time uniquely individualized events had not intervened. There is a difference in kind between the thought which manipulates received objects and essences to derive new ones from their relations and implications, and the thought which generates a new method of observing and classifying them. It is like the difference between readjusting the parts of a wagon to make it more efficient, and the invention of the steam locomotive. One is formal and additive; the other is qualitative and transformative. He knows little who supposes that freedom of thought is ensured by relaxation of conventions, censorships and intolerant dogmas. The relaxation supplies opportunity. But while it is a necessary it is not a sufficient condition. *Freedom* of thought denotes freedom of *thinking;* specific doubting, inquiring, suspense, creating and cultivating of tentative hypotheses, trials or experimentings that are unguaranteed and that involve risks of waste, loss, and error. Let us admit the case of the conservative; if we once start thinking no one can guarantee where we shall come out, except that many objects, ends and institutions are surely doomed. Every thinker puts some portion of an apparently stable world in peril and no one can wholly predict what will emerge in its place.

In approaching the exaggerations of individual mind found in modern philosophy which go by the name of subjectivism and a large part of what is termed idealism, we may profitably recur to ancient thought. The question of the relation of the objective and subjective did not present itself under that name. The problem of the relation of the "natural" and the "positive" covered at least part of the same ground, and in a way closer to experience than does the course taken by much modern philosophy. The "positive" was a term used to cover everything of distinctively human institution, in languages, customs, manners, codes, laws, governments. The issue was whether nature was a norm for these arrangements or whether they were something to which nature should submit. The classic answer was in the former sense. But there were those who regarded nature as raw, crude, wild, and who thought of man and his doings as the standard and measure of nature.

The former conception, under theological sanctions and interpretations, was adopted into the medieval conception of natural law, and made absolutely controlling in morals and politics, wherever not supplemented by revelation, which after all was revelation of a higher nature. To put the problem in terms of the connection between nature and institutions has an advantage over the isolation of the ego by modern philosophy. It acknowledged the social factor. Even when the origin of the positive was sought in the will, in the decrees and enactments of particular persons, the latter were thought of as possessing a socially representative office, as heroes, lawgivers, not as isolated individual minds.

The complete subordination of the positive to natural law in the medieval version of the classic theory involved modern thought in a peculiar embarrassment when interest in humanity as distinct from divinity revived. The institutions which men wished to modify, for which they wished to substitute others or to which they wished to add others of a secular sort, were bound up with divinity, with authoritative natural and revealed law. It was not possible to put institutions as such in contrast to nature, for by accepted theory existing institutions were in the main expressions of the law of nature. The resource which offered itself was to place the mind of the individual as such in contrast to both nature and institutions. This historic fact, reinforced with the conspicuous assertion of medievalism that the individual soul is the ultimate end and ultimate subject of salvation or damnation, affords, it seems to me, the background and source of the isolation of the ego, the thinking self, in all philosophy influenced by either the new science or Protestantism. Descartes as well as Berkeley uses "self" as an equivalent of "mind," and does so spontaneously, as a matter of course, without attempt at argument and justification. If the given science of nature and given positive institutions expressed arbitrary prejudice, unintelligent custom and chance episodes, where could or should mind be found except in the independent and self-initiated activities of individuals? Wholesale revolt against tradition led to the illusion of equally wholesale isolation of mind as something wholly individual. Revolting and reforming thinkers like Descartes little noted how much of tradition they repeated and perpetuated in their very protests and reforms.

An adequate recognition of the empirical historical causes of the exaggeration of the ego in modern philosophy, due to its isolation from social customs, and these from the physical world, makes, it seems to me, criticism of the forms which it has assumed almost unnecessary. Thinkers may start out with a naïve assumption of minds connected with separate individuals. But developments soon show the inadequacy of such "minds" to carry the burden of science and objective institutions, like the family and state. The consequence was revealed to be sceptical, disintegrative, malicious. A transcendental supra-empirical self, making human, or "finite," selves its medium of manifestation, was the logical recourse. Such a conception is an inevitable conclusion, when the value of liberation and utilization of individual capacity in science, art, industry, and politics is a demonstrated em- pirical fact; and when at the same time, individuality instead of being conceived as historic, intermediate, temporally relative and instrumental, is conceived of as original, eternal and absolute. When concrete recon- structions of natural and social objects are thought of as a single and constitutive act, they inevitably become super- natural or transcendental. When the movement ter- minates, as in the later philosophy of Josiah Royce, with a "community of selves," the circle has returned to the empi- rical fact with which it might properly have started out; but the intervening insertion of a transcendent ego re- mains as a plague. It isolates the community of selves from natural existence and in order to get nature again in connection with mind, is compelled to reduce it to a system of volitions, feelings and thoughts.

It remains to mention another historic factor which helps account for the vogue of subjectivism in art and literature, through which it found its way more or less into common belief. Comte several times recurs to the idea that idiocy represents an excess of objectivism, a subordination of feelings and impressions to objects as given, while madness marks an excess of subjectivism. Still more significant is his added remark, that madness has to be construed historically and sociologically. Under primitive conditions all the larger ideas about nature are reveries constructed in the interest of emotions. Myths were fancies, but they were not insanities because they were the only reply to the challenge of nature which existing instrumentalities permitted. Assertion of similar ideas today is insanity, because available intellectual resources and agencies make possible and require radically different adjustments. To entertain and believe fancies which once were spontaneous and general is today a sign of failure, of mental disequilibration. Inability to employ the methods of forming and checking beliefs which are available at a given time, whatever be the source of that inability, constitutes a disorientation. These considerations are not introduced to make the offensive insinuation that philosophic subjectivism is a mode of insanity. and philosophic realism a mode of idiocy. The purpose is to suggest that while the tendency to revery, to intellectual somnambulism, is universal, the use made of revery—which may roughly stand for the subjective element in mind—depends upon contemporary conditions. In one situation fancy generates stories which are consistent with desire and are attractive. These are connected with ceremonies to which, in addition to their immediate good, external efficiency is imputed. They become nuclei about which observations and ideas continually gather; they are centres of mental as well as emotional systematizations. It is no wonder that myths long prevail. When the development of industry and tested inquiry makes it evident

that the actual world will not accept them nor stand for
them, their actuating springs remain in full force and the
river of revery still flows.   It may find public or communicated form in fiction recognized as such, in novel, drama
and poetry which are enjoyed, although their objects are
not believed in.   Or they may remain private, and, with
the play of desires and affections that produce them, constitute a new world enjoyed for its own sake—the "inner
life."

The popular factor in subjectivism, that which renders
philosophic subjectivism intelligible enough to prevent
its being regarded as mere vagary, seems to be a confused
union of two considerations.   On the one hand there is the
recognition, enforced by the course of events, of the constructive power of mind as individual, its re-creative
function in objects of industry, art, and politics.   On the
other hand there is the discovery and exploitation of the
inner life, a new, readily accessible and cheaply enjoyed
esthetic field.   The tales that will not be believed when
they are told and that cannot be told in forms sufficiently
artistic to command the attention of others, may still be
told to one's self and afford relief, consolation and thrill.
Products of fancy that cannot, because of the advance of
knowledge, secure credence as reports of objective events,
are castles in the air, but these castles are impregnable
inner refuges.

The person who knows nothing of sensations or sensa,
as the psychologist and epistemologist talk about them, is
nevertheless aware that objects are other than bare
things to which beliefs must subject themselves.   He is
aware that when things escape his power of control, they
still generate "impressions" which he can entertain in all

sorts of enjoyable and annoying ways.   If he is devoid of ability to regulate conduct in actual employment of objects, this world of impressions will be one in which he loves to dwell.   Its materials are pliable and exact no responsibility.   He may be utterly innocent of the reduction of objects by theorists into conjoined sensations and images; the notion that his table consists largely of images would be to him a wild vagary, contradictory of common-sense.   But he knows very well that the incidents of life may produce fancies in him that are more exciting or more soothing than the incidents themselves.   When there is neither the power to renounce revery nor to use it in any objective embodiment, we have a condition in which soil and atmosphere are prepared to find the spirit of subjective idealism congenial, even if the technical facts adduced and the dialectic employed in its behalf are beyond reach.

Our statements, however, are one-sided, as far as the full scope of the "inner life" is concerned.   It is the home of aspirations and ideals that are noble and that may in time receive fulfillment as well as of figments and airy nothings.   It may be charged with infinite humor and tragedy.   It affords a realm in which king and court fool, prince and pauper, meet as equals.   It is subject-matter for the philosopher as well as for the rebuffed and wistful. Recall the contrast which Royce had drawn between the dominant externalism of the seventeenth century and the spirit of the eighteenth.   "It is no matter whether you are a philosopher and write essays on 'The Principles of Human Knowledge' or whether you are a heroine in an eighteenth century novel, and write sentimental letters to a friend; you are part of the same movement.   The spirit is dissatisfied with the mathematical order, and

feels unfriendliness among the eternities of sevententh-
century thought.   The spirit wants to be at home with
itself, well-friended in the comprehension of its inner
processes.   It loves to be confidential in its heart out-
pourings, keen in its analysis, humane in its attitude
toward life."

We are given to referring the beginnings of subjectivism to Descartes, with his *penseé* as the indubitable
certainty, or to Locke with his simple idea as immediate
object.   Technically or with respect to later dialectical
developments, this reference is correct enough.   But
historically it is wrong.   Descartes' thought is the *nous*
of classic tradition forced inwards because physical
science had extruded it from its object.   Its internality
is a logical necessity of the attempt to reconcile the new
science with the old tradition, not a thing intrinsically
important.   Similarly Locke's simple idea is the classic
Idea, Form or Species dislodged from nature and compelled to take refuge in mind.   For Locke, it is coerced by
external existence and remains coercive for all subsequent
intellectual operations.   The subjective as such is alien
to Locke's way of thinking; his whole bias is against it,
and in favor of what is grounded in nature being a
matter of relations already established.   The "simple idea"
is merely man's available point of contact with the objective order; and in this contact resides its whole import.

From the standpoint of "inner life" the simple idea
became however, a sensation, that is, a feeling, a state
of mind, an intrinsically interesting event having its own
significant career.   If this were true of such a rudimentary thing as blue or soft, how much more significantly it
holds of imagination and emotion.   Inner reveries and

enjoyments constitute freedom to the natural man. Everywhere else is constraint, whether it be of study, of science, family life, industry, or government. The road to freedom by escape into the inner life is no modern discovery; it was taken by savages, by the oppressed, by children, long before it was formulated in philosophical romanticism. The generalized awareness of the fact is new however, and it added a new dimension to characteristically modern experience. It created new forms of art and new theories of esthetics, often promulgated by literary artists who have nothing but contempt for philosophical theories as such. Mr. Santayana is a thinker whose intent and basis are at one with classic thought. But if we note the importance assumed in his thinking by the "inward landscape," there is before us a measure of the pervasive influence of the kind of experience that was seized upon by Romanticism as the exclusive truth of experience.

The function of individualized mind in furthering experiment and invention and the directed reconstruction of events, together with the discovery that objects of sentiment and fancy, although rejected by the order of events in space and time, may form the contents of an inner and private realm, finds its legitimate outcome in the conception of experiencing, and in the discrimination of experiencing into a diversity of states and processes. To the Greeks, experience was the outcome of accumulation of practical acts, sufferings and perception gradually built up into the skill of the carpenter, shoemaker, pilot, farmer, general, and politician. There was nothing merely personal or subjective about it; it was a consolidation, effected by nature, of particular natural occurrences into actualization of the forms of such things as are thus and so usually, now and then, upon the whole, but not necessarily and always. Experience was adequate and final for this kind of thing because it was as much their culminating actualization as rational thought was the actualization of the forms of things that are what they are necessarily. To Aristotle, the copula was a true verb, always affected by tense. Things which fully and completely are, have been, will be, and now are exactly the same; their matter is completely mastered by form. Concerning them we can say "is" with demonstrative certainty: such things are few, though supremely good, and are the objects of science. Of other things we can only say that they have been and are not at the present time, or that though not existing at the present moment they may exist at some unspecified future time. Of them we can say "is" only with a perhaps or a probably, since they are subject to chance. In them matter is not wholly subdued to form. Experience is the actualization through an organic body of just these affairs. Experience was not some person's; it was nature's, localized in a body as that body happened to exist by nature.

As was remarked in the introductory chapter one can hardly use the term "experience" in philosophical discourse, but a critic rises to inquire "Whose experience?" The question is asked in adverse criticism. Its implication is that experience by its very nature is owned by some one; and that the ownership is such in kind that everything about experience is affected by a private and exclusive quality. The implication is as absurd as it would be to infer from the fact that houses are usually owned, are mine and yours and his, that possessive reference so permeates the properties of being a house that nothing intelligible can be said about the latter. It is obvious, however, that a house can be owned only when it has existence and properties independent of being owned. The quality of belonging to some one is not an all-absorbing maw in which independent properties and relations disappear to be digested into egohood. It is additive; it marks the assumption of a new relationship, in consequence of which the house, the common, ordinary, house, acquires new properties. It is subject to taxes; the owner has the right to exclude others from entering it; he enjoys certain privileges and immunities with respect to it and is also exposed to certain burdens and liabilities.

Substitute "experience" for "house," and no other word need be changed. Experience when it happens has the same dependence upon objective natural events, physical and social, as has the occurrence of a house. It has its own objective and definitive traits; these can be described without reference to a self, precisely as a house is of brick, has eight rooms, etc., irrespective of whom it belongs to. Nevertheless, just as for some purposes and with respect to some consequences, it is all important to note the added qualification of personal ownership of real property, so with "experience." In first instance and intent, it is not exact nor relevant to say "I experience" or "I think." "It" experiences or is experienced, "it" thinks or is thought, is a juster phrase. Experience, a serial course of affairs with their own characteristic properties and relationships, occurs, happens, and is what it is. Among and within these occurrences, not outside of them nor underlying them, are those events which are denominated selves. In some specifiable respects and for some specifi-

able consequences, these selves, capable of objective de-
notation just as are sticks, stones, and stars, assume the
care and administration of certain objects and acts in
experience.   Just as in the case of the house, this assumption of ownership brings with it further liabilities and
assets, burdens and enjoyments.

To say in a significant way, "*I* think, believe, desire,
instead of barely *it* is thought, believed, desired," is
to accept and affirm a responsibility and to put forth a
claim.   It does not mean that the self is the source or
author of the thought and affection nor its exclusive seat.
It signifies that the self as a centred organization of energies identifies itself (in the sense of accepting their consequences) with a belief or sentiment of independent and
external origination.   The absurdity of any other conception appears upon examination of such affairs as are
designated by "I do not believe" or "I do not like;" in
them it is obvious that a relationship of incompatibility
between two distinct and denoted objects is contained.

Authorship and liability look in two different ways, one
to the past, the other to the future.   Natural events—
including social habits—originate thoughts and feelings.
To say "*I* think, hope and love" is to say in effect that
genesis is not the last word; instead of throwing the blame
or the credit for the belief, affection and expectation
upon nature, one's family, church, or state, one declares
one's self to be henceforth a partner.   An adoptive act
is proclaimed in virtue of which one claims the benefit of
future goods and admits liability for future ills flowing from the affair in question.   Even in the most "indi-
vidualistic" society some properties remain communal;
and many things, like the bowels of the earth and the

depths of the seas, are unowned by either group or person. The cogent line of defense of the institution of private property is that it promotes prudence, accountability, ingenuity and security, in the production and administration of commodities and resources which exist independently of the relationship of property. In like fashion, not all thoughts and emotions are owned either socially or personally; and either mode of appropriation has to be justified on the basis of distinctive consequences.

Analytic reflection shows that the ordinary conception of causation as a trait belonging to some one thing is the idea of responsibility read backward. The idea that some one thing, or any two or three things, are *the* cause of an occurrence is in effect an application of the idea of credit or blame—as in the Greek αιτία. There is nothing in nature that *belongs* absolutely and exclusively to anything else; belonging is always a matter of reference and distributive assignment, justified in any particular case as far as it works out well. Greek metaphysics and logic are dominated by the idea of inherent belonging and exclusion; another instance of naively reading the story of nature in language appropriate to human association. Modern science has liberated physical events from the domination of the notions of intrinsic belonging and exclusion, but it has retained the idea with exacerbated vigor in the case of psychological events. The elimination of the category from physics and its retention in psychology has provided a seeming scientific basis for the division between psychology and physics, and thereby for the egotism of modern philosophy. Much subjectivism is only a statement of the logical consequences of the doctrine sponsored by psychological "science" of the monopolistic possession of mental phenomena by a self; or, after the idea of an underlying spiritual substance became shaky, of the doctrine that mental events as such constitute all there is to selfhood. For the philosophical implications of the latter idea, as far as privacy, monopoly and exclusiveness of causation and belonging are concerned, are similar to those of the older dogma when it was applied to cosmic nature.

Enough, however, of negation. The positive consequence is an understanding of the shift of emphasis from the experienced, the objective subject-matter, the *what*, to the experiencing, the method of its course, the *how* of its changes. Such a shift occurs whenever the problem of control of production of consequences arises. As long as men are content to enjoy and suffer fire when it happens, fire is just an objective entity which is what it is. That it may be taken as a deity to be adored or propitiated, is evidence that its "whatness" is all there is to it. But when men come to the point of *making* fire, fire is not an essence, but a mode of natural phenomena, an order in change, a "how" of a historic sequence. The change from immediate use in enjoyment and suffering is equivalent to recognition of a method of procedure, and of the alliance of insight into method with possibility of control.

The development of the conception of experiencing as a distinctive operation is akin to the growth of the idea of fire-making out of direct experiences with fire. Fire is fire, inherently just what it is; but making fire is relational. It takes thought away from fire to the other things that help and prevent its occurrence. So with experience in the sense of things that are experienced; they are *what* they are. But their occurrence as experi-

enced things is ascertained to be dependent upon attitudes and dispositions; the manner of their happening is
found to be affected by the habits of an organic individual.
Since myth and science concern the same objects in the
same natural world, sun, moon, and stars, the difference
between them cannot be determined exclusively on the
basis of these natural objects. A differential has to found
in distinctive *ways* of experiencing natural objects; it is
perceived that man is an emotional and imaginative as
well as an observing and reasoning creature, and that
different manners of experiencing affect the status of
subject-matter experienced. Capacity to distinguish between the sun and moon of science and these same things
as they figure in myth and cult depends upon capacity to
distinguish different attitudes and dispositions of the
subject; the heroes of legend and poetry are discriminated from historic characters when memory, imagination and idealizing emotion are taken into the reckoning.
Again, it is discovered that the good of some objects is
connected with one way of experiencing, namely appetite,
while the acquisition of goodness by other objects is
dependent upon the operation of reflection. In consequence, the experienced objects are differentiated as to
their goodness, although good as an essence is unchanged.

The importance of modes of experiencing for control
of experienced objects may be illustrated from economic
theory. A study of various economic essences or concepts is possible:—definition, classification and dialectical
reference to one another of such meanings as value,
utility, rent, exchange, profit, wages, etc. There is also
possible a positivistic study of existential economic
régimes, resulting in description of their structures and

operations. If the presence and operation of dispositions and attitudes be neglected, these alternatives exhaust the field of inquiry. Neither the study of objective essences nor of objective existences is available, however, in problems of polity, in management of economic events. When the "psychological" factor is introduced, say, a study of the effects of certain ways of experiencing, such as incentives, desires, fatigue, monotony, habit, waste-motions, insecurity, prestige, team work, fashion, *esprit de corps*, and a multitude of like factors, the situation changes. Factors that are within control are specified, and a fuller degree of deliberate administration of events is made possible. The objectivity of events remains what it was, but the discovery of the rôle of personal dispositions in conditioning their occurrence, enables us to interpret and connect them in new ways, ways, which are susceptible of greater regulation than were the other ways. Banks, stores, factories do not become psychical when we ascertain the part played in their genesis and operation by psychological factors; they remain as external to the organism and to a particular mind as ever they were, things experienced as are winds and stars. But we get a new leverage, intellectual and practical, upon them when we can convert description of ready-made events and dialectical relation of ready-made notions into an account of a way of occurrence. For a perceived mode of becoming is always ready to be translated into a *method* of production and direction.

Since modern natural science has been concerned with discovery of conditions of production, to be employed as means for consequences, the development of interest in attitudes of individual subjects—the psychological interest—is but an extension of its regular business. Knowledge of conditions of the occurrence of experienced objects is not complete until we have included organic conditions as well as extra-organic conditions. Knowledge of the latter may account for a happening in the abstract but not for the concrete or experienced happening. A general knowledge of dispositions and attitudes renders us exactly the same sort of intellectual and practical service as possession of physical constants. The trouble lies in the inadequacy of our present psychological knowledge. And it is probably this deficiency, which renders such psychological knowledge as we possess unavailable for technological control, which, joined to spontaneous interest in "inner" life, has set off psychological subject-matter as a separate world of existence, instead of a discovery of attitudes and dispositions involved in the world of common experience. In truth, attitudes, dispositions and their kin, while capable of being distinguished and made concrete intellectual objects, are never separate existences. They are always *of*, *from*, *toward*, situations and things. They may be studied with a minimum of attention to the things at and away from which they are directed. The things with which they are concerned may for purposes of inquiry be represented by a blank, a symbol to be specifically filled in as occasion demands. But except as ways of seeking, turning from, appropriating, treating things, they have no existence nor significance.

Every type of culture has experienced resistance and frustration. These events are interpreted according to the bias dominating a particular type of culture. To the modern European mind they have been interpreted as results of the opposed existence of subject and object as independent forms of Being. The notion is now so established in tradition that to many thinkers it appears to be a datum, not an interpretative classification. But the East Indian has envisaged the same phenomena as evidence of the contrast of an illusory world to which corresponds domination by desires and a real world due to emancipation from desires, attained through ascetic discipline and meditation. The Greeks interpreted the same experience on the basis of the cosmic discrepancy of being and becoming, form and matter, as the reluctance of existence to become a complete and transparent medium of meaning. Taken absolutely, the interpretation on the basis of opposition of subject and object has no advantage over the other doctrines; it is a local and provincial interpretation. Taken inherently or absolutely, it has an absurdity from which they are free; for subject and object antithetically defined can have logically no transactions with each other. Taken as a factor in the enterprise of overcoming resistance and reducing the prospects of frustration, statement in terms of distinction of subject and object is intelligible, and is more valuable than the other modes of statement. Object is, as Basil Gildersleeve said, that which objects, that to which frustration is due. But it is also the object*ive;* the final and eventual consummation, an integrated secure independent state of affairs. The subject is that which suffers, is subjected and which endures resistance and frustration; it is also that which attempts subjection of hostile conditions; that which takes the immediate initiative in remaking the situation as it stands. Subjective and objective distinguished as factors in a regulated effort at modification of the environing world have an intelligible meaning. Subjectivism as an "ism" converts this historic, relative and instrumental status and function into something absolute and fixed; while pure "objectivism" is a doctrine of fatalism.

To-day there is marked revival of objectivism, even of externalism. The world of physical science is no longer new and strange; to many it is now familiar; while many of those to whom it is personally unfamiliar take it for granted on authority. To a considerable extent its subject-matter is taking the place of the subject-matter of older creeds as something given ready-made, demanding unhesitating credence and passive acceptance. The doctrine of the opposition of subject and object in knowledge is fading, becoming reminiscent; that sense of strain which is lacking accompanied transition from one set of beliefs to another very different set. Only in politics and economics is the opposition of subject and institutional object poignant. And even in these fields radical and conservative increasingly appeal to objects which are collective, non-individual. The conservative recurs to the objectivism of established institutions, idealized into intrinsic stability; the radical looks forward to the completed outcome of an objective and necessary economic evolution. In spite of the appeal to the catchwords of individualism, private initiative, voluntary abstinence, personal industry and effort, there is more danger at present that the genuinely creative effort of the individual will be lost than there is of any return to earlier individualism. Everything makes for the mass. When private property is talked about, the product of individual labor is no longer meant; but a legally buttressed institution. Capital is no longer the outcome of deliberate personal sacrifice, but is an institution of corporations and finance with massive political and social ramifications. Appeals to secure action of a certain sort may use the old words; but the fears and hopes which are now aroused are not really connected with freedom of individual thought and effort, but with the objective foundations of society, established "law and order."

This resort to an objectivism which ignores initiating and re-organizing desire and imagination will in the end only strengthen that other phase of subjectivism which consists in escape to the enjoyment of inward landscape. Men who are balked of a legitimate realization of their subjectivity, men who are forced to confine innovating need and projection of ideas to technical modes of industrial and political life, and to specialized or "scientific" fields of intellectual activity, will compensate by finding release within their inner consciousness. There will be one philosophy, a realistic one, for mathematics, physical science and the established social order; another, and opposed, philosophy for the affairs of personal life. The objection to dualism is not just that it is a dualism, but that it forces upon us antithetical, non-convertible principles of formulation and interpretation. If there is complete split in nature and experience then of course no ingenuity can explain it away; it must be accepted. But in case no such sharp division actually exists, the evils of supposing there is one are not confined to philosophical theory. Consequences within philosophy as such are of no great import. But philosophical dualism is but a formulated recognition of an impasse in life; an impotence in interaction, inability to make effective transition, limitation of power to regulate and thereby to understand. Capricious pragmatism based on exaltation of personal desire; consolatory estheticism based on capacity for wringing contemplative enjoyment from even the tragedies of the outward spectacle; refugee idealism based on rendering thought omnipotent in the degree in which it is ineffective in concrete affairs;—these forms of subjectivism register an acceptance of whatever obstacles at the time prevent the active participation of the self in the ongoing course of events. Only when obstacles are treated as challenges to remaking of personal desire and thought, so that the latter integrate with the movement of nature and by participation direct its consequences, are opposition and duality rightly understood.

Existentially speaking, a human individual is distinctive opacity of bias and preference conjoined with plasticity and permeability of needs and likings. One trait tends to isolation, discreteness; the other trait to connection, continuity. This ambivalent character is rooted in nature, whose events have their own distinctive indifferencies, resistances, arbitrary closures and intolerances, and also their peculiar openness, warm responsiveness, greedy seekings and transforming unions. The conjunction in nature of whimsical contingency and lawful uniformity is the result of these two characters of events. They persist upon the human plane, and as ultimate characters are ineradicable. Boundaries, demarcations, abrupt, and expansive over-reachings of boundaries impartially and conjunctively mark every phase of human life.

The human individual in his opacity of bias is in so far doomed to a blind solitariness. He hugs himself in his isolation and fights against disclosure, the give and take of communication, as for the very integrity of existence. Even communicable meanings are tinged with color of the uncommunicated; there is a quality of reserve in every publicity. Everything may be done with this irreducible uniqueness except to get rid of it. The sense of it may add a bitter loneliness to experience. It may lead to restless insatiable throwing of the self into every opportunity of external business and dissipation in order to escape from it. It may be cherished, nurtured, developed into a cultivated consolatory detachment from the affairs of life, ending in the delusion of the superiority of the private inner life to all else, or in the illusion that one can really succeed in emancipating himself in his pure inwardness from connection with the world and society. It may express itself in elaborated schemes of self-pity and in bursts of defiant exclamation: Here I stand and cannot otherwise. It may lead to unreasoned loyalty to seemingly lost causes and forlorn hopes—and events may sometimes justify the faith.

Romanticism has made the best and the worst of the discovery of the private and incommunicable. It has converted a pervasive and inevitable color and temper of experience into its substance. In conceiving that this inexpugnable uniqueness, this ultimate singularity, exhausts the self, it has created a vast and somnambulic egotism out of the fact of subjectivity. For every existence in addition to its qualitative and intrinsic boundaries has affinities and active outreachings for connection and intimate union. It is an energy of attraction, expansion and supplementation. The ties and bonds of associated life are spontaneous uncalculated manifestations of this phase of human selfhood, as the union of hydrogen and oxygen is natural and unpremeditated.   Sociability, communication are just as immediate traits of the concrete individual as is the privacy of the closet of consciousness. To define one's self within closed limits, and then to try out the self in expansive acts that inevitably result in an eventual breaking down of the walled-in self, are equally natural and   inevitable acts.   Here is the ultimate "dialectic" of the universal and individual. One no sooner establishes his private and subjective self than he demands it be recognized and acknowledged by others, even if he has to invent an imaginary audience or an Absolute Self to satisfy the demand. And no person taught by experience ever escapes the reflection that no matter how much he does for himself, what endures is only what is done for others: an observation however which is most comforting when it takes the form of attributing desire to serve others to acts which indulge the exclusive self.

In some form or other, the dualism erected between the ego and the world of things and persons represents failure to attain solution of the problem set by this ambiguous nature of the self.   It is a formulated acceptance of oscillation between surrender to the external and assertion of the inner.   In science and in art, especially in the art of intercourse, real solutions occur.   Private bias manages in them to manifest itself in innovations and deviations, which reshape the world of objects and institutions, and which eventually facilitate communication and understanding.   Thereby the final and efficient, the limiting and the expansive, attain a harmony which they do not possess in other natural events.

Thus an individual existence has a double status and import. There is the individual that belongs in a continuous system of connected events which reinforce its activities and which form a world in which it is at home, consistently at one with its own preferences, satisfying its requirements. Such an individual is in its world as a member, extending as far as the moving equilibrium of which it is a part lends support. It is a natural end, not as an abrupt and immediate termination but as a fulfillment. Then there is the individual that finds a gap between its distinctive bias and the operations of the things through which alone its need can be satisfied; it is broken off, discrete, because it is at odds with its surroundings. It either surrenders, conforms, and for the sake of peace becomes a parasitical subordinate, indulges in egotistical solitude; or its activities set out to remake conditions in accord with desire. In the latter process, intelligence is born—not mind which appropriates and enjoys the whole of which it is a part, but mind as individualized, initiating, adventuring, experimenting, dissolving. Its possessed powers, its accomplished unions with the world, are now reduced to uncertain agencies to be forged into efficient instrumentalities in the stress and strain of trial.

The individual, the self, centred in a settled world which owns and sponsors it, and which in turn it owns and enjoys, is finished, closed. Surrender of what is possessed, disowning of what supports one in secure ease, is involved in all inquiry and discovery; the latter implicate an individual still to make, with all the risks implied therein. For to arrive at new truth and vision is to alter. The old self is put off and the new self is only forming, and the form it finally takes will depend upon the unforeseeable result of an adventure.   No one discovers a new world without forsaking an old one; and no one discovers a new world who exacts guarantee in advance for what it shall be, or who puts the act of discovery under bonds with respect to what the new world shall do to him when it comes into vision. This is the truth in the exaggeration of subjectivism. Only by identification with remaking the objects that now obtain are we saved from complacent objectivism. Those who do not fare forth and take the risks attendant upon the formation of new objects and the growth of a new self, are subjected perforce to inevitable change of the settled and close world they have made their own. Identification of the bias and preference of selfhood with the process of intelligent remaking achieves an indestructible union of the instrumental and the final.   For *this* bias can be satisfied no matter what the frustration of other desires and endeavors.

That an individual, possessed of some mode and degree of organized unity, participates in the genesis of every experienced situation, whether it be an object or an activity, is evident.   That the way in which it is engaged affects the quality of the situation experienced is evident. That the way in which it is engaged has consequences that modify not merely the environment but which react to modify the active agent; that every form of life in the higher organisms constantly conserves some consequences of its prior experiences, is also evident.   The constancy and pervasiveness of the operative presence of the self as a determining factor in all situations is the chief reason why we give so little heed to it; it is more intimate and omnipresent in experience than the air we breathe.   Only in pathological cases, in delusions and insanities and social eccentricities, do we readily become aware of it; even in such cases it required long discipline to force attentive observation back upon the self. It is easier to attribute such things to invasion and possession from without, as by demons and devils. Yet till we understand operations of the self as the tool of tools, *the* means in all use of means, specifying its differential activities in their distinctive consequences in varying qualities of what is experienced, science is incomplete and the use made of it is at the mercy of an unknown factor, so that the ultimate and important consequence is in so far a matter of accident. Intentions and efforts bring forth the opposite of what was intended and striven for, and the result is confusion and catastrophe. Thus we are brought to a consideration of the psycho-physical mechanism and functioning of individual centres of action.

CHAPTER SEVEN

NATURE, LIFE AND BODY-MIND

A series of cultural experiences exhibits a series of diverging conceptions of the relation of mind to nature in general and to the organic body in particular. Greek experience included affairs that rewarded without want and struggle the contemplation of free men; they enjoyed a civic life full and rich with an equable adaptation to natural surroundings. Such a life seemed to be upon the whole for those in its full possession a gracious culmination of nature; the organic body was the medium through which the culmination took place. Since any created thing is subject to natural contingency, death was not a problem; a being who is generated shares while he may in mind and eternal forms, and then piously merges with the forces which generated him. But life does not always exist in this happy equilibrium: it is onerous and devastating, civil life corrupt and harsh. Under such circumstances, a spirit which believes that it was created in the image of a divine eternal spirit, in whose everlastingness it properly shares, finds itself an alien and pilgrim in a strange and fallen world. Its presence in that world and its residence in a material body which is a part of that world are an enigma. Again the scene shifts. Nature is conceived to be wholly mechanical. The existence within nature and as part of it of a body possessed of life, manifesting thought and enjoying consciousness is a mystery.

This series of experiences with their corresponding philosophies display characteristic factors in the problem

of life and mind in relation to body. To the Greeks, all
life was psyche, for it was self-movement and only soul
moves itself. That there should be self-movement in a
world in which movement was also up-and-down, to-and-
fro, circular, was indeed interesting but not strange or
untoward. Evidence of the fact of self-movement is
directly had in perception; even plants exhibit it in a
degree and hence have soul, which although only vegetative is a natural condition of animal soul and rational
mind. Organic body occupies a distinctive position in
the hierarchy of being; it is the highest actuality of
nature's physical potentialities, and it is in turn the potentiality of mind. Greek thought, as well as Greek religion,
Greek sculpture and recreation, is piously attentive to
the human body.

In Pauline Christianity and its successors, the body is
earthly, fleshly, lustful and passionate; spirit is Godlike,
everlasting; flesh is corruptible; spirit incorruptible. The
body was conceived in terms of a moral disparagement
colored by supernatural religion. Since the body is
material, the dyslogy extends to all that is material; the
metaphysical discount put upon matter by Plato and
Aristotle becomes in ascetic thought a moral and essential
discount. Sin roots in the will; but occasions for sin
come from the lusts of the body; appetites and desires
spring from the body, distract attention from spiritual
things; concupiscence, anger, pride, love of money and
luxury, worldly ambition, result. Technically, the framework of Aristotelian thought is retained by the scholas-
tics; St. Thomas Aquinas repeats his formulae concerning life and the body almost word for word. But actually
and substantially this formal relationship has been dis-

torted and corrupted through the seduction of spirit by flesh manifest in the fall of man and nature by Adam's sin. Add to moral fear of the flesh, interest in resurrection into the next world for external bliss or woe, and there is present a fullfledged antithesis of spirit and matter. In spite of this antithesis, however, they are conjoined in the body of man. Spirit is simple, one, permanent and indissoluble; matter is multiple, subject to change and dissolution. The possibility of the conjunction of two such opposite things formed a problem. But it would have been a remote, technical problem of no interest save to a few speculative thinkers, were it not given concreteness by the notion of an immortality to be spent in bliss or in woe unutterable, and the dependence of this ultimate destiny upon a life in which lust of the flesh along with the world of ambition and the devil of pride, was a standing temptation to sin and thereby an occasion of eternal damnation.

As long as the Aristotelian metaphysical doctrine persisted that nature is an ordered series from lower to higher of potentialities and actualizations, it was possible to conceive of the organic body as normally the highest term in a physical series and the lowest term in a psychical series. It occupied just that intermediate position where, in being the actualization of the potentialities of physical qualities, body was also potentiality for manifestation of their ideal actualities. Aside from moral and religious questions, there was in medieval thought no special problem attaching to the relation of mind and body. It was just one case of the universal principle of potentiality as the substrate of ideal actuality. But when the time came when the moral and religious

associations of spirit, soul, and body persisted in full
vigor, while the classic metaphysics of the potential and
actual fell into disrepute, the full burden of the question
of the relation of body, nature and man, of mind, spirit,
and matter, was concentrated in the particular problem
of the relation of the body and soul.   When men ceased to
interpret and explain facts in terms of potentiality and
actuality, and resorted to that of causality, mind and
matter stood over against one another in stark unlike-
ness; there were no intermediates to shade gradually the
black of body into the white of spirit.

Moreover, both classic and medieval thought supplied influential empirical impetus to the new conception
in spite of their theoretically divergent foundation.   The
old distinction between vegetative, animal and rational
souls was, when applied to men, a formulation and justification of class divisions in Greek society.   Slaves and
mechanical artisans living on the nutritional, appetitive
level were for practical purposes symbolized by the body—
as obstructions to ideal ends and as solicitations to acts
contrary to reason.   The good citizen in peace and war
was symbolized by the soul proper, amenable to reason,
employing thought, but confining its operations after all
to mundane matters, infected with matter.   Scientific
inquirers and philosophers alone exemplified pure reason,
operating with ideal forms for the sake of the latter.
The claim of this class for inherent superiority was symbolized by *nous*, pure immaterial mind.   In Hellenistic
thought, the three-fold distinction became that of body,
mind or soul and spirit; spirit being elevated above all
world affairs and acts, even moral concerns, having purely
"spiritual" (immaterial) and religious objects.   This doc-

trine fell in with the sharp separation made in Christianity for practical moral purposes, between flesh and spirit, sin and salvation, rebellion and obedience. Thus the abstract and technical Cartesian dualism found prepared for it a rich empirical field with which to blend, and one which afforded its otherwise empty formalism concrete meaning and substance.

The formalism and unreality of the problem remains, however, in the theories which have been offered as its "solutions." They range from the materialism of Hobbes, the apparatus of soul, pineal glands, animal spirits of Descartes, to interactionism, pre-established harmony, occasionalism, parallelism, pan-psychic idealism, epiphenomenalism, and the *élan vital*—a portentous array. The diversity of solutions together with the dialectical character of each doctrine which render it impregnable to empirical attack, suggest that the trouble lies not so much in the solutions, as in the factors which determine statement of the problem. If this be so, the way out of the snarl is a reconsideration of the conceptions in virtue of which the problem exists. And these conceptions have primarily nothing to do with mind-body; they have to do with underlying metaphysical issues:—the denial of quality in general to natural events; the ignoring in particular of temporal quality and the dogma of the superior reality of "causes."

Empirically speaking, the most obvious difference between living and non-living things is that the activities of the former are characterized by needs, by efforts which are active demands to satisfy needs, and by satisfactions. In making this statement, the terms need, effort and satisfaction are primarily employed in a biological sense.

By need is meant a condition of tensional distribution of energies such that the body is in a condition of uneasy or unstable equilibrium. By demand or effort is meant the fact that this state is manifested in movements which modify environing bodies in ways which react upon the body, so that its characteristic pattern of active equilibrium is restored. By satisfaction is meant this recovery of equilibrium pattern, consequent upon the changes of environment due to interactions with the active demands of the organism.

A plant needs water, carbon dioxide; upon occasion it needs to bear seeds. The need is neither an immaterial psychic force superimposed upon matter, nor is it merely a notional or conceptual distinction, introduced by thought after comparison of two different states of the organism, one of emptiness and one of repletion. It denotes a concrete state of events: a condition of tension in the distribution of energies such as involves pressure from points of high potential to those of low potential which in turn effects distinctive changes such that the connection with the environment is altered, so that it acts differently upon the environment and is exposed to different influences from it. In this fact, taken by itself, there is nothing which marks off the plant from the physico-chemical activity of inanimate bodies. The latter also are subject to conditions of disturbed inner equilibrium, which lead to activity in relation to surrounding things, and which terminate after a cycle of changes—a terminus termed saturation, corresponding to satisfaction in organic bodies.

The difference between the animate plant and the inanimate iron molecule is not that the former has something in addition to physico-chemical energy; it lies in the *way* in which physico-chemical energies are interconnected and operate, whence different *consequences* mark inanimate and animate activity respectively. For with animate bodies, recovery or restoration of the equilibrium pattern applies to the complex integrated course or history. In inanimate bodies as such, "saturation" occurs indifferently, not in such a way as to tend to maintain a temporal pattern of activity. The interactions of the various constituent parts of a plant take place in such ways as to tend to continue a characteristically organized activity; they tend to utilize conserved consequences of past activities so as to adapt subsequent changes to the needs of the integral system to which they belong. Organization is a fact, though it is not an original organizing force. Iron as such exhibits characteristics of bias or selective reactions, but it shows no bias in favor of remaining simple iron; it had just as soon, so to speak, become iron-oxide. It shows no tendency in its interaction with water to modify the interaction so that consequences will perpetuate the characteristics of pure iron. If it did, it would have the marks of a living body, and would be called an organism. Iron as a genuine constituent of an *organized* body acts so as to tend to maintain the type of activity of the organism to which it belongs.

If we identify, as common speech does, the physical as such with the inanimate we need another word to denote the activity of organisms as such. Psycho-physical is an appropriate term. Thus employed, "psycho-physical" denotes the conjunctive presence in activity of need-demand-satisfaction, in the sense in which these terms have been defined. In the compound word, the prefix "psycho" denotes that physical activity has acquired additional properties, those of ability to procure a peculiar kind of interactive support of needs from surrounding media. Psycho-physical does not denote an abrogation of the physico-chemical; nor a peculiar mixture of something physical and something psychical (as a centaur is half man and half horse); it denotes the possession of certain qualities and efficacies not displayed by the inanimate.

Thus conceived there is no problem of the relation of physical *and* psychic. There are specifiable empirical events marked by distinctive qualities and efficacies. There is first of all, *organization* with all which is implied thereby. The problem involved is one of definite factual inquiry. Under exactly what conditions does organization occur, and just what are its various modes and their consequences? We may not be able to answer these questions satisfactorily; but the difficulties are not those of a philosophical mystery, but such as attend any inquiry into highly complex affairs. Organization is an empirical trait of some events, no matter how speculative and dubious theories about it may be; especially no matter how false are certain doctrines about it which have had great vogue—namely, those doctrines which have construed it as evidence of a special force or entity called life or soul. Organization is so characteristic of the nature of some events in their sequential linkages that no theory about it can be as speculative or absurd as those which ignore or deny its genuine existence. Denial is never based on empirical evidence, but is a dialectical conclusion from a preconception that whatever appears later in time must be metaphysically unreal as compared with what is found earlier, or from a preconception that since the complex is controlled by means of the simpler, the latter is more "real."

When ever the activities of the constituent parts of an organized pattern of activity are of such a nature as to conduce to the perpetuation of the patterned activity, there exists the basis of sensitivity. Each "part" of an organism is itself organized, and so of the "parts" of the part. Hence its selective bias in interactions with environing things is exercised so as to maintain *itself*, while also maintaining the whole of which it is a member. The root-tips of a plant interact with chemical properties of the soil in such ways as to serve organized life activity; and in such ways as to exact from the rest of the organism their own share of requisite nutrition. This pervasive operative presence of the whole in the part and of the part in the whole constitutes susceptibility—the capacity of feeling—whether or no this potentiality be actualized in plant-life. Responses are not merely selective, but are discriminatory, in behalf of some results rather than others. This discrimination is the essence of sensitivity. Thus with organization, bias becomes interest, and satisfaction a good or value and not a mere satiation of wants or repletion of deficiencies.

However it may be with plants and lower animals, in animals in which locomotion and distance–receptors exist, sensitivity and interest are realized as feeling, even though only as vague and massive uneasiness, comfort, vigor and exhaustion. A sessile organism requires no premonitions of what is to occur, nor cumulative embodiments of what has occurred. An organism with locomotion is as vitally connected with the remote as well as with the nearby; when locomotor organs are accompanied by distance-receptors, response to the distant in space becomes increasingly prepotent and equivalent in effect to response to the future in time.   A response toward what is distant is in effect an expectation or prediction of a later contact. Activities are differentiated into the preparatory, or anticipatory, and the fulfilling or consummatory.   The resultant is a peculiar tension in which each immediate preparatory response is suffused with the consummatory tone of sex or food or security to which it contributes.   Sensitivity, the capacity, is then actualized as feeling; susceptibility to the useful and harmful in surroundings becomes premonitory, an occasion of eventual consequences within life.

On the other hand, a consummation or satisfaction carries with it the continuation, in allied and reinforcing form, of preparatory or anticipatory activities.   It is not only a culmination out of them, but is an integrated cumulation, a funded conservation *of* them.   Comfort or discomfort, fatigue or exhilaration, implicitly sum up a history, and thereby unwittingly provide a means whereby, (when other conditions become present) the past can be unravelled and made explicit.   For it is characteristic of feeling that while it may exist in a formless condition, or without configured distinctions, it is capable of receiving and bearing distinctions without end.   With the multiplication of sensitive discriminatory reactions to different energies of the environment (the differentiation of sense-organs, extero-ceptors and proprio-ceptors) and with the increase in scope and delicacy of movements (the development of motor-organs, to which internal glandular organs for effecting a requisite redistributuion of energy correspond), feelings vary more and more in quality and intensity.

Complex and active animals *have*, therefore, feelings which vary abundantly in quality, corresponding to distinctive directions and phases—initiating, mediating, fulfilling or frustrating—of activities, bound up in distinctive connections with environmental affairs. They *have* them, but they do not know they have them. Activity is psycho-physical, but not "mental," that is, not aware of meanings. As life is a character of events in a peculiar condition of organization, and "feeling" is a quality of life-forms marked by complexly mobile and discriminating responses, so "mind" is an added property assumed by a feeling creature, when it reaches that organized interaction with other living creatures which is language, communication. Then the qualities of feeling become significant of objective differences in external things and of episodes past and to come. This state of things in which qualitatively different feelings are not just had but are significant of objective differences, is mind. Feelings are no longer just felt. They have and they make *sense;* record and prophesy.

That is to say, differences in qualities (feelings) of acts when employed as indications of acts performed and to be performed and as signs of their consequences, *mean* something. And they mean it directly; the meaning is had as their own character. Feelings make sense; as immediate meanings of events and objects, they are sensations, or, more properly, sensa. Without language, the qualities of organic action that are feelings are pains, pleasures, odors, colors, noises, tones, only potentially and proleptically. With language they are discriminated and identified. They are then "objectified;" they are immediate traits of things. This "objectification" is not a miraculous ejection from the organism or soul into external things, nor an illusory attribution of psychical entities to physical things. The qualities never were "in" the organism; they always were qualities of interactions in which both extra-organic things and organisms partake. When named, they enable identification and discrimination of things to take place as means in a further course of inclusive interaction. Hence they are as much qualities of the things engaged as of the organism. For purposes of control they may be referred specifically to either the thing or to the organism or to a specified structure of the organism. Thus color which turns out not to be a reliable sign of external events becomes a sign of, say, a defect in visual apparatus. The notion that sensory affections discriminate and identify themselves, apart from discourse, as being colors and sounds, etc., and thus *ipso facto* constitute certain elementary modes of knowledge, even though it be only knowledge of their own existence, is inherently so absurd that it would never have occurred to any one to entertain it, were it not for certain preconceptions about mind and knowledge. Sentiency in itself is anoetic; it exists as any immediate quality exists, but nevertheless it is an indispensable means of any noetic function.

For when, through language, sentience is taken up into a system of signs, when for example a certain quality of the active relationship of organism and environment is named hunger, it is seen as an organic demand for an extra-organic object. To term a quality "hunger," to name it, is to refer to an object, to food, to that which will satisfy it, towards which the active situation moves. Similarly, to name another quality "red," is to direct an interaction between an organism and a thing to some object which fulfills the demand or need of the situation. It requires but slight observation of mental growth of a child to note that organically conditioned qualities, including those special sense-organs, are discriminated only as they are employed to designate objects; red, for instance, as the property of a dress or toy. The difficulty in the way of identifying the qualities of acts conditioned by proprio-ceptor organs is notoriously enormous. They just merge in the general situation. If they entered into communication as shared means to social consequences they would acquire the same objective distinctiveness as do qualities conditioned by the extero-ceptor organs. On the other hand, the qualities of the latter are just shades of the general tone of situations until they are used, in language, as common or shared means to common ends. Then they are identified as traits of objects. The child has to learn through social intercourse that certain qualities of action mean greediness or anger or fear or rudeness; the case is not otherwise with those qualities which are identified as red, musical tone, a foul odor. The latter may have instigated nausea, and "red" may have excited uneasiness (as blood makes some persons faint); but discrimination of the nauseating object *as* foul odor, and of the excitation *as* red occurs only when they are designated as signs.

The qualities of situations in which organisms and surrounding conditions interact, when discriminated, make sense. Sense is distinct from feeling, for it has a recognized reference; it is the qualitative characteristic of something, not just a submerged unidentified quality or tone. Sense is also different from signification. The latter involves use of a quality as a sign or index of something else, as when the red of a light signifies danger. and the need of bringing a moving locomotive to a stop. The sense of a thing, on the other hand, is an immediate and immanent meaning; it is meaning which is itself felt or directly had. When we are baffled by perplexing conditions, and finally hit upon a clew, and everything falls into place, the whole thing suddenly, as we say, "makes sense." In such a situation, the clew has signification in virtue of being an indication, a guide to interpretation. But the meaning of the *whole* situation as apprehended is sense. This idiomatic usage of the word sense is much nearer the empirical facts than is the ordinary restriction of the word in psychological literature to a single simple recognized quality, like sweet or red: the latter simply designates a case of *minimum* sense, deliberately limited for purposes of intellectual safety-first. Whenever a situation has this double function of meaning, namely signification and sense, mind, intellect is definitely present.

The distinction between physical, psycho-physical, and mental is thus one of levels of increasing complexity and intimacy of interaction among natural events. The idea that matter, life and mind represent separate kinds of Being is a doctrine that springs, as so many philosophic errors have sprung, from a substantiation of eventual functions. The fallacy converts consequences of interaction of events into causes of the occurrence of these consequences—a reduplication which is significant as to the *importance* of the functions, but which hopelessly confuses understanding of them. "Matter," or the physical, is a character of events when they occur at a certain level of interaction. It is not itself an event or existence; the notion that while "mind" denotes essence, "matter" denotes existence is superstition. It is more than a bare essence; for it is a property of a particular field of interacting events. But as it figures in *science* it is as much an essence, as is acceleration, or the square root of minus one; which meanings also express derivative characters of events in interaction. Consequently, while the theory that life, feeling and thought are never independent of physical events may be deemed materialism, it may also be considered just the opposite. For it is reasonable to believe that the most adequate definition of the basic traits of natural existence can be had only when its properties are most fully displayed—a condition which is met in the degree of the scope and intimacy of interactions realized.

In any case, genuine objection to metaphysical materialism is neither moral nor esthetic. Historically speaking, materialism and mechanistic metaphysics—as distinct from mechanistic science—designate the doctrine that matter is the efficient cause of life and mind, and that "cause" occupies a position superior in reality to that of "effect." Both parts of this statement are contrary to fact. As far as the conception of causation is to be introduced at all, not matter but the natural events having matter as a character, "cause" life and mind. "Effects," since they mark the release of potentialities, are more adequate indications of the nature of nature than are just "causes." Control of the occurrence of the complex depends upon its analysis into the more elementary; the dependence of life, sentiency and mind upon "matter" is thus practical or instrumental. Lesser, more external fields of interaction are more manageable than are wider and more intimate ones, and only through managing the former can we direct the occurrence of the latter. Thus it is in virtue of the character of events which is termed matter that psycho-physical and intellectual affairs can be differentially determined. Every discovery of concrete dependence of life and mind upon physical events is therefore an addition to our resources. If life and mind had no mechanism, education, deliberate modification, rectification, prevention and constructive control would be impossible. To damn "matter" because of honorific interest in spirit is but another edition of the old habit of eulogizing ends and disparaging the means on which they depend.

This, then, is the significance of our introductory statement that the "solution" of the problem of mind-body is to be found in a revision of the preliminary assumptions about existence which generate the problem. As we have already noted, fruitful science of nature began when inquirers neglected immediate qualities, the "sense" of events, wet and dry, hot and cold, light and heavy, up and down, in behalf of "primary," namely, signifying, qualities, and when they treated the latter, although called qualities, not as such but as relations. This device made possible a totally different dialectical treatment. Classic science operated in terms of properties already attached to qualitative phenomena of sense and custom. Hence it could only repeat these phenomena in a changed vocabulary;—the vocabulary of sensory forms and forces which were, after all nothing but the already given meanings of things reduplicated. But the new dialectic was that of mathematical equations and functions. It started from meanings which ignored obvious characters or meanings of phenomena; hence it could lead to radically new relationships and generalizations—new in kind, and not merely in detail. No longer was the connection or classification of one color simply with other colors, but with all events involving rhythmic rates of change. Thus events hitherto disjoined were brought together under principles of inclusive formulation and prediction. Temporal qualities were stated as spatial velocities; thereby mathematical functions directly applicable to spatial positions, directions and distances, made it possible to reduce sequence of events into calculable terms. Neglect of temporal qualities as such centered thought upon *order* of succession, an order convertible into one of coexistence.

All this in effect is equivalent to seizing upon relations of events as the proper objects of knowledge. The surrender of immediate qualities, sensory and significant, as objects of science, and as proper forms of classification and understanding, left in reality these immediate qualities just as they were; since they are *had* there is no need to *know* them. But, as we have had frequent occasion to notice, the traditional view that the object of knowledge is reality *par excellence* led to the conclusion that the proper object of science was pre-eminently metaphysically real. Hence immediate qualities, being extruded from the object of science, were left thereby hanging loose from the "real" object. Since their *existence* could not be denied, they were gathered together into a psychic realm of being, set over against the object of physics. Given this premise, all the problems regarding the relation of mind and matter, the psychic and the bodily, necessarily follow. Change the metaphysical premise: restore, that is to say, immediate qualities to their rightful position as qualities of inclusive situations, and the problems in question cease to be epistemological problems. They become specifiable scientific problems: questions, that is to say, of how such and such an event having such and such qualities actually occurs.

Greek science imputed efficacy to qualities like wet and dry, hot and cold, heavy and light and to such qualitative differences in movement as up and down, to and fro, around and around. The world was formulated and explained on the basis of the causal efficacy of these qualities. The scientific revolution of the seventeenth century took its departure from a denial of causal status (and hence of significance for science) of these and all other direct qualities. On account, however, of the conversion of this fact about scientific procedure into a denial of the existence of qualities outside of mind and consciousness, psycho-physical and mental functions became inexplicable anomalies, supernatural in the literal sense of the word. The error of Greek science lay not in assigning qualities to natural existence, but in misconceiving the locus of their efficacy. It attributed to qualities apart from organic action efficiencies which qualities possess only through the medium of an organized activity of life and mind. When life and mind are recognized to be characters of the highly complex and extensive interaction of events, it is possible to give natural existential status to qualities, without falling into the mistake of Greek science. Psycho-physical phenomena and higher mental phenomena may be admitted in their full empirical reality, without recourse to dualistic breach in historic, existential continuity.

When knowing inanimate things, qualities as such may be safely disregarded. They present themselves as intensities and vector directions of movement capable of statement in mathematical terms. Thus their immediate individuality is got around; it is impertinent for science, concerned as the latter is with relationships. The most that can be said about qualities in the inanimate field is that they mark the limit of the contact of historical affairs, being abrupt ends or termini, boundaries of beginning and closing where a particular interaction ceases. They are like a line of foam marking the impact of waves of different directions of movement. They have to be noted and accepted in order to delimit a field of inquiry, but they do not enter into the inquiry as factors or terms.

In life and mind they play an active role. The delimitation or individualization they constitute on this level is not external to events. It is all one with the organization which permeates them, and which in permeating them, converts prior limitations of intensity and direction of energy into actual and intrinsic qualities, or sentient differences. For in feeling a quality exists as quality, and not merely as an abrupt, discrete, unique delimitation of interaction. Red differs from green for purposes of physical science as that which gives specific meaning to two sets of numbers applied to vibrations, or to two different placements of lines in a spectrum. The difference is proleptically qualitative; it refers to a unique difference of potentiality in the affairs under consideration. But as far as calculation and prediction are concerned these differences remain designable by non-qualitative indices of

number and form.   But in an organic creature sensitive
to light, these differences of potentiality may be realized
as differences in immediate sentiency.   To say that they
are *felt*, is to say that they come to independent and intrinsic existence on their own account.   The proposition
does not mean that feeling has been extraneously superadded to something else, or that a mode of extrinsic
cognitive access to a purely physical thing has entered
intrusively into a world of physical things.   "Feeling"
is in general a name for the newly actualized quality
acquired by events previously occurring upon a physical
level, when these events come into more extensive and
delicate relationships of interaction.   More specifically,
it is a name for the coming to existence of those ultimate
differences in affairs which mark them off from one
another and give them discreteness; differences which
upon the physical plane can be spoken of only in anticipation of subsequent realization, or in terms of different
numerical formulae, and different space-time positions
and contiguities.

Thus qualities characteristic of sentiency are qualities
of cosmic events.   Only because they are such, is it possible to establish the one to one correspondence which
natural science does establish between series of numbers
and spatial positions on one hand and the series and spectra
of sensory qualities on the other.   The notion that the
universe is split into two separate and disconnected realms
of existence, one psychical and the other physical, and
then that these two realms of being, in spite of their total
disjunction, specifically and minutely correspond to each
other—as a serial order of numbered vibrations corresponds to the immediately felt qualities of vision of the

prismatic spectrum—presents the acme of incredibility. The one-to-one agreement is intelligible only as a correspondence of properties and relations in one and the same world which is first taken upon a narrower and more external level of interaction, and then upon a more inclusive and intimate level. When we recall that by taking natural events on these two levels and instituting point to point correspondence (or "parallelism") between them, the richer and more complex display of characters is rendered amenable to prediction and deliberate guidance, the intelligibility of the procedure becomes concretely sensible.

Thus while modern science is correct in denying direct efficacy and position in the described sequence of events to say, red, or dry; yet Greek science was correct in its underlying naïve assumption that qualities count for something highly important. Apart from sentiency and life, the career of an event can indeed be fully described without any reference to its having red as a quality,— though even in this case, since description is an event which happens only through mental events, dependence upon an overt or actualized quality of red is required in order to delimit the phenomenon of which a mathematical-mechanical statement is made. Qualities actually become specifically effective however, in psycho-physical situations. Where animal susceptibility exists, a red or an odor or sound may instigate a determinate mode of action; it has selective power in maintenance of a certain pattern of energy-organization. So striking is this fact that we might even define the difference between an inanimate body and a vital and psycho-physical one, by saying that the latter responds to qualities while the former does not.

In this response, qualities become productive of results, and hence potentially significant. That is, in achieving effects, they become connected with consequences, and hence capable of meaning, knowable if not known. This explains the fact that while we are forced to ascribe qualities to events on the physical level, we cannot *know* them on this level; they have when assigned strictly to that level no consequences. But through the medium of living things, they generate effects, which, when qualities are used as means to produce them, are consequences. Thus qualities become intelligible, knowable.

In the higher organisms, those with distance-receptors of ear and eye and, in lesser degree, of smelling, qualities further achieve a difference which is the material basis or substratum of a distinction into activities having preparatory and having consummatory status. "Ends" are not necessarily fulfillments or consummations. They may be mere closures, abrupt cessations, as a railway line may by force of external conditions come to an end, although the end does not fulfill antecedent activities. So there are starts, beginnings which are in no sense preparatory, being rather disturbances and interferences. Events of the physical type have such ends and beginnings which mark them off qualitatively and individually. But as such they are not in any true sense possessed of instrumental nor fulfilling character. They neither initiate nor complete. But when these qualities are realized through organic action, giving rise to acts of utilization, of adaptation (response to quality), they are converted into a series, in which some acts are preparatory and others consummatory. An original contact-activity (including intra-organic disturbances or needs) renders distance receptors open to stimulation; the responses which take place in consequence tend to occur in such a way as to terminate in a further contact-activity in which original need is satisfied.

This series forms the immediate material of thought when social communication and discourse supervene. The beginning not only *is* the initial term in a *series* (as distinct from a *succession*), but it gains the *meaning* of subsequent activity moving toward a consequence of which it is the first member. The concluding term conserves within itself the meaning of the entire preparatory process. Thereby the original status of contact and distance activities is reversed. When activity is directed by distant things, contact activities must be inhibited or held in. They become instrumental; they function only as far as is needed to direct the distance-conditioned activities. The result is nothing less than revolutionary. Organic activity is liberated from subjection to what is closest at hand in space and time. Man is led or drawn rather than pushed. The immediate is significant in respect to what has occurred and will occur; the organic basis of memory and expectation is supplied. The subordination of contact-activity to distance-activity is equivalent to possibility of release from submergence in the merely given, namely, to abstraction, generalization, inference. It institutes both a difference and a connection between matters that prepare the way for other events and the affairs finally appropriated; it furnishes the material for the relation of thing signifying and thing signified— a relation that is actualized when discourse occurs. When this juncture of events is reached, there comes about the distinction mentioned between sense and signification.

The latter denotes the possibility of a later fulfilling sense of things in immediate appropriations and enjoyments. But meanwhile there is a sentience that has to be transformed by subordination to the distance-conditioned activity; which till it is thus transformed is vacant, confused, demanding but lacking meaning. Meanwhile also the distance-conditioned activities acquire as an integral part of their own quality the consequences of their prior fulfilments. They have *significance* with respect to their consequences; but they have perspicuous and coherent *sense* of their own. Thus they become final, and the qualities of contact-activity instrumental. In short, hearing and vision are notoriously the intellectual *and* esthetic senses—an undeniable fact which throws much light on the doctrine of those theorists about value who attempt to divide thought and enjoyable liking from each other in their definitions of value, and who also—quite logically on this premise—sharply separate values into contributory and intrinsic.

The foregoing discussion is both too technical and not elaborately technical enough for adequate comprehension. It may be conceived as an attempt to contribute to what has come to be called an "emergent" theory of mind. But every word that we can use, organism, feeling, psychophysical, sensation and sense, "emergence" itself, is infected by the associations of old theories, whose import is opposite to that here stated. We may, however attempt a recapitulation by premising that while there is no isolated occurrence in nature, yet interaction and connection are not wholesale and homogenous. Interacting-events have tighter and looser ties, which qualify them with certain beginnings and endings, and which mark them off from other fields of interaction.   Such relatively closed fields come into conjunction at times so as to interact with each other, and a critical alteration is effected. A new larger field is formed, in which new energies are released, and to which new qualities appertain.   Regulation, conscious direction and science imply ability to smooth over the rough junctures, and to form by translation and substitution a homogenous medium.   Yet these functions do not abrogate or deny qualitative differences and unlike fields or ranges of operation, from atoms to solar systems.   They do just what they are meant to do: give facility and security in utilizing the simpler manageable field to predict and modify the course of the more complete and highly organized.

In general, three plateaus of such fields may be discriminated.   The first, the scene of narrower and more external interactions, while qualitatively diversified in itself, is physical; its distinctive properties are those of the mathematical-mechanical system discovered by physics and which define matter as a general character.   The second level is that of life.   Qualitative differences, like those of plant and animal, lower and higher animal forms, are here even more conspicuous; but in spite of their variety they have qualities in common which define the psycho-physical.   The third plateau is that of association, communication, participation.   This is still further internally diversified, consisting of individualities.   It is marked throughout its diversities, however, by common properties, which define mind as intellect; possession of and response to meanings.

Each of one of these levels having its own characteristic empirical traits has its own categories.   They are however categories of description, conceptions required to state the fact in question. They are not "explanatory" categories, as explanation is sometimes understood; they do not designate, that is, the operation of forces as "causes." They stick to empirical facts noting and denoting characteristic qualities and consequences peculiar to various levels of interaction. Viewed from this standpoint, the traditional "mechanical" and "teleological" theories both suffer from a common fallacy, which may be suggested by saying that they both purport to be explanatory in the old, non-historical sense of causality. One theory makes matter account for the existence of mind; the other regards happenings that precede the appearance of mind as preparations made for the sake of mind in a sense of preparation that is alleged to explain the occurrence of these antecedents.

Mechanistic metaphysics calls attention to the fact that the latter occurrence could not have taken place without the earlier; that given the earlier, the latter was bound to follow. Spiritualistic metaphysics calls attention to the fact that the earlier, material affairs, prepare the way for vital and ideal affairs, lead up to them; promote them. Both statements are equally true descriptively; neither statement is true in the explanatory and metaphysical meaning imputed to it.

The notion of causal explanation involved in both conceptions implies a breach in the continuity of historic process; the gulf created has then to be bridged by an emission or transfer of force. If one starts with the assumption that mind and matter are two separate things, while the evidence forces one to see that they are connected, one has no option save to attribute the power to make the connection, to carry from one to the other, to one or the other of the two things involved. The one selected is then "cause;" it accounts for the existence of the other. One person is struck by such affairs as that when a match is struck and paper is near-by the paper catches fire, whether any one wished or intended it to do so or not. He is struck by a compulsory power exercised by the earlier over the later; given the lighted match and contiguous paper and the latter *must* burst into flame. Another person is struck by the fact that matches and paper exist only because somebody has use for them; that the intent and purpose of use preceded the coming into being of match and paper. So he concludes that thought, purpose, starts an emission and transfer of force which brought things into existence in order to accomplish the object of thought. Or, if a little less devoted to human analogies, one notes the cunning continuity of nature, how neatly one thing leads up to another, and how elegantly the later registers and takes advantage of what has gone before, and, beholding that the later is the more complex and the more significant, decides that what goes before occurs for the sake of the later, in its behalf, on its account. The eventual has somehow been there from the start, "implicitly," "potentially," but efficaciously enough to attend to its own realization by using material conditions at every stage.

The gratuitous nature of both assumptions is seen if we set out with any acknowledged historic process,—say—the growth from infancy to maturity, or the development of a melodic theme. There are those who regard childhood as merely getting ready for the supreme dignity of adulthood, and there are those who seem quite sure that adult life is merely an unrolling by way of mechanical effects of the "causal" forces found in childhood.   One of the theories makes youth a preliminary and intrinsically insignificant journey toward a goal; the other makes adulthood a projection, on a supernumerary screen, of a plate and pattern previously inserted in the projecting apparatus of childhood or of prenatal condition, or of heredity, or wherever the fixed and separated antecedent be located. Nevertheless the notion of growth makes it easy, I think, to detect the fallacy residing in both views: namely, the breaking up of a continuity of historical change into two separate parts, together with the necessity which follows from the breaking-in-two for some device by which to bring them together again.

The reality *is* the growth-process itself; childhood and adulthood are phases of a continuity, in which just because it is a history, the later cannot exist until the earlier exists ("mechanistic materialism" in germ); and in which the later makes use of the registered and cumulative outcome of the earlier—or, more strictly, *is* its utilization ("spiritualistic teleology" in germ).   The real existence is the history in its entirety, the history as just what it is. The operations of splitting it up into two parts and then having to unite them again by appeal to causative power are equally arbitrary and gratuitous.   Childhood is the childhood *of* and *in* a certain serial process of changes which is just what it is, and so is maturity.   To give the traits of either phase a kind of independent existence, and then to use the form selected to account for or explain the rest of the process is a silly reduplication; reduplication, because we have after all only parts of one and the same original history; silly because we fancy that we have accounted for the history on the basis of an arbitrary selection of part of itself.

Substitute for such growth a more extensive history of nature and call it the evolution of mind from matter, and the conclusion is not different. In the old dispute as to whether a stag runs because he has long and slender legs, or has the legs in order that he may run, both parties overlook the natural descriptive statement; namely, that it is of the nature of what goes on in the world that the stag has long legs and that having them he runs. When mind is said to be implicit, involved, latent, or potential in matter, and subsequent change is asserted to be an affair of making it explicit, evolved, manifest, actual, what happens is that a natural history is first cut arbitrarily and unconsciously in two, and then the severance, is consciously and arbitrarily cancelled. It is simpler not to start by engaging in such manoeuvers.

The discussion gives an understanding of the adaptation of nature and life and mind to one another. A mystery has not seldom been made of the fact that objective nature lends itself to man's sense of fitness, order and beauty; or, in another region of discourse, that objective nature submits to mental operations sufficiently to be known. Or, the mystery is conceived from the other end: it seems wonderful that man should be possessed of a sense of order, beauty and rightness; that he should have a capacity of thinking and knowing, so that man is elevated far above nature and seated with angels. But the wonder and mystery do not seem to be other than the wonder and mystery that there should be such a thing as nature, as existential events, at all, and that in being they should be what they are. The wonder should be transferred to the whole course of things.   Only because an arbitrary breach has previously been introduced by which the world, is first conceived as something quite different from what it demonstrably is, does it then appear passing strange that after all it should be just what it is.   The world is subject-matter for knowledge, because mind has developed *in* that world; a body-mind, whose structures have developed according to the structures of the world in which it exists, will naturally find some of its structures to be concordant and congenial with nature, and some phases of nature with itself.   The latter are beautiful and fit, and others ugly and unfit.   Since mind cannot evolve except where there is an organized process in which the fulfillments of the past are conserved and employed, it is not surprising that mind when it evolves should be mindful of the past and future, and that it should use the structures which are biological adaptations of organism and environment as its own and its only organs.   In ultimate analysis the mystery that mind should use a body, or that a body should have a mind, is like the mystery that a man cultivating plants should use the soil; or that the soil which grows plants at all should grow those adapted to its own physicochemical properties and relations.

The account which has been given will be repeated from a more analytic point of view, starting with evident empirical consideration.   Every "mind" that we are empirically acquainted with is found in connection with some organized body.   Every such body exists in a natural medium to which it sustains some adaptive connection: plants to air, water, sun, and animals to these things and also to plants.   Without such connections, animals die; the "purest" mind would not continue with-

out them.   An animal can live only as long as it draws
nutriment from its medium, finds there means of defence,
and ejects into it waste and superfluous products of its
own making.   Since no particular organism lasts forever,
life in general goes on only as an organism reproduces
itself; and the only place where it can reproduce itself is in
the environment.   In all higher forms reproduction is
sexual; that is, it involves the meeting of two forms.   The
medium is thus one which contains similar and conjunctive forms.   At every point and stage, accordingly, a
living organism and its life processes involve a world or
nature temporally and spatially "external" to itself but
"internal" to its functions.

The only excuse for reciting such commonplaces is that
traditional theories have separated life from nature, mind
from organic life, and thereby created mysteries.   Restore
the connection, and the problem of how a mind can know
an external world or even know that there is such a thing,
is like the problem of how an animal eats things external
to itself; it is the kind of problem that arises only if one
assumes that a hibernating bear living off its own stored
substance defines the normal procedure, ignoring moreover the question where the bear got its stored material.
The problem of how one person knows the existence of
other persons, is, when the relation of mind and life is
genuinely perceived, like the problem of how one
animal can associate with other animals, since other is
other.   A creature generated in a conjunctive union,
dependent upon others (as are at least all higher forms)
for perpetuation of its being, and carrying in its own structure the organs and marks of its intimate connection
with others will know other creatures if it knows itself.

Since both the inanimate and the human environment are involved in the functions of life, it is inevitable, if these functions evolve to the point of thinking and if thinking is naturally serial with biological functions, that it will have as the material of thought, even of its erratic imaginings, the events and connections of this environment. And if the animal succeeds in putting to use any of its thinkings as means of sustaining its functions, those thoughts will have the characters that define knowledge.

In contrast with lower organisms, the more complex forms have distance receptors and a structure in which activators and effectors are allied to distance even more extensively than to contact receptors. What is done in response to things nearby is so tied to what is done in response to what is far away, that a higher organism acts with reference to a spread-out environment as a single situation. We find also in all these higher organisms that what is done is conditioned by consequences of prior activities; we find the fact of learning or habit-formation. In consequence, an organism acts with reference to a time-spread, a serial order of events, as a unit, just as it does in reference to a unified spatial variety. Thus an environment both extensive and enduring is immediately implicated in present behavior. Operatively speaking, the remote and the past are "in" behavior making it what it is. The action called "organic" is not just that of internal structures; it is an integration of organic-environmental connections. It may be a mystery that there should be thinking but it is no mystery that if there is thinking it should contain in a "present" phase, affairs remote in space and in time, even to geologic ages, future eclipses and far away stellar systems. It is only a question of how far what is "in" its actual experience is extricated and becomes focal.

It is also an obvious empirical fact that animals are connected with each other in inclusive schemes of behavior by means of signaling acts, in consequence of which certain acts and consequences are deferred until a joint action made possible by the signaling occurs. In the human being, this function becomes language, communication, discourse, in virtue of which the consequences of the experience of one form of life are integrated in the behavior of others. With the development of recorded speech, the possibilities of this integration are indefinitely widened—in principle the cycle of objective integration within the behavior of a particular organism is completed. Not merely its own distant world of space-time is involved in its conduct but the world of its fellows. When consequences which are unexperienced and future to one agent are experienced and past to another creature with which it is in communication, organic prudence becomes conscious expectation, and future affairs living present realities. Human learning and habit-forming present thereby an integration of organic-environmental connections so vastly superior to those of animals without language that its experience appears to be super-organic.

Another empirical fact follows. Strict repetition and recurrence decrease relatively to the novel. Apart from communication, habit-forming wears grooves; behavior is confined to channels established by prior behavior. In so far the tendency is toward monotonous regularity. The very operation of learning sets a limit to itself, and makes subsequent learning more difficult. But this holds only of a habit, a habit in isolation, a non-communicating habit.

Communication not only increases the number and variety of habits, but tends to link them subtly together, and eventually to subject habit-forming in a particular case to the habit of recognizing that new modes of association will exact a new use of it. Thus habit is formed in view of possible future changes and does not harden so readily. As soon as a child secretes from others the manifestation of a habit there is proof that he is practically aware that he forms *a* habit subject to the requirements of others as to his further habit formations.

Now an animal given to forming habits, is one with an increasing number of needs, and of new relationships with the world about it. Each habit demands appropriate conditions for its exercise and when habits are numerous and complex, as with the human organism, to find these conditions involves search and experimentation; the organism is compelled to make variations, and exposed to error and disappointment. By a seeming paradox, increased power of forming habits means increased susceptibility, sensitiveness, responsiveness. Thus even if we think of habits as so many grooves, the power to acquire many and varied grooves denotes high sensitivity, explosiveness. Thereby an old habit, a fixed groove if one wishes to exaggerate, gets in the way of the process of forming a new habit while the tendency to form a new one cuts across some old habit. Hence instability, novelty, emergence of unexpected and unpredictable combinations. The more an organism learns–the more that is, the former terms of a historic process are retained and integrated in this present phase–the more it has to learn, in order to keep itself going; otherwise death and catastrophe. If mind is a further process in life, a further process of registration, conservation and use of what is conserved, then it must have the traits it does empirically have: being a moving stream, a constant change which nevertheless has axis and direction, linkages, associations as well as initiations, hesitations and conclusions.

The thing essential to bear in mind is that living as an empirical affair is not something which goes on below the skin-surface of an organism: it is always an inclusive affair involving connection, interaction of what is within the organic body and what lies outside in space and time, and with higher organisms far outside. For this reason, organic acts are a kind of fore-action of mind; they look as if they were deliberate and consciously intelligent, because of necessity, intelligent action in utilizing the mechanisms they supply, reproduces their patterns. The evidence usually adduced in support of the proposition that lower animals, animals without language, think, turns out, when examined, to be evidence that when men, organisms with power of social discourse, think, they do so with the organs of adaptation used by lower animals, and thus largely repeat in imagination schemes of overt animal action. But to argue from this fact to the conclusion that animals think is like concluding that because every tool, say a plow, originated from some pre-existing natural production, say a crooked root or forked branch, the latter was inherently and antecedently engaged in plowing. The connection is there, but it is the other way around.

Excuse for dwelling upon the fact that life goes on between and among things of which the organism is but one is because this fact is so much ignored and virtually denied by traditional theories. Consider for example, the definitions of life and mind given by Herbert Spencer:

correspondence of an inner order with an outer order. It implies there is an inner order and an outer order, and that the correspondence consists in the fact that the terms in one order are related to one another as the terms or members of the other order are connected within themselves. The correspondence is like that of various phonographic records to one another; but the genuine correspondence of life and mind with nature is like the correspondence of two persons who "correspond" in order to learn each one of the acts, ideas and intents of the other one, in such ways as to modify one's own intents, ideas and acts, and to substitute partaking in a common and inclusive situation for separate and independent performances. If the organism merely repeats in the series of its own self-enclosed acts the order already given without, death speedily closes its career. Fire for instance consumes tissue; that is the sequence in the external order. Being burned to death is the order of "inner" events which corresponds with this "outer" order. What the organism actually does is to act so as to change its relationship to the environment; and as organisms get more complex and human this change of relationship involves more extensive and more enduring changes in the environmental order. The aim is not to protract a line of organic events parallel to external events, but to form a new scheme of affairs to which both organic and environmental relations contribute, and in which they both partake. Yet all schemes of psycho-physical parallelism, traditional theories of truth as correspondence, etc., are really elaborations of the same sort of assumptions as those made by Spencer: assumptions which first make a division where none exists, and then resort to an artifice to restore the connection which has been willfully destroyed.

If organic life denotes a phase of history in which natural affairs have reached a point in which characteristic new properties appear, and new ways of acting are released because of integration of fields hitherto unlinked, there does not seem to be anything extraordinary in the fact that what is known about the earlier "physical" series is applied to interpret and direct vital phenomena; nor in the fact that this application does not exhaust their character nor suffice wholly for their description. We cannot direct a course of interactions without counting and measuring, but the interactions are more than numbers, spaces and velocities. To explain is to employ one thing to elucidate, clear, shed light upon, put in better order, because in a wider context, another thing. It is thus subordinate to more adequate discourse, which, applied to space-time affairs, assumes the style of narration and description. Speaking in terms of captions familiar in rhetoric, exposition and argument are always subordinate to a descriptive narration, and exist for the sake of making the latter clearer, more coherent and more significant.

Body-mind designates an affair with its own properties. A large part of the difficulty in its discussion—perhaps the whole of the difficulty in general apart from detailed questions—is due to vocabulary. Our language is so permeated with consequences of theories which have divided the body and mind from each other, making separate existential realms out of them, that we lack words to designate the actual existential fact. The circumlocutions we are compelled to resort to—exemplified in the previous discussion —thus induce us to think that analogous separations exist in nature, which can also only be got around by elaborate circuitous arrangements. But body-mind simply designates what actually takes place when a living body is implicated in situations of discourse, communication and participation. In the hyphenated phrase body-mind, "body" designates the continued and conserved, the registered and cumulative operation of factors continuous with the rest of nature, inanimate as well as animate; while "mind" designates the characters and consequences which are differential, indicative of features which emerge when "body" is engaged in a wider, more complex and interdependent situation.

Just as when men start to talk they must use sounds and gestures antecedent to speech, and as when they begin to hunt animals, catch fish or make baskets, they must employ materials and processes that exist antecedently to these operations, so when men begin to observe and think they must use the nervous system and other organic structures which existed independently and antecedently. That the use reshapes the prior materials so as to adapt them more efficiently and freely to the uses to which they are put, is not a problem to be solved: it is an expression of the common fact that anything changes according to the interacting field it enters. Sounds do not cease to be sounds when they become articulate speech; but they do take on new distinctions and arrangements, just as do materials used in tools and machines, without ceasing to be the materials they formerly were. Thus the external or environmental affairs, primarily implicated in living processes and later implicated in discourse, undergo modifications in acquiring meanings and becoming objects of mind, and yet are as "physical" as ever they were.

Unless vital organizations were organizations *of* antecedent natural events, the living creature would have no natural connections; it would not be pertinent to its environment nor its environment relevant to it; the latter would not be usable, material of nutrition and defence. In similar fashion, unless "mind" was, in its existential occurrence, an organization *of* physiological or vital affairs and unless its functions developed out of the patterns of organic behavior, it would have no pertinency to nature, and nature would not be the appropriate scene of its inventions and plans, nor the subject-matter of its knowledge. If we suppose, per impossible or by a miracle, that a separate mind is inserted abruptly in nature, its operation would be wholly dialectical, and in a sense of dialectic which is non-existential not only for the time being, but forever; that is dialectic would be without any *possible* reference to existence. We are so used by tradition both to separating mind from the world and noting that its acts and consequences are relevant to the world-error—aberration and insanity can exist only with respect to relevancy—that we find it easier to make a problem out of the conjunction of two inconsistent premises than to rethink our premises.

Of pure dialectic it is a truism that it is neither materially true nor false, but only self-consistent or else self-contradictory. Were it not for the distorting influence of material bias, of preference that *existence* be thus and so rather than otherwise, and of desire that other creatures should believe as we do or should accept our conclusions, dialectic and calculation would however not be subject even to inconsistency. Some purely logical operations are better than others, even as purely logical, for they have greater scope and fertility, but none are truer or more correct than others. Purely formal errors are impossible, so-called formal fallacies to the contrary notwithstanding. No one ever actually reasoned that since horses are quadrupeds and cows are quadrupeds, horses are cows. If in some cases, it is made to appear that formal reasoning falls into such fallacies, the reason is that material causes are brought in and their operation is overlooked. Dialectical relations are dialectical, not existential and therefore have no causative power; there is nothing in them to generate misconception. The principle of dialectic is identity; its opposite is not inconsistency to say nothing of falsity; it is nonsense. To say that dialectic as such is infallible is only to say it is truistic.

Nevertheless logic or the *use* of meanings in a dialectic manner *is* actually exposed to all sorts of mistakes. For every instance of dialectic is itself existential. Meanings are taken; they are employed for a purpose, just as other materials are; they are combined and disjoined. It is the act of *taking* which enables dialectic to exist or occur, and taking is fallible, it is often mis-taking. Using meanings is a particular act; into this act enter causative factors, physiological, social, moral. The most perfect structure may be employed for purposes to which it is not apt; wrongly employed for the right purpose, it will buckle or default. Thus in dialectic, reasoning may flag because of fatigue; it may take one meaning for another because of perverse sensory appreciations, due to organic maladjustments; haste, due to absence of inhibition, may lead one to take a meaning to be clear when it is cloudy or ambiguous with respect to the purpose for which it is used, although in itself it is neither clear nor obscure; a desire to show off or to confute an opponent may lead to inconsistency and extraneous irrelevancies. Thousands of things may cause fallacies, when meanings truistically infallible because just what they are, are *used* to reach an end or make a conclusion. Self-contradiction assuredly occurs but it is material and active, not formal and non-existential. We contradict ourselves precisely as we contradict another person and for much the same reasons.

The ownership of meanings or mind thus vests in nature; meanings are meanings *of*. The existence of error is proof, not disproof, of the fact that all meanings intrinsically have reference to natural events. The idealist who employs the existence of error and of detection and possible correction of error as evidence of the existence, of a pre-existent truth in which errors are contained in their total relationship, and hence are not errors but constituents of truth, are right in the insistence that error involves objective reference. But in the same way digestion involves food-stuffs; and yet does not prove that there pre-exists a model digestion in which food is perfectly assimilated. Error involves a possibility of detection and corrections because it refers to things, but the possibility has an eventual, not a backward reference. It denotes the possibility of acts yet to be undertaken. Like the criterion of perfect efficiency in respect to machines, the notion of a complete judgment in which errors exist only as a rectified constituent of a perfect truth, is part of the art of examination and invention. Action and reaction are equal, to a hundred per cent of equality; but this formal "law" does not guarantee that in any particular system of action—reaction there is contained perfect efficiency.

Similarly the objective reference of meanings is complete; it is a hundred per cent affair; but it takes errors as well as truth to make up the hundred per cent, as it takes waste as well as efficiency to make up the perfect equality of action and reaction.

We mark off certain uses of meanings as reveries in order to control better the cognitive reference of other meanings. So we mark off certain meanings as purely rational or ideal, as dialectical or non-existential, in order to control better an eventual existential reference. Meaning may *become* purely esthetic; it may be appropriated and enjoyed for what it is in the having. This also involves control; it is *such* a way of taking and using them as to suspend cognitive reference.[1] This suspension is an acquired art. It required long discipline to recognize poetry instead of taking it as history, instruction and prediction. The idea that meanings are originally floating and esthetic and become intellectual, or practical and cognitive, by a conjunction of happy accidents, puts the cart before the horse. Its element of truth is that there is genuine distinction between having a meaning and using it; the element of falsity is in supposing that meanings, ideas, are first had and afterwards used. It required long experience to

[1] This statement does not rest upon a confusion between objects as causal conditions of meanings and objects as cognitively meant. The distinction is a genuine one, not to be slighted. The former connection is antecedent, the latter is subsequential. But meanings or mind have both kinds of connection. Greek myths for example were adequately conditioned in existence; but they also have a diagnostic status. When not taken as meanings of the behavior of gods, they are taken as meanings of Greek life, just as a hallucinatory ghost when not taken as a spiritual apparition is taken as meaning another event, say, a nervous shock. *Having* a meaning is not a reference, but every meaning had is taken **or** used as well as had. "Dialectic" means to take it a certain way.

enforce recognition of the distinction; for originally any meaning had, is had in and for use. To hold an idea contemplatively and esthetically is a late achievement in civilization.

Organic and psycho-physical activities with their qualities are conditions which have to come into existence before mind, the presence and operation of meanings, ideas, is possible. They supply mind with its footing and connection in nature; they provide meanings with their existential stuff. But meanings, ideas, are also, when they occur, characters of a new interaction of events; they are characters which in their incorporation with sentiency transform organic action, furnishing it with new properties. Every thought and meaning has its substratum in some organic act of absorption or elimination of seeking, or turning away from, of destroying or caring for, of signaling or responding. It roots in some definite act of biological behavior; our physical names for mental acts like seeing, grasping, searching, affirming, acquiescing, spurning, comprehending, affection, emotion are not just "metaphors." But while a burnt child may shrink from flame just as the dog cowers at the sight of a stick, a child may in addition, when the conditions involved have become a matter of discourse and are ideas, respond to the burn-giving flame in playful, inventive, curious and investigative ways. He pokes a stick or piece of paper into it; he uses flame and the fact of its painful and burning consequence not just to keep away from it, but to do things with it in ways which will satisfy his want to have to do with fire but without getting burned. Biological acts persist, but have sense, meaning, as well as feeling, tone. Abrupt withdrawal having only negative, protective con-

sequences is turned into significant and fruitful exploration and manipulation. Man combines meanings, like
fire, nearness, remoteness, warmth, comfort, nice, pain,
expansion, softening, so that fire enters into new interactions and effects new consequences. By an intra-organic re-enactment of partial animal reactions to natural
events, and of accompanying reactions to and from others
acquired in intercourse and communication, means-
consequences are tried out in advance without the organism getting irretrievably involved in physical consequences. Thought, deliberation, objectively directed
imagination, in other words, is an added efficacious function
of natural events and hence brings into being new consequences. For images are not made of psychical stuff;
they are qualities of *partial* organic behaviors, which are
their "stuff." They are partial because not fully geared
to extero-ceptor and muscular activities, and hence not
complete and overt.

Domination by spatial considerations leads some
thinkers to ask *where* mind is. Reserving the discussion of
conscious behavior for the next chapter, and accepting
for the moment the standpoint of the questioner (which
ignores the locus of discourse, institutions and social arts),
limiting the question to the organic individual, we may say
that the "seat" or locus of mind—its static phase—is the
qualities of organic action, as far as these qualities have
been conditioned by language and its consequences. It
is usual for those who are posed by the question of "where"
and who are reluctant to answer that mind is "where"
there is a spaceless separate realm of existence, to fall
back in general on the nervous system, and specifically
upon the brain or its cortex as the "seat" of mind. But

the organism is not just a structure; it is a characteristic way of interactivity which is not simultaneous, all at once but serial. It is a way impossible without structures for its mechanism, but it differs from structure as walking differs from legs or breathing from lungs. Prior to communication, the qualities of this action are what we have termed psycho-physical; they are not "mental." The consequences of partaking in communication modify organic ways of acting; the latter attain new qualities.

When I think such meanings as "friend" and "enemy," I refer to external and eventual consequences. But this naming does not involve miraculous "action at a distance." There is something present in organic action which acts as a surrogate for the remote things signified. The words make immediate sense as well as have signification. This something now present is not just the activity of the laryngeal and vocal apparatus. When shortcircuiting through language is carried as far as limitation to this apparatus, words are mere counters automatically used, and language disappears. The ideas are qualities of events in all the parts of organic structure which have ever been implicated in actual situations of concern with extraorganic friends and enemies:—presumably in proprioreceptors and organ-receptors with *all* their connected glandular and muscular mechanisms. These qualities give body and stuff to the activity of the linguistic apparatus. The integration of the qualities of vocal apparatus allied through the nervous mechanism with the qualities of these other events, constitutes the immediate sense of friendliness and animosity. The more intimate the alliance of vocal activity with the total organic disposition toward friends and enemies, the greater is the imme-

diate sense of the words.   The nervous system is in no
sense the "seat " of the idea.   It is the mechanism of the
connection or integration of acts.

"Socrates is mortal" is hardly more than a counter of
logical text-books; S is M will do just as well—or better.
But not so to the disciples of Socrates who had just heard
of his condemnation to death.   The connection of the
auditory act with the totality of organic responses was then
complete.   In some linguistic situations, such emphatic
immediate presence of sense occurs; language is then
poetical.   For other purposes, action is served by elimination of immediate sense as far as possible.   The attitude is prosaic; it is best subserved by mathematical
symbolism; mathematical not signifying something ready
made, but being simply the devices by which mind is
rigidly occupied with instrumental objects, by means of
artificial inhibition of immediate and consummatory qualities, the latter being distracting for the activity in hand.
The consummatory phase cannot be suppressed or eliminated however; nature pitched through the door returns
through the window.   And the common form of its
return today is falling down in worship or in fear before
the resulting mathematico-mechanical object.

In conclusion, it may be asserted that "soul" when
freed from all traces of traditional materialistic animism
denotes the qualities of psycho-physical activities as far as
these are organized into unity.   Some bodies have souls
preeminently as some conspicuously have fragrance, color,
and solidity.   To make this statement is to call attention
to properties that characterize these bodies, not to import
a mysterious non-natural entity or force.   Were there not
in actual existence properties of sensitivity and of marvel-

ously comprehensive and delicate participative response characterizing living bodies, mythical notions about the nature of the soul would never have risen. The myths have lost whatever poetic quality they once had; when offered as science they are superstitious encumbrances. But the idiomatic non-doctrinal use of the word soul retains a sense of the realities concerned. To say emphatically of a particular person that he has soul or a great soul is not to utter a platitude, applicable equally to all human beings. It expresses the conviction that the man or woman in question has in marked degree qualities of sensitive, rich and coordinated participation in all the situations of life. Thus works of art, music, poetry, painting, architecture, have soul, while others are dead, mechanical.

When the organization called soul is free, moving and operative, initial as well as terminal, it is spirit. Qualities are both static, substantial, and transitive. Spirit quickens; it is not only alive, but spirit gives life. Animals are spirited, but man is a living spirit. He lives in his works and his works do follow him. Soul is form, spirit informs. It is the moving function of that of which soul is the substance. Perhaps the words soul and spirit are so heavily laden with traditional mythology and sophisticated doctrine that they must be surrendered; it may be impossible to recover for them in science and philosophy the realities designated in idiomatic speech. But the realities are there, by whatever names they be called.

Old ideas do not die when the beliefs which have been explicitly associated with them disappear; they usually only change their clothes. Present notions about the organism are largely a survival, with changed vocabulary, of old ideas about soul and body.   The soul was conceived as inhabiting the body in an external way.   Now the nervous system is conceived as a substitute, mysteriously within the body.   But as the soul was "simple" and there-fore not diffused through the body, so the nervous system as the seat of mental events is narrowed down to the brain, and then to the cortex of the brain; while many physio-logical inquirers would doubtless feel enormously relieved if a specific portion of the cortex could be ascertained to be *the* seat of consciousness.   Those who talk most of the organism, physiologists and psychologists, are often just those who display least sense of the intimate, delicate and subtle interdependence of all organic structures and processes with one another.   The world seems mad in pre-occupation with what is specific, particular, discon-nected in medicine, politics, science, industry, education. In terms of a conscious control of inclusive wholes, search for those links which occupy key positions and which effect critical connections is indispensable.   But recovery of sanity depends upon seeing and using these specifiable things *as* links functionally significant in a process.   To see the organism *in* nature, the nervous system in the organism, the brain in the nervous system, the cortex in the brain is the answer to the problems which haunt philosophy.   And when thus seen they will be seen to be *in*, not as marbles are in a box but as events are in history, in a moving, growing never finished process. Until we have a procedure in actual practice which demon-strates this continuity, we shall continue to engage in appealing to some other specific thing, some other broken off affair, to restore connectedness and unity—calling the specific religion or reform or whatever specific is the fashionable cure of the period.   Thus we increase the disease in the means used to cure it.[2]

In matters predominantly physical we know that all control depends upon conscious perception of relations obtaining between things, otherwise one cannot be used to affect the other.   We have been marvellously successful in inventing and constructing external machines, because with respect to such things we take for granted that success occurs only upon the conscious plane—that of conscious perception of the relations which things sustain to one another.   We know that locomotives and aeroplanes and telephones and power-plants do not arise from instinct or the subconscious but from deliberately ascertained perception of connections and orders of connections.   Now after a period in which advance in these respects was complacently treated as proof and measure of progress, we have been forced to adopt pessimistic attitudes, and to wonder if this "progress" is to end in the deterioration of man and the possible destruction of civilization.

Clearly we have not carried the plane of conscious control, the direction of action by perception of connections, far enough.   We cannot separate organic life and mind from physical nature without also separating nature from life and mind.   The separation has reached a point where intelligent persons are asking whether the end is to be catastrophe, the subjection of man to the industrial and military machines he has created.   This situation confers peculiar poignancy upon the fact that just where connections and interdependences are most numerous, intimate

[2] See F. Matthias Alexander's Man's Supreme Inheritance, and Conscious Constructive Control.

and pervasive, in living, psycho-physical activity, we most ignore unity and connection, and trust most unreservedly in our deliberate beliefs to the isolated and specific—which signifies that in action we commit ourselves to the unconscious and subconscious, to blind instinct and impulse and routine, disguised and rationalized by all sorts of honorific titles.   Thus we are brought to the topic of consciousness.

CHAPTER EIGHT

EXISTENCE, IDEAS AND CONSCIOUSNESS

In the discussions of the last chapter the word "consciousness" was avoided. It is a word of unsettled signification. Even apart from ambiguities in interpretation, there is no consensus as to what things the word denotes. Two quite different affairs are usually designated by it. On the one hand, it is employed to point out certain qualities in their immediate apparency, qualities of things of sentiency, such as are, from the psychological standpoint, usually termed feelings. The sum total of these immediate qualities present as literal ends or closures of natural processes constitute "consciousness" as an anoetic occurrence. This is consciousness wherever meanings do not exist; that is to say, apart from the existence and employment of signs, or independently of communication. On the other hand, consciousness is used to denote meanings actually perceived, *awareness* of objects: being wide-awake, alert, attentive to the significance of events, present, past, future. It is a lexicographic matter, which will not be discussed, whether the word should be employed to denote two such different affairs. What is important is that the difference in the nature of the things denoted should be registered, and that false ingenuity should not be expended in reducing one to the other.

Our previous discussion enables us, it will appear, to place the two denotations. The existential starting point is immediate qualities. Even meanings taken not as meanings but as existential are grounded in immediate qualities, in sentiencies or "feelings," of organic activities and receptivities. Meanings do not come into being without language, and language implies two selves involved in a conjoint or shared undertaking. Thus while its direct mechanism is found in the vocalizing and auditory apparatuses, this mechanism is in alliance with general organic behavior. Otherwise it becomes a mechanical routine not differing from the "speech" of parrot or a phonographic record. This alliance supplies language with the immediate qualitative "feel" that marks off signs immediately from one another in existence.

The same considerations define the "subconscious" of human thinking. Apart from language, from imputed and inferred meaning, we continually engage in an immense multitude of immediate organic selections, rejections, welcomings, expulsions, appropriations, withdrawals, shrinkings, expansions, elations and dejections, attacks, wardings off, of the most minute, vibratingly delicate nature. We are not aware of the qualities of many or most of these acts; we do not objectively distinguish and identify them. Yet they exist as feeling qualities, and have an enormous directive effect on our behavior. If for example, certain sensory qualities of which we are not cognitively aware cease to exist, we cannot stand or control our posture and movements. In a thoroughly normal organism, these "feelings" have an efficiency of operation which it is impossible for thought to match. Even our most highly intellectualized operations depend upon them as a "fringe" by which to guide our inferential movements. They give us our *sense* of rightness and wrongness, of what to select and emphasize and follow up, and what to drop, slur over and ignore, among the multitude of inchoate meanings that are presenting themselves. They give us premonitions of approach to acceptable meanings, and warnings of getting off the track. Formulated discourse is mainly but a selected statement of what we wish to retain among all these incipient starts, following ups and breakings off. Except as a reader, a hearer repeats something of these organic movements, and thus "gets" their qualities, he does not get the *sense* of what is said; he does not really assent, even though he give cold approbation. These qualities are the stuff of "intuitions" and in actuality the difference between an "intuitive" and an analytic person is at most a matter of degree, of relative emphasis. The "reasoning" person is one who makes his "intuitions" more articulate, more deliverable in speech, as explicit sequence of initial premises, jointures, and conclusions.

Meanings acquired in connection with the use of tools and of language exercise a profound influence upon organic feelings. In the reckoning of this account, are included the changes effected by all the consequences of attitude and habit due to *all* the consequences of tools and language—in short, civilization. Evil communications corrupt (native) good manners of action, and hence pervert feeling and subconsciousness. The deification of the subconscious is legitimate only for those who never indulge in it—animals and thoroughly healthy naïve children— if there be any such. The subconscious of a civilized adult reflects all the habits he has acquired; that is to say, all the organic modifications he has undergone. And in so far as these involve mal-coordinations, fixations and segregations (as they assuredly come to do in a very short time for those living in complex "artificial" conditions), sensory appreciation is confused, perverted and falsified. It is most reliable in just those activities with respect to which it is least spoken of, and least reliable with respect to those things where it is fashionable most to laud it. That is, it operates most successfully in meanings associated with language that is highly technical, affairs remote from fundamental and exigent needs, as in mathematics, or philosophizing far away from concrete situations, or in a highly cultivated fine art. It is surest to be wrong in connection with intimate matters of self-regulation in health, morals, social affairs—in matters most closely connected with basic needs and relationships. Where its use is popularly recommended it is most dangerous. To use feelings which are not the expression of a rectitude of organic action, rectitude that in civilized or artificial conditions is acquired only by taking thought (*taking* thought is radically different to just "thinking"), is to act like an animal without having the structural facilities of animal life. It has the fascination of all easy surrender to fatality and may be eulogized as a return to nature, spontaneity, or to the quasi-divine. It has the charm of lazy and comfortable escape from responsibility; we die, but we die, like animals, upon the field, defeated and mayhap disheartened, but without knowing it.

In a practical sense, here is the heart of the mind-body problem. Activities which develop, appropriate and enjoy meanings bear the same actualizing relation to psychophysical affairs that the latter bear to physical characters. They present the consequences of a wider range of interactions, that in which needs, efforts and satisfactions conditioned by association are operative. In this widened and deepened activity, there are both added resources and values, and added liabilities and defaults. The actualization of meanings furnishes psycho-physical qualities with their ulterior significance and worth. But it also confuses and perverts them. The effects of this corruption are themselves embodied through habits in the psycho-physical, forming one-sided degraded and excessive susceptibilities; creating both disassociations and rigid fixations in the sensory register. These habitual effects become in turn spontaneous, natural, "instinctive;" they form the platform of development and apprehension of further meanings, affecting every subsequent phase of personal and social life.[1]

Thus while the psycho-physical in man, apart from conscious meaning achieves nothing distinguished, the casual growth and incorporation of meanings cause the native need, adjustment and satisfaction to lose their immediate certainty and efficiency, and become subject to all kinds of aberrations. There then occur systematized withdrawals from intercourse and interaction, from what common sense calls "reality": carefully cultivated and artificially protected fantasies of consolation and compensation; rigidly stereotyped beliefs not submitted to objective tests; habits of learned ignorance or systematized ignorings of concrete relationships; organized fanaticisms; dogmatic traditions which socially are harshly intolerant and which intellectually are institutionalized paranoic systems; idealizations which instead of being immediate enjoyments of meanings, cut man off from nature and his fellows.

[1] See the books of Mr. Alexander already referred to, p. 296.

In short, there is constituted what Walter Lippmann has well termed a secondary pseudo-environment, which affects every item of traffic and dealing with the primary environment. Thus the concrete problems of mind-body have their locus and import in the educational procedures by which a normal integration of meanings in organic functions shall be secured and perversions prevented; in the remedial operations of psychiatry, and in social arts and appliances that render intercourse substantial, balanced and flexible.

While on the psycho-physical level, consciousness denotes the totality of actualized immediate qualitative differences, or "feelings," it denotes, upon the plane of mind, actualized apprehensions of meanings, that is, ideas. There is thus an obvious difference between mind and consciousness; meaning and an idea. Mind denotes the whole system of meanings as they are embodied in the workings of organic life; consciousness in a being with language denotes awareness or perception of meanings; it is the perception of actual events, whether past, contemporary or future, *in* their meanings, the having of actual ideas. The greater part of mind is only implicit in any conscious act or state; the field of mind—of operative meanings—is enormously wider than that of consciousness. Mind is contextual and persistent; consciousness is focal and transitive. Mind is, so to speak, structural, substantial; a constant background and foreground; perceptive consciousness is process, a series of heres and nows. Mind is a constant luminosity; consciousness intermittent, a series of flashes of varying intensities. Consciousness is, as it were, the occasional interception of messages continually transmitted, as a mechanical receiving device selects a few of the vibrations with which the air is filled and renders them audible.

The nature of awareness of meanings cannot be conveyed in speech. As with other immediate qualitative existences, words can only hint, point; the indication succeeding when it evokes an actual experience of the thing in question. Such words as apparency, conspicuousness, outstandingness, vividness, clearness, including of course their opposites vague, dim, confused, may assist the evocation. To denote the characteristics of mind a thoroughly different set of names must be used: organization, order, coherence. The relation of mind to consciousness may be partially suggested by saying that while mind as a system of meanings is subject to disorganization, disequilibration, perturbation, there is no sense in referring to a particular state of awareness *in its immediacy* as either organized or disturbed. An idea is just what it is when it occurs. To call it composed or perturbed is to compare one state with another, a comparison which by nature of the case can be made only indirectly on the basis of respective conditions and consequences. Emotional conditions do not *occur* as emotions, intrinsically defined as such; they occur as "tertiary" qualities of objects. Some cases of awareness or perception are designated "emotions" in retrospect or from without, as a child is instructed to term certain perceptual situations anger, or fear, or love, by way of informing him as to their consequences. Immediately, every perceptual awareness may be termed indifferently emotion, sensation, thought, desire: not that it *is* immediately any one of these things, or all of them combined, but that when it is taken in some *reference*, to conditions or to consequences or to both, it has, in that contextual reference, the distinctive properties of emotion, sensation, thought or desire.

The relation between mind and consciousness may be indicated by a familiar happening. When we read a book, we are immediately conscious of meanings that present themselves, and vanish. These meanings existentially occurring are *ideas*. But we are capable of getting ideas from what is read because of an organized system of meanings of which we are not at any one time completely aware. Our mathematical or political "mind" is the system of such meanings as possess and determine our particular apprehensions or ideas. There is however, a continuum or spectrum between this containing system and the meanings which, being focal and urgent, are the ideas of the moment. There is a contextual field between the latter and those meanings which determine the habitual direction of our conscious thoughts and supply the organs for their formation. One great mistake in the orthodox psychological tradition is its exclusive preoccupation with sharp focalization to the neglect of the vague shading off from the foci into a field of increasing dimness.

Discrimination in favor of the clearly distinguished has a certain practical justification, for the vague and extensive background is present in every conscious experience and therefore does not define the character of any one in particular. It represents that which is being used and taken for granted, while the focal phase is that which is imminent and critical. But this fact affords no justification for neglect and denial in theory of the dim and total background consciousness of every distinct thought. If there were a sharp division between the ideas that are focal as we read a certain section of a book and what we have already read, if there were not carried along a sense of the latter, what we now read could not take the form of an idea. Indeed, the use of such words as context and background, fringe, etc., suggests something too external to meet the facts of the case. The larger system of meaning suffuses, interpenetrates, colors what is now and here uppermost; it gives them sense, feeling, as distinct from signification.

Change the illustration from reading a book to seeing and hearing a drama. The emotional as well as intellectual meaning of each presented phase of a play depends upon the operative presence of a continuum of meanings. If we have to remember what has been said and done at any particular point, we are not aware of what is now said and done; while without its suffusive presence in what is now said and done we lack clew to its meaning. Thus the purport of past affairs is present in the momentary cross-sectional idea in a way which is more intimate, direct and pervasive than the way of recall. It is positively and integrally carried in and by the incidents now happening; these incidents are, in the degree of genuine dramatic quality, fulfillment of the meanings constituted by past events; they also give this system of meanings an unexpected turn, and constitute a suspended and still indeterminate meaning, which induces alertness, expectancy. It is this double relationship of continuation, promotion, carrying forward, and of arrest, deviation, need of supplementation, which defines that focalization of meanings which is consciousness, awareness, perception. Every case of consciousness is dramatic; drama is an enhancement of the conditions of consciousness.

It is impossible to tell what immediate consciousness is—not because there is some mystery in or behind it, but for the same reason that we cannot tell just what sweet or red immediately is: it is something had, not communicated and known. But words, as means of directing action, may evoke a situation in which the thing in question is had in some particularly illuminating way. It seems to me that anyone who installs himself in the midst of the unfolding of drama *has* the experience of consciousness in just this sort of way; in a way which enables him to give significance to descriptive and analytic terms otherwise meaningless. There must be a story, some whole, an integrated series of episodes. This connected whole is mind, as it extends beyond a particular process of consciousness and conditions it. There must also be now-occurring events, to which meanings are assigned in terms of a story taking place. Episodes do not mean what they would mean if occurring in some different story. They have to be perceived in terms of the story, as its forwardings and fulfillings. At the same time, until the play or story is ended, meanings given to events are of a sort which constantly evoke a meaning which was not absolutely anticipated or totally predicted: there is expectancy, but also surprise, novelty. As far as complete and assured prediction is possible, interest in the play lags; it ceases to be an observed drama, it is not subsequently in consciousness.

An oft-told tale repeated without change fails to engage perception; it liberates us for attention to another story where development of meanings is as yet incomplete and indeterminate, possessed of suspense and uncertainty. Thus while perceptions are existentially intermittent and discrete, like a series of signal flashes, or telegraphic clicks, yet they involve a continuum of *meaning* in process of formation.   If we became convinced that a succession of flashes or clicks were not a *series* of terms with respect to one and the same unfolding meaning, we should not attend to them or be aware of them.   If on the other hand, there are no variations to compel suspense, no unforseen movement in a new direction; if there is one unbroken luminosity, or one unbroken monotony of sound, there is no perception, no consciousness.

These considerations enable us to give a formal definition of consciousness in relation to mind or meanings. Consciousness, an idea, is that phase of a system of meanings which at a given time is undergoing re-direction, transitive transformation.   The current idealistic conception of consciousness as a power which modifies events, is an inverted statement of this fact.   To treat consciousness as a power accomplishing the change, is but another instance of the common philosophic fallacy of converting an eventual function into an antecedent force or cause. Consciousness *is* the meaning of events in course of remaking; its "cause" is only the fact that this is one of the ways in which nature goes on.   In a proximate sense of causality, namely as place in a series history, its causation is the need and demand for filling out what is indeterminate.

There is a counterpart realist doctrine, according to which consciousness is like the eye running over a field of ready-made objects, or a light which illuminates now this and now that portion of a given field.   These analogies ignore the indeterminateness of meaning when there is awareness; they fail to consider a basic consideration, namely, that while there exists an antecedent stock of meanings, these are just the ones which we take for granted and use: the ones of which we are not and do not need to be conscious. The theory takes as the normal case of consciousness the case where there is a minimum of doubt and inquiry; the case where objects are most familiar and current, and so to speak vouch directly for themselves. It finds consciousness exemplified in being aware of old and often used things (the articles of furniture which figure in most discussions of consciousness) rather than in case of thinking where reflective inquiry is needed in order to arrive at a meaning. It postulates, even though only implicitly, a pre-established harmony of the knower and things known, passing over the fact that such harmony is always an attained outcome of prior inferences and investigations. It assumes a knowing mind wholly guileless, and extraordinarily competent, whose sole business is to behold and register objects just as what they are, and which is unswervingly devoted to its business.

It is hard to believe that such an amiable and optimistic view of the nature of mind could have obtained currency, had it not been for a theology according to which God is perfect mind and man is created in the image of his maker. Even so, however, it could hardly have persisted when science displaced theology, had not science provided a number of cases which satisfy the requirement of the theory, and thereby given it a kind of empirical content and basis. That is, the development of science does present (a) the rise of cognitional interest to a point of prestige, and (b) it supplies eventually many cases of valid cognitive perceptions. Those who concern themselves with inquiry into the nature of consciousness have a strongly developed intellectual interest; this makes it easy for them to postulate a universal concern in knowing objects as the very essence of mind. These persons have rectitude of cognitive bent, acquired through scientific training; and they with ready benevolence, confer similar rectitude upon perception universally. Then when the existence of error, mistake, dreams, hallucinations, etc. is recognized, these things are treated as deviations and exceptions from the normal, to be accounted for by the introduction of complicating factors.

The problem and its solution thus become essentially dialectical. For empirical facts indicate that not error but truth is the exception, the thing to be accounted for, and that the attainment of truth is the outcome of the development of complex and elaborate methods of searching, methods that while congenial to some men in some respects, in many respects go against the human grain, so that they are adopted only after long discipline in a school of hard knocks. Even to put the matter in terms of proportion of erroneous and true perceptions, is to fail to see the chief objection to the theory. For it postulates the primarily cognitive character of awareness or perception. Empirically, however, the characteristic thing about perceptions in their natural estate, apart from subjection to an art of knowing, is their irrelevance to both truth and error; they exist for the most part in another dimension, whose nature may be suggested by reference to imagination, fancy, reverie, affection, love and hate, desire, happiness and misery. This fact, more than the error-problem, proves the artificial character of the spectator, search-light, notion of consciousness.

Empirical evidence in support of the proposition that consciousness of meanings denotes redirection of meanings (which are always ultimately meanings of events) is supplied by obvious facts of attention and interest on one side, and the working of established and assured habits on the other. The familiar does not consciously appear, save in an unexpected, novel, situation, where the familiar presents itself in a new light and is therefore not wholly familiar. Our deepest-seated habits are precisely those of which we have least awareness. When they operate in a situation to which they are not accustomed, in an unusual situation, a new adjustment is required. Hence there is shock, and an accompanying perception of dissolving and reforming meaning. Attention is most alert and stretched, when, because of unusual situations, there is great concern about the issue, together with suspense as to what it will be. We are engaged at once in taking in what *is* happening and looking ahead to what has not yet happened. As far as we can count upon the contemporary conditions *and* upon their outcome, focalization of meaning is absent. That which is taken to be involved *in any event*, in every issue, *no matter what*, we are not aware of. If we consider the entire field from bright focus through the fore-conscious, the "fringe," to what is dim, sub-conscious "feeling," the focus corresponds to the point of imminent need, of urgency; the "fringe" corresponds to things that just have been reacted to or that will soon require to be looked after, while the remote outlying field corresponds to what does not have to be modified, and which may be dependably counted upon in dealing with imminent need.

Hence the proverbial disparity between things in the scale of consciousness and in the scale of consequences is the most conclusive refutation of subjective idealism. The power of a momentary annoyance or flitting amusement to distract a personage from an enduringly serious question is a familiar theme of comedy; a glass of wine or the whine of a mosquito may exclude issues of life and death. Any trivial thing may swell and swell, if it bothers us. To like effect are the standing complaints of moralists that men sacrifice the great good to the lesser, if the latter be close at hand; and their proclamation that reason and freedom are only found when the near-by and the remote good are weighed with equal balance. Tragedy gives the same testimony. While doom impends the tragic hero fatally pursues his way, unheeding of the web closing in upon him, obvious to all others, and oblivious of what should be done to avert destructive destiny.

The *immediately* precarious, the point of greatest immediate need, defines the apex of consciousness, its intense or focal mode. And this is the point of *re*-direction, of *re*-adaptation, *re*-organization. Hence the aptness of James's comparison of the course of consciousness to a stream, in spite of its intermittent character—a fact empirically recognized in his intimation of its rhythmic waxings and wanings—; of his insistence that only an object, not a concrete consciousness which is had twice, or which remains the same; of his analogy of focus and fringe; of his statement of its movements as a series of perchings and flights, of substantial and transitive phases; for meanings are condensed at the focus of imminent re-direction only to disappear as organization is effected, and yield place to another point of stress and weakness.

Empirical confirmation of this conception of consciousness is found in the extreme instability of every perceived object; the impossibility of excluding rapid and subtle change, except at the cost of inducing hypnotic sleep; the passage from being wide awake, awake, drowsy, dreaming and fast asleep, according as an organism is actively partaking, or abstaining from partaking, in the course of events. All that goes by the name of "relativity" of consciousness is to precisely the same effect, including the Weberian principle; perceived changes are those which require a redirection of adaptive behavior. A prior adaptation constitutes a threshold (better called a platform or plateau); what is consciously noted is alteration of one plateau; re-adjustment to another. Similar events may mean cold at one time or place and warmth at another, depending upon the *direction* of organic re-adaptation. Even a tooth-ache is unstable in consciousness for it is notoriously a matter of throbs, pulsations, palpitations, waxings and wanings of intensity, of organic protests and temporary deviations, and of enforced returns—of flights and perchings. The "tooth-ache" which does not change is not the perceived tooth-ache, but the cognitive *object*, the unperceived tooth to which the sequence of all changes is referred.

Confirmation of the hypothesis is found in the fact that wherever perceptual awareness occurs, there is a "moment" of hesitation; there are scruples, reservations, in complete overt action. It seems quite probable that men of the executive type are those of the least subtle and variegated perceptual field; of the lowest degree of consciousness, having the steepest threshold to be crossed in order to induce a state of awareness. We have to "stop and think," and we do not stop unless there is interference. The flood of action at high tide overrides all but the most considerable obstructions. It flows too forcibly and rapidly in one direction to be checked; without inhibition there are no hesitations, crises, alternatives, need of re-direction. Overt action is an enstatement of established organic-environmental integrations. As long as these *can* maintain themselves, they do so; there is then no opportunity for transforming meaning into idea. In completely integrated function there is no room for distinction between things signifying and things signified. Only when behavior is divided within itself, do some of its factors have a subject-matter which stands for present tendencies and for their requirements or indications and implications, while others factors stand for absent and remote objects which, in unifying and organizing activity, complete the meaning of what is given at hand. The readier a response, the less consciousness, meaning, thinking it permits; division introduces mental confusion, but also, in need for redirection, opportunity for observation, recollection, anticipation.

There is then an empirical truth in the common opposition between theory and practice, between the contemplative, reflective type and the executive type, the "go-getter," the kind that "gets things done." It is, however, a contrast between two modes of practice. One is the pushing, slam-bang, act-first and think-afterwards mode, to which events may yield as they give way to any strong force. The other mode is wary, observant, sensitive to slight hints and intimations; perhaps intriguing, timid in public and ruthless in concealed action; perhaps over-cautious and inhibited, unduly subject to scruples, hesitancies, an ineffective Hamlet in performance; or perhaps achieving a balance between immediately urgent demands and remoter consequences, consistent and cumulative in action. In the latter case, there develops a field of perception, rich in hues and subtle in shades of meaning. In the degree in which this occurs, overt action is subordinated to the contribution it renders to sustaining and developing the scope of the conscious field. One lives on a conscious plane; thought guides activity, and perception is its reward. Action is not suppressed but is moderated. Like the scientific experimenter, one acts not just to act, nor rashly, nor automatically, but with a consciousness of purpose and for the sake of learning. Intellectual hesitations and reservations are used to expand and enrich the field of perception, by means of rendering activity more delicate, and discriminatingly adapted.

The notion that highly thoughtful persons are incompetent in action has its proper corrective in another attitude of belief which is expressed in such words as these: "No one can *make* you see this point; but unless you do see it, you won't change your conduct; if you do get the point you will act differently." The first notion, that thought paralyzes, refers to action in gross, the second relates to change in quality of action. Carry to an extreme the experiences indicated by the first proposition, and the result is the so-called automaton or epiphenomenal theory of consciousness; perception is an idle and superficial attachment to a mechanical play of energies. Carry the experiences involved in the other saying to an extreme, and you have the doctrine of the original creativeness of consciousness; it makes objects what they are.

Empirically the situation stands about like this: The use or intent of instruction, advice, admonition, and honest dialectic is to bring to awareness meanings hitherto unperceived, thereby constituting their ideas. The entanglements, misunderstandings and compromised understandings of life are a sufficient commentary on the difficulties in the way of realizing this intent. But experience demonstrates that as far as it is accomplished, conduct is actually changed; to get a new meaning *is* perforce to be in a new attitude. This does not indicate that consciousness or perception is an entity which *makes* the difference. What follows is that perception or consciousness *is*, literally, the difference in process of *making*. Instruction and reproof that are not an idle flogging of the air involve an art of re-directing activity; given this redirection and there is emergence of change in meanings, or perception. There is here no question of priority or causal sequence; intentional change in direction of events *is* transforming change in the *meaning* of those events. We have at present little or next to no controlled art of securing that redirection of behavior which constitutes adequate perception or consciousness. That is, we have little or no art of education in the fundamentals, namely in the management of the organic attitudes which color the qualities of our conscious objects and acts.

As long as our chief psycho-physical coordinations are formed blindly and in the dark during infancy and early childhood, they are accidental adjustments to the pressure of other persons and of circumstances which act upon us. They do not then take into account the consequence of these activities upon formation of habits and habituations. Hence the connection between consciousness and action is precarious, and its possession a doubtful boon as compared with the efficacy of instinct—or structure—in lower animals. Energy is wasteful and misdirected; in the outcome we effect the opposite of what we intended. Consciousness is desultory and casual. Only when organic activity achieves a conscious plane shall we be adequately aware of what we are about. As long as our own fundamental psycho-physical attitudes in dealing with external things are subconscious, our conscious attention going only to the relations of external things, so long will our perception of the external situations be subject at its root to perversion and vitiation. This state of affairs is the source of that apparent disconnection between consciousness and action which strikes us when we begin to reflect. The connecting links between the two are in our own attitudes; while they remain unperceived, consciousness and behavior must appear to be independent of each other. Hence there will be empirical reason for isolating consciousness from natural events. When so isolated, some persons will assert that consciousness is a slavish and capricious shadow of things and others will proclaim that it is their rightful creator and master. Assertions, like those of this discussion, that consciousness is their recognized meaning when they are undergoing purposeful re-direction by means of organic activity will seem to lack full empirical evidence.

It remains to note and deal with two difficulties that have quite probably troubled the reader. In the first place, the discussion has explicitly gone on the basis that *what* is perceived are meanings, rather than just events or existences. In this respect, the view presented agrees with classic teaching, according to which perception, apprehension, lays hold of form, not of matter. I believe this view properly understood is inherently sound; the error in the classic theory lies in its accompanying assumption that all perceptions are intrinsically cognitive. In the second place, the identification of consciousness with perceptive awareness runs counter to the verbal usage of recent psychology and philosophy which limits perception to apprehension (usually valid) of contemporaneously occurring events in "real" space. The latter issue however is not just a matter of propriety of language—about which it would be absurd to argue. It involves the conviction that perception of real things now existing differs *inherently* from other modes of consciousness, such as emotion, thinking, remembering, fancy and imagination. For this conviction, it must be explicitly noted, is contradicted by the conception which has been stated. According to the latter every mode of awareness—as distinct from "feeling"—in its immediate existence is exactly the same sort of thing, namely a remaking of meanings of events. The difference, it is implied, between awareness of present and "real" things and of absent and unreal is extrinsic, not intrinsic to a consciousness. The sequel will reveal that these two points are intimately connected with each other.

When it is denied that we are conscious of *events* as such it is not meant that we are not aware of *objects*. Objects are precisely what we are aware of. For objects are events *with* meanings; tables, the milky way, chairs, stars, cats, dogs, electrons, ghosts, centaurs, historic epochs and all the infinitely multifarious subject-matter of discourse designable by common nouns, verbs and their qualifiers. So intimate is the connection of meanings with consciousness that there is no great difficulty in resolving "consciousness," as a recent original and ingenious thinker has done, into knots, intersections or complexes of universals.[2]

Serious difficulty sets in however when *events* are resolved into such combinations. The matter is referred to here not to be argued; but to indicate that a "realist" has gone even further than the theory now presented goes in identifying the subject-matter of which there is awareness with meanings, or at least with universals which, as simple subject-matter, colors, sounds, etc., and complex, plants, animals, atoms, etc., are precisely the same as meanings. To cause existences in their particularity to disappear into combinations of universals is at least an extreme measure. And the present thesis sticks to the common-sense belief that universals, relations, meanings, are of and about existences, not their exhaustive ingredients. The same existential events are capable of an infinite number of meanings. Thus an existence identified as "paper," because the meaning uppermost at the moment is "something to be written upon," has as many other explicit meanings as it has important consequences recognized in the various connective interactions into which it enters. Since possibilities of conjunction are endless, and since the consequences of any of them may at some time be significant, its potential meanings are en lless. It signifies something to start a fire with; something like snow; made of wood-pulp; manufactured for profit; property in the legal sense; a definite combination illustrative of certain principles of chemical science; an article the inven-

[2] Holt, The Concept of Consciousness.

tion of which has made a tremendous difference in human history, an l so on indefinitely.   There is no conceivable universe of discourse in which the thing may not figure, having in each its own characteristic meaning.   And if we say that after all it is "paper" which has all these different meanings, we are at bottom but asserting that all the different meanings have a common existential reference, converging to the same event.   We are virtually asserting that the *existence* whose usual, standardized meaning in discourse is paper, also has a multitude of other meanings; we are saying in effect that its existence is not exhausted in its being paper, although paper is its ordinary meaning for human intercourse.

Ghosts, centaurs, tribal gods, Helen of Troy and Ophelia of Denmark are as much the meanings of events as are flesh and blood, horses, Florence Nightingale and Madam Curie.   This statement does not mark a discovery; it enunciates a tautology.   It seems questionable only when its significance is altered; when it is taken to denote that, because they are all meanings of events, they all are the same kind of meaning with respect to validity of reference.   Because perception of a ghost does not signify a subtle, intangible form, filling space as it moves about, it does not follow that it may not signify some other existential happening like disordered nerves; a religious animistic tradition; or, as in the play of Hamlet, that it may not signify an enhancement of the meaning of a moving state of affairs.   The existential events that form a drama have their own characteristic meanings, which are not the less meanings of those events because their import is dramatic, not authentically cognitive.   So when men gather in secret to plot a conspiracy, their plans are not the less meanings of certain events because they have not been already carried out; and they remain meanings of events even if the conspiracy comes to naught.

The proposition that the perception of a horse is objectively valid and that of a centaur fanciful and mythical does not denote that one is a meaning of natural events and the other is not. It denotes that they are meanings referable to *different* natural events, and that confused and harmful consequences result from attributing them to the same events. The idea that the consciousness of a horse as now present and of a centaur differ *as* perceptions, or states of awareness, is an illustration of the harm wrought by introspective psychology, which, here as elsewhere, treats *relationships of objects* as if they were inherent qualities of an immediate subject-matter, ignoring the fact that causal relationships to unperceived things are involved. The matter of the cognitive validity of the horse-perception and the cognitive invalidity of the centaur-perception is not an affair of intrinsic difference in the two perceptions, which inspection of the two states of awareness as such can ever bring to light; it is a causal matter, brought to light as we investigate the causal antecedents and consequents of the events having the meanings.

In other words, the difference between assertion of a perception, belief in it, and merely having it is an extrinsic difference; the belief, assertion, cognitive reference is something additive, never merely immediate. Genuinely to believe the centaur-meaning is to assert that events characterized by it interact in certain ways with other now unperceived events. Since belief that centaur has the same kind of objective meaning as has horse denotes expectation of like efficacies and consequences, the difference of validity between them is extrinsic. It is capable of being revealed only by the results of acting upon them. The awareness of centaur meaning is fanciful not simply because part of its conditions lie within the organism; part of the conditions of *any* perception, valid as well as invalid, scientific as well as esthetic, lie within the organism. Nor is it fanciful, simply because it is supposed not to have adequate existential antecedents. Natural conditions, physiological, physical and social, may be specified in one case as in the other. But since the conditions in the two cases are different, consequences are bound to be different. Knowing, believing, involves something additive and extrinsic to having a meaning.

No knowledge is ever merely immediate. The proposition that the perception of a horse is valid and that a centaur is fanciful or hallucinatory, does not denote that there are two modes of awareness, differing intrinsically from each other. It denotes something with respect to causation, namely, that while both have their adequate antecedent conditions, the specific causal conditions are ascertained to be different in the two cases. Hence it denotes something with respect to consequences, namely, that action upon the respective meanings will bring to light (to apparency or awareness) such different kinds of consequences that we should use the two meanings in very different ways. Both acts and consequences lie outside the primary perceptions; both have to be diligently sought for and tested. Since conditions in the two cases *are* different, they operate differently. That is, they belong to different histories, and the matter of the history to which a given thing belongs is just the matter with which knowledge is concerned. The conscious or perceived affair is itself a consequence of antecedent conditions. But were this conscious or apparent (evident, focal) consequence the *only* consequence of the conditions, if there were not other as yet unapparent consequences, we should have absolutely no way to tell in what sequence of events a perception belongs, and hence absolutely no way of determining its validity or cognitive standing. It is because conditions which generate the perception of a horse have other and different consequences than the perception (and similarly of those which generate the idea of the centaur), that it is possible to make a distinction between the value in knowledge of the two ideas. By discovering the different sequential affairs to which they respectively belong we can differentiate their import for knowledge. Failure to recognize this fact is the ultimate condemnation, it may be remarked in passing, of idealistic theories of knowledge, which identify it with immediate consciousness. If an all-inclusive consciousness were to exist, it would be a piece of esthetic scenery, interesting or tedious as the case might be, but having no conceivable cognitive standing.

That a perception is cognitive means, accordingly, that it is used; it is treated as a sign of conditions that implicate other as yet unperceived consequences in addition to the perception itself. That a perception is *truly* cognitive means that its active use or treatment is followed by consequences which fit appropriately into the other consequences which follow independently of its being perceived. To discover that a perception or an idea is cognitively invalid is to find that the consequences which follow from acting upon it entangle and confuse the other consequences which follow from the causes of the perception, instead of integrating or coördinating harmoniously with them. The special technique of scientific inquiry may be defined as consisting of procedures which make it possible to perceive the eventual agreement or disagreement of the two sets of consequences. For experience proves that it is possible for great disparity between them to exist, and yet the conflict not be perceived or else be explained away as of no importance.

Common-sense has no great occasion to distinguish between bare events and objects; objects being events-with-meanings. Events are present and operative *anyway;* what concerns us is their meanings expressed in expectations, beliefs, inferences, regarding their potentialities. The nearest approach that occurs in ordinary life to making the distinction is when there occurs some brute, dumb shock, which we are constrained to interpret, to assign meaning to, that is, to convert into an object. Such situations supply direct empirical evidence of the difference between events and objects; but common-sense does not need to formulate the difference as a distinction. Events have effects or consequences anyway; and since meaning is awareness of these consequences before they actually occur, reflective inquiry which converts an event into an object is the same thing as finding out a meaning which the event already possesses by imputation. It is the essence of common sense, one might say, to treat potentialities as given actualities; since its interest is universally practical, bent upon fruitage, there is no need to note its bent in any particular case. The eventual outcome is for it the "reality" of the present situation.

But not so with philosophic discourse. Philosophy must explicitly note that the business of reflection is to take events which brutely occur and brutely affect us, to convert them into objects by means of inference as to their probable consequences. These are the meanings imputed to the events under consideration. Otherwise philosophy finds itself in a hopeless impasse. For, apart from making a distinction between events and objects, it has no way of differentiating cognitive from esthetic and literary meanings, and within cognitive meanings it has no way of distinguishing the valid from the invalid. The outcome of failure in this respect is exemplified in those discussions which find an inherent and generic cognitive problem in the occurrence of dreams, reveries and hallucinations, a problem other than the scientific one of ascertaining their antecedents and effects. For if intrinsic cognitive intent is ascribed to all perceptions, or forms of awareness, which are alleged to pick out a "reality" to which they refer as an image or sign, dreams, etc., have to be squared to this assumption. Draw the distinction between events and objects, and dream-objects are just what they are, events with one kind of meaning, while scientific-objects are just what they are, events with another kind of meaning, a kind that involves an extrinsic and additive function not contained in dream-objects.

In formulating the distinction between existences and objects of reference, whether cognitive, esthetic or moral, philosophy does not exact that violent break with common sense which is found in the assertion of idealism that events themselves are composed of meanings. Nor does it involve that break with common sense found in epistemological realism, with its assertion of a direct dealing of mind with naked existences unclothed by the intervention of meanings. Philosophy has only to state, to make explicit, the difference between events which are challenges to thought and events which have met the challenge and hence possess meaning. It has only to note that bare occurrence in the way of having, being, or undergoing is the provocation and invitation to thought—seeking and finding unapparent connections, so that thinking terminates when an object is present: namely, when a challenging event is endowed with stable meanings through relationship to something extrinsic but connected.

There is nothing new in the facts contained in this statement. It was an axiom of the classic theory that form, not matter, is the object of knowledge. And many other theories, in spite of the violence with which they nominally protest against the statement that existences as such are not the objects of knowledge, contain the essential facts, though in an incredible form. It is straining at a gnat and swallowing a camel to balk at the proposition that we mentally are concerned with events in their meanings and not in themselves, and at the same time to welcome the proposition that the immediate objects of all consciousness are sensations and complexes of sensations, termed images or ideas. For if by sensations (or by sensa) is meant not mere shocks in feeling, but something qualitative and capable of objective reference, then sensations are but one class of meanings. They are a class of meanings which embody the mature results of elaborate experimental inquiry in tracing out causal dependencies and relationships. This inquiry depends upon prior possession of a system of meanings, physical theories of light, sound, etc., and of knowledge of nervous structures and functions.

The alleged primacy of sensory meanings is mythical. They are primary only in logical status; they are primary as tests and confirmation of inferences concerning matters of fact, not as historic originals.   For, while it is not usually needful to carry the check or test of theoretical calculations to the point of irreducible sensa, colors, sounds, etc., these sensa form a limit approached in careful analytic certifications, and upon critical occasions it is necessary to touch the limit.   The transformation of these ulterior checking meanings into existential primary data is but another example of domination by interest in results and fruits, plus the fallacy which converts a functional office into an antecedent existence.   Sensa are the class of irreducible meanings which are employed in verifying and correcting other meanings.   We actually set out with much coarser and more inclusive meanings and not till we have met with failure from their use do we even set out to discover those ultimate and harder meanings which are sensory in character.

The theory that awareness is intrinsically possessed of cognitive reference and intent is Protean in the forms it has assumed in the history of thought.   One of these forms, that knowledge is recognition, is worth special attention.   The idea that the act of knowing is always one of recognizing or noting is certain to lead the mind astray; dialectically, it breaks upon the impossibility entailed of instituting an initial act of knowing; it commits its holder to a Platonic prior intuition in the realm of eternity.   It is easy to see, however, how the idea suggested itself and gained credence.   Recognition, identified and distinguished meaning, is an indispensable condition of effective experience.   It is a prerequisite of successful practise; except in so far as the situation in which we are to act is distinguished as having a notable character, behavior is hopelessly at a loss. It is a prerequisite to an act of knowing; for without possession of a recognized meaning, there is nothing to know with; there is no indication of the direction inquiry has to take, or of the universe within which inquiry falls. But, recognition is not cognition. It is what the word implicitly conveys; *re*-cognition; not in the sense that an act of cognizing is repeated, but in the sense that there is a reminder of the meaning in which a former experience terminated, and which may be used as an acceptable tool in further activities.

Most theories of knowing which define a knowledge as an immediate noting seem at bottom to rest upon a confusion of widely differing acts: one that of taking cognizance, which means to pay heed to the apparent in terms of non-apparent consequences; and the other that of being re-minded of something previously known, which is then used in the act of true, inferential, cognition. Recognition is re-instatement of a meaning vouched for in some other situation, plus a sense of familiarity, of immediate greeting of welcome or aversion. It is exemplified in the experience of revisiting the scenes of childhood, with the emotional responses which familiar scenes evoke; it is found in the acknowledgments of the thoroughly practical man, who deferentially notes a character of existence as something which, as a practical man, he must take into account in planning his conduct. Recognition is a nod, either of voluntary piety or of coerced respect, not a knowing.

There is another theory which makes "acquaintance" the primary mode of knowledge, and which treats acquaintance–knowledge as wholly immediate. Acquaintance is empirically distinguished from knowing *about* a thing, and from knowing *that* a thing is thus and so. It is genuinely cognitive. But it has its distinctive features because it involves something more than bare presence of an identified meaning; it involves expectancy which is an extrinsic reference; it involves a judgment as to what the object of acquaintance will do in connection with other events. To be acquainted with a man is at least to "know him by sight" as we truly say; it is to use a meaning conditioned by present vision to form a supposition about something not seen: how the man will behave under other circumstances than those of just being seen. To be *acquainted* with a man is to forecast his general life of conduct; it is to have insight into *character*. And insight, as distinct from sight, means that sight is employed to form inferences regarding what is not seen. It passes beyond apparition of meaning. The difference between acquaintance and "knowing about" or "knowing that" is genuine, but it is not a difference between two kinds of knowledge, one immediate and the other mediate. The difference is an affair of accompaniments, contexts and modes of response. The greater intimacy and directness that marks acquaintance is practical and emotional not logical. To be acquainted with anything is to have the kind of expectancy of its consequences which constitutes an immediate readiness to act, an adequate preparatory adjustment to whatever the thing in question may do. To know *about* it is to have a kind of knowledge which does not pass into direct response until some further term has been supplied. Direct readiness to act involves a sense of community; postponed readiness a sense of aloofness. Where there is acquaintance, there is an immediate emotion of participation in the situations in which the object of acquaintance engages, sympathetic or antipathetic according as readiness takes the form of a disposition to favor or to hinder. Knowledge about a historic or literary figure passes into acquaintance when one arrives at a point of imaginative foresight of his prospective conduct and dramatically shares in it. Knowledge that the earth is round becomes acquaintance when, in some juncture of experience, the meaning comes home to us, as we say, or we get a "realizing sense" of it. Acquaintance, then, instead of being a mode of knowledge prior to knowledge about and knowledge that, marks a later stage in which the latter attain full sense and efficacy.

It follows that theories which identify knowledge with acquaintance, recognition, definition and classification give evidence, all the better for being wholly unintended, that we know not just events but events-with-meanings. To assert that knowledge is classification is to assert in effect that kind, character, has overlaid and over ridden bare occurrence and existence. To say that to know is to define is to recognize that wherever there is knowledge there is explicitly present a universal. To hold that cognition is recognition is to concede that likeness, a relation, rather than existence, is central. And to be acquainted with anything is to be aware what it is *like*, in what *sort* of ways it is likely to behave. These features, character, kind, sort, universal, likeness, fall within the universe of meaning. Hence the theories which make them constitutive of knowledge acknowledge that *having* meanings is a prerequisite for knowing. This prerequisite, being universally required, has loomed so large that thinkers have been led to slur over the concrete differential quality of knowledge—a particular act of *taking*, using, responding to, the meanings involved. That curious piece of traditional "analytic" psychology in accordance with which all knowing is a fusion or association of sensation with images is more testimony in the same direction; "associated imagery" being a round about equivalent of events with meaning.

Finally, the notion that knowledge is contemplation is likewise accounted for. To contemplate is consciously to possess meanings; to behold them with relish; to view them so absorbingly as to revel in them. It is a name for the perception of significant characters, plus an emphatic allusion to an accompanying esthetic emotion. Hypotheses which, like the one advanced in this book and chapter, hold that no knowing takes place without an overt act of taking and employing things on the basis of their meanings, have been attacked as over-devoted to keeping busy; as ignoring the place and charm of contemplation. Well, contemplation assuredly has a place. But when it is ultimate, and is a fruition, knowing has stepped out of the picture; the vision is esthetic. This may be better than knowing; but its being better is no reason for mixing different things and attributing to knowledge characters belonging to an esthetic object. Omit the esthetic phase, the absorbing charm of contemplation, and what remains for a theory of knowledge is that meanings must be had before they can be used as means of bringing to apparition meanings now obscure and hidden.

If I were allowed to call to the witness stand but one historic theory to give testimony to prove that while there is no knowing without perception of meaning, yet that having meanings and rolling them over as sweet morsels under the tongue are not knowing, I should summon the venerable doctrine that knowledge is contemplation.

Another difficulty involved in the theory was mentioned; a difficulty contained in the fact that recent theories have limited the signification of perception. In its older usage, it designated any awareness, any "seeing" whether of objects, ideas, principles, conclusions or whatever. In recent literature it is usually restricted to "sense-perception." There can be no quarrel about the meaning of words except a lexicographical quarrel. The issue at stake concerns then not the appropriate use of a word; it concerns certain matters of fact which are implied or usually associated with the present restricted usage. These implications are two: First, there exists a mode of consciousness or awareness which is original, primitive, simple, and which refers immediately and intrinsically to things in space external to the organism at the time of perception. Secondly, this reference is originally, and *ex proprio motu*, cognitive. Now as against these implications, the theory which has been advanced asserts that awareness in the form of auditory and visual perception is, whenever it is cognitive, just as much a matter of inferential judgment, an instance of a way of taking and using meanings, as is any proposition found in the science of physics.

In its general features, argument as to this point is to the same effect as that of the point just discussed. But we may avoid repetition and introduce greater specification by confining ourselves to the factual traits characteristic of perceptions of present objects in space; showing that these, when they are cognitive, are highly selected and artful instances of awareness, not primitive and innocent. The current theory begins with a distinction between peripherally initiated and centrally initiated awareness. Peripheral initiation is the defining mark of such operations as are designated "perceptions." But awarenesses do not come to us labelled "I am caused by an event initiated on the surface of the body by other bodies"; and "I on the contrary originate in an intra-organic event only indirectly connected with surface-changes." The distinction is one made by analytic and classifying thought. This fact is enough to place in doubt the notion that some modes of consciousness are originally and intrinsically "sense-perception."

Moreover, there is no absolute separation between the skin and the interior of the body. No sooner is the distinction drawn than it has to be qualified. As a matter of fact there is no such *thing* as an *exclusively* peripherally initiated nervous event. Internal conditions, those of hunger, blood-circulation, endocrine functions, persistences of prior activities, pre-existent opened and blocked neuronic connections, together with a multitude of other intra-organic factors enter into the determination of a peripheral occurrence. And after the peripheral excitation has taken place, its subsequent career is not self-determined, but is affected by literally everything going on within the organism. It is pure fiction that a "sensation", or peripheral excitation, or stimulus, travels undisturbed in solitary state in its own coach-and-four to enter the brain or consciousness in its purity. A particular

excitation is but one of an avalanche of contemporaneously occurring excitations, peripheral and from proprio-
ceptors; each has to compete with others, to make terms
with them; what happens is an integration of complex
forces.

It requires therefore a highly technical apparatus of
science to discriminate the exact place and nature of a
peripheral stimulation, and to trace its normal course to
just the junction point where it becomes effective for
redirection of activity and thus capable of perception.
"Peripheral origin" marks an interpretation of events, a
discrimination scientifically valid and important, but no
more an original datum than is the spectrum of Betelgeuse.
The same thesis holds good, of course, of the "consciousness" corresponding to the centrally initiated processes.
To suppose that there are inherently marked off different
forms of awareness corresponding to the distinction
arrived at by technical analysis is as flagrant a case of
hypostatizing as can be found. The theory that certain
kinds or forms of consciousness intrinsically have an
intellectual or cognitive reference to things present in
space is merely the traditional theory that knowledge is an
immediate grasp of Being, clothed in the terminology of
recent physiology. While it is offered as if it were established by physiological and psychological research, in
reality it presents an intellectual hold-over, a notion
picked up from early teachings which have not been
subjected to any critical examination; physiology and
psychology merely afford a vocabulary with which to
deck out an unconscionable survival.

Reference to peripheral stimulation of eye or ear or skin
or nose is, whether of the simpler and popular kind or of

the more complex neurological kind, part of the technique of checking up the particular sort of extrinsic reference which should be given to an idea; discovery whether it is to be referred to a past, contemporary or future thing, or treated as due to wish and emotion. Even so, ascertainment of mode of stimulation and origin is always secondary and derived. We do not believe a thing to be "there" because we are directly cognizant of an external origin for our perception; we infer some external stimulation of our sensory apparatus because we are successfully engaged in motor response. Only when the latter fails, do we turn back and examine the matter of sensory stimulation. To say that I am now conscious of a typewriter as the source of sensory stimuli is to make a back-handed and sophisticated statement of the fact that I am engaged in active employment of the typewriter to produce certain consequences, so that what I am aware of is these consequences and the relation to them of parts of the typewriter as means of producing them. As matter of fact, we *never* perceive the peripheral stimuli to which we are at that given time responding.

The notion that these stimuli are the appropriate and normal objects of simple original perceptions represents, as we have just said, an uncritical acceptance by psychologists of an old logical and metaphysical dogma, one having neither origin nor justification within scientific psychology. We are aware only of stimuli to other responses than those which we are now making; we become aware of them when we analyze some performed total act to discover the mechanism of its occurrence. To become aware of an optical or auditory stimulation involved in an act signifies that we now apprehend that an organic change is part of the means used in the act, so that soundness of its structure and working is requisite to efficient performance of the act. I do not usually, for example, hear the sounds made by the striking of the keys; hence I therefore bang at them or strike them unevenly. If I were better trained or more intelligent in the performance of this action, I should hear the sounds, for they would have ceased to be just stimuli and become means of direction of my behavior in securing consequences. Not having learned by the "touch-method," my awareness of contact-qualities as I hit the keys is intermittent and defective. Physiological stimulation of fingers is involved as a condition of my motor response; yet there is no consciousness of contact "sensations" or sensa. But if I used my sensory touch appreciation as means to the proper execution of the act of writing, I should be aware of these qualities. The wider and freer the employment of means, the larger the field of sensory perceptions.

It is usual in current psychology to assert or assume that qualities observed are those of the stimulus. This assumption puts the cart before the horse; qualities which are observed are those attendant upon response to stimuli. We are *observantly* aware (in distinction from inferentially aware) only of what *has* been done; we can perceive what is already there, what *has* happened. By description, a stimulus is not an object of perception, for stimulus is correlative to response, and is undetermined except as response occurs. I am not questioning as a fact of *knowledge* that certain things *are* the stimuli of visual and auditory perception. I am pointing out that we are aware of the stimuli only in terms of our response to them and of the conse-

quences of this response. Argument as to the impossibility
of stimuli being the object of perception is of course dialectical; like all dialectic arguments it is not convincing if
confronted with facts to the contrary. But facts agree.
The whiteness of the paper upon which words are being
written and the blackness of the letters have been constantly operative stimuli in what I have been doing. It
is equally certain that they have not been constantly
perceived objects. If I have perceived them from time
to time, it is in virtue of prior responses of which they were
consequences, and because of the need of employing these
attained consequences as means in further action. In
the laboratory, as in the painter's studio, colors are specific objects of perception. But as perceived, they are
"stimuli" only proleptically and by a shift in the universe
of discourse.[3] The color now and here perceived, in
consequence of an organic adjustment to other stimuli
than color, is in subsequent situations a stimulus to other
modes of behavior, unconscious in so far as just a stimulus; conscious as far as a deliberately utilized means.

When color is perceived, it is in order to paint, or for
matching colors in selection of dress goods, or in an estimate of the harmonious value of the hue of a wall-paper,
or for determining from a spectral line the nature of a
chemical substance. It signifies that we are responding in
such a way as to form or bring into being a stimulus
adequate to operate without being perceived. But in
the meantime in consciousness it is means to an act which

[3] The shift is evident in the fact that stimuli are stated as vibrations
or electro-magnetic disturbance or in similar fashion; now vibrations
are not observed while color the consequence, the effected coordination,
is in direct consciousness.

will effect desired consequences. Shall this color be used? Will this particular piece of goods or pattern of wall paper serve the purpose in view? When such questions are determined, a final stimulus is achieved. What is then perceived is either some further consequence, or this consequence as a means in a new predicament, such as wearing the goods, hanging the wall-paper. The consciousness of stimuli marks the conclusion of an investigation, not an original datum; and what is discovered is not the stimuli to *that* act, the inquiry, but to some other act, past or prospective, and it marks the conversion of *de facto* stimulus into potential means. The question of stimuli is a question of existential causation; and if Hume's lesson had been learned as well as we flatter ourselves it is learned, we should be aware that any matter of causation refers to something extrinsic, to be reached by inquiry and inference.

We conclude, therefore, that while the word "perception" may be limited to designate awareness of objects contemporaneously affecting the bodily organs, there is no ground whatever for the assumption which has usually attended this narrowing of the older meaning of the word: namely, that sense-perception has *intrinsic* properties or qualities marking it off from other forms of consciousness. Much less is there justification for the assumption that such perceptions are the original form of elementary awareness from which other forms of cognitive consciousness develop. On the contrary sensory-perceptual meanings are specifically discriminated objects of awareness; the discrimination takes place in the course of inquiry into causative conditions and consequences; the ultimate need for the inquiry is found in the necessity of discovering what is to be done, or of developing a response suitably adapted to the requirements of a situation. When inquiry reveals that an object external to the organism is now operative and affecting the organism, the pertinency of overt action is established and the kind of overt adjustment that should be made is in evidence. Perceptual meanings (sensory-perceptual) contrast with other meanings in that either (a) the latter cannot be overtly acted upon *now* or immediately, but only at a deferred time, when specified conditions now absent have been brought into being—conceptual meanings—; or (b) that the latter are such that action upon them at *any* time must be of a dramatic or literary or playful sort—non-cognitive meanings. The necessities of behavior enforce very early in life the difference between acts demanded at once, and those pertinent only at a later time; yet making and refining the distinction is a matter of constant search and discovery, not, as the traditional theory presumes, an original and ready-made affair.

Thus we returned to the statement that apart from considerations of use and history there are no original and inherent differences between valid meanings and meanings occurring in revery, desiring, fearing, remembering, all being *intrinsically* the same in relation to events. This fact contains in gist the condemnation of introspection.[4] It makes no difference in principle whether the introspective doctrine takes a dialectical form, as in the Cartesian-Spinozistic logical realism in which intrinsic

[4] It is not asserted that observations *called* introspection have never given results. It *is* claimed that in such cases, the procedure does not conform to the theoretical definition of immediate inspection but involves the results of inquiries into relationships with things not directly present.

self-evidency, clearness, adequacy, or truth, are imputed to some conceptual meanings or ideas; or whether it takes the more usual form of assigning to things appearing in the field of consciousness intrinsic properties which may be read off by direct inspection and thereby used to denominate them as sensory, perceptual, conceptual, imaginative, fantastic, memory, emotional, volitional, etc.   It is asserted that in every case, the basis of classification is extrinsic, an affair dependent upon a study, often hard to make, of generating conditions and of subsequent careers. The denominations are interpretations, and like all interpretations are adequate only when controlled by wide and accurate information as to bodies of fact that are remote and extraneous.   It is not too much to say that the introspective doctrine—much wider in logical scope than so-called introspective psychology— is the last desperate stand and fortress of the classic doctrine that knowledge is immediate grasp, intuition, envisagement, possession.   It is this fact which constitutes the importance of the views that have been criticized. Until they have been criticized, until the assumption of immediate intrinsic differences in the meaning-objects of sensory perceptions, reveries, dreams, desires, emotions, has been expelled, the actual relation of ideas to existences must remain an obscure and confused matter.

If one looks at the net results of physiological inquiry upon psychologist insight, one seems bound to conclude that while potentially they are enormous, actually they consist largely in making more emphatic and conspicuous the old metaphysical problem of the relation of mind and body, and in strengthening a leaning to the parallelistic hypothesis.   The explanation is that they have not been used for what they really are: an important part of our scientific resources with respect to the intelligent conduct of behavior in general, and the discrimination in particular of various kinds of meanings from one another. It is one thing to employ, for example, the distinction between central and peripheral origin of the existence of this and that idea as part of the technique of determining their respective cognitive validities, and quite another to assume that ideas and conscious contents are already intrinsically marked off in themselves (and therefore for direct observation or introspection), and that the problem is simply to find physiological equivalents for their distinction. As far as it is assumed that modes of consciousness are in themselves already differentiated into sensory, perceptual, conceptual, imaginative, retentive, emotional, conative (or may be so discriminated by direct inspection), physiological study will consist simply of search for the different bodily and neural processes that underlie these differences. The outcome is an exacerbation of the traditional mind-body problem; the doctrine of parallelism, instead of being either a scientific discovery or a scientific postulate, is merely a formulation of the original psychological ready-made distinctions plus a more detailed knowledge of physical existential conditions of their occurrence.

If the problem is put as one of a more adequate control of behavior through knowledge of its mechanism, the situation becomes very different. How should we treat a particular meaning: as sound datum for inference, as an effect of habit irrespective of present condition, as an instance of desire, or a consequence of hope or fear, a token of some past psycho-physical maladjustment, or how? Such questions as these are urgent questions in the conduct of life. They are typical of questions which we must find a way of answering if we are to achieve any method of mastering our own behavior similar to that which we have achieved in respect to heat and electricity, coal and iron. And knowledge of the conditions under which our meanings and our modes of taking and using them organically occur is an indispensable portion of the technique of dealing with such questions. In principle, there is no difference between the neurological inquiry and those astronomical inquiries which enable an astronomer to determine the standing and import of some idea in his universe of discourse. The physiological inquiries no more involve a peculiar problem of mind-body than do the astronomical inquiries. Their subject-matter is part of the objective matter-of-fact considerations which extend and buttress inferential conclusions. In concrete subject-matter, they differ, being concerned with organic structures and processes; but this is *only* a difference in concrete subject-matter, like that between astronomical and botanical. The peculiar importance of the physiological material is that in some form it enters as a factor into the occurrence of every meaning and every act, including the astronomical and botanical.

We return, accordingly, from this excursion to the assertion that the objects of revery-consciousness are just as much cases of perceived meanings or ideas of events as are those of sensory perceptual consciousness. *Only*—they are not as *good* objects with respect to direction of subsequent conduct, including the conduct of knowledge. Revery-consciousness, and the influence upon beliefs of affective wishes of which we are not aware, are facts

Given the connection of meanings with environmental-organic integrations (including those of social intercourse) and there is nothing surprising that consciousness should often be of the revery and wish type. We find no great occasion for wonder in the fact that a person who has been taught that the sun moves around the earth, rising above it at sunrise and going under it at sunset, should himself hold that belief. Well, past consummatory experiences have taught the individual many things; they have taught him what conjunctions are agreeable and what disagreeable. Just as past teaching regarding sun and earth have conditioned subsequent behavior, have produced organic modifications in the way of habit which influence subsequent reactions, including interpretations, so with what was taught by having been implicated in a consummatory union of environment and organism. Here too a bias in organic modification is set up; it acts to perpetuate, wherever possible, awareness of fruitions, and to avert perception of frustrations and inconvenient interruptions.

A consciousness which is set on the outside over against the course of nature, which is not a partaker in its moving changes, would have to conform to one or other of two schemes. In one alternative, the consciousness of such a being would be gifted with an infallible spectatorship conjoined with perfect innocency of impartial recordership; it would see and report the world exactly as if it were itself knowingly engaged in producing what it saw and reported. Or, in the other alternative, all consciousness would be so completely irrelevant to the world of which it is outside and beyond, that there would be no common denominator or common multiple. Obviously facts do not agree with either of these suppositions. We dream, but the material of our dream life is the stuff of our waking life. Revery is not first wholly detached from objects of purposeful action and belief, coming later by discipline to acquire reference to them. Its objects consist of the objects of daily concern subjected to a strange perspective, perverted in behalf of a bias. Such empirical facts as these, or the fact that the world of fancy is the ordinary world as we like it to be, as we find it agreeable, is fatal to any theory which seriously asserts the wholesale irrelevance of the material of consciousness to the things of the actual world. Irrelevance exists, but it is relative and specifiable. An idea or emotion is irrelevant not as such, through and through, but because it is a version of the meaning of events which if it were differently edited would be relevant to actions *in* the world to which it belongs.

To par-take and to per-ceive are allied performances. To perceive is a mode of partaking which occurs only under complex conditions and with its own defining traits. Everything of importance hangs upon what particular one of the many possible ways of partaking is employed in a given situation. The organism, wherever possible, participates *à son gré;* its taste and bias are conditioned, in the degree of its susceptibility and retentiveness, upon prior *satisfactions*. If a man has experienced a world which is good, why should not he act to remake a bad world till it agrees with the good world which he has once possessed? And if the task of overt transformation is too great for his powers, why should he not at least act so as to get the renewed *sense* of a good world? These questions express the working logic of human action; the first, the way of objective transformation, is the method of action in the arts and sciences; the second, of action that is fanciful, "wish-fulfilling," romantic, myth-making.

The immense difference between the two modes of action has had to be learned. There is no original and intrinsic difference in the respective modes of conscious-ness accompanying the two kinds of acts. In some mat-ters, the lesson is readily and quickly learned. Such matters constitute the objects of usual every-day sense-perception, the objects of common-sense. Certain organic-integrations have to occur if life is to continue. Suste-nance must be had; destructive enemies must be kept away; the help of others must be availed of. Meanings and ideas connected with these organic-environmental adjust-ments are substantially sound as far as adjustments are successfully made—and within limits they are ordinarily so made, or life ceases. Such gross ideas as a world of things and persons external to our personal wishes and fancies, and as the continuance of energies once set in motion, are so recurrently and emphatically taught that they are never sincerely doubted. Ideas of specific fea-tures of this external world (external to *us*, since it exacts so much of us in effort before it conforms to the needs that are most deeply ourselves), ideas of fire, food, furni-ture, weather and crops, of our friends and enemies, and of our own past and probable future, are so repeatedly presented in the connections of actions and so confirmed by consequences that they become matters of course, substantially valid. They thus form a kind of privileged domain, which, although an island in a sea of ideas where ground is not readily touched, has been by too hasty and impatient theories taken to form the original and inherent constitution of consciousness. In consequence, there is added to genuine natural realism which accepts the casual connection of ideas with events and their potential reference to subsequent events, a specious realistic theory which takes the island for a solid and complete continent. Characteristic traits of the whole continent of mind are then looked upon as if they were only incidental faults and dislocations, to be explained away by dialectic ingenuity; or when the strata of fancy, illusion, error and misinterpretation are realized, wholesale scepticism is indulged in.

Gradually the technique involved in making ordinary organic-environmental adjustments is discovered, and becomes capable of extension to cases where fancy had previously reigned. A larger and larger field of ideas becomes susceptible of analytic objective reference, with the promise of approximate validity. The secret of this technique lies in control of the *ways* in which the organism participates in the course of events. In the case of simple needs and simple environments, existing organic structures practically enforce correct participation; the result is so-called instinctive action. Within this range, modifications undergone by the organism form in the main effective habits. But organic preparation for varied situation having many factors and wide-reaching consequences is not so easily attained. Effective participation here depends upon the use of extra-organic conditions, which supplement structural agencies; namely, tools and other persons, by means of language spoken and recorded. Thus the ultimate buttress of the soundness of all but the simplest ideas consists in the cumulative objective appliances and arts of the community, not in anything found in "consciousness" itself or within the organism.

If any evidence be needed of the artificial character of strictly epistemological discussion it may be found in the fact that it goes on exclusively in terms of an alleged direct contact of "subject" and "object," with total neglect of all the indispensable tools of checking spontaneous beliefs and developing sound ones in their place. Pendulums, lenses, prisms, yard sticks, and pound weights and multiplication and logarithmic tables have a great deal more to do with valid knowing, since they enable the organism to partake with other things in the effecting of consequences, than have bare consciousness or brain and nerves. Without such objective resources to direct the manner of engaging in responsive adaptations, ideas, outside a simple range of constantly tested actions, are at the mercy of any peculiarity of organic constitution and of circumstance; myths are rife and the world is peopled with fabulous personages and is the home of occult forces. Since organic modifications due to past consummatory objects are dominant, since they lead an individual to find or make a world congenial to them; and since man is most at home with his fellows, whether friends or enemies, the world is then taken animistically for the most part. Too many of the traditional ideas of life, soul, mind, spirit, and consciousness, and of the cosmos itself, even in philosophy, are only attenuated versions of this animism, spontaneous, and often gracious even though fantastic, when men lacked instrumentalities by which to direct their active partakings in nature, but which are now graceless and obstructive.

In conclusion, the fact that consciousness of meanings, or having ideas, denotes an exigent re-making of meanings has an import for the theory of nature. Perceptibility is an exponent of contingency as it intersects the regular. The impossibility of "deducing" consciousness from physical laws, the "impassible gulf" between the physical and mental, are in reality but conspicuous cases of the general impossibility of deriving the contingent from the necessary, the uncertain from the regular. The anomaly apparent in the occurrence of consciousness is evidence of an anomalous phase in nature itself. Unless there were something problematic, undecided, still going-on and as yet unfinished and indeterminate, in nature, there could be no such events as perceptions. The point of maximum apparency is the point of greatest stress and undetermined potentiality; the point of maximum of restless shift, is also the point of greatest brightness; it is vivid, but not clear; imminent, urgently expressive of the impending, but not defined, till it has been disposed of and has ceased to be immediately focal. When philosophers have insisted upon the certainty of the immediately and focally present or "given" and have sought indubitable immediate existential data upon which to build, they have always unwittingly passed from the existential to the dialectical; they have substituted a general character for an immediate this. For the immediately given is always the dubious; it is always a matter for subsequent events to determine, or assign character to. It is a cry for something not given, a request addressed to fortune, with the pathos of a plea or the imperiousness of a command. It were, conceivably, "better" that nature should be finished through and through, a closed mechanical or closed teleological structure, such as philosophic schools have fancied. But in that case the flickering candle of consciousness would go out.

The immediate perceptibility of meanings, the very existence of ideas, testifies to insertion of the problematic and hazardous in the settled and uniform, and to the meeting, crossing and parting of the substantial, static, and the transitive and particular. Meanings, characters as such have that solidity, coherence, endurance, and persistent availability, which our idiom calls substance. Yet were this the whole story, meanings not only would not be perceived, but they would not be meanings. They would be tough operative habits, having their own way not to be denied. Organic movements exist to which there occurred in early life meanings so indurated that now they are habits of an over-riding power; meaning has disappeared in bare behavior. It is possible to understand the regret with which some persons contemplate the passage of thought into act; to them it seems the obsequies of an idea; thought has been dissipated in an outward mechanical sequence. Similarly, one may feel that the important and interesting thing in human history is not what men have done, their successes, but what they failed in doing—the desires and imaginings, forbidden execution by the force of events. Ideas are largely the obverse side of action; a perception of what might be, but is not, the promise of things hoped for, the symbol of things not seen. A fixed idea is no idea at all, but a routine compulsion of overt action, perfunctorily and mechanically named idea.

"Pure reason" would thus not be rational at all, but an automatic habit; a substance so stable and pervading as to have no limits and vicissitudes, and hence no perceptibility. "Pure" reasoning is best carried on by fixed symbols, automatically manipulated; its ideal is something approaching the well-devised mechanically operative calculating machine. Unless nature had regular habits, persistent ways, so compacted that they time, measure and give rhythm and recurrence to transitive flux, meanings, recognizable characters, could not be. But also without an interplay of these patient, slow-moving, not easily stirred systems of action with swift-moving, unstable, unsubstantial events, nature would be a routine unmarked by ideas. Adjustment of the slow moving changes of nature to its sudden starts and trepidations, such as gives some degree of order to the latter and as re-adapts the motions of the sluggish and inert core to the volatile surface of hasty movements, makes necessary a conversion of static orders into stable meanings, while it also renders them perceptible, or ideas, as they answer to the flux of things.

Finally, as psycho-physical qualities testify to the presence in nature of needs and satisfactions, of uneasy efforts and their arrest in some limiting termination, so conscious or conspicuously apparent meanings, ideas, are exponents of the deliberate use of the efficacious in behalf of the fulfilling and consummatory, and of the efficient or instrumental nature of the final. This situation is empirically present to us in the arts, and will be discussed in the immediate sequel. For our immediate purpose, it is enough to point out the difference between the explicit natural teleology of classic metaphysics and the implicit teleology of modern science. In the former, the bare *de facto* arrests of nature, which often mark merely exhaustion or else limits imposed by competing energies, were by a *tour de force* assigned eulogistic properties. They were identified with the objects that should be the objects of choice by persons of mature and reflective experience. Thus physics was unwittingly infected by importation of an uncriticized ethic of customary and fixed ends, and of a dialectically ordered hierarchy of fixed means. The identification in modern thought of ends with ends-in-view, with deliberate purpose and planning, of means with deliberately selected and arranged inventions and artifices, is in effect a recognition that the teleology of nature is achieved and exhibited by nature in thinking, not apart from it. If modern theories have often failed to note this implication and have instead contented themselves with a denial of all teleology, the reason is adventitious; it is found in the gratuitous breach of continuity between nature, life, and man.

"This," whatever *this* may be, always implies a system of meanings focussed at a point of stress, uncertainty, and need of regulation. It sums up history, and at the same time opens a new page; it is record and promise in one; a fulfillment and an opportunity. It is a fruition of what has happened and a transitive agency of what is to happen. It is a comment written by natural events on their own direction and tendency, and a surmise of whither they are leading. Every perception, or awareness, marks a "this," and every "this" being a consummation involves retention, and hence contains the capacity of remembering. Every "this" is transitive, momentarily becoming a "that." In its movement it is, therefore, conditioning of what is to come; it presents the potentiality of foresight and prediction. The union of past and future with the present manifest in every awareness of meanings is a mystery only when consciousness is gratuitously divided from nature, and when nature is denied temporal and historic quality. When consciousness is connected with nature, the mystery becomes a luminous revelation of the operative interpenetration in nature of the efficient and the fulfilling.

CHAPTER NINE

EXPERIENCE, NATURE AND ART

Experience, with the Greeks, signified a store of practical wisdom, a fund of insights useful in conducting the affairs of life. Sensation and perception were its occasion and supplied it with pertinent materials, but did not of themselves constitute it. They generated experience when retention was added and when a common factor in the multitude of felt and perceived cases detached itself so as to become available in judgment and exertion. Thus understood, experience is exemplified in the discrimination and skill of the good carpenter, pilot, physician, captain-at-arms; experience is equivalent to art. Modern theory has quite properly extended the application of the term to cover many things that the Greeks would hardly have called "experience," the bare having of aches and pains, or a play of colors before the eyes. But even those who hold this larger signification would admit, I suppose, that such "experiences" count only when they result in insight, or in an enjoyed perception, and that only thus do they define experience in its honorific sense.

Greek thinkers nevertheless disparaged experience in comparison with something called reason and science. The ground for depreciation was not that usually assigned in modern philosophy; it was not that experience is "subjective." On the contrary, experience was considered to be a genuine expression of cosmic forces, not an exclusive attribute or possession of animal or of human nature. It was taken to be a realization of inferior portions of nature, those infected with chance and change, the less *Being* part of the cosmos. Thus while experience meant art, art reflected the contingencies and partialities of nature, while science—theory—exhibited its necessities and universalities. Art was born of need, lack, deprivation, incompleteness, while science—theory—manifested fullness and totality of Being. Thus the depreciatory view of experience was identical with a conception that placed practical activity below theoretical activity, finding the former dependent, impelled from outside, marked by deficiency of real being, while the latter was independent and free because complete and self-sufficing: that is perfect.

In contrast with this self-consistent position we find a curious mixture in modern thinking. The latter feels under no obligation to present a theory of natural existence that links art with nature; on the contrary, it usually holds that science or knowledge is the only *authentic* expression of nature, in which case art must be an arbitrary addition to nature. But modern thought also combines exaltation of science with eulogistic appreciation of art, especially of fine or creative art. At the same time it retains the substance of the classic disparagement of the practical in contrast with the theoretical, although formulating it in somewhat different language: to the effect that knowledge deals with objective reality as it is in itself, while in what is "practical," objective reality is altered and cognitively distorted by subjective factors of want, emotion and striving. And yet in its encomium of art, it fails to note the commonplace of Greek observation—that the fine arts as well as the industrial technologies are affairs of practice.

This confused plight is partly cause and partly effect of an almost universal confusion of the artistic and the esthetic. On one hand, there is action that deals with materials and energies outside the body, assembling, refining, combining, manipulating them until their new state yields a satisfaction not afforded by their crude condition—a formula that applies to fine and useful art alike. On the other hand, there is the delight that attends vision and hearing, an enhancement of the receptive appreciation and assimilation of objects irrespective of participation in the operations of production. Provided the difference of the two things is recognized, it is no matter whether the words "esthetic" and "artistic" or other terms be used to designate the distinction, for the difference is not one of words but of objects. But in some form the difference must be acknowledged.

The community in which Greek art was produced was small; numerous and complicated intermediaries between production and consumption were lacking; producers had a virtually servile status. Because of the close connection between production and enjoyable fruition, the Greeks in their perceptive uses and enjoyments were never wholly unconscious of the artisan and his work, not even when they personally were exclusively concerned with delightful contemplation. But since the artist was an artisan (the term artist having none of the eulogistic connotations of present usage), and since the artisan occupied an inferior position, the enjoyment of works of any art did not stand upon the same level as enjoyment of those objects for the realization of which manual activity was not needed. Objects of rational thought, of contemplative insight were the only things that met the specification of freedom from need, labor, and matter. They alone were self-sufficient, self-existent, and self-explanatory, and hence enjoyment of *them* was on a higher plane than enjoyment of works of art.

These conceptions were consistent with one another and with the conditions of social life at the time. Nowadays we have a messy conjunction of notions that are consistent neither with one another nor with the tenor of our actual life. Knowledge is still regarded by most thinkers as direct grasp of ultimate reality, although the practice of knowing has been assimilated to the procedure of the useful arts;—involving, that is to say, doing that manipulates and arranges natural energies. Again while science is said to lay hold of reality, yet "art" instead of being assigned a lower rank is equally esteemed and honored. And when within art a distinction is drawn between production and appreciation, the chief honor usually goes to the former on the ground that it is "creative," while taste is relatively possessive and passive, dependent for its material upon the activities of the creative artist.

If Greek philosophy was correct in thinking of knowledge as contemplation rather than as a productive art, and if modern philosophy accepts this conclusion, then the only logical course is relative disparagement of all forms of production, since they are modes of practice which is by conception inferior to contemplation. The artistic is then secondary to the esthetic: "creation," to "taste," and the scientific *worker*—as we significantly say—is subordinate in rank and worth to the dilettante who enjoys the results of his labors. But if modern tendencies are justified in putting art and creation first, then the implications of this position should be avowed and carried through. It would then be seen that science is an art, that art is practice, and that the only distinction worth drawing is not between practice and theory, but between those modes of practice that are not intelligent, not inherently and immediately enjoyable, and those which are full of enjoyed meanings. When this perception dawns, it will be a commonplace that art—the mode of activity that is charged with meanings capable of immediately enjoyed possession—is the complete culmination of nature, and that "science" is properly a handmaiden that conducts natural events to this happy issue. Thus would disappear the separations that trouble present thinking: division of everything into nature *and* experience, of experience into practice *and* theory, art *and* science, of art into useful *and* fine, menial *and* free.

Thus the issue involved in experience as art in its pregnant sense and in art as processes and materials of nature continued by direction into achieved and enjoyed meanings, sums up in itself all the issues which have been previously considered. Thought, intelligence, science is the intentional direction of natural events to meanings capable of immediate possession and enjoyment; this direction—which is operative art—is itself a natural event in which nature otherwise partial and incomplete comes fully to itself; so that objects of conscious experience when reflectively chosen, form the "end" of nature. The doings and sufferings that form experience are, in the degree in which experience is intelligent or charged with meanings, a union of the precarious, novel, irregular with the settled, assured and uniform—a union which also defines the artistic and the esthetic. For wherever there is art the contingent and ongoing no longer work at cross purposes with the formal and recurrent but commingle in harmony. And the distinguishing feature of conscious experience, of what for short is often called "consciousness," is that in it the instrumental and the final, meanings that are signs and clews and meanings that are immediately possessed, suffered and enjoyed, come together in one. And all of these things are preëminently true of art.

First, then, art is solvent union of the generic, recurrent, ordered, established phase of nature with its phase that is incomplete, going on, and hence still uncertain, contingent, novel, particular; or as certain systems of esthetic theory have truly declared, though without empirical basis and import in their words, a union of necessity and freedom, a harmony of the many and one, a reconciliation of sensuous and ideal. Of any artistic act and product it may be said both that it is inevitable in its rightness, that nothing in it can be altered without altering all, and that its occurrence is spontaneous, unexpected, fresh, unpredictable. The presence in art, whether as an act or a product, of proportion, economy, order, symmetry, composition, is such a commonplace that it does not need to be dwelt upon. But equally necessary is unexpected combination, and the consequent revelation of possibilities hitherto unrealized. "Repose in stimulation" characterizes art. Order and proportion when they are the whole story are soon exhausted; economy in itself is a tiresome and restrictive taskmaster. It is artistic when it releases.

The more extensive and repeated are the basic uniformities of nature that give form to art, the "greater" is the art, provided—and it is this proviso that distinguishes art—they are indistinguishably fused with the wonder of the new and the grace of the gratuitous. "Creation" may be asserted vaguely and mystically; but it denotes something genuine and indispensable in art. The merely finished is not fine but ended, done with, and the merely "fresh" is that bumptious impertinence indicated by the slang use of the word. The "magic" of poetry—and pregnant experience has poetical quality—is precisely the revelation of meaning in the old effected by its presentation through the new. It radiates the light that never was on land and sea but that is henceforth an abiding illumination of objects. Music in its immediate occurrence is the most varied and etherial of the arts, but is in its conditions and structure the most mechanical. These things are commonplaces; but until they are commonly employed in their evidential significance for a theory of nature's nature, there is no cause to apologize for their citation.

The limiting terms that define art are routine at one extreme and capricious impulse at the other. It is hardly worth while to oppose science and art sharply to one another, when the deficiencies and troubles of life are so evidently due to separation between art and blind routine and blind impulse. Routine exemplies the uniformities and recurrences of nature, caprice expresses its inchoate initiations and deviations. Each in isolation is unnatural as well as inartistic, for nature is an intersection of spontaneity and necessity, the regular and the novel, the finished and the beginning. It is right to object to much of current practice on the ground that it is routine, just as it is right to object to much of our current enjoyments on the ground that they are spasms of excited escape from the thraldom of enforced work. But to transform a just objection against the quality of much of our practical life into a description and definition of practice is on the same plane as to convert legitimate objection to trivial distraction, senseless amusement, and sensual absorption, into a Puritanical aversion to happiness. The idea that work, productive activity, signifies action carried on for merely extraneous ends, and the idea that happiness signifies surrender of mind to the thrills and excitations of the body are one and the same idea. The first notion marks the separation of activity from meaning, and the second marks the separation of receptivity from meaning. Both separations are inevitable as far as experience fails to be art:—when the regular, repetitious, and the novel, contingent in nature fail to sustain and inform each other in a productive activity possessed of immanent and directly enjoyed meaning.

Thus the theme has insensibly passed over into that of the relation of means and consequence, process and product, the instrumental and consummatory. Any activity that is simultaneously both, rather than in alternation and displacement, is art. Disunion of production and consumption is a common enough occurrence. But emphasis upon this separation in order to exalt the consummatory does not define or interpret either art or experience. It obscures their meaning, resulting in a division of art into useful and fine, adjectives which, when they are prefixed to "art," corrupt and destroy its intrinsic significance. For arts that are merely useful are not arts but routines; and arts that are merely final are not arts but passive amusements and distractions, different from other indulgent dissipations only in dependence upon a certain acquired refinement or "cultivation."

The existence of activities that have no immediate enjoyed intrinsic meaning is undeniable. They include much of our labors in home, factory, laboratory and study. By no stretch of language can they be termed either artistic or esthetic. Yet they exist, and are so coercive that they require some attentive recognition. So we optimistically call them "useful" and let it go at that, thinking that by calling them useful we have somehow justified and explained their occurrence. If we were to ask useful for what? we should be obliged to examine their actual consequences, and when we once honestly and fully faced these consequences we should probably find ground for calling such activities detrimental rather than useful.

We call them useful because we arbitrarily cut short our consideration of consequences. We bring into view simply their efficacy in bringing into existence certain commodities; we do not ask for their effect upon the quality of human life and experience. They are useful to make shoes, houses, motor cars, money, and other things which *may* then be put to use; here inquiry and imagination stop. What they also *make* by way of narrowed, embittered, and crippled life, of congested, hurried, confused and extravagant life, is left in oblivion. But to be useful is to fulfill need. The characteristic human need is for possession and appreciation of the meaning of things, and this need is ignored and unsatisfied in the traditional notion of the useful. We identify utility with the external relationship that some events and acts bear to other things that are their products, and thus leave out the only thing that is essential to the idea of utility, inherent place and bearing in experience. Our classificatory use of the conception of some arts as merely instrumental so as to dispose of a large part of human activity is no solving definition; it rather conveys an immense and urgent problem.

The same statement applies to the conception of merely fine or final arts and works of art. In point of fact, the things designated by the phrase fall under three captions. There are activities and receptivities to which the name of "self-expression" is often applied as a eulogistic qualification, in which one indulges himself by giving free outward exhibition to his own states without reference to the conditions upon which intelligible communication depends—an act also sometimes known as "expression of emotion," which is then set up for definition of all fine art. It is easy to dispose of this art by calling it a product of egotism due to balked activity in other occupations. But this treatment misses a more significant point. For all art is a process of making the world a different place in which to live, and involves a phase of protest and of compensatory response. Such art as there is in these manifestations lies in this factor. It is owing to frustration in communication of meanings that the protest becomes arbitrary and the compensatory response wilfully eccentric.

In addition to this type—and frequently mingled with it—there is experimentation in new modes or craftsmanship, cases where the seemingly bizarre and over-individualistic character of the products is due to discontent with existing technique, and is associated with an attempt to find new modes of language. It is aside from the point either to greet these manifestations as if they constituted art for the first time in human history, or to condemn them as not art because of their violent departures from received canons and methods. Some movement in this direction has always been a condition of growth of new forms, a condition of salvation from that mortal arrest and decay called academic art.

Then there is that which in quantity bulks most largely as fine art: the production of buildings in the name of the art of architecture; of pictures in the name of the art of painting; of novels, dramas, etc., in the name of literary art; a production which in reality is largely a form of commercialized industry in production of a class of commodities that find their sale among well-to-do persons desirous of maintaining a conventionally approved status. As the first two modes carry to disproportionate excess that factor of particularity, contingency and difference which is indispensable in all art, deliberately flaunting avoidance of the repetitions and order of nature; so this mode celebrates the regular and finished. It is reminiscent rather than commemorative of the meanings of experienced things. Its products remind their owner of things pleasant in memory though hard in direct-undergoing, and remind others that their owner has achieved an economic standard which makes possible cultivation and decoration of leisure.

Obviously no one of these classes of activity and product or all of them put together, mark off anything that can be called distinctively fine art. They share their qualities and defects with many other acts and objects. But, fortunately, there may be mixed with any one of them, and, still more fortunately, there may occur without mixture, process and product that are characteristically excellent. This occurs when activity is productive of an object that affords continuously renewed delight.

This condition requires that the object be, with its successive consequences, indefinitely instrumental to *new* satisfying events. For otherwise the object is quickly exhausted and satiety sets in. Anyone, who reflects upon the commonplace that a measure of artistic products is their capacity to attract and retain observation with satisfaction under whatever conditions they are approached, while things of less quality soon lose capacity to hold attention becoming indifferent or repellent upon subsequent approach, has a sure demonstration that a genuinely esthetic object is not exclusively consummatory but is causally productive as well. A consummatory object that is not also instrumental turns in time to the dust and ashes of boredom. The "eternal" quality of great art is its renewed instrumentality for further consummatory experiences.

When this fact is noted, it is also seen that limitation of fineness of art to paintings, statues, poems, songs and symphonies is conventional, or even verbal. Any activity that is productive of objects whose perception is an immediate good, and whose operation is a continual source of enjoyable perception of other events exhibits fineness of art. There are acts of all kinds that directly refresh and enlarge the spirit and that are instrumental to the production of new objects and dispositions which are in turn productive of further refinements and replenishments. Frequently moralists make the acts *they* find excellent or virtuous wholly final, and treat art and affection as mere means. Estheticians reverse the performance, and see in good *acts* means to an ulterior external happiness, while esthetic appreciation is called a good in itself, or that strange thing an end in itself. But on

both sides it is true that in being preëminently fructify-
ing the things designated means are immediate satisfactions. They are their own excuses for being just
because they are charged with an office in quickening
apprehension, enlarging the horizon of vision, refining
discrimination, creating standards of appreciation which
are confirmed and deepened by further experiences. It
would almost seem when their non-instrumental character
is insisted upon as if what was meant were an indefinitely
expansive and radiating instrumental efficacy.

The source of the error lies in the habit of calling by the
name of means things that are not means at all; things
that are only external and accidental antecedents of the
happening of something else. Similarly things are
called ends that are not ends save accidentally, since they
are not fulfilments, consummatory, of means, but merely
last terms closing a process. Thus it is often said that a
laborer's toil is the means of his livelihood, although except
in the most tenuous and arbitrary way it bears no relationship to his real living. Even his wage is hardly an end or
consequence of his labor. He might—and frequently
does—equally well or ill—perform any one of a hundred
other tasks as a condition of receiving payment. The
prevailing conception of instrumentality is profoundly
vitiated by the habit of applying it to cases like the above,
where, instead of an operation of means, there is an enforced necessity of doing one thing as a coerced antecedent of the occurrence of another thing which is wanted.

Means are always at least causal conditions; but causal
conditions are means only when they possess an added
qualification; that, namely, of being freely used, because
of perceived connection with chosen consequences. To

entertain, choose and accomplish anything as an end or consequence is to be committed to a like love and care for whatever events and acts are its means. Similarly, consequences, ends, are at least effects; but effects are not ends unless thought has perceived and freely chosen the conditions and processes that are their conditions. The notion that means are menial, instrumentalities servile, is more than a degradation of means to the rank of coercive and external necessities. It renders all things upon which the name of end is bestowed accompaniments of privilege, while the name of utility becomes an apologetic justification for things that are not portions of a good and reasonable life. Livelihood is at present not so much the consequence of a wage-earner's labor as it is the effect of other causes forming the economic régime, labor being merely an accidental appendage of these other causes.

Paints and skill in manipulative arrangement are means of a picture as end, because the picture is *their* assemblage and organization. Tones and susceptibility of the ear when properly interacting are the means of music, because they constitute, make, are, music. A disposition of virtue is a means to a certain quality of happiness because it is a constituent of that good, while such happiness is means in turn to virtue, as the sustaining of good in being. Flour, water, yeast are means of bread because they are ingredients of bread; while bread is a factor *in* life, not just *to* it. A good political constitution, honest police-system, and competent judiciary, are means of the prosperous life of the community because they are integrated portions of that life. Science is an instrumentality of and for art because it is the intelligent factor *in* art. The trite saying that a hand is not a hand except as an organ of the living body—except as a working coördinated part of a balanced system of activities—applies untritely to all things that are means. The connection of means-consequences is never one of bare succession in time, such that the element that is means is past and gone when the end is instituted. An active process is strung out temporarily, but there is a deposit at each stage and point entering cumulatively and constitutively into the outcome. A genuine instrumentality *for* is always an organ *of* an end. It confers continued efficacy upon the object in which it is embodied.

The traditional separation between some things as mere means and others as mere ends is a reflection of the insulated existence of working and leisure classes, of production that is not also consummatory, and consummation that is not productive. This division is not a *merely* social phenomenon. It embodies a perpetuation upon the human plane of a division between need and satisfaction belonging to brute life. And this separation expresses in turn the mechanically external relationship that exists in nature between situations of disturbed equilibrium, of stress, and strain, and achieved equilibrium. For in nature, outside of man, except when events eventuate in "development" or "evolution" (in which a cumulative carrying forward of consequences of past histories in new efficiencies occurs) antecedent events are external transitive conditions of the occurrence of an event having immediate and static qualities. To animals to whom acts have no meaning, the change in the environment required to satisfy needs has no significance on its own account; such change is a mere incident of ego-centric satisfactions. This physically external relationship of antecedents and consequents is perpetuated; it continues to hold true of human industry wherever labor 'and its materials and products are externally enforced necessities for securing a living.   Because Greek industry was so largely upon this plane of servile labor, all industrial activity was regarded by Greek thought as a *mere* means, an extraneous necessity.   Hence satisfactions due to it were conceived to be the ends or goods of purely animal nature in isolation.   With respect to a truly human and rational life, they were not ends or goods at all, but merely "means," that is to say, external conditions that were antecedently enforced requisites of the life conducted and enjoyed by free men, especially by those devoted to the acme of freedom, pure thinking.   As Aristotle asserted, drawing a just conclusion from the assumed premises, there are classes of men who are necessary materials of society but who are not integral parts of it.   And he summed up the whole theory of the external and coerced relationship of means and ends when he said in this very connection that: "When there is one thing that is means and another thing that is end, there is *nothing common* between them, except in so far as the one, the means, produces, and the other, the end, receives the product."

It would thus seem almost self-evident that the distinction between the instrumental and the final adopted in philosophic tradition as a solving word presents in truth a problem, a problem so deep-seated and far-reaching that it may be said to be *the* problem of experience.   For all the intelligent activities of men, no matter whether expressed in science, fine arts, or social relationships, have for their task the conversion of causal bonds, relations of succession, into a connection of means-consequence, into

meanings. When the task is achieved the result is art:
and in art everything is common between means and ends.
Whenever so-called means remain external and servile,
and so-called ends are enjoyed objects whose further
causative status is unperceived, ignored or denied, the
situation is proof positive of limitations of art. Such a
situation consists of affairs in which the problem has *not*
been solved; namely that of converting physical and brute
relationships into connections of meanings characteristic
of the possibilities of nature.

It goes without saying that man begins as a part of
physical and animal nature. In as far as he reacts to
physical things on a strictly physical level, he is pulled
and pushed about, overwhelmed, broken to pieces, lifted on
the crest of the wave of things, like anything else. His
contacts, his sufferings and doings, are matters of direct
interaction only. He is in a "state of nature." As an
animal, even upon the brute level, he manages to subordinate some physical things to his needs, converting them
into materials sustaining life and growth. But in so far
things that serve as material of satisfaction and the acts
that procure and utilize them are not objects, or things-
with-meanings. That appetite as such is blind, is notorious; it may push us into a comfortable result instead of
into disaster; but we are pushed just the same. When
appetite is perceived in its meanings, in the consequences
it induces, and these consequences are experimented
with in reflective imagination, some being seen to be consistent with one another, and hence capable of co-exist-
ence and of serially ordered achievement, others being
incompatible, forbidding conjunction at one time, and
getting in one another's way serially—when this estate

is attained, we live on the human plane, responding to things in their meanings. A relationship of cause-effect has been transformed into one of means-consequence. Then consequences belong *integrally* to the conditions which may produce them, and the latter possess character and distinction. The meaning of causal conditions is carried over also into the consequence, so that the latter is no longer a mere end, a last and closing term of arrest. It is marked out in perception, distinguished by the efficacy of the conditions which have entered into it. Its value as fulfilling and consummatory is measurable by subsequent fulfillments and frustrations to which it is contributory in virtue of the causal means which compose it.

Thus to be conscious of meanings or to have an idea, marks a fruition, an enjoyed or suffered arrest of the flux of events. But there are all kinds of ways of perceiving meanings, all kinds of ideas. Meaning may be determined in terms of consequences hastily snatched at and torn loose from their connections; then is prevented the formation of wider and more enduring ideas. Or, we may be aware of meanings, may achieve ideas, that unite wide and enduring scope with richness of distinctions. The latter sort of consciousness is more than a passing and superficial consummation or end: it takes up into itself meanings covering stretches of existence wrought into consistency. It marks the conclusion of long continued endeavor; of patient and indefatigable search and test. The idea is, in short, art and a work of art. As a work of art, it directly liberates subsequent action and makes it more fruitful in a creation of more meanings and more perceptions.

It is the part of wisdom to recognize how sparse and insecure are such accomplishments in comparison with experience in which physical and animal nature largely have their way.   Our liberal and rich ideas, our adequate appreciations, due to productive art are hemmed in by an unconquered domain in which we are everywhere exposed to the incidence of unknown forces and hurried fatally to unforeseen consequences.   Here indeed we live servilely, menially, mechanically; and we so live as much when forces blindly lead to us ends that are liked as when we are caught in conditions and ends against which we blindly rebel.   To call satisfactions which happen in this blind way "ends" in a eulogistic sense, as did classic thought, is to proclaim in effect our servile submission to accident.   We may indeed enjoy the goods the gods of fortune send us, but we should recognize them for what they are, not asserting them to be good and righteous *altogether*.   For, since they have not been achieved by any art involving deliberate selection and arrangement of forces, we do not know with what they are charged.   It is an old true tale that the god of fortune is capricious, and delights to destroy his darlings after having made them drunk with prosperity.   The goods of art are not the less good in their goodness than the gifts of nature; while in addition they are such as to bring with themselves open-eyed confidence.   They are fruits of means consciously employed; fulfillments whose further consequences are secured by conscious control of the causal conditions which enter into them.   Art is the sole alternative to luck; and divorce from each other of the meaning and value of instrumentalities and ends is the essence of luck. The esoteric character of culture and the supernatural quality of religion are both expressions of the divorce.

The modern mind has formally abjured belief in natural teleology because it found Greek and medieval teleology juvenile and superstitious.   Yet facts have a way of compelling recognition of themselves.   There is little scientific writing which does not introduce at some point or other the idea of tendency.   The idea of tendency unites in itself exclusion of prior design and inclusion of movement in a particular direction, a direction that may be either furthered or counteracted and frustrated, but which is intrinsic.   Direction involves a limiting position, a point or goal of culminating stoppage, as well as an initial starting point.   To assert a tendency and to be fore-conscious of a possible terminus of movement are two names of the same fact.   Such a consciousness may be fatalistic; a sense of inevitable march toward impending doom.   But it may also contain a perception of meanings such as flexibly directs a forward movement.   The end is then an end-in-view and is in constant and cumulative reënactment at each stage of forward movement. It is no longer a terminal point, external to the conditions that have led up to it; it is the continually developing meaning of present tendencies—the very things which as directed we call "means."   The process is art and its product, no matter at what stage it be taken, is a work of art.

To a person building a house, the end-in-view is not just a remote and final goal to be hit upon after a sufficiently great number of coerced motions have been duly performed.   The end-in-view is a plan which is *contemporaneously* operative in selecting and arranging materials. The latter, brick, stone, wood and mortar, are means only as the end-in-view is actually incarnate in them, in form-

ing them. Literally, they *are* the end in its present stage
of realization. The end-in-view is present at each stage
of the process; it is present as the *meaning* of the materials
used and acts done; without its informing presence, the
latter are in no sense "means;" they are merely extrinsic
causal conditions. The statement is generic; it applies
equally at every stage. The house itself, when building
is complete, is "end" in no exclusive sense. It marks the
conclusion of the organization of certain materials and
events into effective means; but these material and events
still exist in causal interaction with other things. New
consequences are foreseen; new purposes, ends-in-view, are
entertained; they are embodied in the coördination of the
thing built, now reduced to material, although significant
material, along with other materials, and thus transmuted
into means. The case is still clearer, when instead of
considering a process subject to as many rigid external
conditions as is the building of a house, we take for illustration a flexibly and freely moving process, such as painting a picture or thinking out a scientific process, when
these operations are carried on artistically. Every process
of free art proves that the difference between means and
end is analytic, formal, not material and chronologic.

What has been said enables us to re-define the distinction drawn between the artistic, as objectively productive,
and the esthetic. Both involve a perception of meanings
in which the instrumental and the consummatory peculiarly intersect. In esthetic perceptions an object inter-
penetrated with meanings is given; it may be taken for
granted; it invites and awaits the act of appropriative
enjoyment. In the esthetic object tendencies are sensed
as brought to fruition; in it is embodied a means-consequence

relationship, as the past work of his hands was surveyed by the Lord and pronounced good. This good differs from those gratifications to which the name sensual rather than sensuous is given, since the former are pleasing endings that occur in ways not informed with the meaning of materials and acts integrated into them. In appreciative possession, perception goes out to tendencies which *have* been brought to happy fruition in such a way as to release and arouse.

Artistic sense on the other hand grasps tendencies as possibilities; the invitation of these possibilities to perception is more urgent and compelling than that of the given already achieved. While the means-consequence relationship is directly sensed, felt, in both appreciation and artistic production, in the former the scale descends upon the side of the attained; in the latter there predominates the invitation of an existent consummation to bring into existence further perceptions. Art in being, the active productive process, may thus be defined as an esthetic perception together with an *operative* perception of the efficiencies of the esthetic object. In many persons with respect to most kinds of enjoyed perceptions, the sense of possibilities, the arousal or excitation attendant upon appreciation of poetry, music, painting, architecture or landscape remains diffuse and inchoate; it takes effect only in direct and undefined channels. The enjoyed perception of a visual scene is in any case a function of that scene in its total connections, but it does not link up adequately. In some happily constituted persons, this effect is adequately coördinated with other endowments and habits; it becomes an integral part of craft, taking effect in the creation of a new object of appreciation. The integration is, however, progressive and experimental, not momentarily accomplished. Thus every creative effort is temporal, subject to risk and deflection. In that sense the difference between the diffuse and postponed change of action due in an ordinary person to release of energies by an esthetic object, and the special and axial direction of subsequent action in a gifted person is, after all, a matter of degree.

Without a sense of moving tendencies which are operative in conjunction with a state of fruition, there is appetitive gratification, but nothing that may be termed appreciation. Sense of moving tendencies supplies thrill, stimulation, excitation; sense of completion, consummation, affords composure, form, measure, composition. Emphasize the latter, and appreciation is of the classic type. This type fits conditions where production is professionalized among technical craftsmen, as among the Greeks; it is adapted to a contemplative enjoyment of the achievements of past ages or remote places, where conditions forbid urge to emulation or productive activity of a similar kind. Any work of art that persistently retains its power to generate enjoyed perception or appreciation becomes in time classic.

In so-called romantic art, the sense of tendencies operative beyond the limits of consummation is in excess; a lively sense of unrealized potentialities attaches to the object; but it is employed to enhance immediate appreciation, not to promote further productive achievement. Whatever is peculiarly romantic excites a feeling that the possibilities suggested go beyond not merely actual present realization, but are beyond effective attainment in any experience. In so far intentionally romantic art is

wilful, and in so far not art.   Excited and uneasy perceptual enjoyment is made ultimate, and the work of art is
accommodated to production of these feelings.   The sense
of unachieved possibilities is employed as a compensatory
equivalent for endeavor in achievement.   Thus when
the romantic spirit invades philosophy the possibilities
present in imaginative sentiment are declared to be the
real, although "transcendental," substance of Being itself.
In complete art, appreciation follows the object and
moves with it to its completion; romanticism reverses the
process and degrades the object to an occasion for arousing a predetermined type of appreciation.   In classicism,
objective achievement is primary, and appreciation not
only conforms to the object, but the object is employed to
compose sentiment and give it distinction.   Its vice,
as an 'ism, is that it turns the mind to what is given;
the given is taken as if it were eternal and wholly separate
from generation and movement.   Art free from subjection to any "ism" has movement, creation, as well as
order, finality.

To institute a difference of *kind* between useful and fine
arts is, therefore, absurd, since art involves a peculiar
interpenetration of means and ends.   Many things are
termed useful for reasons of social status, implying dep-
recation and contempt.   Things are sometimes said to
belong to the menial arts merely because they are cheap
and used familiarly by common people.   These things
of daily use for ordinary ends may survive in later periods,
or be transported to another culture, as from Japan and
China to America, and being rare and sought by con-
noisseurs, rank forthwith as works of fine art.   Other
things may be called fine because their manner of use is

decorative or socially ostentatious. It is tempting to make a distinction of degree and say that a thing belongs to the sphere of use when perception of its meaning is incidental to something else; and that a thing belongs to fine art when its other uses are subordinate to its use in perception. The distinction has a rough practical value, but cannot be pressed too far. For in production of a painting or a poem, as well as in making a vase or a temple, a perception is also employed as means for something beyond itself. Moreover, the perception of urns, pots and pans as commodities may be intrinsically enjoyable, although these things are primarily perceived with reference to some use to which they are put. The only *basic* distinction is that between bad art and good art, and this distinction, between things that meet the requirements of art and those that do not, applies equally to things of use and of beauty. Capacity to offer to perception meaning in which fruition and efficacy interpenetrate is met by different products in various degrees of fulness; it may be missed altogether by pans and poems alike. The difference between the ugliness of a mechanically conceived and executed utensil and of a meretricious and pretentious painting is one only of content or material; in form, both are articles, and bad articles.

Thinking is pre-eminently an art; knowledge and propositions which are the products of thinking, are works of art, as much so as statuary and symphonies. Every successive stage of thinking is a conclusion in which the meaning of what has produced it is condensed; and it is no sooner stated than it is a light radiating to other things —unless it be a fog which obscures them. The antecedents of a conclusion are as causal and existential as those of a building.   They are not logical or dialectical, or an affair of ideas.   While a conclusion follows from antecedents, it does not follow from "premises," in the strict, formal sense.   Premises are the analysis of a conclusion into its logically justifying grounds; there are no premises till there is a conclusion.   Conclusion and premise are reached by a procedure comparable to the use of boards and nails in making a box; or of paint and canvas in making a picture.   If defective materials are employed or if they are put together carelessly and awkwardly, the result is defective.   In some cases the result is called unworthy, in others, ugly; in others, inept; in others, wasteful, inefficient, and in still others untrue, false.   But in each case, the condemnatory adjective refers to the resulting work judged in the light of its method of production.   Scientific method or the art of constructing true perceptions is ascertained in the course of experience to occupy a privileged position in undertaking other arts.   But this unique position only places it the more securely as an art; it does not set its product, knowledge, apart from other works of art.

The existential origin of valid cognitive perceptions is sometimes recognized in form and denied in substance; the name "psychological" is given to the events which generate valid beliefs.   Then a sharp distinction is made between genesis as psychological and validity as logical. Of course lexicographic names are of no special moment; if any one wishes to call the efficient causes of knowledge and truth psychological, he is entitled to do so—provided the actual traits of these causative events are recognized. Such a recognition will note however that psychological does not mean psychic, or refer to events going on exclusively within the head or "subcutaneously." To become aware of an object cognitively as distinct from esthetically, involves external physical movements and external physical appliances physically manipulated. Some of these active changes result in unsound and defective perceptions; some have been ascertained to result usually in valid perceptions. The difference is precisely that which takes place when the art of architecture or sculpture is skilfully conducted or is carried on carelessly, and without adequate appliances. Sometimes the operations productive of tested beliefs are called "inductive;" with an implication in the naming, of discrediting them, as compared with deductive functions, which are assigned a superior exclusive status. Of deduction, when thus defined, the following assertions may be made. First, it has nothing to do with truth about any matter of existence. Secondly, it is not even concerned with consistency or correctness, save in a formal sense whose opposite (as has been previously pointed out) is not inconsistency but nonsense. Thirdly, the meanings which figure in it are the conclusions of prior inquiries which are "inductive," that is, are products of an experimental art of changing external things by appropriate external movements and appliances.

Deduction as it actually occurs in science is *not* deduction as deduction should be according to a common definition. Deduction deals directly with meanings in their relations to one another, rather than with meanings directly referred to existence. But these meanings are what they are in themselves and are related to one another by means of acts of taking and manipulating— an art of discourse. They possess intellectual import and enter fruitfully into scientific method only because they are selected, employed, separated and combined by acts extraneous to them, acts which are as existential and causative as those concerned in the experimental use of apparatus and other physical things.   The *act* of knowing, whether solicitous about inference or about demonstration, is always inductive.   There is only one mode of thinking, the inductive, when thinking denotes anything that actually happens.   The notion that there is another kind called deduction is another evidence of the prevalent tendency in philosophy to treat functions as antecedent operations, and to take essential meanings *of* existence as if they were a kind of Being.   As a concrete operation, deduction is generative, not sterile; but as a concrete operation, it contains an extraneous act of taking and using which is selective, experimental and checked constantly by consequences.

Knowledge or science, as a work of art, like any other work of art, confers upon things traits and potentialities which did not *previously* belong to them.   Objection from the side of alleged realism to this statement springs from a confusion of tenses.   Knowledge is not a distortion or perversion which confers upon *its* subject-matter traits which *do* not belong to it, but is an act which confers upon non-cognitive material traits which *did* not belong to it.   It marks a change by which physical events exhibiting properties of mechanical energy, connected by relations of push and pull, hitting, rebounding, splitting and consolidating, realize characters, meanings and relations of meanings *hitherto* not possessed by them. Architecture does not add to stone and wood something which does not belong to them, but it does add to them properties and efficacies which they did not possess in their earlier state. It adds them by means of engaging them in new modes of interaction, having a new order of consequences. Neither engineering nor fine art limits itself to imitative reproduction or copying of antecedent conditions. Their products may nevertheless be more effectively natural, more "life like," than were antecedent states of natural existence. So it is with the art of knowing and its works.

The failure to recognize that knowledge is a product of art accounts for an otherwise inexplicable fact: that science lies today like an incubus upon such a wide area of beliefs and aspirations. To remove the deadweight, however, recognition that it is an art will have to be more than a theoretical avowal that science is made by man for man, although such recognition is probably an initial preliminary step. But the real source of the difficulty is that the art of knowing is limited to such a narrow area. Like everything precious and scarce, it has been artificially protected; and through this very protection it has been dehumanized and appropriated by a class. As costly jewels of jade and pearl belong only to a few, so with the jewels of science. The philosophic theories which have set science on an altar in a temple remote from the arts of life, to be approached only with peculiar rites, are a part of the technique of retaining a secluded monopoly of belief and intellectual authority. Till the art of achieving adequate and liberal perceptions of the meanings of events is incarnate in education, morals and industry, science will remain a special luxury for a few; for the mass, it will consist of a remote and abstruse body of curious propositions having little to do with life, except where it lays the heavy hand of law upon spontaneity, and invokes necessity and mechanism to witness against generous and free aspiration.

Every error is attended with a contrary and compensatory error, for otherwise it would soon be self-revealing. The conception that causes are metaphysically superior to effects is compensated for by the conception that ends are superior esthetically and morally to means. The two beliefs can be maintained together only by removing "ends" out of the region of the causal and efficacious. This is accomplished nowadays by first calling ends intrinsic values, and then by making a gulf between value and existence. The consequence is that science, dealing as it must, with existence, becomes brutal and mechanical, while criticism of values, whether moral or esthetic, becomes pedantic or effeminate, expressing either personal likes and dislikes, or building up a cumbrous array of rules and authorities. The thing that is needful, discriminating judgment by methods whose consequences improve the art, easily slips through such coarse meshes, and by far the greater part of life goes on in a darkness unillumined by thoughtful inquiry. As long as such a state of thing persists, the argument of this chapter that science is art—like many other propositions of this book—is largely prophetic, or more or less dialectical. When an art of thinking as appropriate to human and social affairs has grown up as that used in dealing with distant stars, it will not be necessary to argue that science is one among the arts and among the works of art. It will be enough to point to observable situations. The separation of science from art, and the division of arts into those concerned with mere means and those concerned with ends in themselves, is a mask for lack of conjunction between power and the goods of life. It will lose plausibility in the degree in which foresight of good informs the display of power.

Evidence of the interpenetration of the efficacious with the final in art is found in the slow emancipation of art from magical rite and cult, and the emergence of science from superstition. For magic and superstition could never have dominated human culture, nor poetry have been treated as insight into natural causes, if means and ends were empirically marked off from each other. The intimacy of their union in one and the same object is that which makes it easy to impute to whatever is consummatory a kind of efficacy which it does not possess. Whatever is final is important; to say this is to enunciate a truism. Lack of instrumentalities and of skill by which to analyze and follow the particular efficacies of the immediately enjoyed object lead to imputation to it of wholesale efficacy in the degree of its importance. To the short-cut pragmatism congenial to natural man, importance measures "reality" and reality in turn defines efficacious power. Loyalties evoked in the passionate citizen by sight of the flag or in the devout Christian by the cross are attributed directly to the intrinsic nature of these objects. Their share in a consummatory experience is translated into a mysterious inner sacred power, an indwelling efficacy. Thus a souvenir of the beloved one, arousing in the lover enjoyment similar to that awakened by the precious one to whom it belonged, possesses delightful, exciting, and consoling efficacies. No matter what things are directly implicated in a consummatory situation, they gain potencies for weal or woe similar to the good or evil which directly marks the situation. Obviously error here resides in the gross and un-discriminating way in which power is attributed; inquiry to reveal the specified elements which form the sequential order is lacking.

It is a commonplace of anthropologists that for the most part clothing originated in situations of unusual awe or prestigious display, rather than as a utility or pro-tection. It was part of a consummatory object, rather than a means to specified consequences. Like the robes of priests, clothes were vestments, and investiture was believed to convey directly to the one ceremonially garbed dread potency or fascinating charm. Clothes were worn to confer authority; a man did not lend his significance to them. Similarly, a victorious hunter and warrior celebrated a triumphant return to camp by affix-ing to his person in conspicuous fashion claws and teeth of the wild beast or enemy that his prowess had subju-gated. These signal proofs of power were integral por-tions of the object of admiration, loyalty and reverence. Thus the trophy became an emblem, and the emblem was endowed with mystic force. From a sign of glory it became a cause of glorification, and even when worn by another aroused the acclaim due to a hero. In time such trophies became the documented seal of prestigious authority. They had an intrinsic causal potency of their own. Legal history is full of like instances. Acts origin-ally performed in connection with, say, the exchange of property, performed as part of the dramatic ceremony of taking possession of land, were not treated as mere evi-dences of title, but as having a mystic power to confer title.

Later, when such things lose their original power and become "mere matters of form," they may still be essen-

tial to the legal force of a transaction, as seals have had to
be affixed to a contract to give it force, even though there
was no longer sense or reason in their use.   Things which
have an efficacy imputed to them simply because they
have shared in some eminent consummatory experience
are symbols.   They are called symbols, however, only
afterwards and from without.   To the devout in politics
and religion they are other than symbols; they are articles possessed of occult potency.   To one man, two
crossed lines are an indication of an arithmetical operation to be performed; to another, they are evidence of the
existence of Christianity as a historic fact, as a crescent
is a reminder of the existence of Islam.   But to another,
a cross is more than a poignant reminder of a tragically
significant death; it has intrinsic sacred power to protect
and to bless.   Since a flag stirs passionate loyalty to
sudden and pervasive ebullition, the flag must have
properties and potencies not possessed by other and
differently configured pieces of cloth; it must be handled
with reverence; it is the natural object of ceremonial
adoration.

   Phenomena like these when manifested in primitive
culture are often interpreted as if they were attempts at a
causal explanation of natural occurrences; magic is said
to be science gone wrong.   In reality, they are facts of
direct emotional and practical response; beliefs, ideas,
interpretations, only come later when responses not being
direct and inevitably appropriate seem to demand
explanation.   As immediate responses they exemplify
the fact that anything involved, no matter how incidentally, in a consummatory situation has the power of arousing the awe, excitement, relief, admiration belonging to

the situation as a whole.   Industry displaces magic, and science reduces myth, when the elements that enter into the constitution of the consummatory whole are discriminated, and each one has its own particular place in sequential order assigned it.   Thus materials and efficacies characteristic of different kinds of arts are distinguished. But because the ceremonial, literary and poetic arts have quite other ways of working and other consequences, than industrial and scientific arts, it is far from following, as current theories assume, that they have no instrumental power at all, or that a sense of their instrumental agency is not involved in their appreciative perception. The pervasive operation of symbolism in human culture is all the proof that is needed to show that an intimate and direct sense of place and connection in a prolonged history enters into the enjoyed and suffered constituents of the history, and especially into the final or terminal members.

Further confirmation of this proposition is found in classic philosophy itself, in its theory that essential forms "make" things *what* they are, even though not causing them to occur.   "Essence," as it figures in Greek theory, represents the mysterious potency of earlier "symbols" emancipated from their superstitious context and envisaged in a dialectic and reflective context.   The essences of Greek-medieval science were in short poetic objects, treated as objects of demonstrative science, used to explain and understand the inner and ultimate constitution of things.   While Greek thought was sufficiently emancipated from magic to deny "efficient" causality to formal and final essences, yet the latter were conceived of as making particular things to be *what* they are, members of natural kinds.   Moreover, by a reversal of causal residence, intrinsic seeking for such forms was imputed to changing events. Thus the ground was prepared for the later frank return of patristic and scholastic thought to a frank animistic supernaturalism. The philosophic theory erred, as did magic and myth, regarding the nature of the efficacy involved in ends; and the error was due to the same causes, namely, failure of analysis into elements. It could not have occurred, were there that sharp division between means and ends, fruitions and instrumentalities, assumed by current thought.

In short, the history of human experience is a history of the development of arts. The history of science in its distinct emergence from religious, ceremonial and poetic arts is the record of a differentiation of arts, not a record of separation from art. The chief significance of the account just given, lies, for our present purpose, in its bearing upon the theory of experience and nature. It is not, however, without import for a theory of criticism. The present confusion, deemed chaos by some, in the fine arts and esthetic criticism seems to be an inevitable consequence of the underlying, even if unavowed, separation of the instrumental and the consummatory. The further men go in the concrete the more they are forced to recognize the logical consequence of their controlling assumptions. We owe it to theories of art prevalent to-day in one school of critics that certain implications, long obscured, of the traditional theory of art and nature have been brought to light. Gratitude for this debt should not be stinted because the adherents of the traditional theory regarding the newer views as capricious heresies, wild aberrations. For these critics, in proclaiming that esthetic qualities in works of fine art are unique, in asserting their separation from not only every thing that is existential in nature but also from all other forms of good, in proclaiming that such arts as music, poetry, painting have characters unshared with any natural things whatsoever:—in asserting such things the critics carry to its conclusion the isolation of fine art from the useful, of the final from efficacious. They thus prove that the separation of the consummation from the instrumental makes art wholly esoteric.

There are substantially but two alternatives. Either art is a continuation, by means of intelligent selection and arrangement, of natural tendencies of natural events; or art is a peculiar addition to nature springing from something dwelling exclusively within the breast of man, whatever name be given the latter. In the former case, delightfully enhanced perception or esthetic appreciation is of the same nature as enjoyment of any object that is consummatory. It is the outcome of a skilled and intelligent art of dealing with natural things for the sake of intensifying, purifying, prolonging and deepening the satisfactions which they spontaneously afford. That, in this process, new meanings develop, and that these afford uniquely new traits and modes of enjoyment is but what happens everywhere in emergent growths.

But if fine art has nothing to do with other activities and products, then of course it has nothing inherently to do with the objects, physical and social, experienced in other situations. It has an occult source and an esoteric character. It makes little difference what the source and the character be called. By strict logic it makes literally no difference. For if the quality of the esthetic experience is by conception unique, then the words employed to describe it have no significance derived from or comparable to the qualities of other experiences; their signification is hidden and specialized to a degree. Consider some of the terms which are in more or less current use among the critics who carry the isolation of art and the esthetic to its limit. It is sometimes said that art is the expression of the emotions; with the implication that, because of this fact, subject-matter is of no significance except as material through which emotion is expressed. Hence art becomes unique. For in works of science, utility and morals the character of the objects forming this subject-matter is all-important. But by this definition, subject-matter is stripped of all its own inherent characters in art in the degree in which it is genuine art; since a truly artistic work is manifest in the reduction of subject-matter to a mere medium of expression of emotion.

In such a statement emotion either has no significance at all, and it is mere accident that this particular combination of letters is employed; or else, if by emotion is meant the same sort of thing that is called emotion in daily life, the statement is demonstrably false. For emotion in its ordinary sense is something called out *by* objects, physical and personal; it is response *to* an objective situation. It is not something existing somewhere by itself which then employs material through which to express itself. Emotion is an indication of intimate participation, in a more or less excited way in some scene of nature or life; it is, so to speak, an attitude or disposition which is a function of objective things. It is intelligible that art should select and assemble objective things in such ways as to evoke emotional response of a refined, sensitive and enduring kind; it is intelligible that the artist himself is one capable of sustaining these emotions, under whose temper and spirit he performs his compositions of objective materials. This procedure may indeed be carried to a point such that the use of objective materials is economized to the minimum, and the evocation of the emotional response carried to its relative maximum. But it still remains true that the origin of the art-process lay in emotional responses spontaneously called out by a situation occurring without any reference to art, and without "esthetic" quality save in the sense in which all immediate enjoyment and suffering is esthetic. Economy in use of objective subject-matter may with experienced and trained minds go so far that what is ordinarily called "representation" is much reduced. But what happens is a highly funded and generalized representation of the formal sources of ordinary emotional experience.

The same sort of remark is to be made concerning "significant form" as a definition of an esthetic object. Unless the meaning of the term is so isolated as to be wholly occult, it denotes a selection, for sake of emphasis, purity, subtlety, of those forms which give consummatory significance to every-day subject-matters of experience. "Forms" are not the peculiar property or creation of the esthetic and artistic; they are characters in virtue of which anything meets the requirements of an enjoyable perception. "Art" does not create the forms; it is their selection and organization in such ways as to enhance, prolong and purify the perceptual experience. It is not by accident that some objects and situations afford marked perceptual satisfactions; they do so because of their structural properties and relations. An artist may work with a minimum of analytic recognition of these structures or "forms;" he may select them chiefly by a kind of sympathetic vibration. But they may also be discriminatively ascertained; and an artist may utilize his deliberate awareness of them to create works of art that are more formal and abstract than those to which the public is accustomed. Tendency to composition in terms of the formal characters marks much contemporary art, in poetry, painting, music, even sculpture and architecture. At their worst, these products are "scientific" rather than artistic; technical exercises, sterile and of a new kind of pedantry. At their best, they assist in ushering in new modes of art and by education of the organs of perception in new modes of consummatory objects; they enlarge and enrich the world of human vision.

Thus, by only a slight forcing of the argument, we reach a conclusion regarding the relations of instrumental and fine art which is precisely the opposite of that intended by seclusive estheticians; namely, that fine art *consciously* undertaken as such is peculiarly instrumental in quality. It is a device in experimentation carried on for the sake of education. It exists for the sake of a specialized use, use being a new training of modes of perception. The creators of such works of art are entitled, when successful, to the gratitude that we give to inventors of microscopes and microphones; in the end, they open new objects to be observed and enjoyed. This is a genuine service; but only an age of combined confusion and conceit will arrogate to works that perform this special utility the exclusive name of fine art.

Experience in the form of art, when reflected upon, we conclude by saying, solves more problems which have troubled philosophers and resolves more hard and fast dualisms than any other theme of thought. As the previous discussion has indicated, it demonstrates the intersection in nature of individual and generic; of chance and law, transforming one into opportunity and the other into liberation; of instrumental and final. More evidently still, it demonstrates the gratuitous falsity of notions that divide overt and executive activity from thought and feeling and thus separate mind and matter. In creative production, the external and physical world is more than a mere means or external condition of perceptions, ideas and emotions; it is subject-matter and sustainer of conscious activity; and thereby exhibits, so that he who runs may read, the fact that consciousness is not a separate realm of being, but is the manifest quality of existence when nature is most free and most active.

CHAPTER TEN

EXISTENCE, VALUE AND CRITICISM

Recent philosophy has witnessed the rise of a theory of value. Value as it usually figures in this discussion marks a desperate attempt to combine the obvious empirical fact that objects are qualified with good and bad, with philosophic deliverances which, in isolating man from nature, qualitative individualities from the world, render this fact anomalous. The philosopher erects a "realm of values" in which to place all the precious things which are extruded from natural existence because of isolations artificially introduced. Poignancy, humor, zest, tragedy, beauty, prosperity and bafflement, although rejected from a nature which is identified with mechanical structure, remain just what they empirically are, and demand recognition. Hence they are gathered up into the realm of values, contradistinguished from the realm of existence. Then the philosopher has a new problem with which to wrestle: What is the relationship of these two "worlds?" Is the world of value that of ultimate and transcendent Being from which the world of existence is a derivation or a fall? Or is it but a manifestation of human subjectivity, a factor somehow miraculously supervening upon an order complete and closed in physical structure? Or are there scattered at random through objective being, detached subsistences as "real" as are physical events, but having no temporal dates and spatial locations, and yet at times and places miraculously united with existences?

Choice among such notions of value is arbitrary, because the problem is arbitrary. When we return to the conceptions of potentiality and actuality, contingency and regularity, qualitatively diverse individuality, with which Greek thought operated, we find no room for a theory of values separate from a theory of nature. Yet if we are to recur to the Greek conceptions, the return must be a return with a difference. It must surrender the identification of natural ends with good and perfection; recognizing that a natural end, a part from endeavor expressing choice, has no intrinsic eulogistic quality, but is the boundary which writes "Finis" to a chapter of history inscribed by a moving system of energies. Failure by exhaustion as well as by triumph may constitute an end; death, ignorance, as well as life, are finalities.

Again, the return must abandon the notion of a predetermined limited number of ends inherently arranged in an order of increasing comprehensiveness and finality. It will have to recognize that natural termini are as infinitely numerous and varied as are the individual systems of action they delimit; and that since there is only relative, not absolute, impermeability and fixity of structure, new individuals with novel ends emerge in irregular procession. It must recognize that limits, closures, ends are experimentally or dynamically determined, presenting, like the boundaries of political individuals or states, a moving adjustment of various energy-systems in their cooperative and competitive interactions, not something belonging to them of their own right. Consequently, it will surrender the separation in nature from each other of contingency and regularity, the hazardous and the assured; it will avoid that relegation of them to distinct orders of Being which is characteristic of the classic tradition.   It will note that they intersect everywhere; that it is uncertainty and indeterminateness that create the need for and the sense of order and security; that whatever is most complete and liberal in being and possession is for that very reason most exposed to vicissitude, and most needful of watchful safeguarding art.

The connotation of "value" in recent thought contains some hint of the changes which experience has compelled in the classic notion of natural ends.   For by implication at least values are recognized to be fugitive and precarious, to be negative and positive, and indefinitely diversified in quality.   Even that metaphysical theory of super-idealism which finds them to be eternal, and the eternal foundation and source of shifting temporal events, bases its argument upon the undeniable insecurity, the interminable elusiveness, the appearance and disappearance, of values in actual experience.   Because of this sense of the evanescence and uncertainty of what used to be called ends but are now called values, the important consideration and concern is not a theory of values but a theory of criticism; a method of discriminating among goods on the basis of the conditions of their appearance, and of their consequences.

Values are values, things immediately having certain intrinsic qualities.   Of them as values there is accordingly nothing to be said; they are what they are.   All that can be said of them concerns their generative conditions and the consequences to which they give rise.   The notion that things as direct values lend themselves to thought and discourse rests upon a confusion of causal categories with immediate qualities.   Objects, for example, may be distinguished as contributory or as fulfilling, but this is distinction of place with respect to causal relationship; it is not a distinction of values. We may be interested in a thing, be concerned with it or like it, for a reason. The reason for appreciation, for an enjoyed appropriation, is often that the object in question serves as a means to something; or the reason is that it stands as the culmination of an antecedent process. But to take into account the reason for liking and enjoyment concerns the cause of the existence of a value, and has nothing to do with the intrinsicalness or nature of the value-quality, which either does or does not exist. Things that are means and things that are fulfillments have different qualities; but so do symphonies, operas and oratorios among themselves. The difference is not one that has anything to do with the immediacy or intrinsicalness of value-quality; it is a difference between one affair and quality and another.

It is self-contradictory to suppose that when a fulfillment possesses immediate value, its means of attainment do not. The person to whom the cessation of a tooth-ache has value, by that very fact finds value in going to a dentist, or in whatever else is means of fulfillment. For fulfillment is as relative to means as means are to realization. Means-consequences constitute a single undivided situation. Consequently when thought and discussion enter, when theorizing sets in, when there is anything beyond bare immediate enjoyment and suffering, it is the means-consequence relationship that is considered. Thought goes beyond immediate existence to its relationships, the conditions which mediate it and the things to which it is in turn mediatory. And such a procedure is criticism. The all but universal confusion in theories of value of determined position in causative or sequential relationship with value proper is indirect testimony to the fact that every intelligent appreciation is also criticism, judgment, of the thing having immediate value. Any *theory* of values is perforce entrance into the field of criticism. Value as such, even things having value, cannot in their immediate existence be reflected upon; they either are or are not; are or are not enjoyed. To pass beyond direct occurrence, even though the passage be restricted to an attempt to define value, is to begin a process of discrimination which implies a reflective criterion. In themselves, values may be just pointed at; to attempt a definition by complete pointing is however bootless. Sooner or later, with respect to positive or negative value, designation will have to include everything.

These remarks are preparatory to presenting a conception of philosophy; namely, that philosophy is inherently criticism, having its distinctive position among various modes of criticism in its generality; a criticism of criticisms, as it were. Criticism is discriminating judgment, careful appraisal, and judgment is appropriately termed criticism wherever the subject-matter of discrimination concerns goods or values. Possession and enjoyment of goods passes insensibly and inevitably into appraisal. First and immature experience is content simply to enjoy. But a brief course in experience enforces reflection; it requires but brief time to teach that some things sweet in the having are bitter in after-taste and in what they lead to. Primitive innocence does not last. Enjoyment ceases to be a datum and becomes a problem. As a problem, it implies intelligent inquiry into the conditions and consequences of a value-object; that is, criticism.   If values were as plentiful as huckleberries, and if the huckleberry-patch were always at hand, the passage of appreciation into criticism would be a senseless procedure.   If one thing tired or bored us, we should have only to turn to another.   But values are as unstable as the forms of clouds.   The things that possess them are exposed to all the contingencies of existence, and they are indifferent to our likings and tastes.

Good things change and vanish not only with changes in the environing medium but with changes in ourselves. Continued perception, except when it has been cultivated through prior criticism, dulls itself; it is soon satiated, exhausted, blasé.   The infinite flippancy of the natural man is a standing theme for discourse by shrewd observers of human nature.   Cultivated taste alone is capable of prolonged appreciation of the same object; and it is capable of it because it has been trained to a discriminating procedure which constantly uncovers in the object new meanings to be perceived and enjoyed.   Add to exhaustion of the organs of perception and enjoyment, all the other organic causes which render enjoyed objects unstable, and then add the external vicissitudes to which they are subjected, and there is no cause to wonder at the evanescence of immediate goods; nor at the so-called paradoxes of pleasure and virtue, according to which they are not secured by aiming at them but by attention to other things;—a fact however, which is not a paradox in a world where nothing is attained in any other way than by attention to its causal conditions.

When criticism and the critical attitude are legitimately distinguished from appreciation and taste, we are in the presence of one case of the constant rhythm of "perchings and flights" (to borrow James' terms), characteristic of alternate emphasis upon the immediate and mediate, the consummatory and instrumental, phases of all conscious experience. If we are misled into ignoring the omnipresence in all observations and ideas of this rhythm, it is largely because, under the influence of formal theories, we attach too elaborate and too remote a signification to "appreciation" and "criticism." Values of some sort or other are not traits of rare and festal occasions; they occur whenever any object is welcomed and lingered over; whenever it arouses aversion and protest; even though the lingering be but momentary and the aversion a passing glance toward something else.

Similarly, criticism is not a matter of formal treatises, published articles, or taking up important matters for consideration in a serious way. It occurs whenever a moment is devoted to looking to see what sort of value is present; whenever instead of accepting a value-object wholeheartedly, being rapt by it, we raise even a shadow of a question about its worth, or modify our sense of it by even a passing estimate of its probable future. It is well upon the whole that we use the terms "appreciation" and "criticism" honorifically, to designate conspicuous instances. But it is fatal to any understanding of them to fail to note that formally emphatic instances are of exactly the same nature as the rhythmic alternation between slight agreeable acceptances, annoyed rejections and passing questionings and estimates, which make up the entire course of our waking experience, whether in revery, in controlled inquiry or in deliberate management of affairs.

The rhythmic succession of the two modes of perception suggests that the difference is one of emphasis, or degree. Critical appreciation, and appreciative, warmly emotionalized criticism occur in every matured sane experience. After the first dumb, formless experience of a thing as a good, subsequent perception of the good contains at least a germ of critical reflection. For this reason, and only for this reason, elaborate and formulated criticism is subsequently possible. The latter, if just and pertinent, can but develop the reflective implications found within appreciation itself. Criticism would be the most wilful of undertakings if the possession and enjoyment of good objects had no element of memory and foresight in it; if it lacked all circumspection and judgment. Criticism is reasonable and to the point, in the degree in which it extends and deepens these factors of intelligence found in immediate taste and enjoyment.

Conscience in morals, taste in fine arts and conviction in beliefs pass insensibly into critical judgments; the latter pass also into a more and more generalized form of criticism called philosophy. How is the assertion of "canons" of taste and criticism compatible with the declaration that there is no discussing tastes? What is meant by a distinction between apparent good and real good? How can the distinction between seeming and being be capable of application to what is good? Is critical appraisal possible without a standard measure of values? Is the standard of values itself a value? Is it derived from the value-objects to which it is applied? If so, what authority does it possess over and beyond that of particular cases? What right has it to pass judgment upon its own source and authors? Does a standard exist transcendentally in independence of concrete cases judged? If so, what is its source, and what is the ground and guarantee of its applicability to alien material? Is taste, immediate appreciation, sense and moral sense, ultimate, its own final judge in every case as it arises? What, in that event, saves us from chaotic anarchy? Is there among men a common measure of value? If so, is it grounded outside of man, in an independent objective form of Being?

Such questions as these, which may be multiplied as one pleases, indicate that no great difficulty would attend an effort to derive all the stock issues of philosophy from the problems of value and their relationship to critical judgment. Whether it be a question of the good and bad in conviction and opinion, or in matters of conduct, or in appreciated scenes of nature and art, there occurs in every instance a conflict between the immediate value-object and the ulterior value-object: the given good, and that reached and justified by reflection; the now apparent and the eventual. In knowledge, for example there are beliefs *de facto* and beliefs *de jure*. In morals, there are immediate goods, the desired, and reasonable goods, the desirable. In esthetics, there are the goods of an undeveloped or perverted taste and there are the goods of cultivated taste. With respect to any of these distinctions, the true, real, final, or objective good is no *more* good as an immediate existence than is the contrasting good, called false, specious, illusory, showy, meretricious, *le faux bon*. The difference in adjectives designates a difference instituted in critical judgment; the validity of the difference between good which is approved and that which is good (immediately) but is *judged bad*, depends therefore upon the value of reflection in general, and of a particular reflective operation in especial. Even if good of the reflective object is different from that of the good of the non-reflective object, it does not follow that it is a better good, much less that it is such a difference in goodness as makes the non-reflective good *bad:*—except upon one proviso, namely, that there is something unique in the value or goodness of reflection.

Either, then, the difference between genuine, valid, good and a counterfeit, specious good is unreal, or it is a difference consequent upon reflection, or criticism, and the significant point is that this difference is equivalent to that made by discovery of relationships, of conditions and consequences. With this conclusion are bound up two other propositions: Of immediate values as such, values which occur and which are possessed and enjoyed, there is no theory at all; they just occur, are enjoyed, possessed; and that is all. The moment we begin to discourse about these values, to define and generalize, to make distinctions in kinds, we are passing beyond value-objects themselves; we are entering, even if only blindly, upon an inquiry into causal antecedents and causative consequents, with a view to appraising the "real," that is the eventual, goodness of the thing in question. We are criticizing, not for its own sake, but for the sake of instituting and perpetuating more enduring and extensive values.

The other proposition is that philosophy is and can be nothing but this critical operation and function become aware of itself and its implications, pursued deliberately and systematically. It starts from actual situations of belief, conduct and appreciative perception which are characterized by immediate qualities of good and bad, and from the modes of critical judgment current at any given time in all the regions of value; these are its data, its subject-matter. These values, criticisms, and critical methods, it subjects to further criticism as comprehensive and consistent as possible. The function is to regulate the further appreciation of goods and bads; to give greater freedom and security in those acts of direct selection, appropriation, identification and of rejection, elimination, destruction which enstate and which exclude objects of belief, conduct and contemplation.

Such a conclusion wears an air of strangeness. It may appear to indicate an attempt by a dialectic trick to make the category of good-and-bad supreme in its jurisdiction over intellectual life and over all objects. This impression will, I think, be readily dissipated by consideration of the actual meaning of what is said. Objects of belief and of refusals to believe are value-objects; for each object is some thing acquiesced in, accepted, adopted, appropriated. This is the same as saying it is found good or satisfactory to believe or disbelieve; truistically, whatever is accepted is as such and in so far good. There is no occult significance in this statement; it is not preliminary to an argument which shall sweep away the properties which objects possess independent of their being objects of belief, or of their being values. It does not annihilate the difference among beliefs; it does not set up the *fact* that an object believed in is perforce found good as if it were a *reason* for belief. On the contrary: the statement is preliminary. The all-important matter is what lies back of and causes acceptance and rejection; whether or no there is method of discrimination and assessment which makes a difference in what is assented to and denied. Properties and relations that *entitle* an object to be found good in belief are extraneous to the qualities that are its immediate good; they are causal, and hence found only by search into the antecedent and the eventual. The conception that there are some objects or some properties of objects which carry their own adequate credentials upon their face is the snare and delusion of the whole historic tradition regarding knowledge, infecting alike sensational and rational schools, objective realisms and introspective idealisms.

Concerning beliefs and their objects taken in their immediacy *"non-disputandum"* holds, as truly as it does concerning tastes and their objects. If a man believes in ghosts, devils, miracles, fortune-tellers, the immutable certainty of the existing economic regime, and the supreme merits of his political party and its leaders, he does so believe; these are immediate goods to him, precisely as some color and tone combinations are lovely, or the mistress of his heart is charming. When the question is raised as to the "real" value of the object for belief, the appeal is to criticism, intelligence. And the court of appeal decides by the law of conditions and consequences. Inquiry duly pursued leads to the enstatement of an object which is directly accepted, good in belief, but an object whose character now depends upon the reflective operations whose conclusion it is. Like the object of dogmatic and uncritical belief, it marks an "end," a static arrest; but unlike it, the "end" is a *conclusion;* hence it carries credentials.

Were not objects of belief immediate goods, false beliefs would not be the dangerous things which they are. For it is because these objects are good to believe, to admit and assert, that they are cherished so intolerantly and unremittingly. Beliefs about God, Nature, society and man are precisely the things that men most cling to and most ardently fight for. It is easier to wean a miser from his hoard, than a man from his deeper opinions. And the tragedy is that in so many cases the *causes* which lead to the thing in question being a value are not *reasons* for its being a good, while the fact that it is an immediate good tends to preclude that search for causes, that dispassionate judgment, which is pre-requisite to the conversion of goods *de facto* into goods *de jure*. Here, again and pre-eminently, since reflection is the instrumentality of securing freer and more enduring goods, reflection is a unique intrinsic good. Its instrumental efficacy determines it to be a candidate for a distinctive position as an immediate good, since beyond other goods it has power of replenishment and fructification. In it, apparent good and real good enormously coincide.

In traditional discussion the fact is overlooked that the subject-matter of belief is a good, since belief means assimilation and assertion. It is overlooked that its immediate goodness is both the obstacle to reflective examination and the source of its necessity. The "true" is indeed set up along with the good and the beautiful as a transcendent good, but the role of empirical good, of value, in the sweep of ordinary beliefs is passed by. The counterpart of this error, which isolates the subject-matter of intellect from the scope of values and valuations, is a corresponding isolation of the subject-matter of esthetic contemplation and immediate enjoyment from judgment. Between these two realms, one of intellectual objects without value and the other of value-objects without intellect, there is an equivocal mid-country in which moral objects are placed, with rival claimants striving to annex them either to the region of purely immediate goods (in this case termed pleasures) or to that of purely rational objects. Hence the primary function of philosophy at present is to make it clear that there is no such difference as this division assumes between science, morals, and esthetic appreciation. All alike exhibit the difference between immediate goods casually occurring and immediate goods which have been reflectively determined by means of critical inquiry. If bare liking is an adequate determinant of values in one case, it is in the others. If intelligence, criticism, is required in one, it is in the others. If the end to be attained in any case is an enhanced and purified immediate appreciative, experienced object, so it is in the others. All cases manifest the same duality and present the same problem; that of embodying intelligence in action which shall convert casual natural goods, whose causes and effects are unknown, into goods valid for thought, right for conduct and cultivated for appreciation.

Philosophic discourse partakes both of scientific and literary discourse. Like literature, it is a comment on nature and life in the interest of a more intense and just appreciation of the meanings present in experience. Its business is reportorial and transcriptive only in the sense in which the drama and poetry have that office. Its primary concern is to clarify, liberate and extend the goods which inhere in the naturally generated functions of experience. It has no call to create a world of "reality" *de novo*, nor to delve into secrets of Being hidden from common-sense and science. It has no stock of information or body of knowledge peculiarly its own; if it does not always become ridiculous when it sets up as a rival of science, it is only because a particular philosopher happens to be also, as a human being, a prophetic man of science. Its business is to accept and to utilize for a purpose the best available knowledge of its own time and place. And this purpose is criticism of beliefs, institutions, customs, policies with respect to their bearing upon good. This does not mean their bearing upon *the* good, as something itself attained and formulated in philosophy. For as philosophy has no private score of knowledge or of methods for attaining truth, so it has no private access to good. As it accepts knowledge of facts and principles from those competent in inquiry and discovery, so it accepts the goods that are diffused in human experience. It has no Mosaic nor Pauline authority of revelation entrusted to it. But it has the authority of intelligence, of criticism of these common and natural goods.

At this point, it departs from the arts of literary discourse. They have a freer office to perform—to perpetuate, enhance and vivify in imagination the natural goods; all things are forgiven to him who succeeds. But philosophic criticism has a stricter task, with a greater measure of responsibility to what lies outside its own products. It has to appraise values by taking cognizance of their causes and consequences; only by this straight and narrow path may it contribute to expansion and emancipation of values. For this reason the conclusions of science about matter-of-fact efficiencies of nature are its indispensable instruments. If its eventual concern is to render goods more coherent, more secure and more significant in appreciation, its road is the subject-matter of natural existence as science discovers and depicts it.

Only in verbal form is there anything novel in this conception of philosophy. It is a version of the old saying that philosophy is love of wisdom, of wisdom which is not knowledge and which nevertheless cannot be without knowledge. The need of an organon of criticism which uses knowledge of relations among events to appraise the casual, immediate goods that obtain among men is not a fact of philosophy, but of nature and life. We can conceive a happier nature and experience than flourishes among us wherein the office of critical reflection would be carried on so continuously and in such detail that no particular apparatus would be needed. But actual experience is such a jumble that a degree of distance and detachment are a pre-requisite of vision in perspective. Thinkers often withdraw too far. But a withdrawal is necessary, unless they are to be deafened by the immediate clamor and blinded by the immediate glare of the scene. What especially makes necessary a generalized instrument of criticism, is the tendency of objects to seek rigid non-communicating compartments. It is natural that nature, variegatedly qualified, should exhibit various trends when it achieves experience of itself, so that there is a distribution of emphasis such as are designated by the adjectives scientific, industrial, political, religious, artistic, educational, moral and so on.

But however natural from the standpoint of causation may be the institutionalizing of these trends, their separation effects an isolation which is unnatural. Narrowness, superficiality, stagnation follow from lack of the nourishment which can be supplied only by generous and wide interactions. Goods isolated as professionalism and institutionalization isolate them, petrify; and in a moving world solidification is always dangerous. Resistant force is gained by precipitation, but no one thing gets strong enough to defy everything. Over-specialization and division of interests, occupations and goods create the need for a generalized medium of intercommunication, of mutual criticism through all-around translation from one separated region of experience into another. Thus philosophy as a critical organ becomes in effect a messenger, a liason officer, making reciprocally intelligible voices speaking provincial tongues, and thereby enlarging as well as rectifying the meanings with which they are charged.

The difficulty is that philosophy, even when professing catholicity, has often been suborned. Instead of being a free messenger of communication it has been a diplomatic agent of some special and partial interest; insincere, because in the name of peace it has fostered divisions that lead to strife, and in the name of loyalty has promoted unholy alliances and secret understandings. One might say that the profuseness of attestations to supreme devotion to truth on the part of philosophy is matter to arouse suspicion. For it has usually been a preliminary to the claim of being a peculiar organ of access to highest and ultimate truth. Such it is not; and it will not lose its esoteric and insincere air until the profession is disclaimed. Truth is a collection of truths; and these constituent truths are in the keeping of the best available methods of inquiry and testing as to matters-of-fact; methods, which are, when collected under a single name, science. As to truth, then, philosophy has no pre-eminent status; it is a recipient, not a donor. But the realm of meanings is wider than that of true-and-false meanings; it is more urgent and more fertile. When the claim of meanings to truth enters in, then truth is indeed pre-eminent. But this fact is often confused with the idea that truth has a claim to enter everywhere; that it has monopolistic jurisdiction. Poetic meanings, moral meanings, a large part of the goods of life are matters of richness and freedom of meanings, rather than of truth; a large part of our life is carried on in a realm of meanings to which truth and falsity as such are irrelevant. And the claim of philosophy to rival or displace science as a purveyor of truth seems to be mostly a compensatory gesture for failure to perform its proper task of liberating and clarifying meanings, including those scientifically authenticated. For, assuredly, a student prizes historic systems rather for the meanings and shades of meanings they have brought to light than for the store of ultimate truths they have ascertained. If accomplishment of the former office were made the avowed business of philosophy, instead of an incidental by-product, its position would be clearer, more intelligent and more respected.

It is sometimes suggested, however, that such a view of philosophy derogates from its dignity, degrading it into an instrument of social reforms, and that it is a view congenial only to those who are insensitive to the positive achievements of culture and over-sensitive to its evils. Such a conception overlooks outstanding facts. "Social reform" is conceived in a Philistine spirit, if it is taken to mean anything less than precisely the liberation and expansion of the meanings of which experience is capable. No doubt many schemes of social reform are guilty of precisely this narrowing. But for that very reason they are futile; they do not succeed in even the special reforms at which they aim, except at the expense of intensifying other defects and creating new ones. Nothing but the best, the richest and fullest experience possible, is good enough for man. The attainment of such an experience is not to be conceived as the specific problem of "reformers" but as the common purpose of men. The contribution which philosophy can make to this common aim is criticism. Criticism certainly includes a heightened consciousness of deficiencies and corruptions in the scheme and distribution of values that obtains at any period.

No just or pertinent criticism in its negative phase can possibly be made, however, except upon the basis of a heightened appreciation of the positive goods which human experience has achieved and offers. Positive concrete goods of science, art and social companionship are the basic subject-matter of philosophy as criticism; and only because such positive goods already exist is their emancipation and secured extension the defining aim of intelligence. The more aware one is of the richness of meanings which experience possesses, the more will a generous and catholic thinker be conscious of the limits which prevent sharing in them; the more aware will he be of their accidental and arbitrary distribution. If instrumental efficacies need to be emphasized, it is not for the sake of instruments but for the sake of that full and more secure distribution of values which is impossible without instrumentalities.

If philosophy be criticism, what is to be said of the relation of philosophy to metaphysics? For metaphysics, as a statement of the generic traits manifested by existences of all kinds without regard to their differentiation into physical and mental, seems to have nothing to do with criticism and choice, with an effective love of wisdom. It begins and ends with analysis and definition. When it has revealed the traits and characters that are sure to turn up in every universe of discourse, its work is done. So at least an argument may run. But the very nature of the traits discovered in every theme of discourse, since they are ineluctable traits of natural existence, forbids such a conclusion. Qualitative individuality and constant relations, contingency and need, movement and arrest are common traits of all existence. This fact is source both of values and of their precariousness; both of immediate possession which is casual and of reflection which is a precondition of secure attainment and appropriation. Any theory that detects and defines these traits is therefore but a ground-map of the province of criticism, establishing base lines to be employed in more intricate triangulations.

If the general traits of nature existed in water-tight compartments, it might be enough to sort out the objects and interests of experience among them. But they are actually so intimately intermixed that all important issues are concerned with their degrees and the ratios they sustain to one another. Barely to note and register that contingency is a trait of natural events has nothing to do with wisdom. To note, however, contingency in connection with a concrete situation of life is that fear of the Lord which is at least the beginning of wisdom. The detection and definition of nature's end is in itself barren. But the undergoing that actually goes on in the light of this discovery brings one close to supreme issues: life and death.

The more sure one is that the world which encompasses human life is of such and such a character (no matter

what his definition), the more one is committed to try to
direct the conduct of life, that of others as well as of himself, upon the basis of the character assigned to the world.
And if he finds that he cannot succeed, that the attempt
lands him in confusion, inconsistency and darkness,
plunging others into discord and shutting them out from
participation, rudimentary precepts instruct him to surrender his assurance as a delusion; and to revise his
notions of the nature of nature till he makes them more
adequate to the concrete facts in which nature is embodied. Man needs the earth in order to walk, the sea
to swim or sail, the air to fly. Of necessity he acts within
the world, and in order to be, he must in some measure
adapt himself as one part of nature to other parts.

In mind, thought, this situation, this predicament
becomes aware of itself. Instead of the coerced adaptation of part to part with coerced failure or success as consequence, there is search for the meaning of things with
respect to acts to be performed, plans and policies to be
formed; there is search for the meaning of proposed acts
with respect to objects they induce and preclude. The
one cord that is never broken is that between the energies
and acts which compose nature. Knowledge modifies
the tie. But the idea that knowledge breaks the tie, that
it inserts something opaque between the interactions of
things, is hardly less than infantile. Knowledge as
science modifies the particular interactions that come
within its reach, because it *is* itself a modification of interactions, due to taking into account their past and future.
The generic insight into existence which alone can define
metaphysics in any empirically intelligible sense is itself
an added fact of interaction, and is therefore subject to

the same requirement of intelligence as any other natural occurrence: namely, inquiry into the bearings, leadings and consequences of what it discovers. The universe is no infinite self-representative series, if only because the addition within it of a representation makes it a different universe.

By an indirect path we are brought to a consideration of the most far-reaching question of all criticism: the relationship between existence and value, or as the problem is often put, between the real and ideal.

Philosophies have usually insisted upon a wholesale relationship. Either the goods which we most prize and which are therefore termed ideal are identified completely and throughout with real Being; or the realms of existence and of the ideal are wholly severed from each other. In the European tradition in its orthodox form the former alternative has prevailed. *Ens* and *verum*, *bonum* are the same. Being, in the full sense, is perfection of power to be; the measure of degrees of perfection and of degrees of reality is extent of power. Evil and error are impotences; futile gestures against omnipotence—against Being. Spinoza restated to this effect medieval theology in terms of the new outlook of science. Modern professed idealisms have taught the same doctrine. After magnifying thought and the objects of thought, after magnifying the ideals of human aspiration, they have then sought to prove that after all these things are not ideal but are real— real not *as* meanings and ideals, but as existential being. Thus the assertion of faith in the ideal belies itself in the making; these "idealists" cannot trust their ideal till they have converted it into existence—that is, into the physical or the psychical, which, since it lacks the properties of the empirically physical and psycho-physical becomes a peculiar kind of existence, called metaphysical.

There are also philosophies, rarer in occurrence, which allege that the ideal is too sacredly ideal to have any point of contact whatever with existence; they think that contact is contagion and contagion infection. At first sight such a view seems to display a certain nobility of faith and fineness of abnegation. But an ideal realm that has no roots in existence has no efficacy nor relevancy. It is a light which is darkness, for shining in the void it illumines nothing and cannot reveal even itself. It gives no instruction, for it cannot be translated into the meaning and import of what actually happens, and hence it is barren; it cannot mitigate the bleakness of existence nor modify its brutalities. It thus abnegates itself in abjuring footing in natural events, and ceases to be ideal, to become whimsical fantasy or linguistic sophistication.

These remarks are made not so much by way of hostile animadversion as by way of indicating the sterility of wholesale conceptions of the relation of existence and value. By negative implication, they reveal the only kind of doctrine that can be effectively critical, taking effect in discriminations which emancipate, extend, and clarify. Such a theory will realize that the meanings which are termed ideal as truly as those which are termed sensuous are generated by existences; that as far as they continue in being they are sustained by events; that they are indications of the possibilities of existences, and are, therefore, to be used as well as enjoyed; used to inspire action to procure and buttress their causal conditions. Such a doctrine criticizes particular occurrences by the particular meanings to which they give rise; it criticizes also particular meanings and goods as their conditions are found to be sparse, accidental, incapable of conservation, or frequent, pliant, congruous, enduring; and as their consequences are found to afford enlightenment and direction in conduct, or to darken counsel, narrow the horizon of vision, befog judgment and distort perspective. A good is a good anyhow, but to reflection those goods approve themselves, whether labelled beauty or truth or righteousness, which steady, vitalize and expand judgments in creation of new goods and conservation of old goods. To common-sense this statement is a truism. If to philosophy it is a stumbling-block, it is because tradition in philosophy has set itself in stiff-necked fashion against discriminations within the realm of existences, on account of the pluralistic implications of discrimination. It insists upon having all or none; it cannot choose in favor of some existences and against others because of prior commitment to a dogma of perfect unity. Such distinctions as it makes are therefore always hierarchical; degrees of greater and less, superior and inferior, in one homogeneous order.

I gladly borrow the glowing words of one of our greatest American philosophers; with their poetry they may succeed in conveying where dry prose fails. Justice Holmes has written: "The mode in which the inevitable comes to pass is through effort. Consciously or unconsciously we all strive to make the kind of world that we like. And although with Spinoza we may regard criticism of the past as futile, there is every reason for doing all that we can to make a future such as we desire." He then goes on to say, "there is every reason also for trying to make our desires intelligent. The trouble is that our ideals for the most part are inarticulate, and that even if we have made them definite we have very little experimental knowledge of the way to bring them about." And this effort to make our desires, our strivings and our ideals, (which are as natural to man as his aches and his clothes) articulate, to define them (not in themselves which is impossible) in terms of inquiry into conditions and consequences is what I have called criticism; and when carried on in the grand manner, philosophy.   In a further essay, Justice Holmes touches upon the relation of philosophy (thus conceived) to our scientific and metaphysical insight into the kind of a world in which we live.

"When we come to our attitude toward the universe I do not see any rational ground for demanding the superlative for being dissatisfied unless we are assured that our truth is cosmic truth, if there is such a thing. . . . . If a man sees no reason for believing that significance, consciousness and ideals are more than marks of the human, that does not justify what has been familiar in French sceptics; getting upon a pedestal and professing to look with haughty scorn upon a world in ruins.   The real conclusion is that the part cannot swallow the whole. . . . . If we believe that we came out of the universe, not it out of us, we must admit that we do not know what we are talking about when we speak of brute matter. We do know that a certain complex of energies can wag its tail and another can make syllogisms.   These are among the powers of the unknown, and if, as may be, it has still greater powers that we cannot understand . . . . why should we not be content?   Why should we employ the energy that is furnished to us by the cosmos to defy it and to shake our fist at the sky?   It seems to me silly."

"That the universe has in it more than we understand, that the private soldiers have not been told the plan of campaign, or even that there is one . . . . has no bearing on our conduct. We still shall fight—all of us because we want to live, some, at least, because we want to realize our spontaneity and prove our powers, for the joy of it, and we may leave to the unknown the supposed final valuation of that which in any event has value to us. It is enough for us that the universe has produced us and has within it, as less than it, all that we believe and love. If we think of our existence not as that of a little god outside, but as that of a ganglion within, we have the infinite behind us. It gives us our only but our adequate significance. If our imagination is strong enough to accept the vision of ourselves as parts inseparable from the rest, and to extend our final interest beyond the boundary of our skins, it justifies even the sacrifice of our lives for ends outside of ourselves. The motive to be sure is the common wants and ideals that we find in man. Philosophy does not furnish motives, but it shows men that they are not fools for doing what they already want to do. It opens to the forlorn hopes on which we throw ourselves away, the vista of the farthest stretch of human thought, the chord of a harmony that breathes from the unknown."

Men move between extremes. They conceive of themselves as gods, or feign a powerful and cunning god as an ally who bends the world to do their bidding and meet their wishes. Disillusionized, they disown the world that disappoints them; and hugging ideals to themselves as their own possession, stand in haughty aloofness apart from the hard course of events that pays so little heed to our hopes and aspirations. But a mind that has opened itself to experience and that has ripened through its discipline knows its own littleness and impotencies; it knows that its wishes and acknowledgments are not final measures of the universe whether in knowledge or in conduct, and hence are, in the end, transient. But it also knows that its juvenile assumption of power and achievement is not a dream to be wholly forgotten. It implies a unity with the universe that is to be preserved. The belief, and the effort of thought and struggle which it inspires are also the doing of the universe, and they in some way, however slight, carry the universe forward. A chastened sense of our importance, apprehension that it is not a yard-stick by which to measure the whole, is consistent with the belief that we and our endeavors are significant not only for themselves but in the whole.

Fidelity to the nature to which we belong, as parts however weak, demands that we cherish our desires and ideals till we have converted them into intelligence, revised them in terms of the ways and means which nature makes possible. When we have used our thought to its utmost and have thrown into the moving unbalanced balance of things our puny strength, we know that though the universe slay us still we may trust, for our lot is one with whatever is good in existence. We know that such thought and effort is one condition of the coming into existence of the better. As far as we are concerned it is the only condition, for it alone is in our power. To ask more than this is childish; but to ask less is a recreance no less egotistic, involving no less a cutting of ourselves from the universe than does the expectation that it meet and satisfy our every wish. To ask in good faith as much as this from ourselves is to stir into motion every capacity of imagination, and to exact from action every skill and bravery.

While, therefore, philosophy has its source not in any special impulse or staked-off section of experience, but in the entire human predicament, this human situation falls wholly within nature. It reflects the traits of nature; it gives indisputable evidence that in nature itself qualities and relations, individualities and uniformities, finalities and efficacies, contingencies and necessities are inextricably bound together. The harsh conflicts and the happy coincidences of this interpenetration make experience what it consciously is; their manifest apparition creates doubt, forces inquiry, exacts choice, and imposes liability for the choice which is made. Were there complete harmony in nature, life would be spontaneous efflorescence. If disharmony were not in both man and nature, if it were only between them, man would be the ruthless overlord of nature, or its querulous oppressed subject. It is precisely the peculiar intermixture of support and frustration of man by nature which constitutes experience. The standing antitheses of philosophic thought, purpose and mechanism, subject and object, necessity and freedom, mind and body, individual and general, are all of them attempts to formulate the fact that nature induces and partially sustains meanings and goods, and at critical junctures withdraws assistance and flouts its own creatures.

The striving of man for objects of imagination is a continuation of natural processes; it is something man has learned from the world in which he occurs, not something which he arbitrarily injects into that world. When he adds perception and ideas to these endeavors, it is not after all he who adds; the addition is again the doing of nature and a further complication of its own domain. To act, to enjoy and suffer in consequence of action, to reflect, to discriminate and make differences in what had been but gross and homogeneous good and evil, according to what inquiry reveals of causes and effects; to act upon what has been learned, thereby to plunge into new and unconsidered predicaments, to test and revise what has been learned, to engage in new goods and evils is human, the course which manifests the course of nature. They are the manifest destiny of contingency, fulfillment, qualitative individualization and generic uniformities in nature. To note, register and define the constituent structure of nature is not then an affair neutral to the office of criticism. It is a preliminary outline of the field of criticism, whose chief import is to afford understanding of the necessity and nature of the office of intelligence.

If I mistake not, the actual animus of subjectivity in modern philosophy is not where its antagonists have placed it. Its actual animus and its obnoxious burden are exemplified in the doctrine of its hostile critics. For they assign to knowledge alone valid reference to existence. Desires, beliefs, "practical" activity, values are attributed exclusively to the human subject; this division is what makes subjectivity a snare and peril. The case of belief is crucial. For it is admitted that belief involves a phase of acquiescence or assertion, it presents qualities which involve *personal* factors; and (whatever definition of value be employed) value. A sharp line of demarcation has therefore to be drawn between belief and knowledge, for the latter has been defined in terms of pure objectivity. The need to control belief is admitted; knowledge figures, even though according to these theories only *per accidens*, as the organon of such control. Practically then, in effect, knowledge, science, truth, is the method of criticizing beliefs. It is the method of determining right participation in beliefs on the part of personal factors. Why then keep up any other distinction between knowledge and beliefs, save that between methodical agencies, efficacious instrumentalities, and the accepted objects which being conclusions, are hence marked by characters due to the method of their production, in contrast with objects of belief blindly and accidentally generated? Why perturbation at the intimation that science is inherently an instrument of critically determining what is good and bad in the way of acceptance and rejection?

I can see but one answer. The realm of desire, belief, search, choice is thought of as "subjective" in a sense which isolates it from natural existence and which makes it an inexplicable irruption. This is the reason for sharp separation of belief and knowledge. Aversion to making science a means of determining the right operation of personal factors, just as the technical and material apparatus of a painter determines his product, is well grounded if the personal is outside of nature. Made a means to something personal conceived in this sense, science loses its objectivity, and becomes infected with the traits which characterize the merely private and arbitrary.

There is involved, however, in the conclusion an unexamined and uncriticized assumption. The reason for isolating doubt, striving, purpose, the variegated colored play of goods and bads, rejections and acceptances, is they do not belong in the block universe which forms the object of generalized knowledge, whether the block be conceived as mechanical or as rational in structure. The argument thus moves in a vicious circle; the question is begged at the outset. If individualized qualities, status arrests, limiting "ends," and contingent changes characterize nature, then they manifest themselves in the uses, enjoyments and sufferings, the searchings and strivings which form conscious experience. These are as realistic, as "objectively" natural, as are the constituents of the object of cognitional experience. There is then no ground for denying or evading the full import of the fact that the latter are the means and the only means of regulative appraisals of values, of their revision, rectification, of their regulated generation and fortification.

The habitual avoidance in theories of knowledge of any reference to the fact that knowledge is a case of belief, operates as a device for ignoring the monstrous consequences of regarding the latter as existentially subjective, personal and private. No such device is available in dealing with esthetic and moral goods. Here the obnoxious one-sided conception operates in full force. The usual current procedure is to link values with likings as merely personal affairs, ignoring the inconvenient fact that the theory logically thereby makes all *beliefs* also matters of arbitrary, undiscussable preference. It is no cause for wonder therefore that there is next to no consensus in esthetic and moral theories. Since their subject-matter is totally segregated from that of science, since they are assigned to independent non-participating realms of existence, the only possible method of achieving agreement has been exiled in advance.

Practically this consequence is intolerable; accordingly it is rarely faced. "Standards" of value suddenly make their appearance to serve as criteria of taste and conscience. The distinction between likings and that which is worth liking, between the desired and the desirable, between the is and the ought, descends out of the blue. There are, it seems, immediate values, but there also are standard values, and the latter may be used to judge and measure immediate goods and bads. Thus the reflective distinction between the true and the false, the genuine and the spurious is brought upon the scene. In strict logic, however, it enters only to disappear. For if the standard is itself a value, then it is by definition only another name for the object of a particular liking, on the part of some particular subjective creature. If the liking for it conflicts with some other liking, the strongest wins. There is no question of false and true, of real and seeming, but only of stronger and weaker. The question of which one *should* be stronger is as meaningless as it would be in a cock-fight.

Such a conclusion puts an end to all attempt at consistency and organization and calls out in reaction an opposite theory. The "standard" is not, it is decided, for us at least, a good. It is rather a principle rationally apprehended. It is that which is "right" rather than that which is good; and since it is the right, it is the standard for judging all goods. If right is also good, the identification subsists in some transcendental realm; in some eternal, non-empirical realm of Being which is also a realm of values. The standard of good thus conceived as a principle of reason and as a form of supreme Being, is set over against the outside of actual desires, striving,

satisfactions and frustrations. It ought to enter into
their determination but for the most part it does not.
The distinction between is and ought is one of kind, and
a separation. It is not surprising that the wheel com-
pletes a full circle, and that the finale is a retort that the
alleged standard is itself but another dignified disguise
for some one's arbitrary liking—the *ipse dixit* of some one
accidentally clothed with extraneous authority.

It is as irritating to have experience of beauty and
moral goodness reduced to groundless whims as to have
that of truth. Common-sense has an inexpugnable
conviction that there are immediate goods of enjoyment
and conduct, and that there are principles by which they
may be appraised and rectified. Common-sense enter-
tains this firm conviction because it is innocent of any
rigid demarcation between knowledge on one side and
belief, conduct and esthetic appreciation on the other.
It is guiltless of the division between objective reality
and subjective events. It takes striving, purposing,
inquiring, wanting, the life of "practice," to be as much
facts of nature as are the themes of scientific discourse;
to it, indeed, the former has a more direct and urgent
reality. Hence it has no difficulty with the idea of rational or objective criticism and rectification of immediate
goods. If it were articulate, it would say that the same
natural processes which generate goods and evils generate
also the striving to secure the one and avoid the other,
and generate judgments to regulate the strivings. Its
weakness is that it fails to recognize that deliberate and
systematized science is a precondition of adequate judgments and hence of adequate striving and adequate choice.
Its organs of criticism are for the most part half-judg-

ments, uncriticized products of custom, chance circumstance and vested interests. Hence commonsense when it begins to reflect upon its own convictions easily falls a victim to traditional theories; and the vicious circle begins over again. It is sound as to the need and possibility of objective criticism of values, it is weak as to the method of accomplishing.

Yet all this time there is an example of the way out in the case of beliefs. There was a time when beliefs about external events were largely matters of what it was found immediately good to accept or reject; as far as there was a distinction made between the immediately good in belief and the real or true, it lay chiefly in the fact that the latter was the object sanctioned by authorities of church and state. Yet it is now all but commonplace that every belief-value must be subjected to criticism; in scientific undertakings, it is a common-place that criticism does not depend upon reference to a transcendent standard truth. The distinction between an immediate belief-value, which is but a challenge to inquiry, and an eventual object of belief that concludes critical inquiry, and has the value of fulfilling the causal relationships discovered, is made in the course of intelligent experiment. The result is a distinction between the apparent and the real good. Gradually a reluctant world is persuaded that meanings so determined define what is good for acceptance and assertion. Meantime beliefs determined by passion, class-interest, routine and authority remain sufficiently prevalent to enforce the perception that it makes all the difference in the world in the value of a belief how its object is formed and arrived at. Thus the lesson is enforced that critical valuations of immediate goods proceed in terms of the generation and consequences of objects qualified with good.

In outward forms, experimental science is infinitely varied. In principle, it is simple. We know an object when we know how it is made, and we know how it is made in the degree in which we ourselves make it. Old tradition compels us to call thinking "mental." But "mental" thought is but partial experimentation, terminating in preliminary readjustments, confined within the organism. As long as thinking remained at this stage, it protected itself by regarding this introverted truncation as evidence of an immaterial reason superior to and independent of body. As long as thought was thus cooped up, overt action in the "outer" natural scene was inevitably shorn of its full meed of meaning; it was to that extent arbitrary and routine. When "outer" and "inner" activity came together in a single experimental operation, used as the only adequate method of discovery and proof, effective criticism, consistent and ordered valuation, emerged. Thought aligned itself with other arts that shape objects by informing things with meanings.

Psychology, which reflects the old dualistic separation of mind from nature, has made current the notion that the processes which terminate in knowledge fare forth from innocent sensory data, or from pure logical principles, or from both together, as original starting points and material. As a natural history of mind this notion is wholly mythological. All knowing and effort to know starts from some belief, some received and asserted meaning which is a deposit of prior experience, personal and communal. In every instance, from passing query to elaborate scientific undertaking, the art of knowing criticizes a belief which has passed current as genuine coin, with a view to its revision. It terminates when freer, richer and more secure objects of belief are instituted as goods of immediate acceptance. The operation is one of doing and making in the literal sense. Starting from one good, treated as apparent and questionable, and ending in another which is tested and substantiated, the final act of knowing is acceptance and intellectual appreciation of what is significantly conclusive.

Is there any reason for supposing that the situation is any different in the case of other values and valuations? Is there any intrinsic difference between the relation of scientific inquiry to belief-values, of esthetic criticism to esthetic values, and of moral judgments to moral goods? Is there any difference in logical method? If we adopt a current theory, and say that immediate values occur where ever there is liking, interest, bias, it is clear that this liking is an act, if not an overt one, at least a dispositional tendency and direction. But most likings, all likings in their first appearance, are blind and gross. They do not know what they are about nor why they attach themselves to this or that object. Moreover, every such act takes a risk and assumes a liability, and does so ignorantly. For there are always in existence rival claimants for liking. To prefer *this* is to exclude *that*. Any liking is choice, unwittingly performed. There is no selection without rejection; interest and bias are selective, preferential. To take this for a good is to declare in act, though not at first in thought, that it is better than something else. This decision is arbitrary, capricious, unreasoned because made without thought of the other object, and without comparison. To say that an object is a good may seem to be an absolute and intrinsic declaration particularly when the assertion is made in direct act rather than in thought. But when we recognize that in effect the assertion is that one thing is better than another thing, the issues shift to something comparative, relational, causal, intellectual and objective. *Immediately* nothing is better or worse than anything else; it is just what it is. Comparison is comparison of things, things in their efficacies, their promotions and hindrances. The better is that which will do more in the way of security, liberation and fecundity for other likings and values.

To make a valuation, to judge appraisingly, is then to bring to conscious perception relations of productivity and resistance and thus to make value significant, intelligent and intelligible. In becoming discriminately aware of the causal conditions of the object liked and preferred, we become aware of its eventual operations. If in the case of esthetic and moral goods, the causal conditions which reflection reveals as determinants of the good object are found to lie within organic constitution in greater degree than is the case with objects of belief, this finding is of enormous importance for the technique of critical judgment. But it does not modify the logic which obtains in knowledge of the relationship of values and valuations to each other. It indicates the particular subject-matter which has to be controlled and used in the conscious art of re-making goods. As inquiries which aim at knowledge start from pre-existent beliefs, so esthetic and moral criticism start from antecedent natural goods of contemplative enjoyment and social intercourse. Its purpose is to make it possible to like and choose knowingly and with meaning, instead of blindly. All criticism worthy of the title is but another name for that revealing discovery of conditions and consequences which enables liking, bias, interest to express themselves in responsible and informed ways instead of ignorantly and fatalistically.

The meaning of the theory advanced concerning the relationship of goods and criticism may be illustrated by ethical theory. Few I suppose would deny that in spite of the attention devoted to this subject by many minds of a high order of intention and intellectual equipment, the outcome, judged from the standpoint of scientific consensus, is rather dismaying. The outcome is due in part to the importance of the subject, its intimate connection with man's deepest concerns, with his most cherished traditions and with the most acutely perplexing problems of his contemporary social life. Objective detachment and development of adequate intellectual instruments are necessarily difficult under such conditions. But I think that we find, amid all the diversity, one common intellectual preconception which inevitably defers the possibility of attainment of scientific method. This is the assumption, implicit or overt, that moral theory is concerned with ends, values rather than with criticism of ends and values; the latter being in fact not only independent of moral theory but not themselves having even moral quality. To discover and define once for all the *bonum* and the *summum bonum* in a way which rationally subserves all virtues and duties, is the traditional task of morals; to deny that moral theory has any such office will seem to many equivalent to denial of the possibility of moral philosophy. Yet in other things repeated failure of achievement is regarded as evidence that we going at the affair in a wrong way. And to a mind willing to surrender the traditional preconception, failure to achieve consensus in method and even in generic conclusions in morals as a branch of philosophy may be similarly explained.

It is not meant of course that the tradition assumes that the good and the highest good are created by moral theory. The assumption is not so bad as that; it is to the effect that it is the province of moral theory to reveal moral goods; to bring them to consciousness and to enforce their character in perception. As empirical fact, however, the arts, those of converse and the literary arts which are the enhanced continuations of social converse, have been the means by which goods are brought home to human perception. The writings of moralists have been efficacious in this direction upon the whole not in their professed intent as theoretical doctrines, but in as far as they have genially participated in the arts of poetry, fiction, parable and drama. Conversion into doctrinal teachings of the imaginative relations of life with which great moral artists have dowered humanity has been the great cause of their ossification into harsh dogmas; illuminating insight into the relations and goods of life has been lost, and an arbitrary code of precepts and rules substituted. Direct appeal of experience concentrated, vivified and intensified by the insight of an artist and embodied in literary creations similar in kind to the revelation of meanings which is the work of any artist, has been treated as a discovery and definition of things true to scientific or philosophic reason.

Meantime the work which theoretical criticism might do has not been done; namely, discovery of the conditions and consequences, the existential relations, of goods which are accepted as goods not because of theory but because they are such in experience.   The cause in large measure is doubtless because the prerequisite tools of physics, physiology and economics were not at hand.   But now when these potential instrumentalities are more adequately prepared they will not be employed until it is recognized that the business of moral theory is not at all with consummations and goods as such, but with discovery of the conditions and consequences of their appearance, a work which is factual and analytic, not dialectic, hortatory, nor prescriptive.   The argument does not forget that there have been would-be naturalistic and empirical ethics which have asserted that goods are such prior to moral conduct as well as to moral theory, and that they become moral only when employed in conduct as objects of reflective choice and endeavor. But the apparent exception proves the rule.   For these forms of moral theory while releasing morals from the obligation of telling man what goods are, leaving that office to life itself, have failed to note that the office of moral philosophy is criticism; and that the performance of this office by discovery of existential conditions and consequences involves a qualitative transformation, a re-making in subsequent action which experimentally tests the conclusions of theory.

Therefore like the Aristotelian ethics, they have been dialectic, defining and classifying in hierarchical order antecedent goods and terminating in a notion of *the* good, the *summum bonum;* or, like hedonistic ethics, they have made a dialectic abstraction of a feature of concrete goods, their pleasantness; and instead of providing a method of analysis of concrete situations have laid down rules of calculation and prescribed policies to be pursued as fixed, not intellectually experimental, results of prior calculations. When they were, like Jeremy Bentham, persons of human sensitiveness to evils from which men suffer in virtue of institutions which may be altered; or, like John Stuart Mill, of genial insight into the constituents of a liberal and humane happiness, they have stirred their generation to beneficent action. But the connection between their theories and the practical outcome was adventitious; their ideas operated when all is said and done as literary rather than as scientific apparatus, as much so as in the case of reforms to which Charles Dickens not meanly contributed.

The implications of the position which has been taken import a "practical" element into philosophy as effective and verifiable criticism, obnoxious to the traditional view. Yet if man is within nature, not a little god outside, and is within as a mode of energy inseparably connected with other modes, interaction is the one unescapable trait of every human concern; thinking, even philosophic thinking, is not exempt. This interaction is subject to partiality because the human factor has bent and bias. But partiality is not obnoxious just because it is partial. A world characterized by qualitative histories with their own beginnings, directions and terminations is of necessity a world in which any interaction is intensive change—a world of partialities, particulars. What is obnoxious in partiality is due to the illusion that there are states and acts which are not also interactions. Immature and undisciplined mind believes in actions which have their seat and source in a particular and separate being, from which they issue. This is the very belief which the advance of intelligent criticism destroys. The latter trans-

forms the notion of isolated one-sided acts into acknowledged interactions. The view which isolates knowledge,
contemplation, liking, interest, value, or whatever from
action is itself a survival of the notion that there are
things which can exist and be known apart from active
connection with other things.

When man finds he is not a little god in his active powers
and accomplishments, he retains his former conceit by
hugging to his bosom the notion that nevertheless in some
realm, be it knowledge or esthetic contemplation, he is
still outside of and detached from the ongoing sweep of
inter-acting and changing events; and being there alone
and irresponsible save to himself, is as a god. When he
perceives clearly and adequately that he is within nature,
a part of its interactions, he sees that the line to be drawn
is not between action and thought, or action and appreciation, but between blind, slavish, meaningless action and
action that is free, significant, directed and responsible.
Knowledge, like the growth of a plant and the movement
of the earth, is a mode of interaction; but it is a mode
which renders other modes luminous, important, valuable,
capable of direction, causes being translated into means
and effects into consequences.

All reason which is itself reasoned, is thus method,
not substance; operative, not "end in itself." To imagine
it the latter is to transport it outside the natural world,
to convert it into a god, whether a big and original one or
a little and derived one, outside of the contingencies of
existence and untouched by its vicissitudes. This is the
meaning of the "reason" which is alleged to envisage
reality *sub specie eternatatis*. It is indeed true that all
relations, all universals and laws as such are timeless.

Even an order of time as an order is timeless, for it is relational. But to give irrelevancy to time the name of eternal in an eulogistic sense, is but to proclaim that irrelevancy to any existence forms a higher kind of existence. Orders, relations, universals are significant and invaluable as objects of knowledge. They are so because they apply to intensive and extensive, individualized, existences; to things of spacious and temporal qualities. Application is not for the sake of something extraneous, for the sake of something designated an utility. It is for the sake of the laws, principles, ideals. Had they not been detached for the purpose of application, they would not have meaning; intent and potentiality of application in the course of events lends them all their significance. Without *actuality* of application, without effort to realise their intent, they are meanings, but they possess neither truth nor falsity, since without application they have no bearing and test. Thus they cease to be objects of knowledge, or even reflection; and become detached objects of contemplation. They may then have the esthetic value possessed by the objects of a dream. But after all we have not left temporal experience, human desire, liking, and passion behind or below us. We have merely painted nature with the colors of an all too local and transitory flight from the hardships of life. These eternal objects abstracted from the course of events, although labeled Reality, in opposition to Appearance, are in truth but the idlest and most evanescent of appearances, born of personal craving and shaped by private fantasy.

Because intelligence is critical method applied to goods of belief, appreciation and conduct, so as to construct, freer and more secure goods, turning assent and assertion

Into free communication of shareable meanings, turning feeling into ordered and liberal sense, turning reaction into response, it is the reasonable object of our deepest faith and loyalty, the stay and support of all reasonable hopes. To utter such a statement is not to indulge in romantic idealization. It is not to assert that intelligence will ever dominate the course of events; it is not even to imply that it will save from ruin and destruction. The issue is one of choice, and choice is always a question of alternatives. What the method of intelligence, thoughtful valuation will accomplish, if once it be tried, is for the result of trial to determine. Since it is relative to the intersection in existence of hazard and rule, of contingency and order, faith in a wholesale and final triumph is fantastic. But some procedure has to be tried; for life is itself a sequence of trials. Carelessness and routine, Olympian aloofness, secluded contemplation are themselves choices. To claim that intelligence is a better method than its alternatives, authority, imitation, caprice and ignorance, prejudice and passion, is hardly an excessive claim. These procedures have been tried and have worked their will. The result is not such as to make it clear that the method of intelligence, the use of science in criticizing and recreating the casual goods of nature into intentional and conclusive goods of art, the union of knowledge and values in production, is not worth trying. There may be those to whom it is treason to think of philosophy as the critical method of developing methods of criticism. But this conception of philosophy also waits to be tried, and the trial which shall approve or condemn lies in the eventual issue. The import of such knowledge as we have acquired and such experience as has been quickened by thought is to evoke and justify the trial.

INDEX

439

Philosophy, Religion

GUIDE TO PHILOSOPHY, C. E. M. Joad. A modern classic which examines many crucial problems which man has pondered through the ages: Does free will exist? Is there plan in the universe? How do we know and validate our knowledge? Such opposed solutions as subjective idealism and realism, chance and teleology, vitalism and logical positivism, are evaluated and the contributions of the great philosophers from the Greeks to moderns like Russell, Whitehead, and others, are considered in the context of each problem. "The finest introduction," BOSTON TRANSCRIPT. Index. Classified bibliography. 592pp. 5⅜ x 8.
T297 Paperbound **$2.00**

HISTORY OF ANCIENT PHILOSOPHY, W. Windelband. One of the clearest, most accurate comprehensive surveys of Greek and Roman philosophy. Discusses ancient philosophy in general, intellectual life in Greece in the 7th and 6th centuries B.C., Thales, Anaximander, Anaximenes, Heraclitus, the Eleatics, Empedocles, Anaxagoras, Leucippus, the Pythagoreans, the Sophists, Socrates, Democritus (20 pages), Plato (50 pages), Aristotle (70 pages), the Peripatetics, Stoics, Epicureans, Sceptics, Neo-platonists, Christian Apologists, etc. 2nd German edition translated by H. E. Cushman. xv + 393pp. 5⅜ x 8.
T357 Paperbound **$1.85**

ILLUSTRATIONS OF THE HISTORY OF MEDIEVAL THOUGHT AND LEARNING, R. L. Poole. Basic analysis of the thought and lives of the leading philosophers and ecclesiastics from the 8th to the 14th century—Abailard, Ockham, Wycliffe, Marsiglio of Padua, and many other great thinkers who carried the torch of Western culture and learning through the "Dark Ages": political, religious, and metaphysical views. Long a standard work for scholars and one of the best introductions to medieval thought for beginners. Index. 10 Appendices. xiii + 327pp. 5⅜ x 8.
T674 Paperbound **$2.00**

PHILOSOPHY AND CIVILIZATION IN THE MIDDLE AGES, M. de Wulf. This semi-popular survey covers aspects of medieval intellectual life such as religion, philosophy, science, the arts, etc. It also covers feudalism vs. Catholicism, rise of the universities, mendicant orders, monastic centers, and similar topics. Unabridged. Bibliography. Index. viii + 320pp. 5⅜ x 8.
T284 Paperbound **$1.85**

AN INTRODUCTION TO SCHOLASTIC PHILOSOPHY, Prof. M. de Wulf. Formerly entitled SCHOLASTICISM OLD AND NEW, this volume examines the central scholastic tradition from St. Anselm, Albertus Magnus, Thomas Aquinas, up to Suarez in the 17th century. The relation of scholasticism to ancient and medieval philosophy and science in general is clear and easily followed. The second part of the book considers the modern revival of scholasticism, the Louvain position, relations with Kantianism and Positivism. Unabridged. xvi + 271pp. 5⅜ x 8.
T296 Clothbound **$3.50**
T283 Paperbound **$1.75**

A HISTORY OF MODERN PHILOSOPHY, H. Höffding. An exceptionally clear and detailed coverage of western philosophy from the Renaissance to the end of the 19th century. Major and minor men such as Pomponazzi, Bodin, Boehme, Telesius, Bruno, Copernicus, da Vinci, Kepler, Galileo, Bacon, Descartes, Hobbes, Spinoza, Leibniz, Wolff, Locke, Newton, Berkeley, Hume, Erasmus, Montesquieu, Voltaire, Diderot, Rousseau, Lessing, Kant, Herder, Fichte, Schelling, Hegel, Schopenhauer, Comte, Mill, Darwin, Spencer, Hartmann, Lange, and many others, are discussed in terms of theory of knowledge, logic, cosmology, and psychology. Index. 2 volumes, total of 1159pp. 5⅜ x 8.
T117 Vol. 1, Paperbound **$2.25**
T118 Vol. 2, Paperbound **$2.25**

ARISTOTLE, A. E. Taylor. A brilliant, searching non-technical account of Aristotle and his thought written by a foremost Platonist. It covers the life and works of Aristotle; classification of the sciences; logic; first philosophy; matter and form; causes; motion and eternity; God; physics; metaphysics; and similar topics. Bibliography. New Index compiled for this edition. 128pp. 5⅜ x 8.
T280 Paperbound **$1.00**

THE SYSTEM OF THOMAS AQUINAS, M. de Wulf. Leading Neo-Thomist, one of founders of University of Louvain, gives concise exposition to central doctrines of Aquinas, as a means toward determining his value to modern philosophy, religion. Formerly "Medieval Philosophy Illustrated from the System of Thomas Aquinas." Trans. by E. Messenger. Introduction. 151pp. 5⅜ x 8.
T568 Paperbound **$1.25**

LEIBNIZ, H. W. Carr. Most stimulating middle-level coverage of basic philosophical thought of Leibniz. Easily understood discussion, analysis of major works: "Theodicy," "Principles of Nature and Grace," "Monadology"; Leibniz's influence; intellectual growth; correspondence; disputes with Bayle, Malebranche, Newton; importance of his thought today, with reinterpretation in modern terminology. "Power and mastery," London Times. Bibliography. Index. 226pp. 5⅜ x 8.
T624 Paperbound **$1.35**

CATALOGUE OF DOVER BOOKS

THE SENSE OF BEAUTY, G. Santayana. A revelation of the beauty of language as well as an important philosophic treatise, this work studies the "why, when, and how beauty appears, what conditions an object must fulfill to be beautiful, what elements of our nature make us sensible of beauty, and what the relation is between the constitution of the object and the excitement of our susceptibility." "It is doubtful if a better treatment of the subject has since been published," PEABODY JOURNAL. Index. ix + 275pp. 5⅜ x 8.
T238 Paperbound **$1.00**

PROBLEMS OF ETHICS, Moritz Schlick. The renowned leader of the "Vienna Circle" applies the logical positivist approach to a wide variety of ethical problems: the source and means of attaining knowledge, the formal and material characteristics of the good, moral norms and principles, absolute vs. relative values, free will and responsibility, comparative importance of pleasure and suffering as ethical values, etc. Disarmingly simple and straightforward despite complexity of subject. First English translation, authorized by author before his death, of a thirty-year old classic. Translated and with an introduction by David Rynin. Index. Foreword by Prof. George P. Adams. xxi + 209pp. 5⅜ x 8. T946 Paperbound **$1.60**

AN INTRODUCTION TO EXISTENTIALISM, Robert G. Olson. A new and indispensable guide to one of the major thought systems of our century, the movement that is central to the thinking of some of the most creative figures of the past hundred years. Stresses Heidegger and Sartre, with careful and objective examination of the existentialist position, values—freedom of choice, individual dignity, personal love, creative effort—and answers to the eternal questions of the human condition. Scholarly, unbiased, analytic, unlike most studies of this difficult subject, Prof. Olson's book is aimed at the student of philosophy as well as at the reader with no formal training who is looking for an absorbing, accessible, and thorough introduction to the basic texts. Index. xv + 221pp. 5⅜ x 8½. T55 Paperbound **$1.50**

SYMBOLIC LOGIC, C. I. Lewis and C. H. Langford. Since first publication in 1932, this has been among most frequently cited works on symbolic logic. Still one of the best introductions both for beginners and for mathematicians, philosophers. First part covers basic topics which easily lend themselves to beginning study. Second part is rigorous, thorough development of logistic method, examination of some of most difficult and abstract aspects of symbolic logic, including modal logic, logical paradoxes, many-valued logic, with Prof. Lewis' own contributions. 2nd revised (corrected) edition. 3 appendixes, one new to this edition. 524pp. 5⅜ x 8. S170 Paperbound **$2.00**

WHITEHEAD'S PHILOSOPHY OF CIVILIZATION, A. H. Johnson. A leading authority on Alfred North Whitehead synthesizes the great philosopher's thought on civilization, scattered throughout various writings, into unified whole. Analysis of Whitehead's general definition of civilization, his reflections on history and influences on its development, his religion, including his analysis of Christianity, concept of solitariness as first requirement of personal religion, and so on. Other chapters cover views on minority groups, society, civil liberties, education. Also critical comments on Whitehead's philosophy. Written with general reader in mind. A perceptive introduction to important area of the thought of a leading philosopher of our century. Revised index and bibliography. xii + 211pp. 5⅜ x 8½.
T996 Paperbound **$1.50**

WHITEHEAD'S THEORY OF REALITY, A. H. Johnson. Introductory outline of Whitehead's theory of actual entities, the heart of his philosophy of reality, followed by his views on nature of God, philosophy of mind, theory of value (truth, beauty, goodness and their opposites), analyses of other philosophers, attitude toward science. A perspicacious lucid introduction by author of dissertation on Whitehead, written under the subject's supervision at Harvard. Good basic view for beginning students of philosophy and for those who are simply interested in important contemporary ideas. Revised index and bibliography. xiii + 267pp. 5⅜ x 8½.
T989 Paperbound **$1.50**

MIND AND THE WORLD-ORDER, C. I. Lewis. Building upon the work of Peirce, James, and Dewey, Professor Lewis outlines a theory of knowledge in terms of "conceptual pragmatism." Dividing truth into abstract mathematical certainty and empirical truth, the author demonstrates that the traditional understanding of the a priori must be abandoned. Detailed analyses of philosophy, metaphysics, method, the "given" in experience, knowledge of objects, nature of the a priori, experience and order, and many others. Appendices. xiv + 446pp. 5⅜ x 8. T359 Paperbound **$2.25**

SCEPTICISM AND ANIMAL FAITH, G. Santayana. To eliminate difficulties in the traditional theory of knowledge, Santayana distinguishes between the independent existence of objects and the essence our mind attributes to them. Scepticism is thereby established as a form of belief, and animal faith is shown to be a necessary condition of knowledge. Belief, classical idealism, intuition, memory, symbols, literary psychology, and much more, discussed with unusual clarity and depth. Index. xii + 314pp. 5⅜ x 8. T235 Clothbound **$3.50**
T236 Paperbound **$2.00**

LANGUAGE AND MYTH, E. Cassirer. Analyzing the non-rational thought processes which go to make up culture, Cassirer demonstrates that beneath both language and myth there lies a dominant unconscious "grammar" of experience whose categories and canons are not those of logical thought. His analyses of seemingly diverse phenomena such as Indian metaphysics, the Melanesian "mana," the Naturphilosophie of Schelling, modern poetry, etc., are profound without being pedantic. Introduction and translation by Susanne Langer. Index. x + 103pp. 5⅜ x 8. T51 Paperbound **$1.25**

CATALOGUE OF DOVER BOOKS

AN ESSAY CONCERNING HUMAN UNDERSTANDING, John Locke. Edited by A. C. Fraser. Unabridged reprinting of definitive edition; only complete edition of "Essay" in print. Marginal analyses of almost every paragraph; hundreds of footnotes; authoritative 140-page biographical, critical, historical prolegomena. Indexes. 1170pp. 5⅜ x 8.

T530 Vol. 1 (Books 1, 2) Paperbound **$2.50**
T531 Vol. 2 (Books 3, 4) Paperbound **$2.50**
2 volume set **$5.00**

THE PHILOSOPHY OF HISTORY, G. W. F. Hegel. One of the great classics of western thought which reveals Hegel's basic principle: that history is not chance but a rational process, the realization of the Spirit of Freedom. Ranges from the oriental cultures of subjective thought to the classical subjective cultures, to the modern absolute synthesis where spiritual and secular may be reconciled. Translation and introduction by J. Sibree. Introduction by C. Hegel. Special introduction for this edition by Prof. Carl Friedrich. xxxix + 447pp. 5⅜ x 8.

T112 Paperbound **$2.25**

THE PHILOSOPHY OF HEGEL, W. T. Stace. The first detailed analysis of Hegel's thought in English, this is especially valuable since so many of Hegel's works are out of print. Dr. Stace examines Hegel's debt to Greek idealists and the 18th century and then proceeds to a careful description and analysis of Hegel's first principles, categories, reason, dialectic method, his logic, philosophy of nature and spirit, etc. Index. Special 14 x 20 chart of Hegelian system. x + 526pp. 5⅜ x 8.

T254 Paperbound **$2.45**

THE WILL TO BELIEVE and HUMAN IMMORTALITY, W. James. Two complete books bound as one. THE WILL TO BELIEVE discusses the interrelations of belief, will, and intellect in man; chance vs. determinism, free will vs. determinism, free will vs. fate, pluralism vs. monism; the philosophies of Hegel and Spencer, and more. HUMAN IMMORTALITY examines the question of survival after death and develops an unusual and powerful argument for immortality. Two prefaces. Index. Total of 429pp. 5⅜ x 8.

T291 Paperbound **$2.00**

THE WORLD AND THE INDIVIDUAL, Josiah Royce. Only major effort by an American philosopher to interpret nature of things in systematic, comprehensive manner. Royce's formulation of an absolute voluntarism remains one of the original and profound solutions to the problems involved. Part One, Four Historical Conceptions of Being, inquires into first principles, true meaning and place of individuality. Part Two, Nature, Man, and the Moral Order, is application of first principles to problems concerning religion, evil, moral order. Introduction by J. E. Smith, Yale Univ. Index. 1070pp. 5⅜ x 8.

T561 Vol. 1 Paperbound **$2.75**
T562 Vol. 2 Paperbound **$2.75**
Two volume set **$5.50**

THE PHILOSOPHICAL WRITINGS OF PEIRCE, edited by J. Buchler. This book (formerly THE PHILOSOPHY OF PEIRCE) is a carefully integrated exposition of Peirce's complete system composed of selections from his own work. Symbolic logic, scientific method, theory of signs, pragmatism, epistemology, chance, cosmology, ethics, and many other topics are treated by one of the greatest philosophers of modern times. This is the only inexpensive compilation of his key ideas. xvi + 386pp. 5⅜ x 8.

T217 Paperbound **$2.00**

EXPERIENCE AND NATURE, John Dewey. An enlarged, revised edition of the Paul Carus lectures which Dewey delivered in 1925. It covers Dewey's basic formulation of the problem of knowledge, with a full discussion of other systems, and a detailing of his own concepts of the relationship of external world, mind, and knowledge. Starts with a thorough examination of the philosophical method; examines the interrelationship of experience and nature; analyzes experience on basis of empirical naturalism, the formulation of law, role of language and social factors in knowledge; etc. Dewey's treatment of central problems in philosophy is profound but extremely easy to follow. ix + 448pp. 5⅜ x 8.

T471 Paperbound **$2.00**

THE PHILOSOPHICAL WORKS OF DESCARTES. The definitive English edition of all the major philosophical works and letters of René Descartes. All of his revolutionary insights, from his famous "Cogito ergo sum" to his detailed account of contemporary science and his astonishingly fruitful concept that all phenomena of the universe (except mind) could be reduced to clear laws by the use of mathematics. An excellent source for the thought of men like Hobbes, Arnauld, Gassendi, etc., who were Descarte's contemporaries. Translated by E. S. Haldane and G. Ross. Introductory notes. Index. Total of 842pp. 5⅜ x 8.

T71 Vol. 1, Paperbound **$2.00**
T72 Vol. 2, Paperbound **$2.00**

THE CHIEF WORKS OF SPINOZA. An unabridged reprint of the famous Bohn edition containing all of Spinoza's most important works: Vol. I: The Theologico-Political Treatise and the Political Treatise. Vol. II: On The Improvement Of Understanding, The Ethics, Selected Letters. Profound and enduring ideas on God, the universe, pantheism, society, religion, the state, democracy, the mind, emotions, freedom and the nature of man, which influenced Goethe, Hegel, Schelling, Coleridge, Whitehead, and many others. Introduction. 2 volumes. 826pp. 5⅜ x 8.

T249 Vol. I, Paperbound **$1.50**
T250 Vol. II, Paperbound **$1.50**

Psychology

YOGA: A SCIENTIFIC EVALUATION, Kovoor T. Behanan. A complete reprinting of the book that for the first time gave Western readers a sane, scientific explanation and analysis of yoga. The author draws on controlled laboratory experiments and personal records of a year as a disciple of a yoga, to investigate yoga psychology, concepts of knowledge, physiology, "supernatural" phenomena, and the ability to tap the deepest human powers. In this study under the auspices of Yale University Institute of Human Relations, the strictest principles of physiological and psychological inquiry are followed throughout. Foreword by W. A. Miles, Yale University. 17 photographs. Glossary. Index. xx + 270pp. 5⅜ x 8. T505 Paperbound **$1.75**

CONDITIONED REFLEXES: AN INVESTIGATION OF THE PHYSIOLOGICAL ACTIVITIES OF THE CEREBRAL CORTEX, I. P. Pavlov. Full, authorized translation of Pavlov's own survey of his work in experimental psychology reviews entire course of experiments, summarizes conclusions, outlines psychological system based on famous "conditioned reflex" concept. Details of technical means used in experiments, observations on formation of conditioned reflexes, function of cerebral hemispheres, results of damage, nature of sleep, typology of nervous system, significance of experiments for human psychology. Trans. by Dr. G. V. Anrep, Cambridge Univ. 235-item bibliography. 18 figures. 445pp. 5⅜ x 8. S614 Paperbound **$2.35**

EXPLANATION OF HUMAN BEHAVIOUR, F. V. Smith. A major intermediate-level introduction to and criticism of 8 complete systems of the psychology of human behavior, with unusual emphasis on theory of investigation and methodology. Part I is an illuminating analysis of the problems involved in the explanation of observed phenomena, and the differing viewpoints on the nature of causality. Parts II and III are a closely detailed survey of the systems of McDougall, Gordon Allport, Lewin, the Gestalt group, Freud, Watson, Hull, and Tolman. Biographical notes. Bibliography of over 800 items. 2 Indexes. 38 figures. xii + 460pp. 5½ x 8¾. T253 Clothbound **$6.00**

SEX IN PSYCHO-ANALYSIS (formerly CONTRIBUTIONS TO PSYCHO-ANALYSIS), S. Ferenczi. Written by an associate of Freud, this volume presents countless insights on such topics as impotence, transference, analysis and children, dreams, symbols, obscene words, masturbation and male homosexuality, paranoia and psycho-analysis, the sense of reality, hypnotism and therapy, and many others. Also includes full text of THE DEVELOPMENT OF PSYCHO-ANALYSIS by Ferenczi and Otto Rank. Two books bound as one. Total of 406pp. 5⅜ x 8. T324 Paperbound **$1.85**

BEYOND PSYCHOLOGY, Otto Rank. One of Rank's most mature contributions, focussing on the irrational basis of human behavior as a basic fact of our lives. The psychoanalytic techniques of myth analysis trace to their source the ultimates of human existence: fear of death, personality, the social organization, the need for love and creativity, etc. Dr. Rank finds them stemming from a common irrational source, man's fear of final destruction. A seminal work in modern psychology, this work sheds light on areas ranging from the concept of immortal soul to the sources of state power. 291pp. 5⅜ x 8. T485 Paperbound **$2.00**

ILLUSIONS AND DELUSIONS OF THE SUPERNATURAL AND THE OCCULT, D. H. Rawcliffe. Holds up to rational examination hundreds of persistent delusions including crystal gazing, automatic writing, table turning, mediumistic trances, mental healing, stigmata, lycanthropy, live burial, the Indian Rope Trick, spiritualism, dowsing, telepathy, clairvoyance, ghosts, ESP, etc. The author explains and exposes the mental and physical deceptions involved, making this not only an exposé of supernatural phenomena, but a valuable exposition of characteristic types of abnormal psychology. Originally titled "The Psychology of the Occult." 14 illustrations. Index. 551pp. 5⅜ x 8. T503 Paperbound **$2.00**

THE PRINCIPLES OF PSYCHOLOGY, William James. The full long-course, unabridged, of one of the great classics of Western literature and science. Wonderfully lucid descriptions of human mental activity, the stream of thought, consciousness, time perception, memory, imagination, emotions, reason, abnormal phenomena, and similar topics. Original contributions are integrated with the work of such men as Berkeley, Binet, Mills, Darwin, Hume, Kant, Royce, Schopenhauer, Spinoza, Locke, Descartes, Galton, Wundt, Lotze, Herbart, Fechner, and scores of others. All contrasting interpretations of mental phenomena are examined in detail — introspective analysis, philosophical interpretation, and experimental research. "A classic," JOURNAL OF CONSULTING PSYCHOLOGY. "The main lines are as valid as ever," PSYCHO-ANALYTICAL QUARTERLY. "Standard reading . . . a classic of interpretation," PSYCHIATRIC QUARTERLY. 94 illustrations. 1408pp. 2 volumes. 5⅜ x 8. Vol. 1, T381 Paperbound **$2.50** Vol. 2, T382 Paperbound **$2.50**

THE DYNAMICS OF THERAPY IN A CONTROLLED RELATIONSHIP, Jessie Taft. One of the most important works in literature of child psychology, out of print for 25 years. Outstanding disciple of Rank describes all aspects of relationship or Rankian therapy through concise, simple elucidation of theory underlying her actual contacts with two seven-year olds. Therapists, social caseworkers, psychologists, counselors, and laymen who work with children will all find this important work an invaluable summation of method, theory of child psychology. xix + 296pp. 5⅜ x 8. T325 Paperbound **$1.75**

Books Explaining Science and Mathematics

WHAT IS SCIENCE?, N. Campbell. The role of experiment and measurement, the function of mathematics, the nature of scientific laws, the difference between laws and theories, the limitations of science, and many similarly provocative topics are treated clearly and without technicalities by an eminent scientist. "Still an excellent introduction to scientific philosophy," H. Margenau in PHYSICS TODAY. "A first-rate primer . . . deserves a wide audience," SCIENTIFIC AMERICAN. 192pp. 5⅜ x 8. S43 Paperbound **$1.25**

THE NATURE OF PHYSICAL THEORY, P. W. Bridgman. A Nobel Laureate's clear, non-technical lectures on difficulties and paradoxes connected with frontier research on the physical sciences. Concerned with such central concepts as thought, logic, mathematics, relativity, probability, wave mechanics, etc. he analyzes the contributions of such men as Newton, Einstein, Bohr, Heisenberg, and many others. "Lucid and entertaining . . . recommended to anyone who wants to get some insight into current philosophies of science," THE NEW PHILOSOPHY. Index. xi + 138pp. 5⅜ x 8. S33 Paperbound **$1.25**

EXPERIMENT AND THEORY IN PHYSICS, Max Born. A Nobel Laureate examines the nature of experiment and theory in theoretical physics and analyzes the advances made by the great physicists of our day: Heisenberg, Einstein, Bohr, Planck, Dirac, and others. The actual process of creation is detailed step-by-step by one who participated. A fine examination of the scientific method at work. 44pp. 5⅜ x 8. S308 Paperbound **75¢**

THE PSYCHOLOGY OF INVENTION IN THE MATHEMATICAL FIELD, J. Hadamard. The reports of such men as Descartes, Pascal, Einstein, Poincaré, and others are considered in this investigation of the method of idea-creation in mathematics and other sciences and the thinking process in general. How do ideas originate? What is the role of the unconscious? What is Poincaré's forgetting hypothesis? are some of the fascinating questions treated. A penetrating analysis of Einstein's thought processes concludes the book. xiii + 145pp. 5⅜ x 8. T107 Paperbound **$1.25**

THE NATURE OF LIGHT AND COLOUR IN THE OPEN AIR, M. Minnaert. Why are shadows sometimes blue, sometimes green, or other colors depending on the light and surroundings? What causes mirages? Why do multiple suns and moons appear in the sky? Professor Minnaert explains these unusual phenomena and hundreds of others in simple, easy-to-understand terms based on optical laws and the properties of light and color. No mathematics is required but artists, scientists, students, and everyone fascinated by these "tricks" of nature will find thousands of useful and amazing pieces of information. Hundreds of observational experiments are suggested which require no special equipment. 200 illustrations; 42 photos. xvi + 362pp. 5⅜ x 8. T196 Paperbound **$2.00**

THE UNIVERSE OF LIGHT, W. Bragg. Sir William Bragg, Nobel Laureate and great modern physicist, is also well known for his powers of clear exposition. Here he analyzes all aspects of light for the layman: lenses, reflection, refraction, the optics of vision, x-rays, the photoelectric effect, etc. He tells you what causes the color of spectra, rainbows, and soap bubbles, how magic mirrors work, and much more. Dozens of simple experiments are described. Preface. Index. 199 line drawings and photographs, including 2 full-page color plates. x + 283pp. 5⅜ x 8. T538 Paperbound **$1.85**

SOAP-BUBBLES: THEIR COLOURS AND THE FORCES THAT MOULD THEM, C. V. Boys. For continuing popularity and validity as scientific primer, few books can match this volume of easily-followed experiments, explanations. Lucid exposition of complexities of liquid films, surface tension and related phenomena, bubbles' reaction to heat, motion, music, magnetic fields. Experiments with capillary attraction, soap bubbles on frames, composite bubbles, liquid cylinders and jets, bubbles other than soap, etc. Wonderful introduction to scientific method, natural laws that have many ramifications in areas of modern physics. Only complete edition in print. New Introduction by S. Z. Lewin, New York University. 83 illustrations; 1 full-page color plate. xii + 190pp. 5⅜ x 8½. T542 Paperbound **95¢**

CATALOGUE OF DOVER BOOKS

BRIDGES AND THEIR BUILDERS, D. B. Steinman & S. R. Watson. Engineers, historians, and every person who has ever been fascinated by great spans will find this book an endless source of information and interest. Greek and Roman structures, Medieval bridges, modern classics such as the Brooklyn Bridge, and the latest developments in the science are retold by one of the world's leading authorities on bridge design and construction. BRIDGES AND THEIR BUILDERS is the only comprehensive and accurate semi-popular history of these important measures of progress in print. New, greatly revised, enlarged edition. 23 photos; 26 line-drawings. Index. xvii + 401pp. 5⅜ x 8. **T431 Paperbound $2.00**

FAMOUS BRIDGES OF THE WORLD, D. B. Steinman. An up-to-the-minute new edition of a book that explains the fascinating drama of how the world's great bridges came to be built. The author, designer of the famed Mackinac bridge, discusses bridges from all periods and all parts of the world, explaining their various types of construction, and describing the problems their builders faced. Although primarily for youngsters, this cannot fail to interest readers of all ages. 48 illustrations in the text. 23 photographs. 99pp. 6⅛ x 9¼. **T161 Paperbound $1.00**

HOW DO YOU USE A SLIDE RULE? by A. A. Merrill. A step-by-step explanation of the slide rule that presents the fundamental rules clearly enough for the non-mathematician to understand. Unlike most instruction manuals, this work concentrates on the two most important operations: multiplication and division. 10 easy lessons, each with a clear drawing, for the reader who has difficulty following other expositions. 1st publication. Index. 2 Appendices. 10 illustrations. 78 problems, all with answers. vi + 36 pp. 6⅛ x 9¼. **T62 Paperbound 60¢**

HOW TO CALCULATE QUICKLY, H. Sticker. A tried and true method for increasing your "number sense" — the ability to see relationships between numbers and groups of numbers. Addition, subtraction, multiplication, division, fractions, and other topics are treated through techniques not generally taught in schools: left to right multiplication, division by inspection, etc. This is not a collection of tricks which work only on special numbers, but a detailed well-planned course, consisting of over 9,000 problems that you can work in spare moments. It is excellent for anyone who is inconvenienced by slow computational skills. 5 or 10 minutes of this book daily will double or triple your calculation speed. 9,000 problems, answers. 256pp. 5⅜ x 8. **T295 Paperbound $1.00**

MATHEMATICAL FUN, GAMES AND PUZZLES, Jack Frohlichstein. A valuable service for parents of children who have trouble with math, for teachers in need of a supplement to regular upper elementary and junior high math texts (each section is graded—easy, average, difficult —for ready adaptation to different levels of ability), and for just anyone who would like to develop basic skills in an informal and entertaining manner. The author combines ten years of experience as a junior high school math teacher with a method that uses puzzles and games to introduce the basic ideas and operations of arithmetic. Stress on everyday uses of math: banking, stock market, personal budgets, insurance, taxes. Intellectually stimulating and practical, too. 418 problems and diversions with answers. Bibliography. 120 illustrations. xix + 306pp. 5⅝ x 8½. **T789 Paperbound $1.75**

GREAT IDEAS OF MODERN MATHEMATICS: THEIR NATURE AND USE, Jagjit Singh. Reader with only high school math will understand main mathematical ideas of modern physics, astronomy, genetics, psychology, evolution, etc. better than many who use them as tools, but comprehend little of their basic structure. Author uses his wide knowledge of non-mathematical fields in brilliant exposition of differential equations, matrices, group theory, logic, statistics, problems of mathematical foundations, imaginary numbers, vectors, etc. Original publication. 2 appendixes. 2 indexes. 65 illustr. 322pp. 5⅜ x 8. **S587 Paperbound $1.75**

*MATHEMATICS IN ACTION, O. G. Sutton. Everyone with a command of high school algebra will find this book one of the finest possible introductions to the application of mathematics to physical theory. Ballistics, numerical analysis, waves and wavelike phenomena, Fourier series, group concepts, fluid flow and aerodynamics, statistical measures, and meteorology are discussed with unusual clarity. Some calculus and differential equations theory is developed by the author for the reader's help in the more difficult sections. 88 figures. Index. viii + 236pp. 5⅜ x 8. **T440 Clothbound $3.50**

*INTRODUCTION TO SYMBOLIC LOGIC AND ITS APPLICATIONS, Rudolph Carnap. One of the clearest, most comprehensive, and rigorous introductions to modern symbolic logic, by perhaps its greatest living master. Not merely elementary theory, but demonstrated applications in mathematics, physics, and biology. Symbolic languages of various degrees of complexity are analyzed, and one constructed. "A creation of the rank of a masterpiece," Zentralblatt für Mathematik und Ihre Grenzgebiete. Over 300 exercises. 5 figures. Bibliography. Index. xvi + 241pp. 5⅜ x 8. **S453 Paperbound $1.85**

*HIGHER MATHEMATICS FOR STUDENTS OF CHEMISTRY AND PHYSICS, J. W. Mellor. Not abstract, but practical, drawing its problems from familiar laboratory material, this book covers theory and application of differential calculus, analytic geometry, functions with singularities, integral calculus, infinite series, solution of numerical equations, differential equations, Fourier's theorem and extensions, probability and the theory of errors, calculus of variations, determinants, etc. "If the reader is not familiar with this book, it will repay him to examine it," CHEM. & ENGINEERING NEWS. 800 problems. 189 figures. 2 appendices; 30 tables of integrals, probability functions, etc. Bibliography. xxi + 641pp. 5⅜ x 8. **S193 Paperbound $2.25**

CATALOGUE OF DOVER BOOKS

THE FOURTH DIMENSION SIMPLY EXPLAINED, edited by Henry P. Manning. Originally written as entries in contest sponsored by "Scientific American," then published in book form, these 22 essays present easily understood explanations of how the fourth dimension may be studied, the relationship of non-Euclidean geometry to the fourth dimension, analogies to three-dimensional space, some fourth-dimensional absurdities and curiosities, possible measurements and forms in the fourth dimension. In general, a thorough coverage of many of the simpler properties of fourth-dimensional space. Multi-points of view on many of the most important aspects are valuable aid to comprehension. Introduction by Dr. Henry P. Manning gives proper emphasis to points in essays, more advanced account of fourth-dimensional geometry. 82 figures. 251pp. 5⅜ x 8.   T711 Paperbound **$1.35**

TRIGONOMETRY REFRESHER FOR TECHNICAL MEN, A. A. Klaf. A modern question and answer text on plane and spherical trigonometry. Part I covers plane trigonometry: angles, quadrants, trigonometrical functions, graphical representation, interpolation, equations, logarithms, solution of triangles, slide rules, etc. Part II discusses applications to navigation, surveying, elasticity, architecture, and engineering. Small angles, periodic functions, vectors, polar coordinates, De Moivre's theorem, fully covered. Part III is devoted to spherical trigonometry and the solution of spherical triangles, with applications to terrestrial and astronomical problems. Special time-savers for numerical calculation. 913 questions answered for you! 1738 problems; answers to odd numbers. 494 figures. 14 pages of functions, formulae. Index. x + 629pp. 5⅜ x 8.   T371 Paperbound **$2.00**

CALCULUS REFRESHER FOR TECHNICAL MEN. A. A. Klaf. Not an ordinary textbook but a unique refresher for engineers, technicians, and students. An examination of the most important aspects of differential and integral calculus by means of 756 key questions. Part I covers simple differential calculus: constants, variables, functions, increments, derivatives, logarithms, curvature, etc. Part II treats fundamental concepts of integration: inspection, substitution, transformation, reduction, areas and volumes, mean value, successive and partial integration, double and triple integration. Stresses practical aspects! A 50 page section gives applications to civil and nautical engineering, electricity, stress and strain, elasticity, industrial engineering, and similar fields. 756 questions answered. 556 problems; solutions to odd numbers. 36 pages of constants, formulae. Index. v + 431pp. 5⅜ x 8.
T370 Paperbound **$2.00**

PROBABILITIES AND LIFE, Emile Borel. One of the leading French mathematicians of the last 100 years makes use of certain results of mathematics of probabilities and explains a number of problems that for the most part, are related to everyday living or to illness and death: computation of life expectancy tables, chances of recovery from various diseases, probabilities of job accidents, weather predictions, games of chance, and so on. Emphasis on results not processes, though some indication is made of mathematical proofs. Simple in style, free of technical terminology, limited in scope to everyday situations, it is comprehensible to laymen, fine reading for beginning students of probability. New English translation. Index. Appendix. vi + 87pp. 5⅜ x 8½.   T121 Paperbound **$1.00**

POPULAR SCIENTIFIC LECTURES, Hermann von Helmholtz. 7 lucid expositions by a pre-eminent scientific mind: "The Physiological Causes of Harmony in Music," "On the Relation of Optics to Painting," "On the Conservation of Force," "On the Interaction of Natural Forces," "On Goethe's Scientific Researches" into theory of color, "On the Origin and Significance of Geometric Axioms," "On Recent Progress in the Theory of Vision." Written with simplicity of expression, stripped of technicalities, these are easy to understand and delightful reading for anyone interested in science or looking for an introduction to serious study of acoustics or optics. Introduction by Professor Morris Kline, Director, Division of Electromagnetic Research, New York University, contains astute, impartial evaluations. Selected from "Popular Lectures on Scientific Subjects," 1st and 2nd series. xii + 286pp. 5⅜ x 8½.   T799 Paperbound **$1.45**

SCIENCE AND METHOD, Henri Poincaré. Procedure of scientific discovery, methodology, experiment, idea-germination—the intellectual processes by which discoveries come into being. Most significant and most interesting aspects of development, application of ideas. Chapters cover selection of facts, chance, mathematical reasoning, mathematics, and logic; Whitehead, Russell, Cantor; the new mechanics, etc. 288pp. 5⅜ x 8.   S222 Paperbound **$1.35**

HEAT AND ITS WORKINGS, Morton Mott-Smith, Ph.D. An unusual book; to our knowledge the only middle-level survey of this important area of science. Explains clearly such important concepts as physiological sensation of heat and Weber's law, measurement of heat, evolution of thermometer, nature of heat, expansion and contraction of solids, Boyle's law, specific heat. BTU's and calories, evaporation, Andrews's isothermals, radiation, the relation of heat to light, many more topics inseparable from other aspects of physics. A wide, non-mathematical yet thorough explanation of basic ideas, theories, phenomena for laymen and beginning scientists illustrated by experiences of daily life. Bibliography. 50 illustrations. x + 165pp. 5⅜ x 8½.   T978 Paperbound **$1.00**

History of Science and Mathematics

THE STUDY OF THE HISTORY OF MATHEMATICS, THE STUDY OF THE HISTORY OF SCIENCE, G. Sarton. Two books bound as one. Each volume contains a long introduction to the methods and philosophy of each of these historical fields, covering the skills and sympathies of the historian, concepts of history of science, psychology of idea-creation, and the purpose of history of science. Prof. Sarton also provides more than 80 pages of classified bibliography. Complete and unabridged. Indexed. 10 illustrations. 188pp. 5⅜ x 8.   T240 Paperbound **$1.25**

A HISTORY OF PHYSICS, Florian Cajori, Ph.D. First written in 1899, thoroughly revised in 1929, this is still best entry into antecedents of modern theories. Precise non-mathematical discussion of ideas, theories, techniques, apparatus of each period from Greeks to 1920's, analyzing within each period basic topics of matter, mechanics, light, electricity and magnetism, sound, atomic theory, etc. Stress on modern developments, from early 19th century to present. Written with critical eye on historical development, significance. Provides most of needed historical background for student of physics. Reprint of second (1929) edition. Index. Bibliography in footnotes. 16 figures. xv + 424pp. 5⅜ x 8.   T970 Paperbound **$2.00**

A HISTORY OF ASTRONOMY FROM THALES TO KEPLER, J. L. E. Dreyer. Formerly titled A HISTORY OF PLANETARY SYSTEMS FROM THALES TO KEPLER. This is the only work in English which provides a detailed history of man's cosmological views from prehistoric times up through the Renaissance. It covers Egypt, Babylonia, early Greece, Alexandria, the Middle Ages, Copernicus, Tycho Brahe, Kepler, and many others. Epicycles and other complex theories of positional astronomy are explained in terms nearly everyone will find clear and easy to understand. "Standard reference on Greek astronomy and the Copernican revolution," SKY AND TELESCOPE. Bibliography. 21 diagrams. Index. xvii + 430pp. 5⅜ x 8.   S79 Paperbound **$1.98**

A SHORT HISTORY OF ASTRONOMY, A. Berry. A popular standard work for over 50 years, this thorough and accurate volume covers the science from primitive times to the end of the 19th century. After the Greeks and Middle Ages, individual chapters analyze Copernicus, Brahe, Galileo, Kepler, and Newton, and the mixed reception of their startling discoveries. Post-Newtonian achievements are then discussed in unusual detail: Halley, Bradley, Lagrange, Laplace, Herschel, Bessel, etc. 2 indexes. 104 illustrations, 9 portraits. xxxi + 440pp. 5⅜ x 8.   T210 Paperbound **$2.00**

PIONEERS OF SCIENCE, Sir Oliver Lodge. An authoritative, yet elementary history of science by a leading scientist and expositor. Concentrating on individuals—Copernicus, Brahe, Kepler, Galileo, Descartes, Newton, Laplace, Herschel, Lord Kelvin, and other scientists—the author presents their discoveries in historical order, adding biographical material on each man and full, specific explanations of their achievements. The full, clear discussions of the accomplishments of post-Newtonian astronomers are features seldom found in other books on the subject. Index. 120 illustrations. xv + 404pp. 5⅜ x 8.   T716 Paperbound **$1.65**

THE BIRTH AND DEVELOPMENT OF THE GEOLOGICAL SCIENCES, F. D. Adams. The most complete and thorough history of the earth sciences in print. Geological thought from earliest recorded times to the end of the 19th century—covers over 300 early thinkers and systems: fossils and hypothetical explanations of them, vulcanists vs. neptunists, figured stones and paleontology, generation of stones, and similar topics. 91 illustrations, including medieval, renaissance woodcuts, etc. 632 footnotes and bibliographic notes. Index. 511pp. 5⅜ x 8.   T5 Paperbound **$2.25**

THE STORY OF ALCHEMY AND EARLY CHEMISTRY, J. M. Stillman. "Add the blood of a red-haired man"—a recipe typical of the many quoted in this authoritative and readable history of the strange beliefs and practices of the alchemists. Concise studies of every leading figure in alchemy and early chemistry through Lavoisier, in this curious epic of superstition and true science, constructed from scores of rare and difficult Greek, Latin, German, and French texts. Foreword by S. W. Young. 246-item bibliography. Index. xiii + 566pp. 5⅜ x 8.   S628 Paperbound **$2.45**

HISTORY OF MATHEMATICS, D. E. Smith. Most comprehensive non-technical history of math in English. Discusses the lives and works of over a thousand major and minor figures, from Euclid to Descartes, Gauss, and Riemann. Vol. I: A chronological examination, from primitive concepts through Egypt, Babylonia, Greece, the Orient, Rome, the Middle Ages, the Renaissance, and up to 1900. Vol. 2: The development of ideas in specific fields and problems, up through elementary calculus. Two volumes, total of 510 illustrations, 1355pp. 5⅜ x 8. Set boxed in attractive container.   T429,430 Paperbound the set **$5.00**

Teach Yourself

These British books are the most effective series of home study books on the market! With no outside help they will teach you as much as is necessary to have a good background in each subject, in many cases offering as much material as a similar high school or college course. They are carefully planned, written by foremost British educators, and amply provided with test questions and problems for you to check your progress; the mathematics books are especially rich in examples and problems. Do not confuse them with skimpy outlines or ordinary school texts or vague generalized popularizations; each book is complete in itself, full without being overdetailed, and designed to give you an easily-acquired branch of knowledge.

TEACH YOURSELF ALGEBRA, P. Abbott. The equivalent of a thorough high school course, up through logarithms. 52 illus. 307pp. 4¼ x 7.　　　　　　　　　　T680 Clothbound **$2.00**

TEACH YOURSELF GEOMETRY, P. Abbott. Plane and solid geometry, covering about a year of plane and six months of solid. 268 illus. 344pp. 4½ x 7.　　　　T681 Clothbound **$2.00**

TEACH YOURSELF TRIGONOMETRY, P. Abbott. Background of algebra and geometry will enable you to get equivalent of elementary college course. Tables. 102 illus. 204pp. 4½ x 7.
T682 Clothbound **$2.00**

TEACH YOURSELF THE CALCULUS, P. Abbott. With algebra and trigonometry you will be able to acquire a good working knowledge of elementary integral calculus and differential calculus. Excellent supplement to any course textbook. 380pp. 4¼ x 7.　　　　T683 Clothbound **$2.00**

TEACH YOURSELF THE SLIDE RULE, B. Snodgrass. Basic principles clearly explained, with many applications in engineering, business, general figuring, will enable you to pick up very useful skill. 10 illus. 207pp. 4¼ x 7.　　　　　　　　　T684 Clothbound **$2.00**

TEACH YOURSELF MECHANICS, P. Abbott. Equivalent of part course on elementary college level, with lever, parallelogram of force, friction, laws of motion, gases, etc. Fine introduction before more advanced course. 163 illus. 271pp. 4½ x 7.　　　T685 Clothbound **$2.00**

TEACH YOURSELF ELECTRICITY, C. W. Wilman. Current, resistance, voltage, Ohm's law, circuits, generators, motors, transformers, etc. Non-mathematical as much as possible. 115 illus. 184pp. 4¼ x 7.　　　　　　　　　　　　　　　　T230 Clothbound **$2.00**

TEACH YOURSELF HEAT ENGINES E. DeVille. Steam and internal combustion engines; non-mathematical introduction for student, for layman wishing background, refresher for advanced student. 76 illus. 217pp. 4¼ x 7.　　　　　　　　　T237 Clothbound **$2.00**

TEACH YOURSELF TO PLAY THE PIANO, King Palmer. Companion and supplement to lessons or self study. Handy reference, too. Nature of instrument, elementary musical theory, technique of playing, interpretation, etc. 60 illus. 144pp. 4¼ x 7.　　T959 Clothbound **$2.00**

TEACH YOURSELF HERALDRY AND GENEALOGY, L. G. Pine. Modern work, avoiding romantic and overpopular misconceptions. Editor of new Burke presents detailed information and commentary down to present. Best general survey. 50 illus. glossary; 129pp. 4¼ x 7.
T962 Clothbound **$2.00**

TEACH YOURSELF HANDWRITING, John L. Dumpleton. Basic Chancery cursive style is popular and easy to learn. Many diagrams. 114 illus. 192pp. 4¼ x 7.　　T960 Clothbound **$2.00**

TEACH YOURSELF CARD GAMES FOR TWO, Kenneth Konstam. Many first-rate games, including old favorites like cribbage and gin and canasta as well as new lesser-known games. Extremely interesting for cards enthusiast. 60 illus. 150pp. 4¼ x 7.　　T963 Clothbound **$2.00**

TEACH YOURSELF GUIDEBOOK TO THE DRAMA, Luis Vargas. Clear, rapid survey of changing fashions and forms from Aeschylus to Tennessee Williams, in all major European traditions. Plot summaries, critical comments, etc. Equivalent of a college drama course; fine cultural background 224pp. 4¼ x 7.　　　　　　　　　　　　T961 Clothbound **$2.00**

TEACH YOURSELF THE ORGAN, Francis Routh. Excellent compendium of background material for everyone interested in organ music, whether as listener or player. 27 musical illus. 158pp. 4¼ x 7.　　　　　　　　　　　　　　　　T977 Clothbound **$2.00**

TEACH YOURSELF TO STUDY SCULPTURE, William Gaunt. Noted British cultural historian surveys culture from Greeks, primitive world, to moderns. Equivalent of college survey course. 23 figures, 40 photos. 158pp. 4¼ x 7.　　　　　　　　　T976 Clothbound **$2.00**

Miscellaneous

THE COMPLETE KANO JIU-JITSU (JUDO), H. I. Hancock and K. Higashi. Most comprehensive guide to judo, referred to as outstanding work by Encyclopaedia Britannica. Complete authentic Japanese system of 160 holds and throws, including the most spectacular, fully illustrated with 487 photos. Full text explains leverage, weight centers, pressure points, special tricks, etc.; shows how to protect yourself from almost any manner of attack though your attacker may have the initial advantage of strength and surprise. This authentic Kano system should not be confused with the many American imitations. xii + 500pp. 5⅜ x 8.
T639 Paperbound **$2.00**

THE MEMOIRS OF JACQUES CASANOVA. Splendid self-revelation by history's most engaging scoundrel—utterly dishonest with women and money, yet highly intelligent and observant. Here are all the famous duels, scandals, amours, banishments, thefts, treacheries, and imprisonments all over Europe: a life lived to the fullest and recounted with gusto in one of the greatest autobiographies of all time. What is more, these Memoirs are also one of the most trustworthy and valuable documents we have on the society and culture of the extravagant 18th century. Here are Voltaire, Louis XV, Catherine the Great, cardinals, castrati, pimps, and pawnbrokers—an entire glittering civilization unfolding before you with an unparalleled sense of actuality. Translated by Arthur Machen. Edited by F. A. Blossom. Introduction by Arthur Symons. Illustrated by Rockwell Kent. Total of xlviii + 2216pp. 5⅜ x 8.
T338 Vol I Paperbound **$2.00**
T339 Vol II Paperbound **$2.00**
T340 Vol III Paperbound **$2.00**
The set **$6.00**

BARNUM'S OWN STORY, P. T. Barnum. The astonishingly frank and gratifyingly well-written autobiography of the master showman and pioneer publicity man reveals the truth about his early career, his famous hoaxes (such as the Fejee Mermaid and the Woolly Horse), his amazing commercial ventures, his fling in politics, his feuds and friendships, his failures and surprising comebacks. A vast panorama of 19th century America's mores, amusements, and vitality. 66 new illustrations in this edition. xii + 500pp. 5⅜ x 8.
T764 Paperbound **$1.65**

THE STORY OF THE TITANIC AS TOLD BY ITS SURVIVORS, ed. by Jack Winocour. Most significant accounts of most overpowering naval disaster of modern times: all 4 authors were survivors. Includes 2 full-length, unabridged books: "The Loss of the S.S. Titanic," by Laurence Beesley, "The Truth about the Titanic," by Col. Archibald Gracie; 6 pertinent chapters from "Titanic and Other Ships," autobiography of only officer to survive, Second Officer Charles Lightoller; and a short, dramatic account by the Titanic's wireless operator, Harold Bride. 26 illus. 368pp. 5⅜ x 8. T610 Paperbound **$1.50**

THE PHYSIOLOGY OF TASTE, Jean Anthelme Brillat-Savarin. Humorous, satirical, witty, and personal classic on joys of food and drink by 18th century French politician, litterateur. Treats the science of gastronomy, erotic value of truffles, Parisian restaurants, drinking contests; gives recipes for tunny omelette, pheasant, Swiss fondue, etc. Only modern translation of original French edition. Introduction. 41 illus. 346pp. 5⅝ x 8⅜.
T591 Paperbound **$1.50**

THE ART OF THE STORY-TELLER, M. L. Shedlock. This classic in the field of effective story-telling is regarded by librarians, story-tellers, and educators as the finest and most lucid book on the subject. The author considers the nature of the story, the difficulties of communicating stories to children, the artifices used in story-telling, how to obtain and maintain the effect of the story, and, of extreme importance, the elements to seek and those to avoid in selecting material. A 99-page selection of Miss Shedlock's most effective stories and an extensive bibliography of further material by Eulalie Steinmetz enhance the book's usefulness. xxi + 320pp. 5⅜ x 8. T635 Paperbound **$1.50**

CREATIVE POWER: THE EDUCATION OF YOUTH IN THE CREATIVE ARTS, Hughes Mearns. In first printing considered revolutionary in its dynamic, progressive approach to teaching the creative arts; now accepted as one of the most effective and valuable approaches yet formulated. Based on the belief that every child has something to contribute, it provides in a stimulating manner invaluable and inspired teaching insights, to stimulate children's latent powers of creative expression in drama, poetry, music, writing, etc. Mearns's methods were developed in his famous experimental classes in creative education at the Lincoln School of Teachers College, Columbia Univ. Named one of the 20 foremost books on education in recent times by National Education Association. New enlarged revised 2nd edition. Introduction. 272pp. 5⅜ x 8. T490 Paperbound **$1.75**

FREE AND INEXPENSIVE EDUCATIONAL AIDS, T. J. Pepe, Superintendent of Schools, Southbury, Connecticut. An up-to-date listing of over 1500 booklets, films, charts, etc. 5% costs less than 25¢; 1% costs more; 94% is yours for the asking. Use this material privately, or in schools from elementary to college, for discussion, vocational guidance, projects. 59 categories include health, trucking, textiles, language, weather, the blood, office practice, wild life, atomic energy, other important topics. Each item described according to contents, number of pages or running time, level. All material is educationally sound, and without political or company bias. 1st publication. Second, revised edition. Index. 244pp. 5⅜ x 8.
T663 Paperbound **$1.50**

CHRONICLES OF THE HOUSE OF BORGIA, Frederick Baron Corvo (Frederick W. Rolfe). In the opinion of many this is the major work of that strange Edwardian literary figure, "Baron Corvo." It was Corvo's intention to investigate the notorious Borgias, from their first emergence in Spain to the Borgia saint in the 16th century and discover their true nature, disregarding both their apologists and their enemies. How well Corvo succeeded is questionable in a historical sense, but as a literary achievement and as a stylistic triumph the "Chronicles" has been a treasured favorite for generations. All the fabulous intrigues and devious currents and countercurrents of the Renaissance come vividly to life in Corvo's work, which is peopled with the notorious and notable personages of Italy and packed with fascinating lore. This is the first complete reprinting of this work, with all the appendices and illustrations. xxi + 375pp. 5⅝ x 8½. **T275 Paperbound $2.00**

ERROR AND ECCENTRICITY IN HUMAN BELIEF, Joseph Jastrow. A thoroughly enjoyable exposé, by a noted psychologist, of the ineradicable gullibility of man. Episodes throughout history —180 A.D. to 1930—that will shock and amuse by revelations of our tendency to fashion belief from desire not reason: the case of "Patience Worth," Ozark woman taking down novels from dictation of 17th-century girl from Devon; "Taxil," perhaps greatest hoaxer of all time; the odic force of Baron Reichenbach; Charles Richet, Nobel Laureate, accepting brazen trickeries of Eusapia Palladino; dozens of other lunacies, crank theories, public tricksters and frauds. For anyone who likes to read about the aberrations of his race. Formerly "Wish and Wisdom." 58 illustrations; 22 full-page plates. Index. xiv + 394pp. 5⅜ x 8½. **T986 Paperbound $1.85**

FADS AND FALLACIES IN THE NAME OF SCIENCE, Martin Gardner. Formerly entitled IN THE NAME OF SCIENCE, this is the standard account of various cults, quack systems, and delusions which have masqueraded as science: hollow earth fanatics, Reich and orgone sex energy, dianetics, Atlantis, multiple moons, Forteanism, flying saucers, medical fallacies like iridiagnosis, zone therapy, etc. A new chapter has been added on Bridey Murphy, psionics, and other recent manifestations in this field. This is a fair, reasoned appraisal of eccentric theory which provides excellent inoculation against cleverly masked nonsense. "Should be read by everyone, scientist and non-scientist alike," R. T. Birge, Prof. Emeritus of Physics, Univ. of California; Former President, American Physical Society. Index. x + 365pp. 5⅜ x 8. **T394 Paperbound $1.50**

MONEY CONVERTER AND TIPPING GUIDE FOR EUROPEAN TRAVEL, C. Vomacka. A small, convenient handbook crammed with information on currency regulations and tipping for every European country including the Iron Curtain countries, plus Israel, Egypt, and Turkey. Currency conversion tables for every country from U.S. to foreign and vice versa. The only source of such information as phone rates, postal rates, clothing sizes, what and when to tip, dutyfree imports, and dozens of other valuable topics. Always kept up to date. 128 pp. 3½ x 5¼. **T260 Paperbound 75¢**

HOW ADVERTISING IS WRITTEN—AND WHY, Aesop Glim. The best material from the famous "Aesop Glim" column in Printer's Ink. Specific, practical, constructive comments and criticisms on such matters as the aims of advertising, importance of copy, art of the headline, adjusting "tone of voice," creating conviction, etc. Timely, effective, useful. Written for the person interested in advertising profession, yet it has few equals as a manual for effective writing of any kind. Revised edition. 150pp. 5⅜ x 8. **T782 Paperbound $1.25**

THE WORLD'S GREAT SPEECHES, edited by Lewis Copeland and Lawrence Lamm. 255 speeches ranging over scores of topics and moods (including a special section of "Informal Speeches" and a fine collection of historically important speeches of the U.S.A. and other western hemisphere countries), present the greatest speakers of all time from Pericles of Athens to Churchill, Roosevelt, and Dylan Thomas. Invaluable as a guide to speakers, fascinating as history both past and contemporary, much material here is available elsewhere only with great difficulty. 3 indices: Topic, Author, Nation. xx + 745pp. 5⅜ x 8. T468 Paperbound $2.75

Pets

CARE AND FEEDING OF BUDGIES (SHELL PARRAKEETS), C. H. Rogers. Sources of information and supply. Index. 40 illustrations. 93pp. 5 x 7¼. **T937 Paperbound 65¢**

THE CARE AND BREEDING OF GOLDFISH, Anthony Evans. Hundreds of important details about indoor and outdoor pools and aquariums; the history, physical features and varieties of goldfish; selection, care, feeding, health and breeding—with a special appendix that shows you how to build your own goldfish pond. Enlarged edition, newly revised. Bibliography. 22 full-page plates; 4 figures. 129pp. 5 x 7¼. **T935 Paperbound 75¢**

OBEDIENCE TRAINING FOR YOUR DOG, C. Wimhurst. You can teach your dog to heel, retrieve, sit, jump, track, climb, refuse food, etc. Covers house training, developing a watchdog, obedience tests, working trials, police dogs. "Proud to recommend this book to every dog owner who is attempting to train his dog," says Blanche Saunders, noted American trainer, in her Introduction. Index. 34 photographs. 122pp. 5 x 7¼. **T938 Paperbound 75¢**

New Books

101 PATCHWORK PATTERNS, Ruby Short McKim. With no more ability than the fundamentals of ordinary sewing, you will learn to make over 100 beautiful quilts: flowers, rainbows, Irish chains, fish and bird designs, leaf designs, unusual geometric patterns, many others. Cutting designs carefully diagrammed and described, suggestions for materials, yardage estimates, step-by-step instructions, plus entertaining stories of origins of quilt names, other folklore. Revised 1962. 101 full-sized patterns. 140 illustrations. Index. 128pp. 7⅞ x 10¾.

T773 Paperbound **$1.85**

ESSENTIAL GRAMMAR SERIES
By concentrating on the essential core of material that constitutes the semantically most important forms and areas of a language and by stressing explanation (often bringing parallel English forms into the discussion) rather than rote memory, this new series of grammar books is among the handiest language aids ever devised. Designed by linguists and teachers for adults with limited learning objectives and learning time, these books omit nothing important, yet they teach more usable language material and do it more quickly and permanently than any other self-study material. Clear and rigidly economical, they concentrate upon immediately usable language material, logically organized so that related material is always presented together. Any reader of typical capability can use them to refresh his grasp of language, to supplement self-study language records or conventional grammars used in schools, or to begin language study on his own. Now available:

ESSENTIAL GERMAN GRAMMAR, Dr. Guy Stern & E. F. Bleiler. Index. Glossary of terms. 128pp. 5⅜ x 8.

T422 Paperbound **$1.00**

ESSENTIAL FRENCH GRAMMAR, Dr. Seymour Resnick. Index. Cognate list. Glossary. 159pp. 5⅜ x 8.

T419 Paperbound **$1.00**

ESSENTIAL ITALIAN GRAMMAR, Dr. Olga Ragusa. Index. Glossary. 111pp. 5⅜ x 8.

T779 Paperbound **$1.00**

ESSENTIAL SPANISH GRAMMAR, Dr. Seymour Resnick. Index. 50-page cognate list. Glossary. 138pp. 5⅜ x 8.

T780 Paperbound **$1.00**

PHILOSOPHIES OF MUSIC HISTORY: A Study of General Histories of Music, 1600-1960, Warren D. Allen. Unquestionably one of the most significant documents yet to appear in musicology, this thorough survey covers the entire field of historical research in music. An influential masterpiece of scholarship, it includes early music histories; theories on the ethos of music; lexicons, dictionaries and encyclopedias of music; musical historiography through the centuries; philosophies of music history; scores of related topics. Copiously documented. New preface brings work up to 1960. Index. 317-item bibliography. 9 illustrations; 3 full-page plates. 5⅜ x 8½. xxxiv + 382pp.

T282 Paperbound **$2.00**

MR. DOOLEY ON IVRYTHING AND IVRYBODY, Finley Peter Dunne. The largest collection in print of hilarious utterances by the irrepressible Irishman of Archey Street, one of the most vital characters in American fiction. Gathered from the half dozen books that appeared during the height of Mr. Dooley's popularity, these 102 pieces are all unaltered and uncut, and they are all remarkably fresh and pertinent even today. Selected and edited by Robert Hutchinson. 5⅜ x 8½. xii + 244p.

T626 Paperbound **$1.00**

TREATISE ON PHYSIOLOGICAL OPTICS, Hermann von Helmholtz. Despite new investigations, this important work will probably remain preeminent. Contains everything known about physiological optics up to 1925, covering scores of topics under the general headings of dioptrics of the eye, sensations of vision, and perecptions of vision. Von Helmholtz's voluminous data are all included, as are extensive supplementary matter incorporated into the third German edition, new material prepared for 1925 English edition, and copious textual annotations by J. P. C. Southall. The most exhaustive treatise ever prepared on the subject, it has behind it a list of contributors that will never again be duplicated. Translated and edited by J. P. C. Southall. Bibliography. Indexes. 312 illustrations. 3 volumes bound as 2. Total of 1749pp. 5⅜ x 8.

S15-16 Two volume set, Clothbound **$15.00**

THE ARTISTIC ANATOMY OF TREES, Rex Vicat Cole. Even the novice with but an elementary knowledge of drawing and none of the structure of trees can learn to draw, paint trees from this systematic, lucid instruction book. Copiously illustrated with the author's own sketches, diagrams, and 50 paintings from the early Renaissance to today, it covers composition; structure of twigs, boughs, buds, branch systems; outline forms of major species; how leaf is set on twig; flowers and fruit and their arrangement; etc. 500 illustrations. Bibliography. Indexes. 347pp. 5⅜ x 8.

T1016 Clothbound **$4.50**

Orientalia

ORIENTAL RELIGIONS IN ROMAN PAGANISM, F. Cumont. A study of the cultural meeting of east and west in the Early Roman Empire. It covers the most important eastern religions of the time from their first appearance in Rome, 204 B.C., when the Great Mother of the Gods was first brought over from Syria. The ecstatic cults of Syria and Phrygia — Cybele, Attis, Adonis, their orgies and mutilatory rites; the mysteries of Egypt — Serapis, Isis, Osiris, the dualism of Persia, the elevation of cosmic evil to equal stature with the deity, Mithra; worship of Hermes Trismegistus; Ishtar, Astarte; the magic of the ancient Near East, etc. Introduction. 55pp. of notes; extensive bibliography. Index. xxiv + 298pp. 5⅜ x 8.
T321 Paperbound **$2.00**

THE MYSTERIES OF MITHRA, F. Cumont. The definitive coverage of a great ideological struggle between the west and the orient in the first centuries of the Christian era. The origin of Mithraism, a Persian mystery religion, and its association with the Roman army is discussed in detail. Then utilizing fragmentary monuments and texts, in one of the greatest feats of scholarly detection, Dr. Cumont reconstructs the mystery teachings and secret doctrines, the hidden organization and cult of Mithra. Mithraic art is discussed, analyzed, and depicted in 70 illustrations. 239pp. 5⅜ x 8.
T323 Paperbound **$1.85**

CHRISTIAN AND ORIENTAL PHILOSOPHY OF ART, A. K. Coomaraswamy. A unique fusion of philosopher, orientalist, art historian, and linguist, the author discusses such matters as: the true function of aesthetics in art, the importance of symbolism, intellectual and philosophic backgrounds, the role of traditional culture in enriching art, common factors in all great art, the nature of medieval art, the nature of folklore, the beauty of mathematics, and similar topics. 2 illustrations. Bibliography. 148pp. 5⅜ x 8.
T378 Paperbound **$1.35**

TRANSFORMATION OF NATURE IN ART, A. K. Coomaraswamy. Unabridged reissue of a basic work upon Asiatic religious art and philosophy of religion. The theory of religious art in Asia and Medieval Europe (exemplified by Meister Eckhart) is analyzed and developed. Detailed consideration is given to Indian medieval aesthetic manuals, symbolic language in philosophy, the origin and use of images in India, and many other fascinating and little known topics. Glossaries of Sanskrit and Chinese terms. Bibliography. 41pp. of notes. 245pp. 5⅜ x 8.
T368 Paperbound **$1.75**

BUDDHIST LOGIC, F.Th. Stcherbatsky. A study of an important part of Buddhism usually ignored by other books on the subject: the Mahayana buddhistic logic of the school of Dignaga and his followers. First vol. devoted to history of Indian logic with Central Asian continuations, detailed exposition of Dignaga system, including theory of knowledge, the sensible world (causation, perception, ultimate reality) and mental world (judgment, inference, logical fallacies, the syllogism), reality of external world, and negation (law of contradiction, universals, dialectic). Vol. II contains translation of Dharmakirti's Nyayabindu with Dharmamottara's commentary. Appendices cover translations of Tibetan treatises on logic, Hindu attacks on Buddhist logic, etc. The basic work, one of the products of the great St. Petersburg school of Indian studies. Written clearly and with an awareness of Western philosophy and logic; meant for the Asian specialist and for the general reader with only a minimum of background. Vol. I, xii + 559pp. Vol. II, viii + 468pp. 5⅜ x 8½.
T955 Vol. I Paperbound **$2.50**
T956 Vol. II Paperbound **$2.50**
The set **$5.00**

THE TEXTS OF TAOISM. The first inexpensive edition of the complete James Legge translations of the Tao Te King and the writings of Chinese mystic Chuang Tse. Also contains several shorter treatises: the T'ai Shang Tractate of Actions and Their Retributions; the King Kang King, or Classic of Purity; the Yin Fu King, or Classic of the Harmony of the Seen and Unseen; the Yu Shu King, or Classic of the Pivot of Jade; and the Hsia Yung King, or Classic of the Directory for a Day. While there are other translations of the Tao Te King, this is the only translation of Chuang Tse and much of other material. Extensive introduction discusses differences between Taoism, Buddhism, Confucianism; authenticity and arrangement of Tao Te King and writings of Chuang Tse; the meaning of the Tao and basic tenets of Taoism; historical accounts of Lao-tse and followers; other pertinent matters. Clarifying notes incorporated into text. Originally published as Volumes 39, 40 of SACRED BOOKS OF THE EAST series, this has long been recognized as an indispensible collection. Sinologists, philosophers, historians of religion will of course be interested and anyone with an elementary course in Oriental religion or philosophy will understand and profit from these writings. Index. Appendix analyzing thought of Chuang Tse. Vol. I, xxiii + 396pp. Vol. II, viii + 340pp. 5⅜ x 8½.
T990 Vol. I Paperbound **$2.25**
T991 Vol. II Paperbound **$2.25**

CATALOGUE OF DOVER BOOKS

EPOCHS OF CHINESE AND JAPANESE ART, Ernest T. Fenollosa. Although this classic of art history was written before the archeological discovery of Shang and Chou civilizations, it is still in many respects the finest detailed study of Chinese and Japanese art available in English. It is very wide in range, covering sculpture, carving, painting, metal work, ceramics, textiles, graphic arts and other areas, and it considers both religious and secular art, including the Japanese woodcut. Its greatest strength, however, lies in its extremely full, detailed, insight-laden discussion of historical and cultural background, and in its analysis of the religious and philosophical implications of art works. It is also a brilliant stylistic achievement, written with enthusiasm and verve, which can be enjoyed and read with profit by both the Orientalist and the general reader who is interested in art. Index. Glossary of proper names. 242 illustrations. Total of 704 pages. 5⅜ x 8½.
T364-5 Two vol. set, paperbound **$5.00**

THE VEDANTA SUTRAS OF BADARAYANA WITH COMMENTARY BY SANKARACHARYA. The definitive translation of the consummation, foremost interpretation of Upanishads. Originally part of SACRED BOOKS OF THE EAST, this two-volume translation includes exhaustive commentary and exegesis by Sankara; 128-page introduction by translator, Prof. Thibaut, that discusses background, scope and purpose of the sutras, value and importance of Sankara's interpretation; copious footnotes providing further explanations. Every serious student of Indian religion or thought, philosophers, historians of religion should read these clear, accurate translations of documents central to development of important thought systems in the East. Unabridged republication of Volumes 34, 38 of the Sacred Books of the East. Translated by George Thibault. General index, index of quotations and of Sanskrit. Vol. I, cxxv + 448pp. Vol. II, iv + 506pp. 5⅜ x 8½.
T994 Vol. I Paperbound **$2.00**
T995 Vol. II Paperbound **$2.00**

THE UPANISHADS. The Max Müller translation of the twelve classical Upanishads available for the first time in an inexpensive format: Chandogya, Kena, Aitareya aranyaka and upanishad, Kaushitaki, Isa, Katha, Mundaka, Taittiriyaka Brhadaranyaka, Svetarasvatara. Prasna — all of the classical Upanishads of the Vedanta school—and the Maitriyana Upanishad. Originally volumes 1, 15 of SACRED BOOKS OF THE EAST series, this is still the most scholarly translation. Prof. Müller, probably most important Sanskritologist of nineteenth century, provided invaluable introduction that acquaints readers with history of Upanishad translations, age and chronology of texts, etc. and a preface that discusses their value to Western readers. Heavily annotated. Stimulating reading for anyone with even only a basic course background in Oriental philosophy, religion, necessary to all Indologists, philosophers, religious historians. Transliteration and pronunciation guide. Vol. I, ciii + 320pp. Vol. II, liii + 350pp.
T992 Vol. I Paperbound **$2.00**
T993 Vol. II Paperbound **$2.00**
The set **$4.00**

Dover publishes books on art, music, philosophy, literature, languages, history, social sciences, psychology, handcrafts, orientalia, puzzles and entertainments, chess, pets and gardens, books explaining science, intermediate and higher mathematics, mathematical physics, engineering, biological sciences, earth sciences, classics of science, etc. Write to:

Dept. catrr.
Dover Publications, Inc.
180 Varick Street, N.Y. 14, N.Y.